P9-APH-168

Detroit

Comparative American Cities

A series edited by Joe T. Darden

Detroit

Race and Uneven Development

Joe T. Darden

Richard Child Hill

June Thomas

Richard Thomas

Temple University Press · Philadelphia

Temple University Press, Philadelphia 19122

Published 1987

Printed in the United States of America

∞ The paper used in this publication meets the minimum requirements of American National Standard for Information Sciences—Permanence of paper for Printed Library Materials, ANSI Z39.48-1984

Library of Congress Cataloging-in-Publication Data

Detroit, race and uneven development.

(Comparative American cities)

Includes index.

1. Detroit (Mich.)—Economic conditions. 2. Detroit (Mich.)—Race relations. 3. Detroit (Mich.)—Social conditions. 4. Afro-Americans—Michigan—Detroit—Economic conditions. 5. Afro-Americans—Housing—Michigan—Detroit—. 6. Urban renewal—Michigan—Detroit.—I. Darden, Joe T. II. Series.

HC108.D6D47 1987 305.8′009774′34 86-30188

ISBN 0-87722-485-4 (alk. paper)

Contents

List of Maps, Figures, and Tables

Maps

Figures

Tables

Preface

Angles of Vision

This book is an interdisciplinary effort by a team of researchers associated with Urban Affairs Programs at Michigan State University (MSU). As with all approaches to understanding the city, interdisciplinary investigations have special strengths and some weaknesses. We think the special strength of *Detroit: Race and Uneven Development* comes from our attempt to bridge disparate methods and disciplines. Disciplines represented here include sociology, geography, history, and planning. And the cross-cutting methodological dimensions informing our research and analyses range from positive to normative and from historical to futuristic.

By offering many angles of vision, we hope to capture much of the richness, the complexity, and the contradiction of urban life. But a strength can be a weakness too. So we must also note at the outset that our book is probably less consistent in style, method, and argument than a work turned out by a single author or by a team from a single discipline would have been.

Pulling our act together has not been easy. It took more hours of discussion than we can or care to enumerate. But our quest for coherence was aided by our shared concerns and sensibilities. Our objective throughout this project has been to understand the human damage done by inequality, in order that we might contribute to the creation of a more just city. And our belief at the end, as at the beginning of our investigation of metropolitan Detroit, is that the best scholarly path to that goal is the one charted by interdisciplinary, holistic, historical, and critical signposts.

Several graduate assistants offered help with the research necessary to complete this work. These include Angela Braithwaite, Jo Dohoney, Cleopatra Jones, and Melvin Williams. In addition, Marie McNutt's secretarial prowess with our word processor greatly eased the journey through numerous drafts of the book. Thanks are also extended to Urban Affairs Programs for its support. Cartographic assistance was provided by Cindy Brewer of the Center for Cartographic Research and Spatial Analysis, under the directorship of Michael Lipsey of the Department of Geography at Michigan State University. The figures in Chapter 5 were compiled by Sherman K. Hollander. We sincerely appreciate these contributions.

We also appreciate the cooperation of Michael Band, Graphics Editor of the *Detroit News*, in allowing us the use of the illustrations on Population Shift in Metro Detroit, 1960–1980 and Shift in Assessed Valuation in Metro Detroit, 1960–1980. The illustrations were extremely valuable. We also thank Sally Pratt for providing editorial assistance.

For us this book has been a way of learning more about the modern metropolis and about metropolitan Detroit. We each have benefited mightily from the opportunity to test our ideas and findings against the knowledge possessed by other members of the research team. During myriad discussions—sometimes freewheeling, sometimes minutely focused—we have tried to weld our diverse angles of vision into an intelligible whole. We hope this book proves to be a way of learning about metropolitan Detroit for the reader as well.

Series Preface

The Comparative American Cities series grew out of a need for more comparative scholarly works on America's urban areas in the post-World War II era. American cities are storehouses of potential assets and liabilities for their residents and for society as a whole. It is important that scholars examine the nation's metropolitan areas to assess trends that may affect economic and political decision-making in the future.

The books have a contemporary approach, with the post-World War II period providing historical antecedents for current concerns. Each book generally addresses the same issues, although the peculiarities of the local environments necessarily shape each account. The major areas of concern include uneven regional development, white middle-class suburbanization, residential segregation of races and classes, and central-city issues such as economic disinvestment, black political power, and the concentration of blacks, Hispanics, and the poor. Each city in the series is viewed within the context of its metropolitan area as a whole. Taken together, these studies describe the spatial redistribution of wealth within the metropolises—the economic decline of central cities and the economic rise of the suburbs—a redistribution facilitated by the massive construction of interstate highways in the 1950s, 1960s, and 1970s.

Since World War II the metropolitan areas included in this series have been increasingly affected by uneven economic and social development and by conflict between cities and suburbs and between the white majority and the growing nonwhite minority. The central cities of each metropolitan area have also been losing jobs to the suburbs. There has been a tendency toward growing income inequality between cities and suburbs and between blacks and whites. Economic growth and decline have followed closely the racial composition of neighborhoods—that is, black neighborhoods have declined, while white neighborhoods have generally grown.

All of these studies assess the ways central-city governments have responded to these issues. In recent years most central-city elected officials have attempted to provide services and employment opportunities on a more equitable basis and to implement a more balanced and progressive economic development agenda. Most central-city mayors have been elected with the strong support of minorities, and the mayors have often cooperated with the business elite in attempts to stimulate more economic growth and to save the cities from further economic decline. Since this decline is related to structural changes in the economy within the context of uneven development, however, attempts at preventing the flow of jobs to the suburbs have largely failed, and the economic and social gap continues to widen.

There are no quick solutions to the economic, racial, and political problems of the cities in these studies. Though high-technology industries may play a part in each city's future, it is unlikely that they will produce as many jobs as are needed, or reduce the racial differences in unemployment rates. Blacks and other minorities who have limited spatial access to the areas of high-tech industries may not receive a fair share of their benefits.

Each city's plight is deeply rooted in America's problems of free-market economic investment, racial prejudice and discrimination, and the outmoded political structure that continues to separate the city from the suburbs, one suburb from another, the rich from the poor, and blacks from whites. As long as this structure remains, there is a strong probability that the situation will worsen, as population mobility continues to reinforce patterns of economic, social, and racial inequality, contributing to more racial and class conflict.

The problems of urban America require the immediate attention of government officials and the citizenry of this nation. New solutions involving changes in the political structure are long overdue. Our hope is that comparative studies such as these might provide the impetus for informed decisions and policies that will address the underlying problems besetting America's major urban areas.

Joe T. Darden, Series Editor
Comparative American Cities

Detroit

1

Detroit

An Overview

This book explores some of the major factors in the post–World War II evolution of one of the mightiest industrial metropolises of twentieth-century North America. It argues that the current state of the city of Detroit and its region—spatial inequality of industry and commerce, chronic racial and class segregation, regional political fragmentation—is a logical result of trends that have gradually escalated throughout the post–World War II era. It explains major trends by focusing specifically upon factors that have led to economic decentralization and racial segregation. In doing so, the book does not offer a global description of the city or its region, nor does it present background or explanatory material on all of its conditions or problems. Rather it looks at some of the basic aspects of recent city development that one must understand in order to begin to comprehend where Detroit has been and where it is going.

Although the city of Detroit first developed and grew as a center of trade and commerce, the automobile assembly line and a burgeoning automobile industry turned Detroit into a modern metropolis. Detroit and its jobs attracted immigrants from all over the United States as well as the world. The manufacturing sector was the irresistible lighthouse that drew the Irish, Poles, Italians, Finns, Hungarians, and blacks.

These ethnic groups set up their own enclaves in areas close to the central business district, enclaves in which the language and culture of the old country flourished intact. As foreign immigration declined, especially after World War I, domestic immigration increased, bringing thousands of rural southern black and white farmers and agricultural workers to serve Detroit's assembly lines. Gradually many of the European ethnic enclaves dispersed and assimilated, and their members bought newer and better housing farther from the central business district. But for many years the dispersion maintained ethnic and class lines. As late as 1940 distinctive white ethnic settlements remained fairly stable, including a large Polish enclave centered in Hamtramck and west Detroit; several German neighborhoods in northeast Detroit; a Hungarian settlement in the Delray area of southwest Detroit; and English, Scottish, and Jewish enclaves in the northwest area to the west of Woodward Avenue.[1]

After World War II the city population transformed in at least two fundamental ways. First, decentralization accelerated as more and more manufacturing firms, commercial establishments, and middle-class residents (especially white families of northern European ancestry) moved to the suburbs. Second, immigration of blacks from the South increased, transmuting the percentage of blacks in the city population from 9.2 percent in 1940 to 28.9 percent in 1960 and 63.1 percent in 1980.[2] One trend reinforced the other, as increasing black in-migration generated even more white out-migration. Although some whites of eastern and southern European ancestry remained in city ethnic enclaves—and in recent decades Middle Eastern immigrants to the city rekindled its familiar lighthouse function—many upwardly mobile residents left the city for working-class, middle-class, or upper-class suburbs in the larger metropolitan area, and fewer and fewer nonblacks moved into the city. Neighborhood shops and downtown department stores shut down as emigrants outnumbered immigrants and the population of the city plummeted. Sections of the larger metropolis boomed economically, but Detroit city, once a paragon of industrial prowess and a polyglot of ethnic diversity, lost firms yearly. Both city and region developed ever more blatant racial and class segregation daily. The core city became heavily black and poor. The largely white suburbs divided along class lines. Those blacks who moved out of the city, spurred by the search for a better life and repelled by mounting decay, became resegregated in suburban enclaves.

These trends continued during the decade of the 1970s. Between 1970 and 1980 the Standard Metropolitan Statistical Area (SMSA) expanded from three counties to six, but the population of the three core counties that made up the 1970 SMSA declined by 160,000 people. This three-county loss of 3.8 percent was caused almost entirely by population decline in the central city, which had lost 311,000 people. While some areas of the city remained intact and stable, in other areas blocks disappeared as people abandoned homes, which the city then had to demolish. This led to further decline in neighboring property values and the inability to sell housing units, which led to additional decline. All of these trends depressed remaining residential and commercial property values.

Those who remained were the poorest of the poor. The percentage of persons in the city of Detroit who fell below the official U.S. poverty line rose from 14.9 percent in 1969 to 21.9 percent in 1979. In 1979, of those 436,891 poor persons in the SMSA, 258,575—or three out of every five poor people—lived in the city.[3] As in many industrial cities in the Northeast and Midwest, it was left to the city administration to provide services to an increasingly poor population. At the same time industries and more well-to-do residents left the municipal boundaries. State government assistance became necessary to rescue the city's public school system, which virtually collapsed for want of revenue. The old story of not enough money to deal with extensive decay played full stage in Detroit, with wearisome familiarity.

Yet Detroit remained isolated within its metropolitan area. Although thoughts of metropolitan governance or financial sharing publicly surfaced occasionally, no serious attempt gained anything close to success. Wealthy suburbanites seemed content to continue to play status musical chairs, with upwardly mobile residents moving from suburb to suburb, depending on job status and current fashion. Working-class suburbanites seemed preoccupied with their concept of maintaining property values, through subtle exclusion of blacks, and with keeping their own enclaves from falling into the expanding pit of declining manufacturing employment and advancing residential decay. Black city politicians seemed content with black political power and unwilling to sacrifice that power for the unknown territory of regional governance.

Meanwhile cosmetic attempts to "revitalize" sections of the city, such as the refurbishment of portions of the central business district, brought small successes but on the whole failed to counter significantly the ongoing trends of decentralization and disinvestment.

John H. Mollenkopf suggests that three broad kinds of cities exist.[4] One kind includes those new cities of the South that had little or no industrial legacy but grew up based on administrative and service activities or on new high-technology industries. A second group includes cities that were industrial centers before 1930 but in recent years developed strong corporate, banking, and service sectors, such as New York, Boston, Chicago, and San Francisco. According to Mollenkopf's typology, Detroit would fall within the third group: cities that have never managed to become administrative and service nodes to the extent necessary to offset the loss of manufacturing functions. These are the cities most hurt by the transformation of the postindustrial economy.

The problem with placing Detroit within this third category—and, in a broader sense, the problem with the typology—is that it applies only to the central city and only if one views that central city as divorced from the rest of the region. The administrative and service functions Mollenkopf refers to also take place in the Detroit region, but they are centered in the suburban municipalities of Southfield, Troy, and Dearborn, among others. To focus only on the central city is to fail to fully understand the nature of the region's economy. Detroit's older economic and political pattern was based on strong central-city manufacturing and retail sectors, but the current metropolitan pattern is dispersed and multicentric, much like that of Los Angeles. The problem in the Detroit metropolis is one of uneven regional development, rather than unmitigated regional decline. The political economy of the city of Detroit is dependent upon the political economy of the Detroit metropolis.

This book offers modest insights into why uneven regional development characterizes that metropolis. It suggests that disinvestment, suburbanization, and racial segregation strongly influence the status of the central city and its suburbs. Two major perspectives underlie the approach taken in this book. First the post-war evolution of the city of Detroit must be understood within the particular framework of its region and the uneven variations within that region. Second one must thoroughly understand the role of race in order to comprehend the spatial and political development of the city and its region.

As explained in Chapter 2, for the first portion of the post–World War II era, the regional framework was one of duality, with the central city marked by sustained economic and population decline and suburban areas characterized almost completely by growth. To a large extent this dual model is still relevant: Total property valuation and population have risen in suburban counties and fallen in the central city. Chapter 2 begins by describing the steep downhill slide of the economy of the city of Detroit. A massive freeway system became the conduit for the flight of the worker and the work place, and Detroit's share of the region's population, jobs, and wealth plummeted. Eventually, all major shopping areas were located in the suburbs, symbols of the emasculated power of the central business district.

In spite of such obvious duality, by the late 1970s a multicentric mode of growth was evident. Some industrial suburbs lost factories, while various nodes of commerce arose and flourished in other suburbs in the metropolis. In some contexts it became less and less relevant to talk about the central city versus the suburbs, for much depended on which portions of the central city one was addressing as well as which particular suburbs. For example, Livingston County has not experienced nearly as much growth as Oakland County, and significant disinvestment has occurred in the downriver suburbs. On the other hand, investment dollars are beginning to pour into the riverfront of the city of Detroit, although development within the city is uneven.

Chapter 2 is the primary locus for explaining this regional political economy, but it is also an important ingredient in other chapters. For example, in Chapter 3, which covers patterns of race and class disparity, a conscious attempt has been made to avoid treating all suburbs as monolithic. Although it was important to look at variations between the central city and the suburbs as a whole, patterns of racial and income dispersion differed by suburbs. On the whole, suburbanization in the Detroit region has been a white phenomenon. A measure of racial segregation between municipalities shows that municipal segregation has actually increased, because when black suburbanization has taken place, it has centered in a few suburbs. Southfield, Warren, and Dearborn, all contiguous to Detroit, have experienced different rates and levels of suburbanization, and different suburbs vary widely in socioeconomic status. Even though most metropolitan poverty has become concentrated in the central city, poverty clusters exist in two of the least-developed counties of the six-county SMSA and in several key municipalities in the backwaters of metropolitan economic growth.

It is in the context of politics and policy that we suggest that one logical approach to uneven economic development in the region would be greater regional political cooperation. As the last portion of Chapter 6 explains, efforts to implement meaningful regional governance schemes have not been especially successful. The regional municipalities and counties have formed a council of governments and a regional transportation authority, as well as other single-purpose agencies, and groups of governments have cooperated in various endeavors throughout the years. But attempts to implement strong fiscal reform or to establish a true regional government have simply failed.

One explanation for the failure of many such attempts is that racial estrangement has characterized the region for many years. Thus the first perspective of the book, that problems of and solutions for the metropolis must be viewed within the context of the regional political economy, connects with the second perspective, that issues of race, racial conflict, and racial cooperation are critical.

Just as several chapters reflect the regionalist perspective, so too do several chapters reflect the racial perspective. Racial issues have played a crucial role in defining the parameters of change in the Detroit metropolis. All of the influential decisions that have shaped the metropolis and all of the proposals for future development touch in some sense upon the issues of race and racial interaction. The fragmentation that the city and metropolis suffer is racial as well as economic and political, and solutions to Detroit's problems must overcome the racial divisiveness that has characterized much of its history.

Chapter 3 begins the analysis of the role of race by examining the spatial evidence of racial and income segregation, with a strong emphasis on race. The high levels of racial segregation in the region cannot be explained by variables such as housing value or rental costs. For example, in 1980 the location of low-rent and low-value housing explained only 36 percent of the variation in black residence in the six-county SMSA. Quite often rents and housing prices paid by blacks were disproportionately higher than those paid by whites, but blacks remained segregated because of other factors. It is not sufficient to view residential patterns of the Detroit metropolis solely as reflections of homeowners' ability to pay.

What such patterns do reflect is explained largely in Chapter 4's discussion of the history of interracial conflict and cooperation in the region. The chapter describes the historical context of white opposition to black influx. Embodied in such classic confrontations as the 1940s battle over Detroit's Sojourner Truth housing project, this opposition caused many whites to move to suburbs such as Dearborn, which erected virtually airtight walls against blacks. A leapfrog pattern of black residence developed largely because of varying levels of acceptance among white neighborhoods and municipalities. White suburban enclave building, assisted by laws of incorporation, became so strong that some municipalities lost federal housing and community funds rather than open the enclave.

Yet a parallel phenomenon existed: Many white citizens sincerely attempted to support the concept and reality of fair housing. In some suburbs, notably Oak Park, interracial harmony and cooperation developed to such a high level that many began to believe that Detroit might one day become a metropolis of truly multiracial communities.

Chapter 5's discussion of city redevelopment policies does not focus as heavily on race but does suggest that early redevelopment projects aggravated problems of racial estrangement within the city of Detroit. The first half of that chapter describes the urban renewal era, during which the city administration destroyed a number of black and white ethnic communities in various attempts to wipe out slums or allow resident institutions to expand. Black residents of the Gratiot, Medical Center, and University City projects paid an especially high price. Urban renewal seriously crippled the viability of scores of black businesses, and its relocation policies so alienated black residents that resentment lingered for years.

The racial theme is also important to the last core chapter, "Politics and Policy," in which we explain the complexities involved in trying to initiate any kind of political transformation in the region. First we describe the rise of black political power in the city through sketches that demonstrate the profound difficulties black politicians faced in their attempts to develop that power. For many years whites simply did not support black candidates. Black reaction to this lack of reciprocal support sometimes came in the form of coalition-building efforts but often translated instead into efforts to build strong black political organizations. White suburban isolationism reached new heights with the 1970s controversies over bussing, especially with court-ordered school desegregation plans. This combination of black political turf building and white isolationism lays the explanatory groundwork for the last section of that chapter, which describes the futile attempts to establish strong regional governance and cooperation.

So our two perspectives, in the final analysis, join hands. While urban problems and solutions must be understood in their regional context, one can explain neither problem nor solution without understanding the pattern of race and the history of racial interaction.

One final point is that the changes found in the Detroit metropolis cannot be blamed upon some natural process of evolution over which humans as decision makers had no control. It is obvious that Detroit is a city in which even the postindustrial functions of a strong service-sector economy and an office building–oriented central business district have faltered. It is also obvious that the region has continuously been characterized by problems of uneven development and racial estrangement. But this process is not a natural one like that of some organism undergoing predictable stages of growth. Rather, the changes in the Detroit metropolis are affected by deliberate collective actions and subject to reversal by people, governments, and institutions.

This fact is obvious in all of the chapters, although it is emphasized in some more than others. In the context of economic development, we see that the very same people who have aided the decentralization of economic growth in the Detroit region have now decided, it appears, to focus some of that growth on the riverfront. In the context of racial segregation, conflict, and cooperation, we see that groups of individuals developed actions that caused severe racial estrangement, and yet groups also developed healing mechanisms. In the context of city redevelopment policy, we see that the city government is making a series of crucial decisions—most specifically in its attempts to balance industrial, neighborhood, and central business district/riverfront development—that it hopes will reverse the trends of disinvestment. And the relevance of politics and policy is obvious: It is in the political and policy arenas that much, though not all, of the decision making can be made. Policy action cannot solve the problems of Detroit, but it can certainly alleviate them.

Yet the book's discussion of city redevelopment policy shows that effort alone may not be sufficient if it takes place only in the political arena or involves only some portions of the city or metropolis. Redevelopment policy in Detroit, for example, has been a steep uphill battle against the forces of depopulation and disinvestment. As a result, the residents of the city have sometimes been reduced to fighting over the crumbs dropped from the table of regional economic development.

What is needed for Detroit is a new vision, one based on more equitable economic development and more intense racial and political cooperation. In the final chapter we do not offer the vision so much as project how much has yet to be accomplished. But it is our sincere hope that the people of Detroit move toward such a vision, which cannot really be defined for them but which they must themselves develop.

2

Uneven Development in Metropolitan Detroit

Our purpose in this chapter is to trace uneven development—the spatial trajectory of investment and disinvestment, economic growth and decline—in metropolitan Detroit since the Second World War. We begin with Detroit in the late 1940s, when the spatial path taken by an expanding auto industry, abetted by federal transportation and housing policies, yielded massive suburbanization. Auto decentralization, then the reorganization of commercial capital from downtown to regional shopping centers gave birth to two Detroits. One, the Detroit metropolitan area as a whole, had a thriving economy. The other, the central city, became home for hundreds of thousands of poor and unemployed people.

This peculiar postwar pattern of uneven urban development is by now a familiar story in the United States. In growing numbers industrial and commercial companies moved their capital from the central city to the suburbs and beyond. The central city came to be surrounded by mostly white suburbs of an affluent professional or more modest working-class character. Meanwhile private disinvestment created a crisis for the central city indexed in jobs lost, schools impoverished, houses dilapidated, stores abandoned, crimes committed, taxes increased, services reduced. As capital and jobs moved elsewhere, the central city came to be increasingly populated by minorities, by poor people, and by the aged—by people, that is, who often share a marginal relationship to the process of economic production and exchange. And to be marginal to the economy is to have few political resources and little influence with the government.

Yet, paradoxically, even as industrial and commercial corporations abandoned the city, new private investment (backed by public "incentives") was targeted to the redevelopment of downtown. New administrative, financial, cultural, and recreational activities for the downtown gentry bloomed, even as life in the rest of the city wilted. Since relations of conflict tend to follow lines of inequality, this dualistic pattern of uneven development tended to pit the city against the suburbs, and neighborhoods against downtown.

Of course, this dual development model never fully captured what was going on, but until recently it seemed a reasonable enough approximation for many urban areas, including Detroit. By the mid-1970s, however, deviations from that urban trajectory were just too big to ignore. The changes afoot didn't displace the earlier development pattern so much as they came to overlay it, making uneven metropolitan development more complicated and more intricate.

First, there has been the rise of downtowns in the suburbs. Younger metropolises, like Los Angeles and Houston, seem almost to have started out that way, but now central cities in older metropolitan areas like Detroit have lost ground in the competition for central place with business centers on their periphery. This further weakens the central city, even as it further fragments the metropolitan area.

Second, there has been widespread disinvestment from inner-ring industrial suburbs—that is, from those working-class satellite communities that developed during the 1950s and 1960s, nourished, in no small measure, by capital that had once resided in the central city. When the crises in the U.S. metal-bending industries struck in the 1970s, disinvestment spread out from the central city, upriver and downriver, into the industrial suburbs of Detroit. Many residents in Detroit's working-class suburbs now confronted similar economic problems to those afflicting their central-city counterparts. Even so, economic reorganization in response to the industrial crisis is bringing with it a spatial redistribution of capital that continues to advantage selected suburbs; most notably, high-technology replacements for inner-city Detroit's flagging industries are congregating in outlying research parks.

Detroit officials hope to beat rival suburbs at their own game by pursuing a corporate-center redevelopment strategy on the downtown riverfront. But suburban competition is stiff, and corporate mergers keep picking up Detroit's capital and putting it elsewhere, so this development strategy entails big risks. And should riverfront redevelopment succeed, it remains to be seen whether the economic benefits will spread out to those in Detroit who need them most.

These changes—downtown decentralization, suburban industrial decline, regional competition for high-technology business investment—suggest some others. For one thing, traditional central-city divisions between downtown and neighborhood (and among neighborhoods) are now metropolitan in scope, but they occur in a context of heightened political fragmentation and race and class segregation. This is so because suburban downtowns and research parks are walled off from the rest of the metropolis by municipal boundaries in a way that had no parallel in the division between central-city downtown and neighborhoods in an earlier era. And since industrial suburbs can't fall back on the kind of diversified tax base that has helped sustain the central city through the worst of times, urban disinvestment can create even greater trauma for them than it has for their central-city neighbor. So new urban conflicts arise as suburbs vie more intensely with one another for capital investment and for their share of the region's tax base. New conflicts open up new possibilities for regional alliances, as impoverished working-class communities in the suburbs and the central city confront forces that seem bent on erasing their future.

How, then, has the postwar process of uneven development unfolded in metropolitan Detroit?

The Motor City

Location economists tell us that *export* industries oriented toward regional, national, and international markets form the dynamic core of any metropolitan economy. But export industries aren't self-sufficient; they require *complementary* industries, those that provide materials to be processed by export industries and those that use the products of export industries for further processing. Together, export and complementary industries also generate local *service* industries, those that meet the immediate, daily sustenance needs of urban workers and residents.[1] So understood, Detroit has a metal-bending economy largely based upon one export industry, motor vehicle production, and three complementary industries: nonelectrical machinery, fabricated metals, and primary metals. Most of the machine tools, foundry products, metal stampings, machinery, and sheet steel these complementary industries make end up in the automobile plants, so for most of this century the Motor City's economic prosperity has followed that of the car companies.[2]

Why Detroit?

At the turn of the century, auto production was spread over New England and the mid-Atlantic and midwestern states. Yet by 1910 Detroit's auto predominance was so well-established that it would stand unchallenged for nearly three-quarters of a century. Why did the auto industry concentrate in southeast Michigan?

The structure of the auto industry is composed of several elements: *Raw materials* go into the *production* of components, which are *assembled* into finished vehicles for *distribution and sale*. These products must be *designed and engineered* and the production process *financed and coordinated* from beginning to end.

Many factors can shape the way auto companies arrange and rearrange these elements in space. For one thing, car production is a "discrete process" industry, so parts can be manufactured in different places and then assembled into the final product. For another, autos are "transport sensitive" goods, so economies in transport costs can be realized by assembling the product near consumers. Then too, the auto industry has heretofore had a voracious appetite for ferrous metals and has tended to sink its manufacturing facilities into soil laden with limestone and iron ore. And perhaps most important of all, auto profits are contingent upon achieving economies of scale, most particularly in engine casting, dieing, and stamping.[3]

The auto industry was drawn to southeastern Michigan by the natural and industrial terrains. Located on an isthmus between Lake St. Clair and Lake Erie, Detroit was a navigation point where western railroad barons, Canadian merchants, and Great Lakes shippers met, mingled, and engaged in diversified business. Detroit was also midway between the iron ore fields of northern Michigan and the coal fields of Appalachia—the stuff of which steel is made. Detroit had blast furnaces and brass foundries, and the city's factories turned out stoves, gasoline engines, farm implements, marine equipment, and carriages—all forerunners of the auto industry. Early automobiles were loaded with brass, and axles and springs were modeled from railroad cars. But the automobile's true parent was the carriage, for carriage making provided bodies, wheels, and the assembly principle.[4]

The structural parallels between carriage making and the auto industry ran close. Both included components production and contracting, both were assembly operations, and each had similar market and dealer networks. Carriage components—wheels, axles, bodies, and furnishings—found ready use in car manufacture. Contractors for components did the majority of the work in each industry. Sales and distribution channels were similar, since both required a network of dealers. And each product had to be assembled. Southern Michigan and northern Indiana were home territory for the carriage industry. Flint, just north of Detroit, was its capital.

William C. Durant, carriage manufacturer and salesman, lived and worked in Flint. And Durant's firm was a forerunner to General Motors.[5]

At the beginning the auto industry was carved up among hundreds of independent carmakers, demand for cars was spread over a wide area, and local entrepreneurs responded to local opportunities. But spatial dispersion among many independent carmakers quickly gave way to spatial concentration among a few large companies. By 1920 fewer than a dozen firms were doing substantial business in automobiles. The same economies of scale that led to industrial concentration among a handful of firms led to spatial concentration in southeast Michigan. The right mix of minerals and waterways, and the economic matrix provided by the carriage and marine gasoline-engine industries, enabled Michigan producers to make less expensive cars and expand their markets at the expense of competitors. Parts contractors were nearby. Assembly production was well understood. Parts specialization and the assembly line allowed for economies of scale. New supplier firms specializing in rubber products, auto bodies, carburetors, engines, radiators, fans, pumps, and gaskets flocked to Michigan to get in on the rising demand. And as market demand followed the population from east to west, Detroit reaped further locational advantages.[6]

By 1920 Michigan was the center of the auto industry. Located there were the steel mills, foundries, and engine plants nourishing the assembly line. In 1925, 55 percent of all wage earners in the auto and parts industries lived in Michigan. Just a decade earlier that figure had been only 23 percent. The number of auto workers in Michigan had risen from 2,735 in 1904, to 67,500 in 1914, to 234,500 in 1925.[7]

The Spatial Logic of Auto Production

Detroit grew with the auto industry, and the auto industry grew according to a kind of leapfrog spatial logic. Car factories were built next to railroad lines, in open space but not too far from an available labor force. Once built, an auto plant attracted complementary metal and machinery industries, then residential subdivisions. So as the auto industry expanded, the Motor City sprawled, farther and farther out.

Detroit's first mass-production facilities were located near the river on the east side of the city. When Henry Ford built the Highland Park plant in 1913, northwest industrial and residential expansion followed. Ford later built the Rouge plant to the southwest, and around it grew one of the world's largest manufacturing complexes. World War II brought another wave of factory construction and spatial growth, but in the suburban

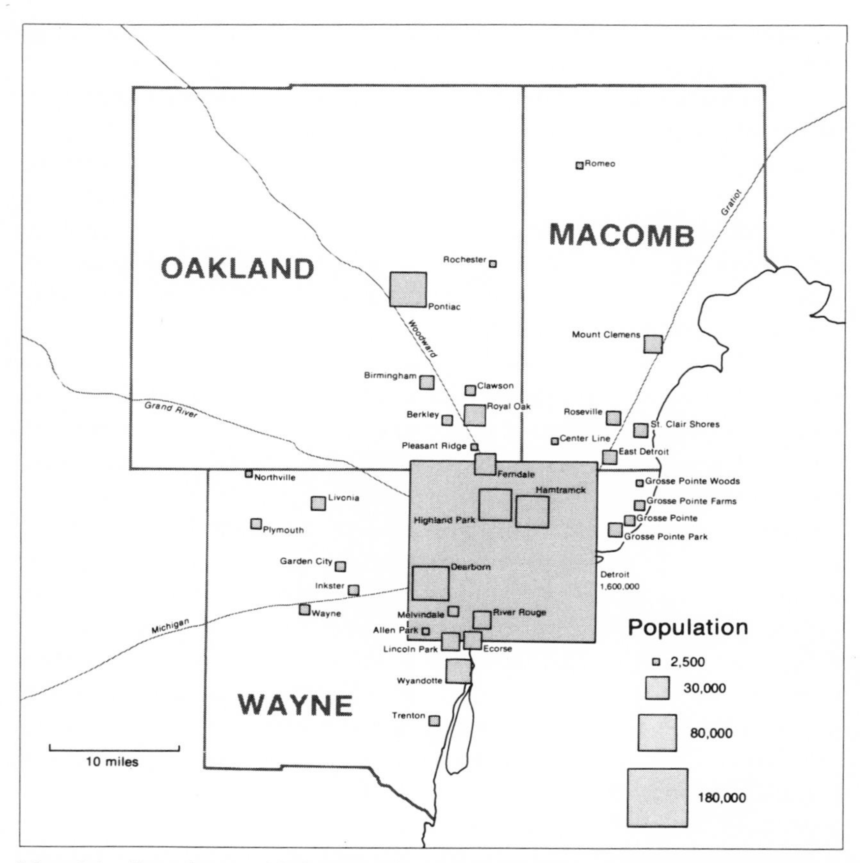

Map 2.1 Detroit area 1940 population: Standard Metropolitan Statistical Area municipalities over 2,500

Source: U.S. Department of Commerce, Bureau of the Census, 1950.

periphery. Past location considerations—rail lines, undeveloped land, and proximity to a labor force—were now supplemented by a national defense policy urging the dispersal of war production to satellite cities as a protection against potential atomic attack. Between 1947 and 1955 the Big Three (Ford, Chrysler, and General Motors) constructed some 20 new plants in suburban Detroit.[8] As in the past, complementary metal and machinery industries clustered around the new factories, and residential growth and services followed industrial expansion.

Government policy further stimulated emigration from Detroit to the suburbs in the early 1950s. The federal government financed construction of a huge freeway network. And the Federal Housing Administration in-

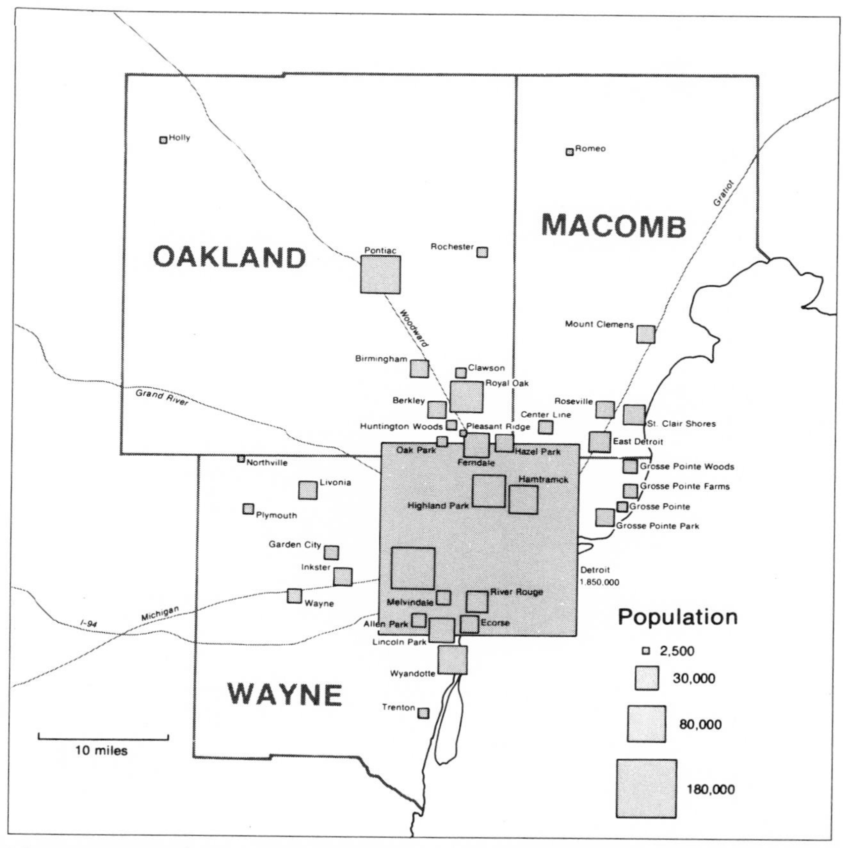

Map 2.2 Detroit area 1950 population: Standard Metropolitan Statistical Area municipalities over 2,500

Source: U.S. Department of Commerce, Bureau of the Census, 1950.

sured loans for new suburban homes while often redlining older areas in the central city.

The freeway system provided a funnel for suburban immigration. Manufacturing plants relocated to suburban industrial corridors. Commercial establishments flocked to suburban shopping malls. Warehouse facilities left lofts at points of central-city railway convergence for single-story buildings at points of suburban interstate freeway convergence. And as the auto industry continued to decentralize, some central-city neighborhoods became blue-collar dormitories for workers commuting to suburban plants.[9]

Maps 2.1 to 2.5 graphically reveal the explosion of population and the

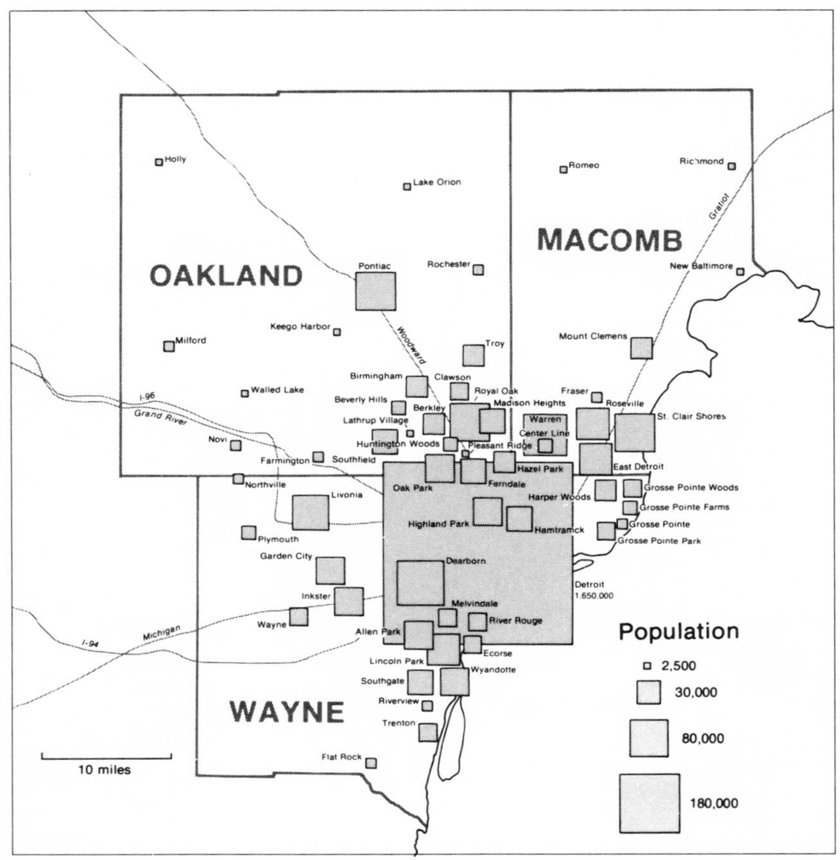

Map 2.3 Detroit area 1960 population: Standard Metropolitan Statistical Area municipalities over 2,500
Source: U.S. Department of Commerce, Bureau of the Census, 1980.

proliferation of municipalities in the Detroit suburbs during the four decades from 1940 to 1980. As rails and roads sliced through postwar Detroit, suburban residential corridors fronting the main highway arteries alternated with industrial corridors fronting the major railroad lines. Working-class suburbs—like Center Line, Warren, Sterling Heights, and Utica in Macomb County, and Melvindale, East Dearborn, Inkster, and Wayne in Wayne County—clustered in the industrial corridors, often in a chaotic fashion, often without central service facilities. More privileged suburbs—like Pleasant Ridge, Huntington Woods, Berkley, Birmingham, and Bloomfield Hills along the Woodward Corridor in Oakland County—where auto administrators and professionals set up residence, tended to

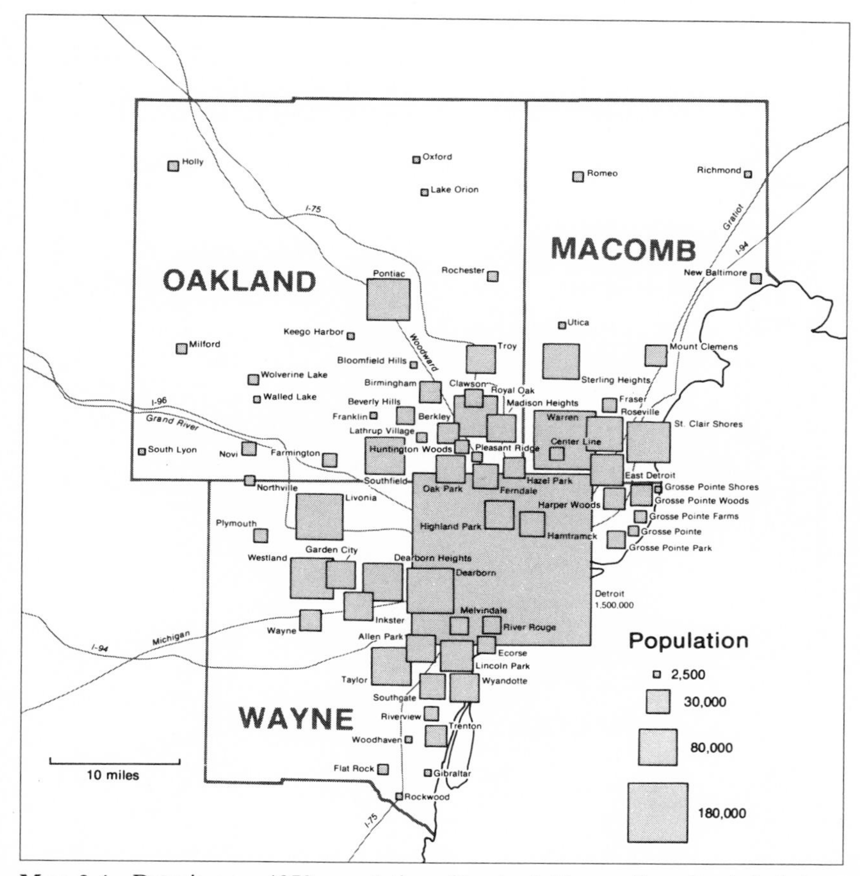

Map 2.4 Detroit area 1970 population: Standard Metropolitan Statistical Area municipalities over 2,500

Source: U.S. Department of Commerce, Bureau of the Census, 1980.

cluster along radial causeways, usually in a less haphazard fashion and often with established services.[10]

The Flight to Suburbia

The Motor City's population peaked in 1952 at 1.85 million. By 1960 the number of people residing in the central city had fallen to 1.67 million. During the next 20 years Detroit lost nearly half a million people, while surrounding suburban counties gained over a million new residents. Detroit's share of the region's population dropped accordingly, from 42.3 percent in 1960 to 27.6 percent in 1980.[11] (See Figure 2.1.)

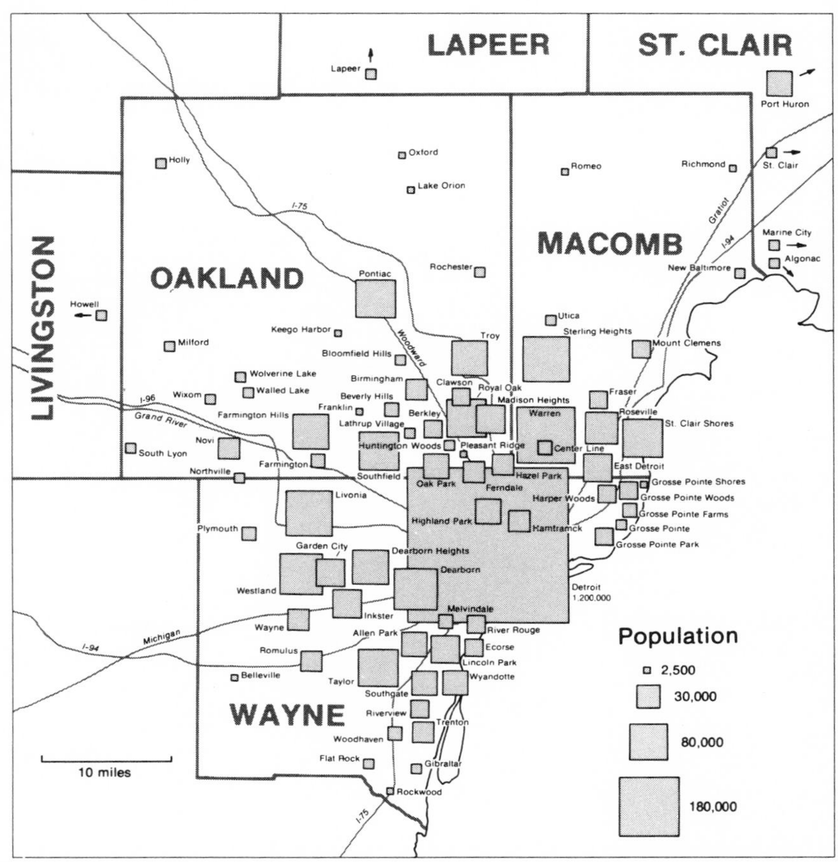

Map 2.5 Detroit area 1980 population: Standard Metropolitan Statistical Area municipalities over 2,500

Source: U.S. Department of Commerce, Bureau of the Census, 1980.

Population shifts of this magnitude suggest a massive movement of capital from central city to suburbia. And that's precisely what happened. Figure 2.2 shows just how sweeping the changes in the distribution of assessed property values between Detroit and surrounding suburban counties were during the two decades from 1960 to 1980. In 1960 the central city possessed half the region's property wealth, and its closest suburban competitor, the rest of Wayne County, ranked a very distant second. By 1980 Detroit's share of the region's property value had shrunk to just 16.5 percent, and the central city ranked fourth on the regional totem pole, far behind suburban Oakland and Macomb counties.

Just how steep an economic slide the Motor City has taken is indicated

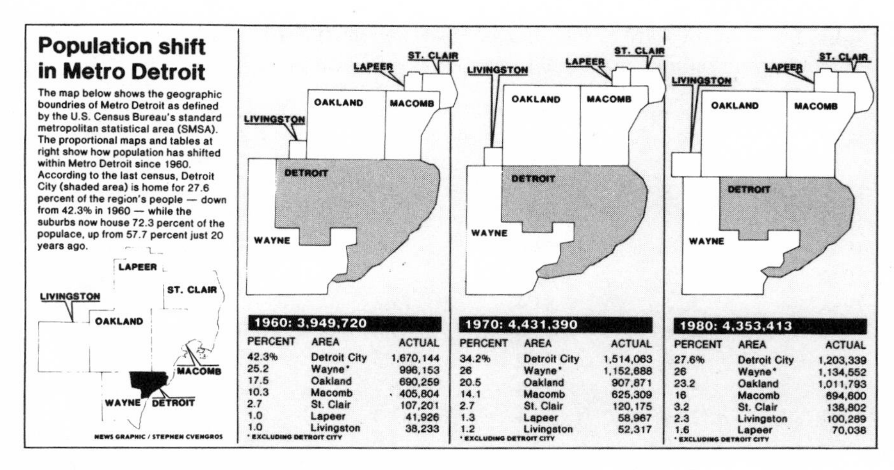

Figure 2.1 Population shift in metro Detroit, 1960–1980
Source: Detroit News, Graphic division/Stephen Czvengros.

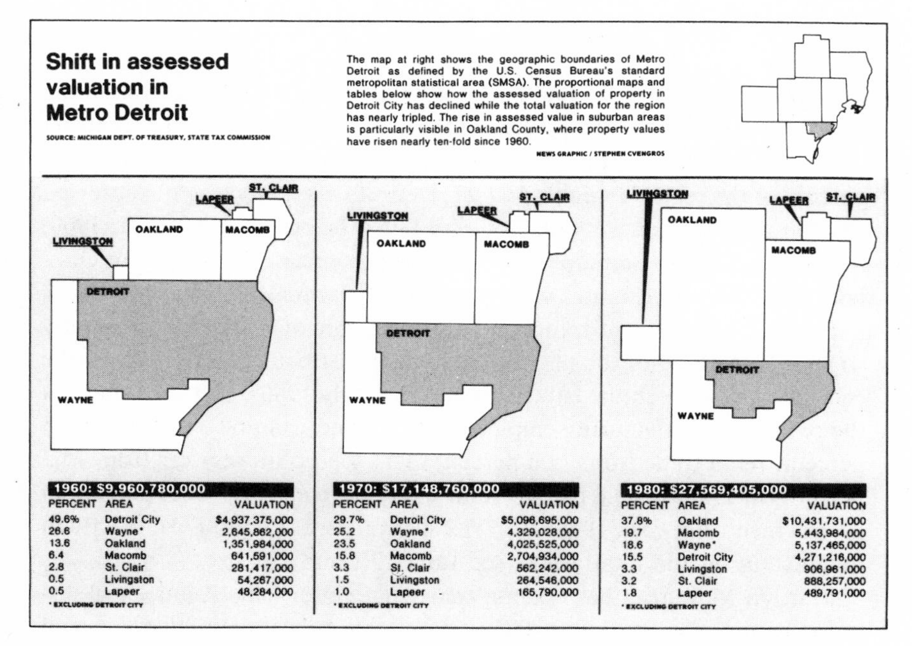

Figure 2.2 Shift in assessed valuation in metro Detroit, 1960–1980
Source: Michigan Department of Treasury, State Tax Commission. *Detroit News*, Graphic division/Stephen Cvengros.

Table 2.1 Detroit share of total Standard Metropolitan Statistical Area employment in selected industrial sectors, 1929–1982 (in percentage)

Year	Manufacturing (%)	Retail (%)	Service (%)	Wholesale (%)	Four-sector total (%)
1929	75.2	82.2		94.8	
1939	57.7	77.9		92.0	
1948	60.3	72.6		90.1	
1954	53.5	63.3		76.8	
1958	50.5	54.4	75.3	74.1	55.6
1963	40.6	43.4	65.8	68.6	45.8
1967	35.8	38.2	60.5	57.9	40.4
1972	33.4	28.5	46.7	44.5	34.7
1977	27.9	20.1	33.3	32.3	27.1
1982	25.0	15.4	23.6	29.6	22.4

Source: Data for 1929–1954 are adapted from Raymond Vernon, "The Changing Economic Function of the Central City," in James Q. Wilson (ed.), *Urban Renewal: The Record and the Controversy* (Cambridge, Mass.: Massachusetts Institute of Technology Press, 1966), pp. 6–15. Data for 1958–1982 are from the U.S. Department of Commerce, *Census of Business*, various years, (Washington, D.C.: U.S. Government Printing Office).

by comparing Figures 2.1 and 2.2. In 1960 Detroit had 42.3 percent of the area's population and 49.6 percent of the area's wealth. By 1980 the central city had 27.6 percent of the region's population matched by only 16.5 percent of the region's wealth. In fact, Detroit's economy was so depressed in 1980 that its assessed valuation had fallen below what it was in 1960, and this during the same period when property values in suburban Oakland and Macomb counties were rising nearly tenfold.

Postwar employment trends in various sectors of the Detroit economy suggest something of the magnitude of disinvestment experienced by the central city. Between the late 1940s and the early 1980s, Detroit's share of the region's manufacturing employment dropped from 60.3 percent to 25 percent, retail trade from 72.6 percent to 15.4 percent, services from 75.3 percent (in 1958) to 23.6 percent, and wholesale trade from 90.1 percent to 29.6 percent. Between 1958 and 1982 Detroit lost 187,100 jobs, mostly in manufacturing and retail trade (see Tables 2.1 and 2.2).

Marilyn Morehead has taken a somewhat closer look at industrial disinvestment in Detroit by analyzing data provided by the U.S. Census of Manufactures at five-year intervals over the period 1947–1977.[12] She identified two big postwar waves of central-city industrial disinvestment. During the forties and the fifties, trends in manufacturing employment and investment in central Detroit were pretty much the same as those in the

Table 2.2 Employment loss in selected economic sectors, city of Detroit, 1958–1982

Sector	Year	Change in employment (in thousands)	Percent change
Manufacturing	1958–1963	−3.8	−1.9
	1963–1967	+8.5	+4.2
	1967–1972	−28.7	−13.7
	1972–1977	−21.7	−15.0
	1977–1982	−47.6	−31.1
	1958–1982	−98.7	−48.3
Retail	1958–1963	−22.4	−23.7
	1963–1967	+3.2	+4.4
	1967–1972	−12.5	−16.6
	1972–1977	−14.3	−22.8
	1977–1982	−10.6	−21.9
	1958–1982	−56.6	−60.0
Services	1958–1963	+2.8	+6.4
	1963–1967	+6.0	+12.8
	1967–1972	−1.1	−2.2
	1972–1977	−9.0	−17.5
	1977–1982	+5.7	+13.5
	1958–1982	−2.6	−5.1
Wholesale	1958–1963	−1.1	−2.4
	1963–1967	+0.2	0
	1967–1972	−11.1	−24.8
	1972–1977	−8.9	−26.4
	1977–1982	−8.1	−32.7
	1958–1982	−29.0	−63.5
Four-sector total	1958–1963	−24.5	−6.3
	1963–1967	+17.9	+4.9
	1967–1972	−53.4	−14.0
	1972–1977	−59.3	−18.0
	1977–1982	−60.6	−22.5
	1958–1982	−187.1	−47.3

Source: Derived from U.S. Department of Commerce, *Census of Business*, various years, (Washington, D.C.: U.S. Government Printing Office).

metropolitan area as a whole. But after the deep recession of 1958, there was a significant change. From 1958 to 1963 Detroit's share of the SMSA's new capital expenditures fell from 44 percent to 30 percent. Metropolitan manufacturing employment grew from 295,800 to 329,700, while manufacturing jobs in the central city fell from 145,200 to 141,400.

Between 1963 and 1967, years when the economy boomed along with the war in Vietnam, both the city and the SMSA added industrial jobs, but city jobs did not grow as fast, so Detroit's share of metropolitan employment continued to drop. Between 1967 and 1972 manufacturing employment and capital investment fell in both the city and the SMSA. Then came the next major wave of central-city capital flight. Between 1972 and 1977 Detroit lost 15 percent of its manufacturing jobs, while the SMSA gained slightly. In this five-year period Detroit's share of metropolitan industrial investment dropped from 30 to 22 percent. All told, metropolitan industrial investment targeted to Detroit fell from 44 percent in 1958 to 22 percent in 1977—a decline of 50 percent in just two decades.

If anything, commercial disinvestment in Detroit has been more catastrophic for the city than has industrial abandonment. Certainly it is more visible to the eye. All one has to do is drive downtown, around the empty Kern block, then by the demolished remains of Crowley's Department Store, and past Hudson's shuttered downtown emporium—the three grand pillars of downtown Detroit's once thriving commercial district. Then turn onto one of Detroit's major thoroughfares—Grand River, Woodward, or Gratiot—and go to the city's limits. The panorama includes hundreds of vacant lots, boarded up buildings, and storefronts ready for a bulldozer. Then turn onto an expressway: You can take the John Lodge, for example, and go to the Northland Shopping Center, where over 30 new stores have been added to help Northland compete with the posh Fairlane Town Center in Dearborn, a shopping mall accessible *via* the Southfield Expressway. Similar comparisons with other suburban shopping havens could readily be made. Such comparisons show what is significant: the mass migration of commercial capital from central city to "regional" shopping centers.

The J. L. Hudson Company, long Detroit's dominant retail power and the nation's number two retail leader after Macy's during most years since World War II, is a perfect case illustration of commercial disinvestment in the Motor City. In the 1940s Hudson's 25-story, block-square, 2 million-square-foot downtown building generated three times the sales of its nearest Detroit competitor.[13] But by 1950 Detroit's population was growing mostly on the fringes of the city. Downtown Detroit had become increasingly congested, as 100,000 cars competed daily for 15,000 central business district parking spaces, and plans were in the works for the John Lodge and I-94 expressways.

In 1951 the Hudson Company decided to build Northland Shopping Center where the new Lodge Expressway intersected Eight Mile Road, and the Eastland Shopping Center in Harper Woods near Grosse Pointe and the planned Ford Expressway. Completed in 1953, Northland was the first regional shopping center with a "hub design," that is, with an anchor department store at the center of a cluster of smaller stores. Northland was an immediate success, and for 15 out of the next 16 years it was number one in sales among the nation's shopping centers.

Hudson's downtown sales peaked at $154 million in 1953, about the same time the city of Detroit reached its high-water population mark. By 1959 Hudson's sales had fallen to $117 million, a 24 percent decline in six years. But by then Hudson's transfer of capital from downtown to Northland and Eastland was paying off handsomely. Combined sales at the Northland and Eastland shopping centers came to $103 million, more than offsetting the decline in sales at the downtown store.

In 1969 the J. L. Hudson Company merged with the Dayton Corporation of Minneapolis to become the nation's seventh largest nonfood retailer. Hudson's initiated the merger because it was growing slowly and needed capital. So the J. L. Hudson Company became the J. L. Hudson Division of the Dayton-Hudson Corporation, a subsidiary now with 18 stores in three states and 10,000 employees. Decision-making power, once concentrated in downtown Detroit, was transferred to the new corporate headquarters in Minneapolis. Then, in 1978, the Dayton-Hudson Corporation sold Northland, Eastland, Westland, Southland, and five other shopping centers to the Equitable Life Assurance Society of New York. So the Hudson Department Stores are now owned by a Minneapolis firm, and the shopping centers they anchor are owned by a New York Insurance Company.[14]

In January 1983 the Dayton-Hudson Corporation closed its downtown Detroit department store, citing declining sales and increased operating costs. Then, in March 1984, the Minnesota corporation announced that its last remaining central-city operation, the Hudson Division headquarters, would be combined with the Dayton Corporation headquarters in Minneapolis, and the rest of Hudson's corporate staff would leave the city. Mayor Coleman Young charged the Dayton-Hudson Corporation with "pulling up stakes and moving out" of a city that had helped it grow into one of the nation's largest department store chains. But it was City Council President Erma Henderson who seemed to sum up the move best. "Unfortunately,"

Table 2.3 Trends in location of retail sales and the 20 major shopping areas (MSAs), city of Detroit and suburbs, 1958–1977

	Location of sales				Location of MSAs			
	Sales ($1000)		Percentage		Number		Percentage	
Year	City	Suburbs	City	Suburbs	City	Suburbs	City	Suburbs
1958	524.1	273.1	65.7	34.3	10	10	50	50
1963	417.5	680.4	38.0	62.0	5	15	25	75
1967	473.7	954.0	33.2	66.8	5	15	25	75
1972	386.5	1,489.1	20.6	79.4	3	17	15	85
1977	241.7	2,228.7	9.8	90.2	1	19	5	95

Source: David Snyder, "Commercial Disinvestment," *DARE City Life Task Force Report*, Detroit, Mich., 1981.

she was quoted as saying, "the people who miss it the most are those who are abandoned by Hudson's. . . . I'm talking about the blacks, the poor, and the elderly who are unable or can't afford to go to the suburban shopping centers. I guess these people didn't fit into their plans."[15]

Indeed they didn't, but then, as the Census of Retail Trade figures in Table 2.3 demonstrate, Hudson's was merely making its contribution to a more general trend. Between 1958 and 1977 Detroit's share of the commercial sales generated by the region's 20 major shopping areas dropped from 65.7 percent to 9.8 percent. In 1958 10 of the region's 20 major shopping areas were located in the city of Detroit. By 1977 that number had dropped to 1, and with the closing of Hudson's in 1983, the central city—with a population of 1.2 million people—was no longer home to even 1 major regional shopping area.[16]

Beyond Suburbia

Relocation from city to suburb largely set the pattern of uneven urban development in the Detroit region during the 1950s and 1960s. But by the mid-1970s another unsettling economic issue began to demand public attention: capital flight to other regions and abroad. The Great Lakes manufacturing empire was crumbling in the face of regional and international shifts in business investment and employment growth. In 1972 Detroit's civic elite commissioned a study of the exodus of capital from the Motor City. The study's conclusion was alarmingly simple: With dated production facilities, a public infrastructure in poor condition, high taxes, and a strongly unionized and aggressive labor force, Detroit would be hard pressed to retain business activity, let alone attract new capital investment.[17]

For the first time since the Great Depression, slump levels of unemployment failed to dissipate with national economic expansion. Detroit's central city lost nearly a quarter-million jobs and one-fifth of its population during the 1970s. With one-third of the city lacking any earned income and 60 percent receiving some form of public assistance; with taxes rising, capital fleeing, and property values stagnating; with municipal workers let go and public services curtailed, fiscal crises became routine.

Then, in 1980, the U.S. auto industry experienced an economic slide unparalleled since the Great Depression. The car giants lost $3.5 billion, 250,000 workers were laid off, and an additional 450,000 lost their jobs in supplier industries. Economic recession, rising energy prices, a saturated U.S. market for gas-guzzling cars, and increased foreign competition sent the Big Three's profits plummeting. With their survival at stake, the auto giants mounted a reorganization strategy of a depth and scope unprecedented in the industry. Their plan included changes in product design, global concentration and centralization of capital in fewer firms, redesign of the labor process in relationship to new technologies, and transformation in the industry's international division of labor.[18]

The global reorganization of the auto industry has meant massive job loss, severe reductions in social services, major labor concessions, and a declining standard of living.[19] In 1978 auto companies employed 735,000 hourly workers in the United States; by the spring of 1984 that figure had dropped to 565,000—a decline of 170,000 industrial jobs. One hundred and five thousand of those auto workers were on indefinite layoff; the remaining 65,000 had simply disappeared from the United Auto Workers' (UAW) rolls.[20]

Between 1960 and 1980 the Japanese auto industry grew from the smallest to the largest in the world. The Japanese advantage came primarily from a home-centered, export-oriented production system, which generated higher productivity and therefore allowed domestic companies to produce cars for much less than their international competitors. Of all the auto companies in Japan, Toyota is the most successful. Despite stiff export barriers in western Europe and the voluntary restraint agreement with the United States, Toyota made big profits while Western companies incurred big losses during the steep recession of 1979–1982.[21] Japanese competitors now call the company, the "Toyota bank," because its profits have been so large that it can finance most of its spending on plant and equipment from internal funds.[22]

The Toyota system maximizes manufacturing efficiency by keeping inventory to an absolute minimum; by making sure each step of the manufacturing process is done correctly the first time, even though the assembly line runs slower as a result; and by continually reducing the amount of human labor that goes into each car. The Toyota advantage in time, space, and money was graphically illustrated in a recent study by Ford Motor Company. When Ford compared Toyota plants with similar manufacturing facilities in western Europe and North America, the corporation discovered that (1) because of inventory-saving techniques, Toyota's production per worker was three times that of Ford's, (2) a Toyota engine plant takes up 300,000 square feet compared with 900,000 at a comparable Ford facility, (3) from 80 to 85 percent of the Toyotas coming off the line had no defects, as compared with an average of seven to eight defects per car at Ford, (4) because of Toyota's heavy investment in backup tooling, the time required to change a standard die took five to ten minutes at Toyota, as compared with three to four hours at Ford.[23]

This time, economic crisis and disinvestment have hit Detroit's central city and industrial suburbs alike. It seems that the economic premises upon which the Motor City and its industrial satellites developed—inexpensive energy, a hegemonic corporate position in national and international auto markets, and expanding employment opportunities in industries linked to car production—have run their course and now are subjects for economic historians. Meanwhile city officials throughout the region are seeking a development model that will ensure their communities an economic future.

One Detroit, Two Detroits, Many Detroits

By the early 1950s the "leapfrog" spatial logic of auto expansion, abetted by federal transportation and housing policies, yielded massive suburbanization in the Detroit region. Auto industry decentralization, then the reorganization of commercial capital from downtown to regional shopping centers, gave birth to two Detroits. One, the Detroit metropolitan area, was thriving economically, stimulated by high levels of capital investment. It contained nearly half of Michigan's population. Residents of this Detroit were mostly white, they lived in single-family houses located in the suburbs, and they earned an income above the state average. But the other Detroit, the central city, had become more and more like a segregated urban enclave during the decades following World War II.[24] Home to hundreds of thousands of poor and unemployed people, the city was now pitted against the suburbs in a classic American pattern of uneven urban development.

Table 2.4 Employment by type of industry: Macomb, Oakland, and Wayne counties, 1981 (percentage)

Employment	Michigan (%)	Macomb (%)	Oakland (%)	Wayne (%)
Construction	4	3	5	3
Manufacturing	36	46	25	36
Wholesale trade	6	4	9	6
Retail trade	20	22	21	17
Finance	6	3	9	6
Service	22	18	26	25
Transportation	5	3	5	7
Base totals	2,760,060	204,359	409,884	738,866

Source: James Jacobs, "Small Business and Economic Development in Macomb County," Macomb Community College, Center for Community Studies, Detroit, Mich., 1983, table 6.

Note: The first two columns do not add up to 100 percent due to rounding.

Then came global economic crisis and the international reorganization of the U.S. auto and steel industries in the late 1970s. Deindustrialization spread out from the central city into suburban Detroit. And residents in Detroit's industrial, working-class suburbs have come to share many problems with their central-city neighbors. Yet, at the same time, many suburban financial, commercial, and research and development enclaves are booming. This suggests a new pattern of uneven urban development linked to a reorganized division of labor in the international economy. This pattern is characterized less by a single, fundamental division between two Detroits—the central city and its suburbs—than by multiple divisions among many competing subcenters. A swing through Detroit's suburban ring, starting to the north and ending in the south, should help get this point across.

The Northern Industrial Belt: Macomb County

Macomb County, due north from the city of Detroit, well reveals the inroads industrial decline has made into suburban life. As Table 2.4 indicates, Macomb is considerably more industrialized than other counties in the Detroit region. In fact, Macomb is one of the most industrialized areas in the United States. There are, for example, more industrial jobs in Macomb County than in Pittsburgh, Cleveland, Buffalo, or Cincinnati. Some 46 percent of Macomb's population is employed in manufacturing: half in

Table 2.5 Population of Macomb County 1900–1980

Year	Population	Numerical change (from previous decade)	Percentage change (from previous decade)
1900	33,244	+1,431	+4.5
1910	32,606	−638	−1.9
1920	38,103	+5,497	+16.9
1930	77,146	+39,043	+102.5
1940	107,638	+30,492	+39.5
1950	184,961	+77,323	+71.8
1960	405,804	+220,843	+119.4
1970	625,309	+219,505	+54.1
1980	688,230	+62,921	+10.1

Source: James Jacobs, "The Urbanization of Macomb County," Macomb Community College, Detroit, Mich., 1981, table 9.

major auto plants and most of the rest in chemical, glass, machine, and metal fabrication and other "hardware manufacturing" that complements auto production.[25] Today suburbs in the southern end of Macomb County are sharing the same problems as the city of Detroit: a declining economy, growing unemployment and welfare caseloads, the closing of schools, and a rising crime rate.[26]

Macomb is traversed by one of Detroit's major industrial corridors, Van Dyke and Mound Road. Heavy industry started setting up shop there in the 1930s: Rotary Electric Steel Corporation (now Jones and Laughlin) in 1933, Chrysler's truck plant in 1938, and General Electric's Metallurgical Products Division in 1940. They all settled on the border of Detroit, close to workers commuting from the central city by bus or trolley.

World War II gave Macomb County another boost. In 1940 the U.S. Navy built a manufacturing plant on Mound Road. In 1951 the army built a tank plant there and located the headquarters of its Tank Automotive Command adjacent to it. In 1940 General Motors began building its Tech Center in the corridor, and this stimulated growth in Macomb's suburbs just to the north: Warren, Sterling Heights, Fraser, and Clinton Township. Gradually, Macomb County became a center for a skilled-labor machine industry linked to auto manufacturers and host to many small tool and die shops and auto parts companies. By 1976 the county had over 100,000 manufacturing jobs.

But between 1970 and 1980 Macomb's population increased by only 10 percent, the county's lowest growth rate since the first decade of this century. And all the cities in the southern end of the county—East Detroit,

Table 2.6 Population change, southern Macomb County suburbs, 1970–1980

Suburbs	1970 population	1980 population	Percent change
East Detroit	45,920	38,220	−16.8
St. Clair Shores	88,093	75,470	−14.3
Warren	179,260	159,504	−11.0
Roseville	60,529	54,214	−10.4
Center Line	10,379	9,498	−8.5
Total	384,181	336,906	−12.3

Source: Computed from 1980 figures in *Detroit News* article, July 10, 1980.

Roseville, Center Line, St. Clair Shores, and Warren—actually decreased in population (see Tables 2.5 and 2.6). Macomb's factories were now moving to lower-wage, rural areas in the Sunbelt and abroad.[27]

Between 1970 and 1977 the market value of industrial property in Macomb County dropped by 5.6 percent.[28] By 1979 the county had 94 fewer manufacturing plants than at its 1967 industrial peak—a decline of 10 percent. Then, as the economy slumped between 1979 and 1982, Macomb lost 21 percent of its manufacturing jobs; that added up to 41 percent of county employment in transportation equipment, 25 percent of county employment in fabricated metal parts, and 15 percent of county employment in nonelectrical machinery.[29]

By March 1981 Macomb's unemployment rate was 15.3 percent, more than double that of the metropolitan area as a whole. Some 21,000 Macomb residents were drawing regular unemployment, and 6,300 more were drawing extended unemployment benefits. For the tens of thousands of Macomb workers who had exhausted their unemployment insurance, welfare was the only alternative. By February 1981 over 42,600 people were subsisting on welfare in Macomb County.[30]

According to the Michigan Employment Security Commission (MESC), most Macomb County unemployment recipients were between the ages of 20 and 34. The vast majority had been employed in the machine trades and in structural occupations—the jobs most severely affected by the current crisis and reorganization of the U.S. auto industry. The employment prospects for these workers, MESC analysts concluded, were "extremely poor."[31]

If there is an urban center to Macomb County, the city of Warren is it. Warren has 25 percent of Macomb's population, labor force, and housing.

The city has 30 percent of the county's assessed valuation and 61 percent of Macomb's industrial property. Incorporated in 1957, Warren grew pell-mell into a sprawling, formless suburban mass. Today Warren is Michigan's third largest city, behind Detroit and Grand Rapids.

Warren is also a white city, part of the barrier reef that whites erected to wall blacks into the central city. Out of 157,000 Warren residents, just 300 are blacks and 1,500 are Hispanics. Warren's workers are just about evenly split between white- and blue-collar, skilled and unskilled trades: Twenty percent are laborers, 15 percent are in the skilled trades, and 13 percent are in the service industries. Most Warren residents own their own homes and have moderate incomes.

Warren's auto-related economy was hard hit by the economic crisis beginning in 1979. Since then scores of small tooling, auto parts, and machine shops have closed down. The city lost another $7 million in annual tax revenues when the Jones and Laughlin steel mill shut its doors in 1983. Unemployment reached a high of 20.1 percent in 1982, although by mid-1984 it had dropped to 11 percent, slightly above Michigan's 10.3 percent rate. Since Warren's property tax levy, at 12.25 mills, ranks among the state's lowest (Detroit's, for example, is 32.4 mills), the economic trauma ushered in severe fiscal problems for the city too. Since 1981 Warren has eliminated nearly 10 percent of its municipal work force.[32]

The fallout from the economic crisis has widened the gap between Warren's north and south ends. The south end, bordering the city of Detroit, is a decayed commercial and residential area with high crime rates. Here porno shops and other small, on-the-margin businesses cluster in overcrowded, dilapidated buildings. Here, too, deteriorated wood-frame houses line unpaved, hole-pocked streets. The south end is split off from the rest of Warren by Interstate 696, a thoroughfare some Warren residents refer to as the "Mason-Dixon line." Warren's north end is prosperous, safe, affluent. Here neat, split-level brick ranch homes cluster about a fine old Victorian neighborhood dating from 1850. The GM Tech Center, the city's civic center, high-rise office buildings, and several new restaurants fill out the rest of north Warren's landscape.

For years Warren refused to seek urban renewal or Community Development Block Grants funds. City residents feared Washington would tie the grants to a demand that Warren build public housing, and public housing would attract low-income, minority residents. In 1970, when Warren residents voted to pass over $30 million in federal urban renewal funds to rehabilitate substandard wooden homes on the city's south side, *Time Magazine* called Warren the nation's most racist city.[33]

Today Warren's City Council no longer rejects federal redevelopment funds, and city officials are pinning their hopes for an economic turnaround on a $500 million Chrysler "Dodge City" project targeted for the south end. In return for a $50.5 million city tax abatement, Chrysler has promised to construct a new stamping and assembly complex for pickup trucks. But "Dodge City" helps Warren retain only 4,000 jobs the city would have lost had Chrysler decided to relocate truck production elsewhere. Warren's urban planners are also dreaming about a new downtown, built around the city's civic center and eventually including a mini-convention center, an auditorium, a cultural center, a central library, and a heliport.

The Northwest Passage: Oakland County

The development model Warren officials have in mind, no doubt, is provided by their neighbors to the west, in Oakland County. The northwestern suburbs of Oakland County have enjoyed a phenomenal growth in population and corporate business during the past two decades. Oakland County's population grew 11.5 percent between 1970 and 1980—the highest county growth rate in Michigan and a rate higher than that in 99 percent of U.S. counties. Oakland County's per-person income ranks 19th among all 3,137 counties in the United States, and Oakland trails only Manhattan in the list of the wealthiest counties with more than a million people.[34]

Avenues express the character of Oakland County as they do the rest of the region. Southfield Road, for example, passes through Southfield and other northwest suburbs like Lathrup Village, Beverly Hills, and Birmingham, all of which number among the wealthiest communities in the United States.[35] At one time Southfield Road was a wide residential street, but it lost its homey character when the property between the major mile roads attracted office and retail investment. Now low-slung office blocks and faceless buildings with clashing fake colonial, Victorian, and modern designs house racket clubs, synagogues, and professional consultants of every variety. Apartment and condo complexes, with names like Le Chateau and Balmoral Club, crowd around shopping centers built on acres of asphalt.[36]

Detroit architecture critic Robert Benson has noted how Southfield Road gives off an impression of indecision that carries over to the communities along its path. Neither truly residential, nor fully commercial, Southfield Road is a formless combination of the two—a reflection, perhaps, of hypermobility and rootlessness among its "new class" inhabitants. Mobility and rootlessness are also expressed in an expanding suburban divorce rate and rising numbers of well-to-do singles, with lifestyles to match, all of which pervades the culture of northwest suburbs like Southfield, Farmington Hills, Birmingham, and Troy.

At five o'clock most any work day, thousands of pin stripe–clad business executives and decked-out clerical workers leave dozens of high-rise office towers and edge their Detroit specials (mainly Mark IV's and Mustangs, it seems) onto the Northwestern Highway. Their immediate destination, as charted by area social columnists, is singles bars with names like Excalibur, Carlos Murphy's, Tequila Willie's, and TGI Friday's. Later, perhaps, they will travel north and west to disco spots like Ginopolis's, Mr. Laff's, Archibald's, Bennigan's, and Fanny's. These suburbanites reside in complexes like Somerset Park in Troy, Muirwood in Farmington Hills, Franklin Park Towers in Southfield. And they socialize in groups like Birmingham Singles and Somerset Singles Ski Club, which offer weekly tennis, volleyball, ski trips, dances, weekend excursions, and discussion sessions.[37]

Suburban gentry concentrated in this density indicate one reason why Oakland County now claims to be the business center of southeastern Michigan. Oakland County suburbs—Southfield, Troy, Farmington Hills, Pontiac, Birmingham, and Bloomfield Hills—number six out of the ten cities in metropolitan Detroit with over 1 million square feet of office space. Oakland County now possesses half of all the office space in the seven-county region. Oakland's total office footage now tops Detroit's. In fact, just two Oakland County suburbs, Southfield and Troy, now have a combined 24.6 million square feet compared with Detroit's 25.3 million. Although 200,000 fewer people reside in Oakland County than in the city of Detroit, assessments suggest Oakland County has well over double the wealth of the Motor City.[38] Indexed by numbers of major corporations and professional people occupying big chunks of office space, Oakland County now occupies the central place in the region, according to institutional properties analysts.[39]

Downtown in Oakland County is Southfield. Incorporated in 1958, Southfield's rural landscape was rapidly transformed into subdivisions, office high-rises, and business headquarters. With 75,568 residents in 1980, Southfield was the 17th largest city in Michigan, but with 15 million square feet of office space, Southfield ranked 8 in size of tax base. A fifth of *Fortune*'s 500 largest corporations have world, national, or regional headquarters in Southfield.[40]

Southfield has been positioned to grow because of its accessibility to major highways (including Telegraph, Southfield Expressway, Northwestern Highway, and the I-696 freeway) and because of Oakland County's reputation as a high-status location for lawyers, accountants, consultants, and other professionals. Southfield's latest building boom includes 18 new buildings along a six-mile stretch of the Northwestern Highway, coming to 3 million square feet of office space and $135 million worth of construction. Southfield now has more office buildings than Detroit (142 as compared with 116), but its rents are still lower. Rents average between $8.50 and $15.50 a square foot as compared with an average Detroit rent of $15.50.[41]

Yet in the metropolitan real estate game, Southfield's era of rapid growth is already past. Eighty-four percent of its land is now developed, and "urban" problems are encroaching upon the city: declining school enrollments, clogged transportation arteries, aging housing, and an obsolete government structure. Worried about "suburban flight," Southfield influentials established the 2001 Committee in the late 1970s. Made up of some 200 business, government, and community representatives and divided into 11 subcommittees, the 2001 Committee's task was to chart Southfield's future and stake out a position of leadership in competition with other cities in the region.

Southfield's principal Oakland County competitor is Troy, its neighbor to the north. Twenty-five thousand people work along the four-mile strip of Big Beaver Road, known as Troy's "Golden Corridor." The corridor contains 6 million square feet of office space, occupied by major corporate headquarters like K-Mart International, Volkswagen of North America, Ziebart, Ex-Cello, and Kelly Services and by offices of such nationally known professionals as architect Minoru Yamasaki. Corporate headquarters, three major hotels, high-tech industries, and sprawling residential developments were lured to Troy by advantages like the I-75 expressway for ease in commuting, two small airports for handling corporate air traffic, and an ample and skilled work force. Troy takes in more tax dollars per capita than any other city in the country, even though the city has a five-mill tax rate ceiling.[42] And developer A. Alfred Taubman is now building Somerset North in Troy—a futuristic, bilevel shopping mall with adjoining offices, hotel, and residences.

Yet Troy officials are already worried that their businesses will leave for an even more welcoming spot on the suburban frontier. So they have developed a strategy they claim will prevent Southfield's "mistakes." Rather than developing rows of small offices, which have high turnover rates, or building high-rises, which bring traffic congestion, Troy's emphasis is on low-rise "campus centers" with wide green spaces in between.[43]

Troy's prime business attractions—the nearby I-75 highway, lots of big corporate offices, and good hotels—suggest the Golden Corridor is designed more for the automobile and easy access for out-of-town business clients than it is for local residents and community institutions. And many developers now seem to think that Troy has peaked. The city has reached two-thirds of its planned 120,000 population; 30 percent of its office and industrial space is still there for development, but this land is less desirable than that which preceded it. Eleven Troy businesses have recently relocated —several to neighboring Rochester Hills, where land is less expensive, tax rates are lower, and tax abatements are easier to get.[44]

Northwest suburbanites have also put together an ambitious countywide economic development plan. With a projected 20 percent increase in the labor force by 1990, Oakland officials calculate that the county will need 90,000 new jobs to keep its unemployment rate at 6 percent.[45] And Oakland County is now competing with other parts of southeast Michigan for high-technology research centers and production facilities.

The attraction Oakland officials are now touting most is a 1,700-acre high-technology park adjacent to Oakland University. The Oakland Technology Park spans Auburn and Rochester Hills and is bounded by I-75, University Drive, Adams Road, and the M-59 freeway. The park's promoters talk about producing 20,000 jobs in five to ten years, by attracting $1 billion from companies wanting to invest in the "work place of the twentieth century." The property is owned by Oakland University, Oakland Community College, Comerica, Inc., and an investment group led by builder Samuel Frankel.[46]

The county hopes Oakland Technology Park will serve as an important link in a high-tech corridor rivaling the national significance of Boston's Route 128 and Santa Clara County's Silicon Valley. In Oakland's version, the high-tech focus is on advanced manufacturing technology, particularly automation processes. Oakland University will work with industry to train students in the repair of microprocessors and diesel engines, and the university has built a $1 million robotics demonstration center to give students direct experience with industrial robots.

Comerica has started the park development off by breaking ground for a $45 million computer and operations center expected to employ 1,000 workers within a year. General Motor's new corporate subsidiary, Electronic Data Systems (EDS) also plans to build a big computer center in the park. EDS designs, installs, and operates business information systems for corporate and government clients throughout the world. Since its merger with General Motors, EDS has been making a big splash in the Oakland County real estate market. EDS is after space for the 1,200 employees the company is moving to the Detroit area, for the 4,000 local workers

GM has transferred to EDS, and for the 2,000 new employees the company plans to hire in southeast Michigan. Thus far EDS has signed a three-year lease for a new two-story building in Bloomfield Township, and the company has taken over six of nine floors in Travelers Tower II in the Southfield Civic Center.[47]

GMF Robotics has also opted to locate its new $20 million headquarters in the Oakland County Technology Park. GMF Robotics, with $70 million in sales in 1984, is one of the leading robotics firms in the United States. Right now GMF primarily makes computer-controlled painters, and the U.S. auto industry is 60 percent of its market. A joint venture between GM and Fujitsu Fanuc, Ltd. of Japan, GMF was chased by dozens of communities in Michigan and in other states before it set its sight on land just south of Quail Ridge, a subdivision of $200,000 homes in Oakland Technology Park.[48]

Chrysler Corporation recently gave the biggest boost to Oakland County's plans for becoming the center of high technology in the region. Chrysler has decided to build a $500 million corporate research center adjacent to Oakland University in the park. Chrysler's effort to match the GM and Ford tech centers will provide research opportunities for Oakland University computer science and engineering faculty members and internships and prospective employment for Oakland University students, and it will strengthen Oakland County's ties to the high-technology dimension of the international auto industry.[49]

All this high-tech development activity also bodes added riches for some of the state's biggest real estate investors. Troy developer Samuel Frankel and a partnership of 35 investors, including Max Fisher and federal judge Avern Cohn and his former silk-stocking law partners, Honigman, Miller, and Schwartz, own an 806-acre chunk of property in the park, and they stand to make an enormous sum of money when they sell it. The group's holding was initially purchased for $806 an acre in 1969. In 1982 the Frankel group sold 16 acres for $16,000 an acre; that's a 2,000 percent profit, and it puts a value of some $13 million on the original $650,000 investment.[50]

The Region in Microcosm: Suburban Wayne County

The portion of Wayne County lying outside the city of Detroit fills out the region's southwestern suburban landscape. Suburban Wayne's share of the region's population has hovered around 25 percent since 1960, but the county's suburbs have steadily lost ground in wealth and income to their northern neighbors (see Figures 2.1 and 2.2). It's more accurate, though, to argue that suburban Wayne County reflects, in microcosm, the pattern of uneven development that now besets the region as a whole. Some Wayne suburbs have suffered massive disinvestment, yet others are challenging Oakland County's growing financial and commercial domination over the region.

Ford's Fairlane In the early 1970s, Fairlane, a planned, 2,360-acre residential/office/commercial "new town within the town" of Dearborn, joined the regional tug of war for business supremacy in southeastern Michigan. Dearborn fronts the southwest border of Detroit; downtown Detroit is 15 minutes to the east, and the Detroit Metropolitan Airport is 15 minutes to the west. When the Ford Motor Company's Land Development subsidiary decided to build Fairlane, it received full cooperation from the city of Dearborn. This isn't surprising, since Ford Motor Company already provided over half of Dearborn's tax revenues.[51]

Fairlane land was Henry Ford I's birthplace, his boyhood home, and later the site for his Fair Lane Mansion and Fair Lane Estate. Between 1908 and 1911 Henry Ford purchased 2,100 acres of farm and woodland in Dearborn Township. Shortly thereafter Henry and Clara Ford settled at Fair Lane to escape the social confines of exclusive Grosse Pointe and the daily pressures of Ford's industrial empire. Ford was a nature lover, and Fair Lane was his personal wilderness retreat. There Ford walked with naturalist friends along secluded paths and across grounds populated by deer and songbirds that he'd imported from England.[52]

A priceless retreat for the founding entrepreneur, Fair Lane became a priceless development plum for his corporate successor. Ford Motor Company started planning Fairlane in 1968 to fill in the empty spaces left over from Ford's other developments in Dearborn: the Ford Motor Company World Headquarters, the Ford Research and Engineering Center, the Ford Division Headquarters, the Ford Rouge Plant, the Fair Lane Estate, and Greenfield Village. Fairlane is touted to be the largest contiguous, privately owned piece of urban real estate in the nation.[53] The following number among the key elements making up the Fairlane development:

The *Fairlane Transportation Center* consists of 27 acres containing the regional reservation center for United Airlines, the administrative offices and data processing center for the Automobile Club of Michigan, a planned high-rise "theme tower," additional offices, a heliport, and a rapid-rail transit system.

The *Fairlane Office Park* consists of a 160-acre business cluster centering upon Parklane Towers, a 15-story twin office block. The towers contain a half-million square feet of office space and overlook an expanse of greenery and water. Insurance companies, ad agencies, law firms, and financial institutions inhabit Parklane, and so do the Detroit, Toledo, and Ironton Railroad and the Ford Motor Land Development Corporation. A covered mini-mall connects the buildings with a row of fancy boutiques and shops offering diverse business services.

The *Fairlane Town Center* consists of 282 acres developed around the posh Hyatt Regency Dearborn and the Fairlane Shopping Mall. The Hyatt Regency—designed by Charles Luckman Associates, a national planning and architectural firm—has a 13-story atrium; an interior, plant-filled courtyard; five stainless-steel-and-glass elevator bubbles connecting 11 floors of guest rooms; complete banquet and convention facilities, including a ballroom that seats 1,000; and a scenic rooftop lounge overlooking the Ford empire at one revolution per hour. Outside, a heliport stands near the front entrance. Eight hundred employees keep the hotel functioning.

A half-mile to the northeast is the Fairlane Shopping Mall, one of the largest shopping centers in the Midwest. The mall features 1.8 million square feet of enclosed, climatically controlled shopping area. It is anchored by 4 department stores set amidst 160 smaller shops. Waterworks, art displays, and plantings decorate this trilevel palace of consumption built by the Al Taubman Company. Patrons of the hotel and shopping center can make the journey between them in 71 seconds on a People Mover: The driverless, rubber-tired, computer-controlled, pollution-free vehicles move at 20 miles an hour between stations in front of the hotel and inside the shopping mall.

In the northwest corner of Town Center, next to the University of Michigan's Dearborn campus and the Henry Ford Community College, is the Henry Ford Hospital. This ambulatory care center offers provisions for 24-hour physician care, radiology facilities, laboratory, pharmaceutical, and dental services, and ambulatory surgery.

Fairlane East is an array of luxury apartments and condominiums overlooking rolling "land mounds" and, for $2,000 extra, a lake. The condos offer features like cabinets with "hand-rubbed finish by the Indiana Amish," fireplaces, patios, two-car garages with automatic door openers, trash mashers, and a security system that includes a gate guarded around the clock. Residents have access to a lakeside community center and, if they are so inclined, to membership in the nearby Fairlane Club—a $7 million private athletic club that boasts 18 tennis courts, 8 bowling lanes, 4 racket ball courts, 2 swimming pools, billiard tables, handball courts, a whirlpool, an all-sport pro shop, a dining room, a ballroom, cocktail bars and grills, card rooms, a library, a youth lounge, an observation deck, locker rooms, shower rooms, sauna and steam rooms, exercise rooms, and massage rooms.

Fairlane Commerce Park is a 165-acre light-industry park housing headquarters for Applied Handling, Inc., distribution centers for the Nestlé Company and Interstate United Corporation, an office and display center for the Sheet Metal Air Conditioning Contractors Association, and a multi-tenant facility built by the Ford Motor Land Development Corporation. Fairlane also hosts a 350,000-square-foot automated bulk-mail center for the U.S. Postal Service—a facility designed to speed up the sorting of second-, third-, and fourth-class mail and parcel post.

Fairlane once rested upon a natural flood plain of the Rouge River. But after a flood on the plain in 1947, which did little damage to Dearborn, the U.S. Army Corps of Engineers came up with a plan to prevent future flooding in the lower Rouge Valley. The project—bitterly opposed by area environmentalists—straightened, deepened, paved, and realigned a six-mile stretch of the Rouge River. Now a concrete ditch speeds the runoff of water from the flood plain during heavy rains. Ford's Fairlane development is the main benefactor of this $40 million, publicly funded project, which protects areas like Fairlane East and Commerce Park from nature's hazards.

Many of the firms in Fairlane came from downtown Detroit: United Airlines, the Automobile Club of Michigan, and J. Walter Thompson Advertising Agency, to name a few.[54] Some 40 percent of Parklane Towers was first filled by businesses that either moved to Fairlane from Detroit or added new offices in Fairlane. Offices in Parklane rent for less than on the riverfront. Fairlane is closer to where corporate executives live, has plentiful parking, and is distant from central-city problems. The Fairlane Shopping Mall is also designed to draw customers from great distances, including Detroit. According to Ford developers, the mall is designed to "create the nice feeling that will attract people from as far away as . . . 50 miles . . . for an all-day shopping experience."[55]

Downriver Fairlane's future seems rosy indeed. Yet barely a stone's throw away from Ford's affluent headquarters city stands a cluster of industrial communities so hard hit by disinvestment and decay that their name has come to symbolize deindustrialization in the Detroit region.

Downriver is a collection of blue-collar communities nestled against one another along the Detroit River, south and west from the central city of

Table 2.7 Population trends in downriver communities, 1950–1980

Communities	1950	1960	1970	1980
Allen Park	12,329	37,494	40,747	34,196
Brownstown Township	na	na	na	7,040
Ecorse	17,948	17,328	17,515	14,447
Flat Rock	1,931	4,696	5,643	6,853
Gibraltar	nd	2,196	3,842	4,458
Grosse Isle Township	nd	nd	8,306	9,320
Lincoln Park	29,310	53,933	52,984	45,105
Melvindale	9,483	13,089	13,862	12,322
River Rouge	20,549	18,147	15,947	12,912
Riverview	1,432	7,237	11,342	14,569
Rockwood	1,044	2,026	3,225	3,346
Southgate	nd	29,404	33,909	32,058
Taylor	nd	nd	70,020	77,568
Trenton	6,222	18,439	24,127	22,762
Woodhaven	nd	na	3,566	10,902
Wyandotte	36,846	43,519	41,061	34,006

Source: U.S. Department of Commerce, Bureau of the Census, 1980 census tracts, Detroit, Mich. *Census of Population and Housing* (Washington, D.C.: U.S. Government Printing Office, 1983).

Note: na = not available; nd = not defined.

Detroit—cities whose combined population came to about 340,000 in 1980. At the turn of the century the Downriver Corridor became a steel supplier for the auto industry and later a plant location for car builders and parts suppliers in search of large plots of inexpensive land fronting a waterway. Downriver also became home for immigrants from Europe and the southern United States who came to work in the plants and mills.[56]

Fourteen municipalities and two townships cluster along the Downriver Corridor, one of the Motor City's principal rail arteries. Ranging in size from 2.4 square miles (River Rouge) to 23.3 square miles (Taylor), all 16 communities combined take up 120 square miles of land south of the central-city border.

Downriver boomed during the 1950s. But population growth slowed during the 1960s and in some communities even declined (see Table 2.7). By the 1970s Downriver had become the population loss leader among areas in the region. Downriver's oldest industrial communities, Ecorse and River Rouge, are closest to the central city, and they lost the most people. In fact, they were number two and number three on Michigan's list of most rapidly declining city populations. On the other hand, Downriver's southernmost cities, those farthest from central Detroit, continued to grow during the 1970s.[57]

Some Downriver communities have more factories than others, but heavy industry is their common lifeline. Downriver dependence on heavy industry is extraordinary, even when gauged against the metal-bending Motor City. In 1980, for example, 22 percent of U.S. workers and 33 percent of metropolitan Detroit workers were employed in manufacturing; but the figure for Downriver was 37 percent, and it went as high as 45 percent in Ecorse and 47 percent in Gibraltar.[58]

Now all that may be history. Downriver's economy centers upon steel and other closely linked industries that "begin at the furnace," like auto producers and suppliers and manufacturers of industrial chemicals. Strong pressures are working to restructure the U.S. steel industry in ways that are tearing Downriver communities apart. In 1982 U.S. steel producers lost a colossal $3 billion—their worst record since the Great Depression. And 1983 brought slight improvement. The forces behind these dismal figures include a relatively stagnant domestic market, rising foreign competition because of the internationalization of steel production, and new technologies that allow for new methods of steel production.[59]

By the early 1980s the ripple effect from plant closings, cutbacks, and concessions threatened to swamp Downriver. The complete toll in disrupted communities and dislocated lives defies calculation. But job trends from 1976 to 1983 among Downriver's largest industrial plants suggest something of the magnitude of deindustrialization Downriver. In 1980 DANA Corporation closed its Ecorse plant and BASF shut down its Wyandotte factory. By 1981 Downriver's major factories employed 13,435 fewer workers, a 36 percent decline since 1979. And the downward slide continued. By 1983 four more major plants had closed: Firestone Steel, Ford Casting, McLouth Steel (in Gibraltar), and Whitehead and Kales. Job loss in Downriver's major factories now came to 14,750, a 40 percent decline since 1979.[60]

Cycles of boom and bust set the rhythm of life in industrial communities. But Downriver now confronts a different kind of crisis. Unemployment benefits and belt tightening don't suffice when months of unemployment turn into years. Reports from social service agencies and community groups trace the social ramifications of disinvestment Downriver. Many people required temporary food and shelter. A new emergency hot line averaged 30 calls a day. Alcoholism, emotional problems, and family violence rose.

Still, by 1982, only 38 percent of those eligible for social services in Downriver's communities had actually applied for assistance.[61]

Downriver residents share a regional consciousness born of three generations' experience with heavy industry's booms and busts. But recent crises in steel and auto industries have compelled local governments, businesses, unions, and social service agencies to translate that collective identity into collective organization—in the form of the Downriver Community Conference (DCC)—to combat industrial decline and the attendant social crises that beset the entire region.[62] Founded in 1977, the Downriver Community Conference is an intergovernmental planning and development organization. The DCC is organized like a corporation, governed by a board of directors made up of the mayors and supervisors of the 16 Downriver communities, and run by a paid staff. The Downriver Community Conference's most important programs now fall into three areas: (1) economic development, (2) employment and training, and (3) community services. DCC's foray into economic development includes public relations campaigning to promote the Downriver image, lobbying for changes in state legislation to improve Michigan's business climate, forestalling store and plant closings by means of a "business retention team," enticing business investment with brochures promising tax abatements and other sorts of financial assistance, and assisting businesses with permits and zoning through an ombudsman service. DCC's Government Marketing Division provides assistance to businesses wishing to procure government contracts. The DCC also runs a business incubator program, lodged in the Downriver Business Venture Center, where new businesses can reduce operating costs by sharing office machines, secretarial help, and a conference room.[63] The aim of DCC's employment and training program is to "return workers, as expeditiously as possible, to quality jobs in the labor market." To that end the DCC has established and is attempting to expand a labor exchange network, whereby the organization mediates between "supply employers" (those who fire) and "demand employers" (those who hire). DCC now boasts of a network of 200 demand employers, most of whom are in Michigan.[64]

The Downriver Community Conference also offers and helps coordinate several community services through the downriver Human Service Coalition, which includes the Department of Social Services; hospitals; and agencies dealing with mental health, substance abuse, aging, information and referral, and domestic violence. The DCC offers a hotline referral system to help workers cope with the stress of losing their jobs. And

DCC's hot line services also include a health referral network, whereby local doctors offer some appointments, hospitals offer some bed space, and pharmacies offer some prescriptions free or at reduced prices to the unemployed.

The DCC's economic development program is premised on the principal that the best way to create jobs is by offering public incentives to increase private profits. And the DCC boasts about generating $20 million in contracts for local companies and hundreds of jobs.[65] But deindustrialization Downriver has thrown thousands out of work. And should DCC's most ambitious plans come to pass, they will still fall short of what would be required to restore Downriver's economy.[66]

Fairlane and Downriver present starkly contrasting images of suburbia. And suburban Wayne County evokes, within itself, a pattern of uneven development among communities that characterizes the Detroit region as a whole. Nonetheless, mightn't one say that Fairlane offers a model for renewed development that can be mimicked by the region's more economically depressed areas? City officials in Detroit seem to think so, and they are marshalling their riverfront resources to make their wish come true.

Coming Full Circle: Renaissance on the Riverfront

Detroit is where it is because of its strategic location on the Great Lakes. The city's name comes from the French word "étroit," which means the "strait." In this case "l'étroit" is the river that connects Lake Erie with Lake Huron. The French founded Detroit in 1701 as a military stronghold to control fur trade on the lakes, and ever since, the strait has been the geographic spine of the city. For a long time the Detroit River was the city's economic backbone too.[67]

For more than two centuries the riverfront was Detroit's window on the world. Streets along the eastern riverfront—with names like St. Aubin, Beaubien, Campau, and Chene—hail back to the early ribbon farmers, who cultivated long, narrow strips of land, each jutting out from the river to give them access to water and transportation. By 1900 the rhythm of life on those streets was orchestrated by ships docking and unloading cargo at riverside piers, by railroad cars arriving at waterfront storage depots, and by ferries and lake-bound cruise boats coming and going. Factories and warehouses crowded the river's edge—Parke-Davis, Berry Brothers Varnish, Michigan Stove, Lauhoff Brothers, Company Roller Mill Works, Detroit Dry Dock, Detroit Car Works, and Russell Wheel and Foundry, to name a few.[68] Crammed against waterfront work places were saloons, bordellos, boardinghouses, and small hotels. And along the riverfront's congested side streets were one- and two-story frame houses, butcher shops, bakeries, barber shops, shoemakers' shops, blacksmitheries, and grocery and dry goods stores.

But as Detroit began to assume the trappings of a Motor City, the early captains of industry looked to land in the interior for room to grow. As the importance of the railroad diminished, freight and shipping companies also left. With the completion of the bridge and tunnel connecting Detroit to Windsor, the international ferry service folded up too. Later, interstate freeways accelerated the flight of capital and imagination to suburbia. The exodus from the riverfront eventually left the city with miles of shoreline blighted by dilapidated buildings, rusted tracks, and vacant, littered lots. Front door to the city for two centuries, the Detroit River now staked out the Motor City's backyard.

Ironically, Detroit officials are again banking on the river to revitalize their city. They hope a redeveloped, mixed-use riverfront will pull people back to the inner city to live as well as work. And some very wealthy corporations and business magnates are putting big money behind that image of the city's future. But the city's public officials and their private partners aren't trying to entice just anyone down to the water's edge: Their primary target is the young urban professional earning $20,000 to $40,000 a year. Developers reason there are plenty of people like that among the 110,000 workers downtown and among the 450,000 city residents who live within five miles of the water's edge.[69]

Planning for the Detroit riverfront isn't new; it actually began in the 1940s. A salient feature of the city's 1951 master plan was a 3.5-mile park promenade and riverfront drive running east from the downtown civic center, past Belle Isle—the idyllic island park designed by Frederick Law Olmsted, the landscape architect who created New York's Central Park—all the way to the Grosse Pointes. But the riverfront ranked below other municipal development priorities during the 1950s and 1960s, including the civic center complex (Cobo Hall, the Veterans Memorial Building, Ford Auditorium, and the City-County Building), the Lafayette and Elmwood Park residential developments, and construction in the New Center area of midtown. But as New York, San Diego, Portland, Seattle, San Francisco, St. Louis, Baltimore, and Boston rediscovered the magnetic power of their waterfronts during the 1970s, the attention of Detroit's development establishment naturally turned in that direction too.

There is no doubt city officials and the plans they formulate will exert influence over the path future development will follow in Detroit. For example, the municipality now controls an estimated 20 to 30 percent of the land on the eastern riverfront.[70] The city can use its condemnation, leasing, and quick-take powers (the last allows the city to undertake rapid condemnation and clearance of a site even while litigation over condemnation awards is pending) to help determine what goes where on the waterfront. And city officials have sizable economic incentives at hand—low-cost financing, grants, loans, and tax abatements—to coax private developers to play the game according to the city's blueprints. Even so, leading parts in the urban redevelopment drama still go to the barons of private capital and the corporations they control. The story of riverfront development well illustrates the way power is wielded in Detroit and the unresolved problems still bound up with that kind of revitalization strategy.

The Renaissance Center

In the winter of 1970, 23 executives gathered for a meeting at the Michigan Avenue headquarters of the Detroit Chamber of Commerce. Included were Henry Ford II; Detroit financier Max Fisher; high-ranking executives from the auto companies, banks, and utilities; and well known retailers like J. L. Hudson and Harry B. Cunningham, chairman of K-Mart, Inc. Detroit's mayor and the governor of Michigan were also there. Out of that meeting emerged a new redevelopment organization, Detroit Renaissance. Max Fisher, Henry Ford II, and Robert Surdam (president of the National Bank of Detroit) were appointed to co-chair the organization, and they hired Robert McCabe (second in command at New York's Urban Development Corporation) to run the daily affairs of Detroit Renaissance.[71]

In 1971 Fisher, Taubman, and Henry Ford II privately commissioned, through Detroit Renaissance, a high-priced study of the future of riverfront development. What they had in mind was a Detroit answer to Chicago's waterfront: a spine of parks, stores, office buildings, shops, and high- and low-rise housing, running all the way from Belle Isle to the Ambassador Bridge linking Detroit to Windsor. And they wanted Detroit Renaissance to buy and control that riverfront property. They were particularly interested in 100 riverfront acres then owned by the bankrupt Penn Central Railway.[72]

What was needed first, the Detroit Renaissance group concluded, was a development project of such a magnitude as to change the image of downtown and thereby counter the attractions of suburbia, arrest ten years of disinvestment, and provide a catalyst for the renewal of the central city.

Encouraged by Henry Ford and Max Fisher, Wayne Doran, head of Ford Land Development Corporation, acquired 50 acres from Penn Central for just such a riverfront project.[73] The project was Henry Ford's Renaissance Center, known as the "RenCen" among Detroiters. It is a multitowered, 33-acre megastructure containing offices, a hotel, restaurants, shops, and entertainment facilities. Plans for the RenCen—a third larger than New York's Rockefeller Center and three times the size of Atlanta's Peachtree Center—were presented to the Detroit Common Council in November 1971 and to the Detroit business community at an Economic Club luncheon in May 1972. Ground was broken for the Renaissance Center Phase I on May 22, 1973.[74]

Henry Ford took the leadership of the Renaissance Center project right from the start. By the late 1960s Ford had little financial stake in the central city: The Ford Land Development Corporation was building Fairlane (the Ford Motor Company's headquarters community in suburban Dearborn), and Henry's brother William Clay Ford had decided to move his Detroit Lions football team from downtown to suburban Pontiac in Oakland County. Local leaders kept asking Ford what his company was going to do about disinvestment in Detroit. The Motor City had nothing comparable to the Golden Triangle in Pittsburgh or the Peachtree Center in Atlanta, and it seemed all too apparent to Detroit's near-majority-black community that big business cared little for the future of their city.[75]

After deciding to mastermind the RenCen project, Henry Ford turned over the technical development details to Wayne Doran, president of the Ford Land Development Corporation (a subsidiary of Ford Motor Company) and took upon himself responsibility for raising the money to finance the riverfront project. Ford's method of raising capital for the Renaissance Center speaks volumes about the way power can be wielded by corporate chieftains. Ford got the business involvement and financing he wanted by soliciting corporations dependent upon the auto industry for their continued prosperity.

The rules governing fund raising in the Motor City were set in 1949, when Detroit's business establishment organized the nation's most successful United Fund. The rule of thumb is that if the auto companies get involved, the other corporations will follow. So Ford needed one critical ally: General Motors Chairman Richard Gerstenberg. Ford met Gerstenberg over lunch in the 14th-floor dining room of GM's headquarters on Grand Boulevard. There the two auto magnates discussed the relationship between corporation and community, scanned drawings of the RenCen project, and talked over GM's own $25 million investment in the adjacent

New Center area. When General Motors decided to join the Renaissance group in December 1972, it brought along a trail of potential corporate investors too.[76]

Ford organized a limited partnership, designating the Downtown Development Corporation, an offshoot of Ford Motor Land Development Corporation, to be the managing partner. He then put together a list of large firms that had reasons for seeing Detroit succeed. Companies based in Detroit were ranked at the top; then came outside corporations that had a sizable stake in Detroit through their business with the auto industry. Ford sent the chief executive of each company a letter of invitation to meet with him at company headquarters in Dearborn. He gave each executive a sales talk and a confidential report outlining the tax advantages that could accrue from investing in the riverfront development. The capital outlay, Ford experts further argued, could be recouped in nine years. Profits would be shared in proportion to equity investment.[77]

In the end Ford put together a 51-member Renaissance Center partnership, the largest private investment group ever assembled in the United States for an urban real estate project.[78] Among the corporate partners, 38 (75 percent) gained all or a substantial portion of their business from the auto industry. Apart from Ford Motor Company (which put up 61 percent of the original cash investment), these companies invested nearly $120 million and guaranteed almost $2 million more in loans. Taken together, this combine of automakers, suppliers, and servicers had annual sales in cars, parts, and accessories of nearly $135 billion, equivalent to about one-quarter of the federal budget that year.[79]

Construction money for the Renaissance Center came from a $200 million loan financed by a consortium of 28 banks, including 7 in Detroit and others in New York, Philadelphia, Chicago, and San Francisco. The loan was arranged by Robert Surdam, chair of the National Bank of Detroit and co-chair of Detroit Renaissance. The National Bank of Detroit put up the largest bank sum, $27 million. The mortgage to pay off the $200 million construction loan was the largest first mortgage loan ever made for a real estate project and came mostly from insurance companies: Aetna Life Insurance ($50 million), Equitable Life Assurance Society of the United States ($50 million), John Hancock Life Insurance Company ($50 million), and Travelers Insurance Company ($30 million). Ford Motor Credit Company put in the remaining $20 million.[80]

A study of corporate interlocks has revealed a well-established network of relationships among the 51 RenCen partners. A corporate interlock is a channel of communication and common interest among firms. It occurs when a member of the board of directors of one corporation sits on the board of directors of another corporation. There was a total of 242 interlocking directors among the 51 RenCen corporations. Nearly 40 percent of those interlocks were with the six financial institutions.[81]

The financial power held by the network of corporate investors is impressive indeed. But the biggest commitment by far came from Ford Motor Company. Ford put up $112.6 million, nearly one-third of the total cost of the first phase of the RenCen project. That sum included $81.6 million of the cash investment; a $5 million loan to the RenCen partnership by Ford Motor Credit Company; a loan guarantee of $6 million by a Ford subsidiary, the Downtown Development Corporation; and Ford Motor Credit Company's $20 million contribution to the long-term mortgage.

Elite Streets

Henry Ford hired John Portman to design the Renaissance Center. Portman's architectural trademarks include soaring sunlit lobbies, exterior glass elevators, majestic fountains, and garden atmospheres. Portman also designed Atlanta's Peachtree Center, the Embarcadero Center in San Francisco, and megastructures in Fort Worth, Los Angeles, Chicago, New York, London, Paris, and Brussels. Portman is famous for designing "total environments," and he likes to talk about "putting people on their feet again so they can walk to church and the drugstore" all within a single urban complex.[82]

In Portman's view, Detroit—an industrial city with a blighted central business district—did not provide much in surroundings to "lean on." So what was needed was something in size and shape that could stand alone. Portman therefore designed an "urban village" to bring as many of the city's functions within walking distance as possible, preferably all under one roof.[83]

The Renaissance Center stands at the base of Detroit's central business district and extends along the Detroit River. RenCen Phase I is composed of five towers—a 73-story cylindrical, glass-walled hotel encircled by four, 39-story octagon-shaped office buildings. The four office towers contain 2.2 million square feet of rentable floor space. The hotel has 1,400 guest rooms and a full complement of meeting rooms, ballrooms, and restaurants. On the top 3 floors a rooftop restaurant and a cocktail lounge revolve one complete turn every hour. On a clear day one can see for 30 miles.[84]

The five towers emerge from a massive, landscaped podium positioned over the streets that cross the site. In effect, the podium becomes a four-story-high "pedestrian island" connecting hotel to office towers and providing space for restaurants, shops, theaters, and parking. The RenCen is fronted on the city side by concrete bunkers, which house the heating and cooling plants. The bunkers, designers explain, were located outside to save space inside the buildings and to provide a sound barrier against city traffic.[85]

Inside the Renaissance Center a seemingly endless expanse of space rises from the base of the central hotel cylinder. A glass-roofed court is surrounded by several levels of balconied corridors and crisscrossed by bridges. Circular seating pods extend over a landscape of fountains, sculptures, trees in planters, and a pool that resembles a moat. The seating pods are accessible by cantilevered stairways and by escalators. Shops are located along hallways formed by segments of octagons—an intentional design strategy to keep people moving at angles, not in straight lines, to maximize exposure to shopping, eating, and drinking establishments.[86]

The Renaissance Center has received scant praise from Detroit's architecture critics. Several blocks from the heart of downtown, separated from the city's edge by a broad ten-lane boulevard and two-story bunkers, the dramatically modern RenCen towers are detached and aloof above their surroundings. The RenCen has been called a "fortress for whites to work in while the rest of the city goes to hell around them" and a "Noah's Ark for the middle class," among other epithets. Depictions of this kind highlight the RenCen's walled, protective, and exclusive exterior as well as a layout that provides easy parking access for motoring suburbanites and tourists but turns massive abutments to central-city pedestrians on the side facing downtown. The RenCen's self-contained interior also seems designed to take Detroit out of mind by taking the city out of sight.[87]

Portman acknowledges that the interior of the RenCen is a heavily landscaped "other world," set in the midst of the urban environment yet isolated from it. But the objective, he has argued, was to lift "private space" above an amplified, multilevel "public space." "Our cities," Portman has decried, "have run nature and humans out. We need to bring trees, water, fountains, flowers, sculpture and other human amenities back into the city." But as Detroit architecture columnist Robert Benson has noted, "Portman did not bring trees, water, fountains, flowers, and sculpture into the public space of the city, since none of these things is in sight *outside* of the building; rather they were brought into a limited private investor's world."[88]

According to Portman's assessment of Detroit, people wouldn't go to the RenCen unless they were barricaded inside to feel safe.[89] Indeed, at full strength RenCen has a larger security staff than half the nation's police forces. RenCen's first director of safety was the former deputy chief of the Detroit Police Department. And the security chief oversees a specially designed Central Control Center (housed below the boiler bunker) to provide around-the-clock monitoring of fire and intrusion, using closed-circuit television surveillance, a two-way radio and pager network, and direct telephone communications with the city police and fire departments.[90]

According to William G. Conway, megastructures like the RenCen are the architect's vision of a controlled environment.[91] They respect neither the texture nor the geography of the city. Rather, the design of the megastructure suggests hostility toward the city it is supposed to save. By turning a massive wall to Detroit, the RenCen says it wants to stand alone. The RenCen poses a barrier to all pedestrian movement except for the people inside, who meander through a mazelike, high-security environment that attempts to emulate elite streets: North Michigan Avenue, Rodeo Drive, Fifth Avenue. But in substituting the suburban enclave for the urban street, the megastructured city actually reduces the amenities offered by public places.

Going Broke

Henry Ford II's personal commitment to the RenCen grew as he became more involved in the project, and so did the commitment of his company. The Ford family owns 9 percent of the stock in Ford Motor Company and controls 40 percent of the company's voting shares.[92] When RenCen management ran into difficulty attracting tenants, the Ford Motor Company leased an entire office tower—34 floors of office space—nearly triple the space it originally planned to occupy. The company filled up the tower by transferring several Dearborn operations to the riverfront: Ford Division General Offices, the Lincoln Mercury Division General Offices, the Glass Division General Offices, the Industrial Engine Operations, the Ford Aerospace Communications Corporation, the Ford Export Corporation, North America Automotive Operations Sales Group, the Office of the General Counsel, and Ford Marketing Services. All together Ford relocated 1,700 Dearborn employees to Detroit, 700 more than originally scheduled. And Ford Motor Company became the RenCen's largest tenant, with triple the office space of Manufacturers National Bank, the megastructure's second largest occupant.[93]

When Ford's suburban employees reacted unfavorably to the proposed move from Dearborn to the Renaissance Center, expressing worries about crime and security, the long commute, Detroit's income tax, and working long distances from their families, the company responded with a promise to pay raises to cover the tax and commuting costs. Ford also took employees on a bus tour to the RenCen, where they learned they would be scrutinized by TV monitors when working late at night and could be escorted out of the building by security personnel. Ford acquired 12 acres of land east of the RenCen for free employee parking and put an employee cafeteria inside the tower.[94]

When construction overruns pushed up costs by $100 million, Henry Ford returned to the 50 equity partners for more capital. When Ford was unable to secure sufficient mortgage financing, the Ford Motor Credit Company assumed $20 million of the mortgage. Ford originally planned to invest $6 million in the Renaissance Center, but his company's total outlay eventually came to $300 million—perhaps the largest civic investment ever made by one corporation.

The Renaissance Center started losing money right from the beginning, and each year the red ink rose higher. In 1978 the RenCen partnership lost $27.2 million; in 1979, $30.3 million; in 1980, $33.3 million; in 1981, $40 million.[95] All told, RenCen operating losses came to $130 million between 1977 and 1982, and at a time when the Ford Motor Company was losing billions of dollars in its auto operations.[96] In August 1980, with heavy operating losses and enormous long-term debts, the RenCen partnership began making only partial payments to the holders of its $197 million first mortgage. The RenCen partnership then negotiated new financing arrangements to lighten the debt burden. But the lenders' price for refinancing was to reduce by 20 years the time period in which the total loan had to be repaid, from 2013 to 1993. So after 1982, for 10 years the RenCen partners would have to make monthly payments of $2.6 million—almost twice the size of the payments on which they had already defaulted.[97]

In April 1982 Henry Ford II announced that the RenCen would be sold, at a loss, to an investor group headed by a Chicago real estate tycoon. The buyers wanted the RenCen primarily for its tax advantages—depreciation allowances, investment credits, and operating-loss deductions. But the investor group couldn't raise sufficient capital to pay the negotiated price of $505 million.[98]

On January 1, 1983, the RenCen partnership defaulted again, this time on the second mortgage.[99] The second mortgage secured the unpaid interest on the original $197 million mortgage and was part of the renegotiation deal signed with the lenders in 1981.[100] Two weeks later Hartman Financial Services, Ltd. (which included investors from the original-purchase loan group) offered $275 million for the RenCen—less than the total debt of $290 million and an enormous drop from the $505 million offer in April 1982.[101]

The creditors, it seemed, were in a bind. A takeover hardly assured profits under their management. But if they foreclosed and put RenCen up for sale, there was a big doubt as to whether anyone with the money would come forth to buy it at anything approximating the money that had gone into constructing it. On February 27, 1983, RenCen's five insurance and credit company lenders—Aetna Life Insurance Company, Equitable Life Assurance Society of the United States, Travelers Insurance Company, John Hancock Life Insurance Company, and Ford Motor Credit Company—agreed to trade the $200 million in debts they held and pick up another $13 million in liabilities for 53 percent ownership of Renaissance Center.[102]

The new partnership of creditors now calls itself the Renaissance Center Venture. Originally, the Ford Motor Land Development Corporation owned 65 percent, and the other 50 limited partners owned 35 percent of the RenCen. Under the new agreement Ford owns 30 percent, the limited partners own 17 percent, and the mortgage holders own 53 percent. The equity held by Ford and the original partners is merely symbolic, because under the new agreement only the equity held by the lenders can pay a return if the RenCen should become profitable, and only the lenders' equity will be repaid should the RenCen be sold. Downtown realtors put the value of the RenCen at less than $200 million, since the original partnership could not meet payment on a mortgage for that amount. And many doubt the RenCen will ever make money.[103]

The Renaissance Center was billed as a catalyst for the physical regeneration of downtown and the spiritual regeneration of the whole city. But the RenCen faced problems from the beginning. The heart of the matter was Detroit's depressed downtown real estate market—the most salient indicator of the central city's weak position in the regional economy. The RenCen opened in the wake of closing decisions by three major retailers, including one of only two remaining downtown department stores. Detroit's last central business district (CBD) department store, Hudson's, closed in 1983. Two of the five largest downtown hotels had shut their doors in the previous two years, and a third had gone into receivership. And the central business district was largely deserted after six o'clock in the evening.[104]

The effect of the Renaissance Center was to increase prime downtown office space 28 percent in a market already short of prime tenants. No big industrial corporations were yet headquartered on the riverfront. General Motors was three miles to the north; Chrysler was in Highland Park, an incorporated city within the city of Detroit; Ford, American Motor Corporation, and most big suppliers were in the suburbs. The city's major banks and utilities occupied their own buildings. So the RenCen depended upon attracting tenants that provide services to big business: law firms, accounting firms, advertising agencies, and branch offices of insurance companies. RenCen space was originally offered at $9.60 per square foot when the market value for other downtown buildings was $10.00 to $12.00 per square foot.[105] Rents eventually rose to $13.00 a square foot, but the RenCen needed $18.00 to $20.00 just to cover costs.[106]

Even at that, RenCen's below-market rents were bringing little new business downtown. Thirty percent of RenCen's tenants came from the suburbs, but they nearly all belonged to Ford Motor Company. The RenCen originally hosted high-fashion specialty boutiques designed to cater to affluent suburbanites, hotel guests, and well-placed office workers. But this strategy also failed, as a list of shops that closed since the RenCen opened readily reveals: Cartier, Charles Jourdan, Emanuel Ungaro, Hattie's Boutique, Courreges, Van Dyke's, and Ramayah Arts. The RenCen management has now changed the marketing focus of its stores from high fashion to goods priced more in reach of the average Detroit resident. It has also set out to simplify the mazelike interior and modify the fortresslike exterior of Detroit's waterfront monolith.[107]

Riverfront West

If the worth of a development project is measured less by the profits it earns on its own than by the new activity it triggers around it, then the RenCen can't be judged a total disaster. For there is no doubt that Ford's megastructure has helped stimulate new construction and redevelopment activity along the downtown riverfront. An important case in point is Riverfront West.

In 1974 Henry Ford's Detroit Renaissance colleague, Max Fisher, entered a partnership with Penn Central and Southfield builder Adolph Komer to hold onto another 36 riverfront acres south of the Windsor Tunnel.[108] Fisher bought out Komer and the railroad in 1978 and formed a partnership with Alfred Taubman called Riverfront Associates. Riverfront Associates then set in motion Riverfront West, a $78 million high-rise apartment complex, the largest private investment on the Detroit riverfront after the Renaissance Center.

Max Fisher and Al Taubman go back a long way, at least as far as the early 1950s, when oil entrepreneur Fisher hired contractor Taubman to build Speedway Gasoline stations for his Aurora (later to become Marathon) Gasoline Company. Taubman went on to become a czar of the suburban shopping malls and is reputed by *Forbes* magazine to be the wealthiest person in Michigan.[109] As for Max Fisher, he has been described by a White House appointments secretary as "probably the most prominent Republican in the country."[110] Apart or in tandem, Max Fisher and Al Taubman number among the biggest property owners and the most influential developers in the Detroit region.

Max and His Pal Al Son of Jewish immigrant parents, Al Taubman grew up in Michigan during the depression, first in Pontiac, then in Sylvan Lake. The senior Taubman was a custom-home builder, and Al studied fine art in college until he dropped out to become a builder too. The elder Taubman built custom homes, but young Al struck out for the urban frontier and became a builder of suburbia.

Al Taubman became a shopping mall developer and suburban landlord in the boom years of the 1950s and 1960s. He built his first shopping center, North Flint Plaza, in 1952. But in the ensuing years A. Alfred Taubman's empire has come to include the Taubman Company headquarters in Troy; 21 major shopping malls, including Fairlane Town Center, Lakeside, Twelve Oaks, and Briarwood in the Detroit area and others spread around the country; a broadcast company; the A & W fast-food chain; the Michigan Panthers football team; and Sotheby's, the aristocratic British art dealer and auction house.[111]

According to the classification scheme used by shopping mall trade journals, Al Taubman is a "silk-stocking purveyor." Taubman likes to describe his malls as possessing "total depth," by which he means they are multilevel with glass-encased elevators; waterfalls; sculptures in atriums; marble facing on the floors; and branches of world city boutiques like Krun Chocolate Shops, Brooks Brothers Clothiers, and Saks Fifth Avenue. Taubman was among the first developers to build malls with two and three levels connected by a network of ramps, elevators, and escalators, so as to guarantee equal traffic and therefore equal rents on each level.

Taubman accumulated his fortune by repeatedly risking the profits from his finished centers on financing for new, larger malls. Taubman's Woodfield Mall, built in suburban Chicago in 1970, illustrates his frontier developer style. Built at a cost of $90 million and containing 2 million square feet, Woodfield was then the world's largest shopping center. Yet Taubman built Woodfield in a small community of 18,000 people, on the periphery of the Chicago metropolitan area. Taubman was out to create suburban growth, not to follow it.[112]

Al Taubman's risk-taking proclivities are also revealed in the famous Irvine land deal. Taubman led a group of investors in a bidding war against Mobil Oil Corporation for a 77,000-acre tract of land, part of the Irvine Ranch in Orange County, California. Among the investors in the group were Henry Ford II; Max Fisher; Milton Petrie, a New Jersey retailer; and New York real estate barons Charles Allen, Jr., and Henry Allen. When Taubman cajoled reluctant members of the investment group to raise their bid to a stunning $337 million, Mobil dropped out. In the spring of 1983 the group sold the Irvine land for an estimated three times the original investment. Taubman's 15 percent share alone is said to have come to $150 million.[113]

Al Taubman is building Riverfront West with Max Fisher, his mentor and friend, who is also the son of Jewish immigrant parents.[114] Fisher's father and two partners began the Keystone Oil Company in Detroit, a small refinery where they cleaned and reclaimed used lubricating oil and then sold it back to the industries they bought it from. After earning a business degree from Ohio State, Max joined the company as a salesman. Under Max's leadership the company modified the Keystone plant to refine crude oil for gasoline, kerosene, and fuel oil. Then the company entered into a joint venture with Aurora Gasoline Company, which refined and sold gas to Detroit service stations. Max Fisher's objective was to turn Aurora-Keystone into a fully integrated oil company, one that owns both the supply and the demand ends of the oil market.[115]

During World War II Fisher's company provided industrial fuel oil for Detroit's arsenal of democracy. Pipelines were built directly from the Aurora refinery to the Ford River Rouge complex in Dearborn. And by the time the company had finished buying the 680 service stations in the Speedway 79 chain, Aurora had become the largest independent oil company in the Midwest. Possessing large quantities of scrap steel, Fisher's company also had the goods when oil drillers were desperately seeking pipe and fittings in the steel-scarce early postwar years. Later Aurora bought into the rich Albion-Scipio oil field in southern Michigan and built a refinery in Muskegon. In 1959 Aurora sold out to Marathon Oil for 875,000 shares of Marathon stock, a sum equal to $36.5 million. Max Fisher's stock share came to 38 percent, and he still owns Marathon stock valued at $70 million in today's market.[116]

Max Fisher's personal fortune is now estimated at $225 million[117] and is made up of that huge block of Marathon Oil stock and $10 million worth of United Brands stock (United Brands owns Chiquita bananas and Sun Harvest lettuce and at one time owned A & W products, now owned by Al Taubman).[118] Fisher has also dealt extensively in real estate, including a one-time interest in the Fisher building in Detroit and part ownership of the Irvine Ranch. Fisher has been a major landowner in Troy, where he is a partner with Al Taubman in the 2,000-unit Somerset Mall Apartments and where he owns Somerset Inn in a limited partnership with Henry Ford II. When Kresge Corporation sought land for its K-Mart World Headquarters in Troy, the corporation bought it from Max Fisher.[119]

Fisher has retired as president of Marathon Oil Company and as chairman of United Brands, but he still retains directorships on the boards of several corporations, including Owens Illinois, Dayco Corporation, Manufacturing National Corporation (which owns Manufacturers National Bank in Detroit), Michigan Bell Telephone Company, and the Fruehauf Corporation.[120]

Max Fisher started translating his economic wealth into political power when he took up fund raising for big charities like the United Jewish Appeal and the United Fund. Fisher has raised millions for Jewish charities, and he single-handedly financed Israel's petrochemical industry in the 1950s with a $16 million investment. Since then he has been an unofficial financial advisor to the Israeli government.[121]

When Fisher chaired the Jewish Welfare Federation of Detroit, he raised nearly $6 million, the most in the organization's history. That kind of fund-raising acumen raised eyebrows among United Fund organizers in Detroit. Henry Ford II and a few other industrialists had launched the United Fund in 1948, and ever since, it had been dominated by WASP executives and bankers. When Fisher was placed on the board of the United Fund, it broke a precedent, and it also signaled Fisher's membership in corporate Detroit—a tightknit old-boy network that did not easily admit newcomers, especially Jews with no connections to the city's car czars. When Fisher chaired the United Fund in 1961, it hit a record $19.5 million in contributions, with plenty of Jewish support, and it became the largest individual community charity in the country. In 1965 Fisher was elected general chair of the United Jewish Appeal, the biggest voluntary fund-raising organization in the United States.[122]

Fisher headed Republican Party fund raising in Michigan in 1962. George Romney was elected governor that year, and he began a 20-year moderate Republican dynasty in Michigan. Max Fisher went on to become a big-time fund-raiser for Richard Nixon and then Gerald Ford. Fisher personally gave $150,000 to the Nixon campaign in 1968 and $250,000 in 1972.[123] In 1980 Fisher put together a $1,000-a-ticket Reagan fund-raiser in Detroit, which garnered $330,000 from the likes of William Agee, then chair of Bendix Corporation; Thomas Murphy, then chair of General Motors; and Al Taubman, Fisher's ofttime partner. In this way Fisher became the most influential Jewish leader in the Republican party. And as a party finance controller, Fisher also has had a great deal to say about who does and who does not run for political office on the Republican ticket.

Through his extraordinarily successful charitable and political fund raising, Fisher has paved a road of friends and favors from Detroit's City Hall to the Lansing Statehouse and into the Oval Office in Washington, D.C.[124] It was Max Fisher who originated the idea for Detroit Renaissance, Inc., and it was Max Fisher who served as its first chairman in 1970. It was also Max Fisher who encouraged Henry Ford II to undertake the Renaissance Center project. And when Max Fisher decided to build Riverfront West, down the strait from the RenCen, that project also became a kind of textbook case in the application of power to realize an urban development project.

Riverfront Politics Located on a ten-acre site on East Jefferson, just west of the Joe Louis Arena, Riverfront West is a twin-towered, 29-story apartment complex. Rents for the 604 units range from $475 for the smallest one-bedroom apartment on the first 5 floors, to $2,100 a month for the largest two-bedroom on the top 5 floors. Riverfront West amenities include a view of the Detroit River, tennis courts atop the parking garage, a glass-enclosed swimming pool, a 77-boat marina, a health club, a gatehouse with private access, around-the-clock security, and a downtown People Mover stop near the front door.[125]

Construction money for Riverfront West came from a loan of $40 million administered by Manufacturers National Bank of Detroit. Development bonds were issued by the Detroit Downtown Development Authority and purchased by the Chemical Bank of New York. The bonds were guaranteed by the Federal Housing Administration until completion of the buildings. Then the Government National Mortgage Association bought the mortgage, thus providing the funds to redeem the bonds. All together two banks, one city agency, and two federal agencies were involved in this end of the project.

When it came to making his way through the development maze, it helped that Max Fisher was on the board of directors of Manufacturers

National Bank of Detroit. It helped that the board members of the Downtown Development Authority overlapped with board members on Detroit Renaissance, Inc. And it helped that Fisher was in a position to call personally on Republican agency heads in Washington, D.C., to get action on various facets of the Riverfront development. In 1981, for example, Fisher paid a visit to Drew Lewis, head of the Urban Mass Transportation Authority (someone Fisher had worked closely with in the Reagan campaign), to urge a favorable decision on the federal grant for a People Mover that was to connect his apartment complex to the rest of downtown Detroit.[126]

When it came to state government support, Fisher received strong backing from then Republican governor William Milliken, an outspokenly grateful beneficiary of Fisher's fund-raising expertise. And state representative William Ryan, a Democrat from Detroit, sponsored special state legislation authorizing Detroit to grant a 12-year tax abatement to Riverfront West. Known around the state capitol as the "Max Fisher Bill," the tax abatement sailed through the Statehouse in 1976 with hardly a whimper of opposition.

Opposition to Riverfront West did emerge locally, however. Fisher's fancy riverfront apartments blocked public access to the waterfront, and this angered the United Conservation Clubs representing some 200,000 sports enthusiasts in Michigan. Also the 12-year tax abatement was estimated to save Fisher and his partners (and cost the city of Detroit) $700,000 a year in taxes. City council member Ken Cockrel, an outspoken critic of tax abatements, and DARE (Detroit Alliance for a Rational Economy), the political organization that helped get Cockrel elected, put together a petition campaign opposing the tax break. Antiabatement campaigners wore T-shirts sporting the slogan, "No Tax Break for Riverfront West; Tax Max and his Pal Al." All told, Fisher's Riverfront West spurred special T-shirts, petition drives, hearings, zoning, and state legislation. But in the end, Max and his Pal Al got their abatement, and two new spires were added to Detroit's shoreline.

The Warehouse District

Today's most important chunk of riverfront real estate is the Warehouse District, sometimes referred to as Rivertown, an area along the river that runs east from the Renaissance Center to Belle Isle. Right now most of the 323 acres in the Warehouse District is home for abandoned and boarded up buildings, decrepit old factories, vacant land littered with rusting metal, and streets laid down during World War II. But the city's plans for the eastern riverfront project a starkly different image: high-style living in luxury high-rises, lofts, and quaint carriagehouse condos; new-class couples strolling along gas-lit cobblestone streets lined with flower stalls and sidewalk cafes, as they make their way to a live concert in a riverfront park; fitness buffs biking riverfront trails; and the return of Great Lakes cruisers, sailboats, water taxis, and trolleys going downtown.[127]

The city of Detroit began laying the soil for the blossoming of the Warehouse District in 1976, by acquiring land to build three linked eastern riverfront parks. One, Chene Park, has already been completed. Chene is an "adult park," which serves people who work near it and the 16,000 residents of Elmwood Park and Lafayette Park north of Jefferson Avenue. By all indications Chene Park has been an unqualified success. Crowds flock to concerts in the park's outdoor amphitheater. Workers eat lunch on its sea wall. Lovers stroll its grassy knolls. Viewed from Chene's slopes, the Detroit River can be seen linking Belle Isle, Windsor, downtown Detroit, and the Ambassador Bridge in one sweeping vista.[128] The two riverfront parks to come—St. Aubin and Mt. Elliot—will house summer arts festivals, marinas, and a replica of the Globe Theater, which will be leased by Wayne State University for dramatic productions.

The private catalyst to redevelopment of the eastern riverfront is River Place, a turn-of-the-century "old town in town" now under construction by the Stroh Company. When Stroh began shopping around for a new headquarters site, the vacated Parke-Davis office building on the eastern riverfront attracted the company's attention. Parke-Davis began building its pharmaceutical complex in the Warehouse District in 1873. When the company abandoned the site a few years ago, it left vacant its main office and 47 surrounding buildings. The city convinced Stroh to buy the whole complex and turn it into a $159 million development including the company headquarters, red-brick offices, apartments, and a retail market built around a village square.[129]

In size and financial importance, River Place is the biggest private development in the Detroit area since the RenCen. But the project also has considerable historical and architectural significance. Preservation architect James Steward Polshek is designing River Place. Polshek is dean of the Graduate School of Architecture and Planning at Columbia University. His firm directed the renovation of Carnegie Hall and the U.S. Custom House in New York. Polshek is planning the rehabilitation of seven existing buildings, including some designed by Alfred Kahn, and he is building five new ones. In Polshek's view, River Place is "the most significant collection of 19th and 20th century industrial buildings on a single site in this country."[130]

All told, River Place is to be a 21-acre riverfront village. The first phase was to move Stroh's corporate offices to the site. The second phase, completed in the summer of 1985, is a $50 million renovation of two buildings to be leased for office and retail use. Phases to follow include additional buildings for office and retail use, a 500-unit apartment complex, and a 300-unit hotel.[131]

The objective is to transform these historical buildings into a vital, urban quarter with around-the-clock activity—one rivaling Boston's Fanueil Hall–Quincy Market, San Francisco's Ghiradelli Square, and Baltimore's Harbor Place. Thus far River Place has received accolades from architects and neighboring residents. The project is neither a barricaded fortress nor a gaudy palace of consumption, but a well-designed, outdoor public place sometimes offering vistas of the river and sometimes of downtown Detroit, as well as its own architectural attractions.

Stroh's River Place has triggered related activity in the Warehouse District. A case in point is the Harborside development, cosponsored by American Natural Resources Company (ANR) and Michigan Consolidated Gas. Harborside is a housing–shopping center project on the Detroit River between the River Place and Mt. Elliot Park developments. The project's first phase includes a ten-story, 100 unit apartment building as well as an 85,000-square-foot shopping center. But developers predict Harborside will eventually include over 1,000 housing units at a cost of some $200 million.[132]

The Detroit Renaissance

Crisis and decentralization in the auto industry and competition from suburbs in filling office space and attracting retail business have taken a devastating toll on the city of Detroit. Detroit is now trying to meet the crisis and the competition by transforming itself from a metal-bending, Motor City into a modern metropolis that fits the global corporate image: a financial, administrative, and professional services center for auto and related industries; a research and development site for new growth industries; and a commercial haven offering luxury consumption opportunities to young corporate managers, educated professionals, convention goers, and tourists.

Riverfront redevelopment is the linchpin in Detroit's corporate-center redevelopment strategy, for the city is attempting to create a "golden arch" beginning at the riverfront and radiating through the central business district to a Central Functions cultural area. The city is aiming to foster upper-income neighborhoods within this arch, and the city has set about constructing a transportation system to knit activities in the arch into a unified whole.[133]

Mayor Coleman Young says he doesn't want Detroit's riverfront to become yet another Gold Coast. He wants 15 to 20 percent of waterfront housing for moderate- and low-income people. That remains to be seen. As for now, if one goes across the strait and looks at Detroit's skyline from Windsor's opposing shore, one sees—lined up in a row left to right—Max and Al's Riverfront West, Coleman Young's Joe Louis Arena, Henry Ford's Renaissance Center, Stroh's River Place, and ANR's Harborside. Just that glance says a lot about who wields power over Detroit's development. But what happened recently to ANR suggests just how precarious a hold Detroit, or any city, has on its own economic future, so long as the forces in command are located in private board rooms rather than in public places.

ANR is a Detroit-based holding company dealing in natural gas pipelines, trucking, and oil and gas exploration. ANR and its chairman, Arthur Seder, Jr., have played a critical part in the city's quest to refurbish the downtown. In 1983 ANR moved some 1,000 of its pipeline operations employees into Tower 500, one of two nearly vacant, 21-story office buildings in the second phase of the Renaissance Center. That move raised the occupancy of RenCen Phase II from 38 percent to 90 percent. Then, in September 1984, ANR arranged to buy Towers 500 and 600 from Ford Land Development and the Rockefeller Group.[134]

In March 1985 ANR fell victim to a hostile takeover by Coastal Corporation, a Houston-based natural gas company. As part of the buy-out accord, Coastal agreed to retain most ANR employees and its Detroit headquarters and operations for two years.[135] But after that it's anyone's guess. The biggest loser in Coastal's corporate raid on ANR may well turn out to be the city of Detroit.

Conclusion

We have traced the changing pattern of economic growth and decline in metropolitan Detroit through time and through space. A story about so large a topic, told in so limited a space could only be a sketch. Even so, our foray into the Motor City's space economy, past and present, does point the way toward a more refined conception of uneven development in Detroit than the one we started with. And our analysis raises some critical issues too.

Viewed along the dimensions of time and space, the trajectory of economic development in metropolitan Detroit during this century can, we think, be usefully divided into three periods: (1) the Era of City Building, 1913–1950, (2) the Era of Suburbanization, 1951–1978, and (3) the Era of Regional Competition, 1979 to the present. One period doesn't give way to the next so much as each new period forms a layer upon the ones that came before. So the picture stays the same even as it changes.

The *Era of City Building* in Detroit coincides with the creation of the assembly line and mass production. When Henry Ford built his "crystal palace" in Highland Park in 1913, the modern factory system was born. From then on, the auto industry expanded according to a well-defined spatial logic: a factory, then complementary plants and residential development clustered along industrial corridors following railroad lines. Commercial districts emerged along highway arteries paralleling the industrial corridors. The Motor City grew in the wake of an expanding auto industry, outward from the river—north, west, south—into the landed interior. Development was unevenly distributed across an inner city where housing was old and the poor were concentrated, a middle city where land use was mixed and in transition, and in an outer city where the urban gentry lived in large homes clustered around schools and parks, according to a city plan. The era of city building was dominated by the spatial logic of industrial expansion.

The *Era of Suburbanization* can be dated from 1951, the year the central city's population peaked and the year Hudson's decided to build the Northland Shopping Center. The United States experienced unparalleled economic growth during the early postwar years, and the logic of industrial expansion stayed the same, but now it extended beyond the city limits. The Big Three built 20 new auto plants in the Detroit area during the decade following World War II—all beyond the boundaries of the central city. Complementary industries, commercial development, and residential subdivisions followed, like metal shavings drawn to a magnet. But this time it was the suburbs that boomed, not the central city.

Industrial organization didn't change much, but two new development forces were at work during the Era of Suburbanization: federal policy and the reorganization of commercial capital. The federal government underwrote suburban growth by financing a massive freeway system and by providing mortgage loans, insurance, and tax deductions for new home buyers. Also critical to the suburban trajectory was the way commercial capitalists reorganized their business operations from downtown emporiums and strips to regional shopping malls located on the periphery of the metropolis. Indeed, if the spatial logic of industrial expansion and mass production can be said to have dominated the Era of City Building, then the Era of Suburbanization was dominated as much by the reorganization of commercial capital and federally subsidized mass consumption as by anything else.

As industrial growth extended to the suburbs and as commercial capital concentrated on the urban periphery, the principal axis of uneven development shifted from cities within the city to the line that divided the city from its suburbs. In Detroit that line became a racial barrier, as the division between central city and suburb came to coincide all too closely with that between black and white.

The *Era of Regional Competition* can be dated from 1979, the year the auto industry experienced its worst depression since the big one in 1929. International economic crisis brought on by world overproduction and increasing international competition is now spawning reorganization in the basic manufacturing industries. To maintain profitability, industrial corporations are shifting blue-collar production work abroad and automating it at home. They are concentrating their domestic capital on administration, research and development, and high-value, high-technology operations. The upshot is a corresponding reorganization of the regional economy according to a new spatial logic.

Capital flight and automation have dealt a hard blow to Detroit's industrial suburbs. But as corporations concentrate their capital on administration, research, and high technology, a new type of regional growth pole has emerged. Epitomized by Silicon Valley outside of San Francisco and Route 128 outside of Boston, it is the science city, or the technopolis, as the Japanese like to call it. At the core of the technopolis are universities with strong science and engineering faculties, government-subsidized research parks, and closely linked, high-technology companies specializing in high-value production. The Oakland Technology Park, billed as the "work place of the twenty-first century," fits this blueprint to a tee. The Era of Regional Competition is dominated neither by industrial nor by commercial capital. Rather, the driving force seems to be the creation of new information technologies and their application to all sectors of the economy.

The relationship between work and residence is also changing, particularly among the "new class" of trend-setting professionals. Commuting is valued less; more people want to live nearer their place of work, in planned "new or old towns in town" like Fairlane and River Place. Moreover, when suburbs like Warren grow to number among Michigan's largest cities, when outlying financial centers like Southfield surpass Detroit's central business district in office space, and when industrial communities like those downriver are hit as hard by disinvestment as any industrial area inside the Motor City, the very distinction between central city and suburbs fades away.

Instead, a region of interdependent yet relatively autonomous cities is emerging. Knit together by a regional division of labor, these cities remain deeply divided along lines of race, class, and municipal boundary. The principal fault line of uneven development no longer runs among areas within the city, nor between the city and its suburbs, but rather it travels among competing cities within a region of cities. In the Era of Regional Competition there is no longer one Detroit, nor two Detroits; there are many Detroits.

Yet amidst these periods of change the critical issues always seem to remain the same. New urban development continues to be targeted to the privileged few. Power over urban development continues to be concentrated among a handful of individuals and corporations whose reach spans the metropolis and beyond. And urban development continues to be uneven, unpredictable, and precarious, since the most important development decisions are made in private offices, not in public places.

What our analysis suggests, as much as anything else, is that an effective and balanced urban redevelopment strategy will have to be a regional, public strategy. And that raises another sticky issue: Will the current shake up in the regional economy provide the impetus for heretofore antagonistic groups to overcome their race and class divisions to form new alliances for regional change? We can't assess this possibility until we take a closer look at patterns of race and class inequality, the history of racial conflict and cooperation, and past redevelopment efforts in metropolitan Detroit —subjects toward which we now turn our attention.

3

Patterns of Race and Class Disparity

The preceding chapter focused on uneven economic development and the changing patterns of economic growth and decline over time and through space in metropolitan Detroit. The trajectory of economic development was traced through three periods between 1913 and the present, emphasizing the periods covering the Era of Suburbanization (1951–1978) and the Era of Regional Competition (1979 to the present). Throughout these periods uneven development has remained in the hands of powerful people and corporations and has tended to serve the privileged few. Most of the development has been occurring in the Northwest Passage of Oakland County. On the other hand, the upriver and downriver suburbs have been experiencing economic decline. Uneven economic development has been a persistent characteristic of the metropolitan Detroit landscape.

Uneven economic development, therefore, is related to patterns of race and class. This chapter examines the spatial patterns of race and class in metropolitan Detroit. The findings show that the patterns of race and class often parallel the patterns of uneven economic development.

Patterns of Race

Detroit and its suburbs combine to form a metropolis where 4.35 million people live. (See Map 2.5.) The Detroit city of 1.2 million comprises 27.6 percent of the population and 85 percent of the region's blacks. In contrast, the suburbs are where 72.4 percent, or 3.15 million people live; 88 percent are whites and 4.2 percent are blacks.[1]

Most blacks originally moved to metropolitan Detroit from Arkansas, Alabama, the Carolinas, Georgia, Mississippi, and Louisiana. They were in search of new occupations. Most were hoping to escape the racial discrimination in employment so prevalent in the South. What they found, however, meant their dream would be deferred. Discrimination in employment also existed in the North.

By the outbreak of World War II, black and white workers had become institutionalized into a dual labor market with the majority of black workers restricted to foundry work, general labor, and janitorial jobs. As long as blacks were in the hot, dirty "nigger jobs," most white workers felt secure. But as soon as war production policies placed blacks in so-called white jobs, all hell broke loose. White workers began engaging in "hate strikes" protesting the introduction of blacks into white jobs. Patriotism to many white workers certainly did not mean abandoning their white-skin privileges. As one white worker said during a walkout at the Packard Plant, "I'd rather see Hitler and Hirohito win than work next to a nigger."[2]

Throughout the war white workers engaged in hate strikes to protest the upgrading and transferring of black workers to jobs from which they had been excluded by tradition. One of the worst of these hate strikes occurred in 1944, when 39,000 white workers walked out of the Packard Plant, closing it down, because black workers were put in previously all-white jobs.[3] Unlike the blacks who migrated to Detroit during World War I, many blacks who populated the Motor City during and after World War II sought employment outside traditional black occupations.[4] These black expectations were peaking just at the time when many white employers were re-establishing the racial dual labor market and deliberately pitting black workers against white workers to increase production.[5]

After the war some employers lost little time in returning to their former racist employment practices. By June 1948 close to 65 percent of all job openings in Detroit contained written discriminatory specifications, and those that did not discriminate in written form did so at the gate. In December 1953 out of a sample of 417 job orders in manufacturing, 82.7 percent contained specifications for white workers only, and of a sample of 115 clerical, sales, and professional job orders, 82.6 percent asked for white workers. As expected, the greatest demand for blacks was in domestic and personal service employment.[6]

A study of black employment by the mayor's Interracial Committee in 1951 reported that in large retail stores blacks worked as elevator operators, doorkeepers, maids, janitors, and stock handlers. No blacks were employed as sales clerks. Blacks worked in every capacity in the restaurant business as a whole but were in segregated occupations in most individual restaurants. Blacks in business offices worked as janitors, messengers, and maintenance people. The only blacks working for the major white newspapers were maintenance people, elevator operators, and doorkeepers. Driver/salespeople for most businesses had to be white. Common trucking and private bus transportation companies did not use black drivers, and only black cab companies hired black cabbies. Blacks were almost invisible in the licensed building trades. In short, in 1951 the majority of blacks were confined to low-status jobs.[7]

Between 1943 and 1953—as a result of labor demands and an assortment of social change strategies involving a coalition of labor, church, black, and liberal organizations—incremental changes occurred in Detroit's dual labor market. The interracial struggle for a local and state Fair Employment Practice Commission contributed to these changes, as did the back-room negotiations by the Detroit Urban League. The picketing of individual stores by radical groups such as the Communist party kept the pressure on and contributed in opening jobs for blacks.[8]

Gradually, as a result of these efforts, blacks began obtaining employment in previously all-white jobs. By 1950 black nurses were becoming visible in white hospitals. Black sales personnel were also being hired by Cunningham's drug stores, and black faces showed up among bank employees. The J. L. Hudson Department Store hired its first blacks in sales personnel in 1953, and the *Detroit Free Press*, reacting in part to social pressure, became the first major white newspaper in the city to hire a black reporter.[9] The Michigan Bell Telephone Company, however, represented by far the best example of racial integration in employment during this period. It began gradually hiring blacks in skilled and unskilled employment until it had achieved a policy of integration.[10]

Racial discrimination in employment continued throughout the 1950s and 1960s in the face of a continuous surge of black expectation and politicalization. In 1956, 15 of Detroit's largest department stores refused to hire black sales personnel. Blacks with college degrees were operating elevators and pushing brooms. Four years later, on the eve of the second stage of the Civil Rights Movement, none of Detroit's three big radio stations (WJR, WWJ, WXYZ) employed blacks as disc jockeys or as technical or secretarial personnel.[11] The election of liberal mayor Jerome Cavanaugh in 1960, with much black support, helped increase employment opportunities for blacks in Detroit. Cavanaugh began his tenure as mayor by issuing an executive order guaranteeing equal employment opportunities and granting the Civil Service and Community Relations Commission responsibility for implementing the order. In November 1962 he issued a directive that provided for systematic monitoring of firms doing business with the city to insure that they complied with Michigan's Fair Employment Practices Law, passed in 1955.[12]

Cavanaugh's bold initiative in equal employment opportunity generated contrasting views in the black community. A writer for the *Michigan*

Chronicle heaped praise upon the mayor: "Detroiters should be proud that the years of devoted labor and concern by thousands of people of good will throughout our city came to fruition in that courageous act of the Chief Executive."[13] A writer for another black newspaper viewed Cavanaugh a bit differently. Acknowledging that the mayor had appointed many more blacks than any other mayor, the writer commented, "It is by no means something over which Negroes, who represent nearly 30 percent of the population and are commanding less than 10 percent of meaningful city positions, should feel smug."[14]

As early as 1951 black United Auto Workers (UAW) members who were also members of the Detroit Negro Labor Council were becoming increasingly resentful over the failure of the Walter Reuther leadership to aggressively push for the upgrading of black UAW workers in the auto factories. They were also upset over the fact that no black served on the UAW's International Executive Board. The rift between the black workers and the white UAW leadership widened when the black labor organization began a petition drive for a citywide referendum for a local Fair Employment Practices Commission (FEPC) ordinance (which failed), prompting the UAW leadership to order all UAW members who signed the petitions to withdraw their names. Widening the rift even further, the UAW leadership characterized the black petition drive as an "irresponsible communist inspired approach."[15]

This serious break in the ranks of one of the most viable interracial relationships in the city highlighted the sensitive problem that often plagues such unequal balances of power. In such relationships the structure and strategy of interracial cooperation are often determined by the racial groups commanding the most power. Thus the white-dominated UAW, pursuing some of the same goals as its black UAW membership, still reserved the right to call the shots on certain vital issues. Black UAW members who felt alienated by this unequal distribution of power and decision making within this UAW model of interracial cooperation sought their independence in black labor organizations such as the Negro Labor Council (NLC) and the Trade Union Leadership Council (TULC), founded in 1951 and 1957 respectively. The TULC was founded to fight racial discrimination within organized labor, including the UAW, but later expanded its interests to include nonunion members and job training.[16] This move toward independence by black trade unionists was less an indication of their frustration with interracial cooperation than it was the need to take the lead in their own struggle, from an independent organizational base from which they could then renegotiate the structure and nature of future interracial relationships.

Black Protest

Blacks and whites participated in the 1963 sit-in at the First Federal Savings and Loan Association to protest unfair hiring practices. An interracial group also participated in the 1964 picketing of the General Motors (GM) building.[17] Far more blacks than whites participated in the GM demonstration, a fact that bothered white minister and social activist Malcolm Boyd. However, National Association for the Advancement of Colored People (NAACP) National Labor Secretary Herbert Hill, also white, made up for the lack of whites with his rousing speech: "We will show GM that while it is a powerful corporation, it is not more powerful than the people. We will show them that it is not a sovereign unto itself."[18]

The struggle against racial discrimination in employment continued throughout the 1960s, with conflict being an essential aspect of the overall strategy. Picketing became the common tactic of protest groups. Downtown stores, such as Crowley-Milner, often refused to change their hiring policies until pressured to do so by picketing and boycotting. Even the giant GM Corporation, under threat of a black boycott of its products, increased the pace of integrating blacks into all its divisions.[19] The pressure was kept on GM and other Detroit automobile companies by the National Industry Negotiating Committee of the NAACP, whose purpose was to increase the number of blacks in the technical, professional, and managerial levels of the auto industry.[20] In 1963 Mayor Cavanaugh ordered the Civil Rights Commission to conduct a report on the status of blacks in the police and fire departments. The completed report disclosed that both departments were deficient in the hiring and upgrading of blacks. Of 5,017 employees in the police department, only 337—7 percent—were nonwhite. Only whites held professional or managerial positions in the department. Nonwhite employment in the fire department was worse. Only 55 nonwhites were employed out of a total work force of 1,861—a mere 3 percent. The fire department, however, did have 1 nonwhite in the professional and managerial category.[21] Low minority employment in the fire and police departments reflected employment patterns evident throughout municipal government. In fact, the dual labor market that characterized the private sector often duplicated itself in the public sector. Certain city departments, such as housing and welfare, that interacted with black communities tended to hire a high percentage of blacks. Public works also traditionally hired a high percentage of blacks because of its need for menial workers. In contrast, black employees were practically nonexistent in the city controller and purchases and supplies departments.[22]

Seven years later, in 1970, this nonwhite employment pattern remained basically unchanged. Although a survey in 1968 showed that blacks made up 43 percent of the city's employees, indicating that the "city's record as an equal opportunity employer was good," the police, fire, and building and safety engineering departments were still far below the city average in nonwhite employment.[23]

The reluctance of these departments to change set the stage for a series of racial conflicts over employment. In March of 1974, just months after Detroit elected its first black mayor, Coleman Young, one of the city's top black officials exploded in anger over the extent of racial discrimination in city jobs: James Watts, commissioner of the Detroit Department of Public Works, told other city officials at a mayor's budget hearing, "Blacks get the end of the stick, the lowest jobs. . . . We've been screwed in this town for years." Appointed by Mayor Young, Watts headed the second largest department in the city, second only to the police department. "If the black community knew what they were getting in city government," Watts said, "they would burn this town down. We'd have a revolution."[24] But the town was not burned down, and the black community did not flare up in revolution. Instead, blacks waited to see what changes Young would institute to correct the black employment situation in slow-moving city departments such as the fire and police departments. Mayor Young instituted an affirmative action policy that had a revolutionary impact on the police department.

In 1967 blacks made up only 5 percent of the police department. In July of that year Detroit experienced the bloodiest rebellion in a half-century and the costliest, in terms of property damage, in U.S. history. When it ended, 33 people were dead, 347 injured, 3,800 arrested. About 5,000 people were homeless—most of them black. Well over 1,000 buildings had been burned to the ground and 2,700 businesses ransacked. The total damage soared to $50 million. All this triggered by a police raid on a "blind pig" in the black ghetto.[25] During the rebellion white police deliberately shotgunned to death 3 unarmed black men in the Algiers Motel. Two of the men were shot while lying or kneeling.[26] When the story of this police slaughter of unarmed black men was made public, police–black community relations became even worse.

Thirty-three of the persons killed during the rebellion were black; 10 were white. According to official accounts, 17 people who died—of whom 2 were white—were looters. Police officers killed 20; the National Guard killed between 7 and 9; the army killed 1. Two people died at the hands of rioters. Store owners killed several people.[27]

Compared with earlier "race riots," the black rebellion or "civil disorder" in Detroit in the summer of 1967, while racial in character, was not interracial. The black rebellion "involved action within Negro neighborhoods against symbols of white American society—authority and property—rather than against white persons."[28]

Although a police raid on a "blind pig" triggered the disorder, the rebellion itself "developed out of an increasingly disturbed social atmosphere, in which typically a series of tension-heightening incidents over a period of weeks or months became linked in the minds of many in the Negro community with a shared network of underlying grievances."[29] In other words, the black rebellion of 1967 was more than a riot or civil disorder in the minds of black participants. It stemmed from a long train of racial abuses heaped upon the black community over the years.

Who were these black rebels or rioters? Surprisingly, to some white and black observers, the typical black participants in the disorder were not habitual criminals, bums, hoodlums, or alienated members of the so-called underclass. Rather, they tended to be teenagers who had lived in Detroit all of their lives, who had dropped out of school, yet who were a bit more educated than many of their peers. One key factor was that they also tended to be underemployed or unemployed. Another factor, perhaps the most critical one in explaining their participation in the rebellion, was their racial pride. In addition, these typical participants harbored hostility against both whites and middle-class blacks and were, "though informed about politics, highly distrustful of the political system and of political leaders."[30]

Unfortunately, these black rioters received most if not all of the media attention. While they were rioting, other blacks walked the streets of burning neighborhoods urging rioters to "cool it." These "counter-rioters" shared some of the attitudes of the vast majority of blacks in the riot area, who neither rioted nor took action against those involved in rioting. These counter-rioters were from typically better-educated and higher-income classes than either the rioters or the majority of nonrioting blacks.[31]

Throughout the chaos of the "riots," as most whites saw them, and the "rebellions," as many blacks viewed them, negotiations occurred between white officials and representatives of the black community including both established black leaders and militant young blacks. These negotiations focused on specific grievances related to "the rebellion," as well as how authorities should handle the disorder.[32]

The black civil disorders of 1967 left a bad taste in everyone's mouth. White police feared blacks even more now that they knew how volatile the racial situation really was in Detroit. Yet many white police officers continued rubbing salt in the wounds of racial discord. In 1967 the black rebellion in Detroit and the disclosure of the Algiers Motel murders destroyed almost all hope for better police–black community relations as well as for better race relations in general. White police officers flocked into the National Rifle Association, using their membership to buy carbines for the next black rebellion. Private citizens began buying guns in record numbers. And suburban housewives were seen on TV practicing their pistol shooting.[33] White suburbanites trembled as they heard Detroit's radical black preacher the Reverend Albert B. Cleage, Jr., give a sermon on the black struggle at the memorial service for those killed in the rebellion: "We are engaged in a nation-wide rebellion, seeking to become what God intended that we should be—free men with control of our destiny, the destiny of black men."[34]

People interested in interracial cooperation found themselves "struggling up a slippery slope." The New Detroit Committee, set up after the rebellion and made up of Detroit's upper-class liberals, could do little to calm the growing fear and hatred between white police officers and black citizens. In 1968, two months after the assassination of Dr. Martin Luther King, which totally demoralized the shrinking ranks of interracial cooperation, white police assaulted marchers in downtown Detroit and later beat several middle-class black youths attending a high school affair. The police commissioner acted boldly in both cases, disciplining one policeman in the first attack and nine in the second. A year later a white policeman was killed and another one wounded, when police attacked the New Bethel Baptist Church, located in the middle of a black ghetto. Police arrested 143 men, women, and children and took them to jail, where they were later released by black judge George Crockett. White police picketed Crockett's court, demanding that he be removed, and the state senate approved two resolutions criticizing his action in the incident. Even the state judicial tenure committee got into the act by announcing that it would also review Crockett's conduct. Nothing came of this campaign. And when the Detroit Commission on Community Relations released its study of the New Bethel incident, it condemned both the killing of the policemen and the police raid. The commission was especially critical of the Detroit Police Officers' Association's campaigns for so-called law and order and the removal of Judge George Crockett, characterizing such campaigns as symbolizing "the spectre of the police state and paramilitary government of a colonial people."[35]

The decade of the 1970s opened ominously for black community–police relations. In 1971 the Detroit Police Department established the most controversial police unit in Detroit's history. This new police unit was called STRESS (Stop the Robberies; Enjoy Safe Streets) and was made up of white decoys dressed as drunks and derelicts and sent to work in mostly black high-crime areas. Predictably, most of the people killed by the unit were black. STRESS, therefore, came to symbolize just more of the same; namely, white police killing black people under the guise of fighting crime. But if STRESS contributed to more friction between white police and blacks, it also contributed to the politicalization of the black community, which led to the election of Coleman Young, the first black mayor of Detroit. Young's vow to abolish STRESS rallied blacks to support his election. After his election Young wasted little time in eliminating STRESS, which probably more than any single act contributed to the reduction of racial conflict and ushered in a new era of black community–police relations.[36] The pressure of a black mayor and the emergence of blacks in key municipal jobs radically changed the structure and nature of interracial conflict and cooperation, unlike in the past, when such relations revolved around white power centers only.

By 1976, three years after the election of Coleman Young, the police department not only had a black chief, its first, but the percentage of blacks in the department had grown to 25 percent, clear proof of the influence of black political power.[37]

The cost of this dramatic improvement in black employment in the police department was growing racial tensions and conflicts between white and black police officers. Many young, white, male officers, lacking a sense of the police department's racial history, felt victimized by the affirmative action policy. On the other hand, many nonwhite and women officers knew instinctively that they would not have jobs had it not been for black political power and affirmative action policy.

As soon as hard times hit the city, many of the younger black officers who were last hired were first fired. They went to court, and a federal judge temporarily ruled that under the city's affirmative action policy, minority workers could not be laid off. Instead, white officers with more seniority would have to be laid off. In May 1975 the racial tension surrounding this situation turned into open conflict, when close to 1,000 white officers picketed the federal building where the preceedings were taking place. Someone threw a beer can, and a fight ensued in which a black officer was beaten by off-duty white officers.[38] Conflicts over affirmative action continued. Almost ten years later the U.S. Supreme Court ruled that seniority takes precedence over affirmative action gains by minorities.[39] Nevertheless, racial disparity in social and economic life persists.

Racial Disparity in Social and Economic Life

Most blacks and whites in metropolitan Detroit are socially and economically unequal. Since 1948 metropolitan Detroit unemployment has always been worse for blacks than for whites, with the rate for black males ranging from a low of 1.5 times that of white males to as much as 4 times as high.[40] Major contributors to black unemployment in metropolitan Detroit have been large cutbacks in sales jobs, brought about by the closing of retail outlets in Detroit city, and general reductions in service jobs. For instance, 31 percent of nonwhite sales workers were unemployed, as compared with 3.8 percent unemployment among white sales workers, in 1983. In service jobs, too, the black unemployment rate is substantially higher, at 15.5 percent or twice that of the white unemployment rate of 7.4 percent.[41] And these figures do not include the many blacks who have become so discouraged they quit seeking work.

Not only is a higher percentage of whites employed but they also earn about one-third more than blacks in metropolitan Detroit. Median incomes in 1979, for instance, placed whites at $20,568 compared with $13,695 for blacks.

In metropolitan Detroit 27 percent of the black households received some type of public assistance in 1980, compared with 6.8 percent for whites. And, whereas 25 percent of all blacks were living below the defined level of poverty in 1980, only about 7 percent of whites were. Furthermore, 44 percent of the black households with only a female head of family present were below the poverty level, compared with 24 percent for white women raising families as single parents.[42]

Underscoring the financial differences, in 1980 more than 50 percent of the white family households received interest, dividend, or rental income, a sign of investment capital and savings, compared with only 13.6 percent of the black households in metropolitan Detroit receiving such income. Such disparity is perpetuated by racially segregated housing.

Racial Residential Segregation between Municipalities, 1940–1980

The preceding discussion has firmly established the extent of black/white disparity in metropolitan Detroit, a disparity that is maintained, intensified, and perpetuated by racial residential segregation. This section examines the pattern of residential segregation over time and at different scales. Segregated housing is the last barrier to the achievement of racial equality.

In Detroit and other large urban areas, metropolitan fragmentation has emerged as an important variable in understanding the uneven spatial distribution of various racial and social population groups. This fragmentation, which involves a decentralization of economic and political activity, enables those who are financially able and white to reside in municipalities in the urban fringe (i.e., the suburbs), where they can isolate themselves from the racial and class mixture of the central city.

Such status-homogeneous suburban municipal enclaves are possible because of their ability to incorporate as separate municipalities and focus their political and economic power on the maintenance of neighborhood stability.[43] Often the effort to maintain stability involves the exclusion of groups on the basis of race and class. This section examines the unevenness in the distribution of the black population between municipalities throughout metropolitan Detroit. The aim is to determine whether blacks have become more evenly distributed since 1940. The subunits for analysis are municipalities with at least 2,500 people in 1980.

If the black population were evenly distributed, then every municipality would have the same proportion of blacks and whites and the index of dissimilarity would be zero.[44] As the black population and the white population differ in spatial distribution, the index of dissimilarity increases; that is, the larger the index, the greater the inequality in spatial distribution between blacks and whites over the municipalities.

In 1940 the index of dissimilarity was only 17 percent, indicating a low level of unevenness in the spatial distribution of blacks and whites. Of all the blacks in the 34 incorporated places with a population of 2,500 or more, 89.9 percent lived in Detroit. However, 75.8 percent of all whites also lived there.

Between 1940 and 1950 the black population became more unevenly distributed, increasing the index of dissimilarity to 26.6 percent. (See Table 3.1.) Another increase in the index occurred between 1950 and 1960, sending it to 44.4 percent. The increase in segregation was due in part to the fact that 8 (or 42 percent) of the 19 places that became incorporated

Table 3.1 The pattern of racial segregation between municipalities, 1940–1980

Year	Index of dissimilarity black v. total white	Number
1940	17.0	34
1950	26.6	39
1960	44.4	58
1970	32.8	73
1980	75.3	84

Source: Computed by the authors from data obtained from the U.S. Department of Commerce, Bureau of the Census, 1940, 1950, 1960, 1970, and 1980 final population and housing unit counts, Detroit, Mich., *Census of Population and Housing.* (Washington, D.C.: U.S. Government Printing Office).

Note: Compare Tables 3.1 and 3.5. Most of the indexes of dissimilarity are larger for the SMSA (column 1) in Table 3.5. The larger indexes can in part be attributed to the smaller subunits used. The indexes in Table 3.5 are based on census tracts, which are smaller than municipalities. As a general rule, the smaller the subunits used, the greater the expected index of dissimilarity.

between 1950 and 1960 were all-white municipalities. (See Table 3.2.) Such all-white suburban communities included Lathrup Village, Fraser, Milford, Riverview, New Baltimore, Richmond, Walled Lake, and Lake Orion. Of all the blacks in the 58 incorporated places in 1960, 88 percent lived in Detroit compared with 66 percent of all whites. Between 1960 and 1970 the index of dissimilarity declined to 32.8 percent. The reason for the decline in segregation is not clear. It may have been related to the fact that blacks were slightly better represented in the newly established incorporated places. Only 4, or 27 percent, of the 15 new places were all white. Ninety percent of all blacks in the 73 incorporated places in 1970 resided in Detroit, whereas only 63 percent of all whites resided there. Between 1970 and 1980 the index of dissimilarity increased to 75.3 percent. This substantial increase was probably related to the overwhelming shift in the white population from the central city to the suburbs. Since most blacks did not participate in the suburban shift, residential segregation increased. Of all the blacks in the 84 incorporated places in 1980, 87 percent lived in Detroit, compared with only 18 percent of all whites. (See Table 3.2 for the number of places added by decade.)

In sum, the spatial distribution between blacks and whites has become

Table 3.2 Places added to Detroit's Standard Metropolitan Statistical Area and the population by race, 1950–1980

1950			1960			1970			1980		
	Population			Population			Population			Population	
Places	White	Black	Places	White	Black	Places	White	Black	Places	White	Black
Hazel Park	17,757	5	Beverly Hills Village	8,626	7	Bloomfield Township	3,603	31	Algonac	4,339	1
Holly Village	2,660	2	Farmington	6,877	3	Dearborn Heights	79,720	12	Brighton	4,152	5
Huntington Woods	4,921	27	Flat Rock	4,694	2	Franklin	3,333	8	Howell	6,870	4
Livonia	17,513	8	Fraser	7,026	0	Gibraltar	3,315	1	Lapeer city	6,017	26
Oak Park	5,258	9	Harper Woods	19,968	3	Grosse Pointe	2,890	7	Marine City	4,387	1
			Keego Harbor	2,755	2	Lake Orion Heights	2,545	0	Marysville	7,288	0
			Lake Orion	2,698	0	Oxford	2,528	0	Metamora	551	0
			Lathrup Village	3,556	0	Rockwood	3,114	2	North Branch	889	0
			Madison Heights	33,257	13	South Lyon	2,673	0	Port Huron	30,940	2,127
			Milford	4,320	0	Sterling Heights	61,077	38	St. Clair city	4,739	0
			New Baltimore	3,148	0	Taylor	69,680	20			
			Novi	6,374	9	Utica	3,487	5			
			Richmond	2,667	0	Westland	84,099	2,234			
			Riverview	7,232	0	Wolverine Lake Village	4,284	0			
			Southfield	31,435	34	Woodhaven	3,313	1			
			Southgate	29,377	1						
			Troy	19,025	3						
			Walled Lake	3,547	0						
			Warren	89,072	19						

Source: U.S. Department of Commerce, Bureau of the Census, 1950, 1960, 1970, and 1980, final population and housing counts, Detroit, Mich., *Census of Population and Housing*, (Washington, D.C.: U.S. Government Printing Office).

more uneven since 1940. In 1940 the index of dissimilarity was only 17 percent. By 1980 the index had increased to 75.3 percent. It is apparent that over a 40-year period blacks and whites have been moving in different directions throughout metropolitan Detroit. William H. Frey's analysis of the migration patterns of blacks and whites during the 1950s and 1960s shows that the white population followed a fairly well-established life-course pattern of city to suburb destination selection.[45] The black population, in contrast, displayed extremely low levels of suburban selection at all ages. Growth outside the city of Detroit during the postwar period has consisted almost entirely of whites. As Table 3.2 shows, 50 incorporated places were added to Detroit's metropolitan area during a 30-year period. The population of those places consisted of 737,007 whites and only 4,852 blacks. Thus, blacks constituted less than 1 percent of the newly incorporated suburban places. Furthermore, 90 percent of the 4,852 blacks lived in Westland and Port Huron. While the black population probably would have preferred the suburbs, especially during the childbearing stage, its low level of suburban selection was due to a lack of access rather than preference.[46] The migration data suggest that the extremely low levels of suburban selection that characterized the black population in the aggregate did not vary appreciably across age categories[47] or across any other socioeconomic measures during the postwar years, as did the levels of suburban selection in the white population.[48] The evidence clearly suggests that it was the various forms of racial discrimination in housing practiced by real estate brokers, financial organizations, and government institutions that prevented black residence in the suburbs.[49]

The Federal Housing Administration (FHA) insurance program, for example, which subsidized the growth of the Detroit suburbs, primarily benefited white middle- and working-class residents. The reason is that the FHA adopted a segregationist policy and refused to insure projects that did not comply. The common belief of white appraisers was that racial integration of the suburbs would lower property values. Although there was no evidence for this assumption, it was an official Federal Housing Administration policy.[50] White appraisers were told to look for physical barriers between racial groups or to find and honor racially restrictive covenants. Race was officially listed as a valid reason for rejecting a mortgage.[51] Thus, while the FHA provided an important service for young, white families, it viewed blacks as a liability on its appraisal balance sheet and denied them equal access to the Detroit suburbs.

Most of all, the FHA and Veterans Administration (VA) mortgage insurance programs shaped and reinforced the racial and economic segregation of suburbia. These programs, for example, allowed nonwhites to hold only 2 percent of the guaranteed mortgages in 1950. They allowed families to become homeowners with virtually no down payment, but rarely offered black veterans the same opportunity to obtain this new housing in the suburbs and thus build their equity.

At the same time, the federal government also subsidized the preparation of comprehensive plans for these emerging suburbs. Under these programs there was usually no requirement for balanced growth of all income groups in the metropolitan region. Thus, competition was rampant between suburban communities for the most effective combinations of public and private actions to insulate themselves from the less-affluent and racially different people living in the city.[52]

As new suburban municipalities have become incorporated, they have been populated primarily by whites. Suburban expansion from 1940 to 1970 was synonymous with white expansion. Only recently, since 1970, have blacks experienced significant participation in the suburbanization process. Because the number of blacks in most suburbs in 1970 was very small, clearly most of the change during the decade can be attributed to movement into the suburbs. The pattern of black suburbanization has varied from a high of 6,739 percent in Southfield to a low of 3 percent in Mount Clemens. In 11 suburbs the rate of black suburbanization exceeded 1,000 percent. In addition to Southfield, the suburbs experiencing the highest rates of black suburbanization were Taylor (6,230), Oak Park (5,197), Southgate (4,450), Lincoln Park (4,420), Troy (4,180), Wayne city (3,911), Madison Heights (1,500), Shelby Township (1,275), Waterford Township (1,252), and Trenton (1,050). (See Table 3.3.) All of these suburbs are in Wayne and Oakland counties.

In contrast to expected trends, blacks also left certain suburbs during the decade. For example, the black population declined in Harrison Township, Plymouth Township, and Grosse Pointe Farms (−37, −38, and −56 percent respectively) during the decade. It appears, then, that black suburbanization in Detroit is multidimensional, encompassing a range of patterns and dynamics of growth. Some suburbs experienced tremendous black gains during the decade, others experienced average growth, and some declined. Caution is advised, however, in interpreting the percentage change in Table 3.3 because of the small population base.

Several attempts have been made to identify the types of suburbs with evidence of black residence or growth.[53] Not one of these studies has provided typologies that are totally applicable to black suburbanization in Detroit. Harold X. Connally's characterization of black suburbanization

Table 3.3 Spatial variation in black suburbanization in Detroit, 1970–1980

Suburban municipality	Number of blacks, 1970	Number of blacks, 1980	Percent change 1970–1980
Southfield	102	6,976	6,739
Taylor	20	1,266	6,230
Oak Park	72	3,814	5,197
Southgate	6	273	4,450
Lincoln Park	5	226	4,420
Troy	15	642	4,180
Wayne	28	1,123	3,911
Madison Heights	15	240	1,500
Shelby Township	12	165	1,275
Waterford Township	33	446	1,252
Trenton	2	23	1,050
West Bloomfield	26	226	769
Canton Township	64	514	703
Fraser	2	15	650
Dearborn	13	83	539
Sterling Heights	38	204	437
Dearborn Heights	12	63	425
Redford Township	17	87	412
Royal Oak	26	116	346
Brownstown Township	99	395	299
Allen Park	29	109	276
Farmington Hills	83	310	274
Berkley	4	13	225
Livonia	41	108	163
Birmingham	18	44	144
Garden City	10	24	140
Warren	132	297	125
Avon Township	132	292	121
East Detroit	13	26	100
Clinton Township	1,296	2,489	92
Wyandotte	18	29	61
Romulus	2,767	4,333	57
Chesterfield Township	136	188	38
Ferndale	89	117	32
Pontiac	22,670	28,532	26
Highland Park	19,609	23,443	20
Inkster	17,189	19,994	16

Table 3.3 (*Continued*)

Suburban municipality	Number of blacks, 1970	Number of blacks, 1980	Percent change 1970–1980
Port Huron	1,857	2,127	15
St. Clair Shores	167	181	8
Mount Clemens	3,324	3,437	3
Westland	2,234	2,200	−2
Roseville	606	569	−6
Hamtramck	3,270	2,751	−16
Harrison Township	737	467	−37
Plymouth Township	487	301	−38
Grosse Pointe Farms	43	19	−56

Source: Computed by the authors from data obtained from the U.S. Department of Commerce, Bureau of the Census, 1970 Census tracts final report, Detroit, Mich., *Census of Population and Housing* (Washington, D.C.: U.S. Government Printing Office, 1972); U.S. Bureau of the Census, PHC 80-v-24, Detroit, Mich., 1980, *Census of Population and Housing Advance Reports*, (Washington, D.C.: U.S. Government Printing Office, 1981).

as "physical expansion of inner city ghettos into contiguous [suburban] areas" does have partial applicability.[54] However, physical expansion, often called "spill over," is inadequate as a complete model to explain the process of black suburbanization in Detroit. It does not explain why blacks move to some nearby suburbs and not to others of the same distance or why there are numerous cases of leapfrogging to more distant suburbs.[55]

The typology presented here views suburbanization as a reflection of black social and spatial mobility. It assumes that black social mobility is facilitated by growing suburbs and restricted by declining suburbs. It assumes that black spatial mobility is facilitated by proximity to the central city and restricted by distance. Thus, the relevant question can be stated thus: Are blacks moving to (1) growing, contiguous (to Detroit) suburbs, (2) declining, contiguous suburbs, (3) growing, noncontiguous suburbs, or (4) declining, noncontiguous suburbs? This typology takes into account the concentric zone sector and multiple nucleus pattern of movement of the black population. Types 1 and 2 are examples of the concentric and sector pattern of movement. The typology also considers black movement to separate nodes with consequent movement within and away from such multiple nodes. Types 3 and 4 thus reflect a multiple-nucleus pattern of black movement.

A Typology of Suburbanization in Detroit

The definitions used in this typology are as follows:

Type 1 Suburbs—Growing and Contiguous. These suburbs are growing in *total* population and are either located on Detroit's border or less than one mile away.

Type 2 Suburbs—Declining and Contiguous. These suburbs are declining in *total* population and are located on Detroit's border or less than one mile away.

Type 3 Suburbs—Growing and Noncontiguous. These suburbs are growing in *total* population and are located one mile or more from Detroit's border.

Type 4 Suburbs—Declining and Noncontiguous. These suburbs are declining in *total* population and are located one mile or more from Detroit's border.

Based on the typology above, the distribution of the black population in 44 suburbs of Detroit is as follows: Two, or 4.5 percent, of the places are Type 1 suburbs; that is, they are contiguous to Detroit and growing. Since there is a higher than average increase in new housing units, black movement into these suburbs involves more than does black movement into units vacated by whites. Southfield, which experienced the highest rate of black suburbanization between 1970 and 1980, is the typical example of the Type 1 suburb. (See Table 3.4.) Eleven, or 25 percent, of the suburbs are in the Type 2 category. These suburbs represent the typical example of blacks primarily replacing whites in existing units. Few, if any, new housing units are being built in these suburbs. Although black movement may be concentric or sectorial, ghettoization appears inevitable. Thirteen, or 29.5 percent, of the suburbs are in the Type 3 category. These suburbs are evolving as distinct and separate nodes away from Detroit. The number of new housing units being built is above average for the metropolitan areas. Black suburbanization in these areas is obviously not due to physical expansion. Most is due to leapfrogging from Detroit to these more distant areas. The most representative example of suburbanization of blacks in Detroit is the Type 4 suburb. Eighteen, or 41 percent, of the suburbs are in this category. Few new housing units are being built, and blacks are primarily replacing whites in existing units. Despite the recent movement of blacks to suburban Detroit, blacks constituted only 4.2 percent of the suburban population in 1980. The place of residence for the majority of blacks is still the central city.

Table 3.4 A typology of suburbanization in Detroit

Suburban places	Distance from Detroit	Rate of growth	Rate of decline
Type 1			
Southfield	0	9.1	
Sterling Heights	0	77.6	
Type 2			
Dearborn	0		−13.0
Dearborn Heights	0		−15.4
East Detroit	0		−16.6
Ferndale	0		−15.0
Grosse Pointe Farms	0		−9.8
Hamtramck	0		−20.5
Highland Park	0		−21.3
Lincoln Park	0		−14.9
Oak Park	0		−14.2
Redford Township	0		−18.7
Type 3			
Avon Township	13	66.4	
Brownstown Township	7	149.0	
Canton Township	9	340.9	
Chesterfield Township	20	94.9	
Clinton Township	7	48.2	
Fraser	5	22.7	
Harrison Township	8	26.1	
Shelby Township	12	32.1	
Taylor	4	10.8	
Troy	6	70.2	
Waterford Township	13	9.0	
Wayne city	10	0.5	
West Bloomfield Township	8	46.9	
Type 4			
Allen Park	3		−16.1
Berkley	3		−14.8
Birmingham	6		−17.1
Garden City	3		−14.9
Inkster	3		−8.8
Livonia	3		−4.8
Madison Heights	2		−8.4
Mount Clemens	9		−8.2
Plymouth Township	8		−15.1
Pontiac	11		−10.0
Port Huron	42		−5.1

Table 3.4 (*Continued*)

Suburban places	Distance from Detroit	Rate of growth	Rate of decline
Roseville	2		−10.3
Royal Oak	1		−17.8
St. Clair Shores	1		−13.5
Southgate	3		−5.5
Trenton	6		−5.7
Westland	3		−2.5
Wyandotte	2		−17.2

Source: Computed by the authors from data obtained from the U.S. Department of Commerce, Bureau of the Census, PHC 80-v-24, Detroit, Mich., 1980 *Census of Population and Housing Advance Reports*, (Washington, D.C.: U.S. Government Printing Office, 1981).

Note: Two suburbs, Romulus and Farmington Hills, were established after 1970. Thus, they are excluded from the analysis. The total sample size is 44 suburbs.

Furthermore, the few blacks who have escaped to the suburbs have not escaped segregation. Since 1950 blacks in the suburbs of Detroit have been more segregated from whites residentially than blacks in the city of Detroit have been. The pattern in the suburbs was toward increasing segregation from 1940 to 1970. The index of dissimilarity increased from 80.9 percent to 92.2 percent during the 30-year period. Between 1970 and 1980 black suburban segregation dropped to 83.9 percent. Even so, blacks in the suburbs in 1980 remained more segregated than the black residents in the city of Detroit. (See Table 3.5.) Unlike in the suburbs, segregation in the city has been declining since 1940. The pattern of suburbanization for blacks, therefore, has been different from that of most racial and ethnic groups. For the latter, suburbanization has usually meant a reduction in residential segregation. For blacks, suburbanization has resulted in continued segregation.

The Pattern of Race within Detroit, 1940–1980

In 1940 there were 1,472,000 whites and 149,000 blacks in Detroit. Most blacks were restricted to a ghetto just east of Woodward Avenue, from the Detroit River to the Highland Park city limits. Seventy percent of the black population lived there. Such concentration of blacks in a single area

Table 3.5 Residential segregation of blacks in the Detroit Standard Metropolitan Statistical Area (SMSA), central city, and suburbs, 1940–1980

Year	Indexes of dissimilarity		
	SMSA	Central city	Suburbs
1940	83.7	83.5	80.9
1950	84.0	81.1	87.4
1960	87.4	80.4	89.8
1970	88.9	78.2	92.2
1980	85.8	67.4	83.9

Source: Computed by the authors from data obtained from the U.S. Department of Commerce, Bureau of the Census, 1940, 1950, 1960, 1970, and 1980 census tracts, Detroit, Mich., *Census of Population and Housing* (Washington, D.C.: U.S. Government Printing Office).

was reflected in the 83.5 percent index of dissimilarity (See Table 3.5). the area where most blacks lived was euphemistically termed "Paradise Valley."[56] It was an area of overcrowded and dilapidated housing, high unemployment, low incomes, and low educational attainment. It was also the area in which the Detroit race riot of 1943 occurred.[57] There were two smaller concentrations of blacks: One area was on the near west side, and the other was the Northlawn community, a semirural area at the northern boundary of the city and Wyoming Avenue. Over time the black population expanded into areas where fewer blacks resided, and segregation between the races declined an average 4 percentage points per year. The Northlawn area, however, was one community where black expansion into surrounding areas was prevented by race-conscious whites, who built an eight-foot wall to stop the expansion of blacks. As long as strong resistance to black expansion persisted, residential segregation remained high. Thus, between the 30-year period from 1940 to 1970, segregation declined by only 5.3 percentage points. On the other hand, during the 10-year period from 1970 to 1980, segregation decreased 10.8 percentage points. White resistance to black expansion has given way to white flight to the suburbs. The decline in segregation therefore may be temporary, as most of the buyers of units vacated by whites are blacks instead of other whites.

In 1940 the metropolitan area (Wayne, Oakland, and Macomb counties) had a black population of 170,000 and a white population of 2 million. Residential segregation was very high (See Table 3.5). As in the pattern in the suburbs, blacks and whites throughout the metropolitan area experienced increasing residential segregation from 1940 to 1970. Even though the level of segregation declined slightly between 1970 and 1980, blacks and whites within the metropolitan area remained highly segregated in 1980, with an index of dissimilarity of 85.8 percent. (See Table 3.5.)

In sum, between 1940 and 1980 most blacks and whites have continued to live in separate neighborhoods in the city of Detroit, the suburbs, and the entire metropolitan area. An uneven spatial distribution of blacks has been the rule. How much of the spatial distribution of blacks could be attributed to the cost of housing?

The Spatial Distribution of Blacks and Housing Cost, 1960–1980

Given the fact that blacks usually have a lower average economic status than whites, let us assume that most black homeowners live in low-value housing and most black renters in low-rent housing, while most whites live in high-value and high-rent housing. Does this assumption allow us to conclude that the spatial distribution of blacks is merely a function of the spatial distribution of low-value and low-rent housing?

Regression analyses of the effects of housing cost on the spatial distribution of blacks are presented for the years 1960, 1970, and 1980. These are the years when the most rapid suburbanization occurred and the metropolitan area assumed major significance *vis-à-vis* the central city.

To ascertain the relative significance of housing cost in explaining the uneven spatial distribution of blacks, "percent black" by census tracts was regressed against "percent low-value housing" and "percent low-rent housing" by census tracts.[58]

The reason for regressing "percent black" by census tracts with housing value and rent instead of income is that income does not precisely reflect what a black person actually pays for housing. For example, let us assume that a given white person earns $22,000 a year and a given black person $18,000. Both might pay $300 per month rent for a house. This phenomenon, in which blacks are denied economic equality in certain areas (income) but have forced equality in others (cost of housing), is common in cities and suburbs throughout the United States. Furthermore, even at equal levels of education and occupation, blacks earn less income than whites on the average, and the gap continues to widen. This fact, together with the higher proportion of blacks at lower levels of education and occupation, leaves no doubt that racial economic inequality in terms of income is still very much in existence. However, the fact that blacks earn less than whites does not necessarily indicate that blacks pay less than whites for housing. To measure the influence of housing cost on the spatial distribution of blacks, it is much more meaningful and more precise to focus on the actual cost of the housing than on the income of the occupants.[59] Nevertheless, even when authors have used income as a variable to explain the spatial distribution of blacks, income has accounted for very little of it.[60]

The variables "low-value housing" and "low-rent housing" were coded for the regression analysis by computing the percentage of housing in each tract that was below the SMSA's median housing value and median housing rent. For example, if no housing in the tract had a value below the median for the SMSA, the figure for the variable would be 0 percent. On the other hand, if all of the housing in the tract had a value below the median value for the SMSA, the figure for the variable would be 100 percent. In other words, dollar values of housing and rent were not coded; instead, the percentage of the housing in each tract that was low-value or low-rent was used.

Regression analysis was carried out for the central city, the suburbs, and the SMSA of Detroit for 1960, 1970, and 1980, and the results are presented in Table 3.6. In the table the coefficient of multiple correlation, R, indicates the total strength of the relationship between the dependent and the independent variables. The coefficient of determination, R^2, provides an estimate of the proportion of the total spatial variation in the dependent variable that can be explained by the independent variables.

In 1960 the location of low-rent and low-value housing together explained only 17 percent of the total spatial variation in the dependent variable, leaving 83 percent unexplained.

In the suburbs the location of low-value and low-rent housing together explained only 14 percent of the total spatial variation in the dependent variable, leaving 86 percent unexplained.

Finally, for the total SMSA, the location of low-rent and low-value housing failed to explain very much of the uneven distribution of blacks in 1960. Together the variables explained only 20 percent of the total spatial variation in the dependent variable, leaving 80 percent unexplained.

Thus, housing cost or the location of low-rent and low-value housing explained from 14 to 20 percent of the uneven distribution of blacks in Detroit and its surrounding suburbs in 1960.

Table 3.6 The relationship between the location of blacks and the location of low-rent housing (LRH) and low-value housing (LVH), 1960, 1970, and 1980

Variable	1960			1970			1980		
	Regression coefficient (β)	Unexplained variation	Correlation coefficient	Regression coefficient (β)	Unexplained variation	Correlation coefficient	Regression coefficient (β)	Unexplained variation	Correlation coefficient
Central city									
Percentage of LRH	.4837	83%	$R = .4060$*	.8395	64%	$R = .5997$*	.2739	96%	$R = .1910$
Percentage of LVH	.1645		$R^2 = .1648$	−.2507		$R^2 = .3596$	.1179		$R^2 = .0364$
Suburbs							a .3994	57%	$R = .6529$*
							.5282		$R^2 = .4263$
Percentage of LRH	.1599	86%	$R = .3755$*	.3051	75%	$R = .5037$*	b .4058	55%	$R = .6702$*
Percentage of LVH	.1010		$R^2 = .1410$	.0654		$R^2 = .2538$	.5445		$R^2 = .4491$
SMSA							a .3853	67%	$R = .5730$*
							.4953		$R^2 = .3283$
Percentage of LRH	.3231	80%	$R = .4434$*	.7135	52%	$R = .6891$*	b .3983	64%	$R = .6004$*
Percentage of LVH	.2764		$R^2 = .1966$	.001		$R^2 = .4749$	.5195		$R^2 = .3605$

Source: Computed by the authors from data derived from the U.S. Department of Commerce, Bureau of the Census, 1960 Census tracts, final report, PHC (1)-40, Detroit, Mich. (Standard Metropolitan Statistical Area) *Census of Population and Housing* (Washington, D.C.: U.S. Government Printing Office); U.S. Bureau of the Census, 1970 Census tracts, final report, PHC (1)-58, Detroit, Mich. (Standard Metropolitan Statistical Area) *Census of Population and Housing* (Washington, D.C.: U.S. Government Printing Office); U.S. Bureau of the Census. 1980 Summary Tape File 4 *Census of Population and Housing* (Washington, D.C.: U.S. Government Printing Office).

* Significant at the .001 level

a. For 1980, Suburbs and SMSA for Wayne, Oakland, and Macomb counties.

b. For 1980, Suburbs and SMSA for Wayne, Oakland, Macomb, Livingston, Lapeer, and St. Clair counties.

In 1970 the location of low-rent and low-value housing together explained 36 percent of the total spatial variation in the dependent variable, leaving 64 percent unexplained in the central city. Clearly, cost had a stronger influence on the spatial distribution of blacks in 1970 than in 1960; however, a large amount, 64 percent, remained unexplained.

Together, the location of low-rent and low-value housing explained 25 percent of the total spatial variation in the dependent variable, leaving 75 percent still unexplained in the suburbs.

In the SMSA in 1970 the location of low-rent housing together with low-value housing accounted for 48 percent of the total spatial variation in the dependent variable, leaving 52 percent unexplained. Thus, housing cost explained more of the spatial distribution of blacks in 1970 than in 1960. Nevertheless, the bulk, 52 percent, of the distribution of blacks could not be explained by housing cost.

By 1980 the location of low-rent and low-value housing virtually ceased to be important factors in explaining the distribution of central-city blacks. Together the variables explained only 4 percent of the total spatial variation in the dependent variable, leaving 96 percent unexplained.

In the suburban area of Wayne, Oakland, and Macomb counties, the location of low-rent and low-value housing together explained only 43 percent of the total spatial variation, leaving 57 percent unexplained. In the expanded suburban area, which includes the additional counties of Livingston, Lapeer, and St. Clair, the variables together explained 45 percent of the variation, leaving 55 percent unexplained.

In the SMSA (Wayne, Oakland, and Macomb) the location of low-rent and low-value housing together explained 33 percent of the total spatial variation in the dependent variable, leaving 67 percent unexplained. In the six-county SMSA the variables together explained 36 percent of the total spatial variation in the dependent variable, leaving 64 percent unexplained.

Housing value, therefore, does not explain the uneven distribution of the black and white populations. Indeed in some suburban municipalities, black-occupied housing units have a higher value than white-occupied housing units, as shown in Table 3.7. Table 3.7 also shows that among the housing units in southern Macomb County, the median value of black-occupied units exceeded the value of white-occupied units in East Detroit and Warren. The median housing value of black-occupied units exceeded the value of white-occupied units in seven of ten suburban municipalities in Oakland County. Suburban municipalities where the black-occupied housing units had a higher median value than white-occupied units in-

Table 3.7 Occupied housing units by race in selected suburbs of Detroit, 1980[a]

Suburban municipality	Median value ($)			Median contracted rent ($)		
	Black	White	Difference	Black	White	Difference
Oakland County						
Avon Township	104,700	81,400	23,300	325	302	23
Berkeley	na	39,500		na	237	
Birmingham	60,000	77,800	−17,800	500+	354	146
Farmington Hills	106,300	86,600	19,700	392	363	29
Ferndale	22,500	27,400	−4,900	153	235	−82
Madison Heights	na	39,600		269	261	8
Oak Park	45,500	39,600	5,900	327	268	59
Pontiac	25,100	47,400	−22,300	197	231	−34
Royal Oak	45,000	44,600	400	316	270	46
Southfield	74,000	66,300	7,700	379	366	13
Troy	100,500	82,800	17,700	364	347	17
Waterford Township	49,400	47,600	1,800	283	285	−2
West Bloomfield Township	na	200,000	na	na	436	
Southern Macomb County						
Center Line	na	38,900		na	132	
East Detroit	40,000	38,800	1,200	na	248	
Roseville	24,500	37,400	−12,900	151	242	−91
St. Clair Shores	37,500	46,500	−9,000	158	269	−111
Warren	51,300	47,300	4,000	253	260	−7
Downriver communities						
Allen Park	na	48,200		na	272	
Brownstone Township	38,800	56,300	−17,500	258	251	7
Ecorse	24,600	21,800	2,800	147	165	−18
Flat Rock	na	47,900		230	211	19
Gibraltar	na	51,600		na	254	
Grosse Isle Township	na	89,500		na	292	
Lincoln Park	na	34,500		263	275	−12
Melvindale	na	29,900		275	228	47
River Rouge	23,700	19,600	4,100	124	157	−33
Riverview	77,500	53,900	23,600	280	254	26
Rockwood	na	46,800		na	252	
Southgate	32,500	42,200	−9,700	282	284	−2
Taylor	37,500	37,100	400	276	245	31
Trenton	na	56,200		282	235	47

Table 3.7 (*Continued*)

Suburban municipality	Median value ($)			Median contracted rent ($)		
	Black	White	Difference	Black	White	Difference
Woodhaven	na	65,500		276	265	11
Wyandotte	na	35,100		165	192	−27

Source: U.S. Department of Commerce, Bureau of the Census, Detroit, Mich., 1980, *Census of Housing: Characteristics of Housing Units* (Washington, D.C.: U.S. Government Printing Office, 1982), Vol. 1, ch. A, pt. 24.

a. Includes suburbs with populations of 2,500 or more.

na = not available.

cluded Avon Township, Farmington Hills, Oak Park, Royal Oak Township, Southfield, Troy, and Waterford Township.

The value of black-occupied units also exceeded the value of white-occupied units in four of six downriver municipalities: Ecorse, River Rouge, Riverview, and Taylor.

On the average the rent paid by blacks exceeded the rent paid by whites for units located in the suburbs of Oakland County, such as Avon Township, Birmingham, Farmington Hills, Madison Heights, Oak Park, Royal Oak Township, Southfield, and Troy.

Furthermore, the median rent paid by blacks exceeded the rent paid by whites in the downriver municipalities of Brownstown Township, Flat Rock, Melvindale, Riverview, Taylor, Trenton, and Woodhaven. Clearly, then, housing cost is not the primary reason blacks are highly segregated from whites. Yet blacks have remained disproportionately concentrated in the central city, whereas most whites have relocated to the suburbs.

The Consequences of Residential Segregation

Such differential concentration of blacks in the central city has serious social and economic consequences. Jobs and other economic opportunities have been shifting to the suburbs and to nonmetropolitan areas. Detroit, like other central cities, will continue to offer decreasing opportunities for social and economic mobility.

Another consequence is related to the differential accessibility to mortgage and home-improvement loans. Although Michigan's Anti-Redlining

Act prohibits geographic discrimination in the making of mortgage and home-improvement loans, the number, percentage, and type of loan are not evenly distributed in metropolitan Detroit.[61] Instead, the racial composition of census tracts or neighborhoods is related to the pattern of lending.

In 1983 the number and total volume of mortgage loans in metropolitan Detroit *increased* above 1982 levels. However, the percentage of loans made between 1982 and 1983 in moderate-to-high-minority tracts *decreased* for every loan category reported. Moderate-to-high-minority tracts are defined as tracts with more than 5 percent minority population.[62] Between 1982 and 1983 the FHA Farm Home Administration (Fm Ha) and VA loans made in moderate-to-high-minority tracts, as a percentage of the metropolitan area total, decreased from 14.4 to 11.5 percent. Conventional loans declined from 15.7 to 12.8 percent, and home-improvement loans dropped from 14.1 to 13.9 percent.[63]

Additionally, the percentages of FHA, Fm Ha, VA, and conventional loans made in 1983 in moderate-to-high-minority tracts were lower than the percentages of single-family structures in those tracts. Clearly, residents living in moderate-to-high-minority tracts are receiving less than their fair share of mortgage loans.

Between 1979 and 1983 the percentages of conventional loans and home-improvement loans denied in moderate-to-high-minority tracts or neighborhoods were higher than the percentages of loan applications denied in low-minority tracts.[64] It appears that in moderate-to-high-minority tracts, lenders are applying lending standards that are different from those applied in low-minority tracts.

Furthermore, based on foreclosure data from Michigan's Department of Commerce, such differential lending patterns cannot be economically justified.[65] The results refute a frequent assumption that lending in moderate-to-high-minority tracts constitutes higher economic risk. In sum, one probable consequence of living in racially segregated or moderate-to-high-minority neighborhoods is differential treatment by lenders in the allocation of conventional and home-improvement loans. When lending practices and policies are differentially applied on the basis of location and race, such practices and policies may affect the quality of housing and the quantity of homeownership.

Because blacks in metropolitan Detroit are disproportionately located in the central city, a higher percentage of blacks compared with whites are likely to live in older, overcrowded housing. Of the 119,491 black-occupied housing units in metropolitan Detroit in 1980, 40.8 percent were built in

1939 or earlier. Only 18.8 percent of the 225,475 white-occupied housing units were built in 1939 or earlier.[66]

Since most older housing is disproportionately located in areas of high population density, there is often a relationship between older housing and overcrowded living conditions. On the average, in 1980, blacks in owner-occupied housing in metropolitan Detroit were 2.7 times more likely than whites to live in overcrowded conditions.[67] The condition of blacks in renter-occupied housing was not much better. Blacks, on the average, were 2.4 times more likely than whites to live in overcrowded housing.

As stated previously, mortgage loans are not distributed evenly throughout metropolitan Detroit. It is more difficult to secure a loan in moderate-to-high-minority tracts or neighborhoods. This differential accessibility to mortgage loans can be a significant factor in explaining the differential rates of homeownership between blacks and whites in metropolitan Detroit. In 1980, 52.7 percent of the black-occupied units in metropolitan Detroit were owned, compared with 76 percent of the white-occupied units—a difference of 23.3 percentage points.

The economic impact of the differential rates of black and white homeownership should not be underestimated. Restrictions on homeownership opportunities have far-reaching implications, since homeownership is related to wealth accumulation. For example, the average house purchased with an FHA 203 mortgage in 1949 (a time when few FHA mortgages were issued to blacks) had a value of $8,286 and a mortgage of $7,101. If a 30-year-old household head had purchased this house with a 20-year mortgage, and assuming no appreciation or depreciation, the savings would have amounted to more than $7,000, and the purchaser would have owned the house by age 50. Assuming that the value increased by a conservative 2.5 percent per year, the purchaser would have accumulated assets worth at least $16,000, a considerable accumulation that could be borrowed against for children's college education or simply held until retirement.[68]

Since homeownership is subsidized by the federal government through tax deductibility of mortgage interest and property taxes, the federal and state governments must take the responsibility to assure that racial restrictions are eliminated. During each fiscal year the federal government foregoes revenues of several billion dollars as a result of federal income-tax provisions enabling homeowners to take itemized deductions for mortgage interest and property taxes paid on their owner-occupied homes. In fiscal year 1980, for example, the amount lost to the federal treasury was $14.6 billion.[69]

Since the opportunities for securing a mortgage may be greater in the suburbs, let us return to suburban Detroit to examine its differential rates of racial movement.

Differential Patterns of Racial Mobility in the Suburbs

Racial mobility between 1970 and 1980 followed four patterns: (1) the decline of the white population and the increase of the black population, (2) the increase of whites and blacks, (3) the decline of whites and blacks, and (4) the increase of whites and the decline of blacks.

Despite Oakland County's high level of economic development, several municipalities experienced white population declines between 1970 and 1980. Among these suburbs were Berkley, Birmingham, Ferndale, Madison Heights, Oak Park, Pontiac, Royal Oak Township, and Southfield. Although each suburb experienced an increase in the black population, the numbers were insufficient to offset the white population loss in every suburb except Southfield.

Southfield: A Racially Tolerant Suburb

In terms of racial mobility, Southfield has been an exception. From 1970 to 1980 more than 6,000 blacks were added to Southfield's population, a number clearly sufficient to offset the loss of 2,000 whites. Southfield had the highest number and percentage increase in black population of any Detroit suburb. Thus, Southfield was the only suburb bordering Detroit to grow between 1970 and 1980. Had it not been for the substantial increase in the black population, Southfield too would have declined over the decade. Unlike some of its sister suburbs, such as Dearborn and Warren, which over the years have become known for their less than hospitable attitudes toward blacks, Southfield decided to resist the mass white racial hysteria and, instead, worked toward becoming a multiracial city. As a result, Southfield and Oak Park are two of the most racially and culturally representative suburbs in the metropolitan area. The politics of Southfield are discussed in detail later in the book.

Suburbs in Oakland County that have experienced increases in blacks and whites over the decade include Avon Township, Farmington Hills, Troy, Waterford Township, and West Bloomfield Township. These suburbs are located an average distance of 8.4 miles from Detroit's border.

Unlike the Northwest Passage of Oakland County, southern Macomb

County has been experiencing a white population decline with very little black population gain. One suburb, Roseville, experienced population declines by whites and blacks. Such population losses are not surprising, given the dependence of these suburbs on heavy manufacturing, where the unemployment rates have been very high. The average unemployment rate in 1980 for the five suburban communities was 12.6 percent.

Warren: A Racially Hostile Suburb

Unlike Southfield, Warren fell victim to mass white racial hysteria and allowed itself to become a refuge for panic-stricken working-class whites fleeing the east side of Detroit. In the minds of those unfortunate people, "the black hordes" had chased them out of east side Detroit and deprived them of "their rights" to live in a racially segregated community. No wonder Warren has resorted to a multitude of efforts to maintain its racial isolation. (See Chapter 4.)

Interestingly enough, Detroit blacks owned property in the area where Warren now sits 30 years before its incorporation as a city in 1957. The Detroit Memorial Park, situated on Thirteen Mile Road and Ryan in a beautiful 80-acre cemetery, was owned and operated by blacks. In 1970 only 28 black families lived in Warren, and 20 of them resided in a U.S. government housing project called Center Line Gardens, located between Eleven Mile and Twelve Mile roads. In 1980 the black population of Warren was 297.

Racial mobility in downriver communities involved white population losses and small black gains in Allen Park, Lincoln Park, Melvindale, Southgate, Trenton, and Wyandotte. Areas experiencing growth by whites and blacks included Brownstown Township, Flat Rock, Gibraltar, Riverview, Taylor, and Woodhaven. These suburbs are located at an average distance of six miles from Detroit's border.

River Rouge and Ecorse: Industrial Suburbs with Historically Black Concentrations

Two suburbs experienced population losses by whites and blacks. These were River Rouge and Ecorse. The former is on Detroit's border, and the latter is less than one mile away. Thus, there is a positive relationship between distance from Detroit's border and white population growth. On the other hand, there appears to be an inverse relationship between distance from Detroit and black population growth in the suburbs. The first blacks in the downriver communities of River Rouge and Ecorse did not come from Detroit as part of the wave of black suburbanization in the 1970s and 1980s, as was the case in other Detroit suburbs. Blacks were living in both cities as far back as World War I. They probably came directly from the South to work in the manufacturing plants located in the area. Great Lakes Steel set up operations in Ecorse in 1931, paving the way for other key industrial developments in the city. By the time Ecorse became incorporated in 1942, it had assumed a significant role in the downriver economy. The black community had also grown during the period, numbering between 500 and 600.[70] Historically, therefore, blacks in both Ecorse and River Rouge do not fit the pattern of post–World War II black suburbanization, since many lived in these industrial cities long before Detroit developed suburbs as we know them today.

In sum, there have been differential patterns of residential location and mobility by race in the metropolitan area of Detroit. Three patterns can be described:

First is the concentric pattern, in which most white growth is occurring on the periphery or in outer zones at greater distances from Detroit's border. On the other hand, suburbs vacated by whites are experiencing black population increases, with the greatest increases occurring in those suburbs near Detroit's border.

Second is a sector pattern, in which most growth by whites and blacks is occurring in the northwest sector of Oakland County. This is the area of highest economic development. It is also the sector where most of the elites—professionals, managers, and administrators—reside.

And third is a multiple-nucleus pattern. The black population is not evenly distributed throughout the metropolitan area. Instead, most blacks can be found in the central city and in only a few suburbs. Thus there is the dominant nucleus—the central city—and smaller nuclei such as Pontiac, Inkster, Ecorse, and River Rouge. Historically, each smaller nucleus has maintained a sizable black population. Furthermore, each municipality has evolved primarily as a satellite city in contrast to the evolution of residential suburbs.

Patterns of Class

As indicated in the preceding section, metropolitan fragmentation is an effective tool that has been utilized by several suburban municipalities to

Table 3.8 City / metropolitan disparity in household income for the 33 largest U.S. metropolitan areas, 1983

Area	Disparity rank	Metro income	City income	Difference
Detroit	1	$33,241	$21,556	$11,685
Oakland	2	33,401	23,305	10,096
Cleveland	3	29,277	19,261	10,016
St. Louis	4	29,321	19,389	9,932
Minneapolis	5	32,917	23,714	9,203
Baltimore	6	29,731	20,816	8,915
Washington, D.C.	7	38,629	29,893	8,736
Chicago	8	32,679	24,205	8,474
Atlanta	9	29,976	21,531	8,445
Boston	10	29,191	21,221	7,970
Philadelphia	11	28,473	20,867	7,606
Miami	12	27,945	20,381	7,564
St. Paul	13	32,917	25,539	7,378
Milwaukee	14	31,510	24,268	7,242
Buffalo	15	26,370	19,286	7,084
Cincinnati	16	28,764	21,903	6,861
Denver	17	33,525	26,994	6,531
New York	18	29,573	23,238	6,335
San Francisco	19	33,401	27,131	6,270
Phoenix	20	29,301	23,301	6,000
Pittsburgh	21	28,618	22,888	5,730
Fort Worth	22	31,630	25,991	5,639
Portland	23	29,627	24,814	4,813
New Orleans	24	28,210	23,464	4,746
Seattle	25	31,788	27,054	4,734
Kansas City	26	29,925	25,475	4,450
Columbus	27	27,533	23,220	4,313
Houston	28	36,390	33,020	3,370
Los Angeles	29	31,025	28,460	2,565
Indianapolis	30	29,210	27,038	2,172
Dallas	31	31,630	29,610	2,020
San Antonio	32	25,061	23,085	1,976
San Deigo	33	29,012	28,077	935

Source: Detroit News, January 6, 1985.

isolate their governments racially and to maintain racially homogeneous enclaves. Metropolitan fragmentation also equips suburban municipalities with the tools to isolate themselves socially and economically, thus denying the poor equal access. Such actions often result in the uneven spatial distribution of social and economic classes.

This section examines the unevenness in the distribution of population groups by income, occupation, and education. The aim is to determine the extent of social and economic disparities between municipalities throughout metropolitan Detroit. The subunits for analysis are municipalities that had at least 2,500 people in 1980. It has been widely known that inequality exists between Detroit and the suburbs generally. What may not be generally known is that the $11,685 gap in average household income between the overall region of metropolitan Detroit ($33,241) and Detroit city ($21,556) in 1983 was the widest of the 33 largest metropolitan areas in the United States (See Table 3.8).

Furthermore, often overlooked is the fact that social and economic inequality is also very prevalent between individual suburban municipalities. In other words, a mere central city/suburban comparison is insufficient to really unveil the hidden dimensions of class inequality within metropolitan Detroit. A comparison between individual municipalities is also necessary. The data suggest that widespread intermunicipal socioeconomic inequality exists in metropolitan Detroit. Such inequality can be measured by income, occupational status, and level of educational attainment.

Median family income within metropolitan Detroit in 1980 ranged from $75,000 and above in Bloomfield Hills, a suburb in Oakland County, to $13,180 in Highland Park, a municipal enclave surrounded by Detroit. The median family income of the wealthiest municipality was 5.7 times the median family income of the poorest. The remaining nine municipalities that make up the top ten wealthiest municipalities are Grosse Pointe Shores ($62,819), Franklin ($53,480), Grosse Pointe Farms ($42,252), Beverly Hills Village ($41,923), Lathrup Village ($39,647), Grosse Pointe ($37,864), Huntington Woods ($36,461), Grosse Pointe Woods ($35,673), and Grosse Pointe Park ($35,527). (See Table 3.9.) The wealth is concentrated in Oakland County and the east coast suburban communities in Wayne County.

The remaining nine poorest municipalities, as measured by median family income, are Fraser ($14,381), Hamtramck ($16,462), Detroit ($17,033), Lapeer ($17,276), Port Huron ($18,618), River Rouge ($18,618), Pontiac ($18,630), Marine City ($18,790), and Hazel Park ($19,495). Most of the poverty is concentrated in Detroit, Pontiac, and Port Huron and the less-developed areas of Lapeer and St. Clair counties.

Table 3.9 Class and race inequality in metropolitan Detroit, 1980

Municipality	Total population	SMSA's popula- tiuon (%)	Median family income ($)	SMSA's profes- sionals (%)	SMSA's college graduate (%)	white (%)	non-white (%)
Detroit	1,203,339	27.65	17,033	16.42	15.92	34.4	65.6
Warren	161,134	3.70	26,535	3.24	2.30	98.2	1.8
Sterling Heights	108,999	2.50	29,662	2.88	2.43	97.4	2.6
Livonia	104,814	2.41	31,673	3.24	3.29	98.5	1.5
Dearborn	90,660	2.08	26,935	2.72	2.98	98.4	1.6
Westland	84,603	1.94	25,216	1.61	1.47	95.8	4.2
Taylor	77,568	1.78	23,932	1.00	0.77	96.2	3.8
Pontiac	76,715	1.76	18,630	0.80	0.72	57.8	42.2
St. Clair Shores	76,210	1.75	26,817	1.78	1.38	98.8	1.2
Southfield	75,568	1.74	31,603	3.76	4.33	88.3	11.7
Royal Oak	70,893	1.63	26,421	2.78	2.67	98.6	1.4
Dearborn Heights	67,706	1.56	27,639	1.59	1.35	98.2	1.8
Troy	67,102	1.54	34,192	3.37	3.91	94.5	5.5
Roseville	54,311	1.25	23,173	0.74	0.44	97.6	2.4
Lincoln Park	45,105	1.04	27,171	0.58	0.46	98.0	2.0
East Detroit	38,280	0.88	23,843	0.62	0.46	99.1	0.9
Garden City	35,640	0.82	26,895	0.50	0.56	99.0	1.0
Madison Heights	35,375	0.81	24,650	0.67	0.51	96.9	3.1
Inkster	35,190	0.80	20,170	0.46	0.36	42.0	58.0
Allen Park	34,196	0.79	29,411	0.89	0.74	98.1	1.9
Wyandotte	34,006	0.78	23,042	0.49	0.40	98.9	1.1
Port Huron	33,981	0.78	18,618	0.61	0.56	91.1	8.9
Southgate	32,058	0.74	27,299	0.61	0.48	97.5	2.5
Oak Park	31,537	0.73	24,447	1.05	1.17	85.7	14.3
Highland Park	27,909	0.64	13,180	0.31	0.30	14.2	85.8
Ferndale	26,227	0.60	19,919	0.47	0.57	97.9	2.1
Trenton	22,762	0.52	30,148	0.63	0.65	99.0	1.0
Novi	22,525	0.52	30,169	0.87	0.95	97.8	2.2
Birmingham	21,689	0.50	33,968	1.40	1.99	98.6	1.4
Hamtramck	21,300	0.49	16,462	0.21	0.20	82.2	17.8
Wayne	21,159	0.49	23,913	0.32	0.27	93.4	6.6
Hazel Park	20,914	0.48	19,495	0.20	0.11	98.0	2.0
Grosse Pointe Woods	18,886	0.43	35,673	1.01	1.26	98.9	1.1
Mount Clemens	18,806	0.43	21,354	0.37	0.35	80.0	20.0
Berkley	18,637	0.42	24,667	0.50	0.50	98.8	1.2
Harper Woods	16,361	0.37	25,343	0.46	0.43	99,0	1.0
Clawson	15,103	0.35	27,031	0.37	0.32	98.9	1.1

Table 3.9 (*Continued*)

Municipality	Total population	SMSA's population (%)	Median family income ($)	SMSA's professionals (%)	SMSA's college graduate (%)	white (%)	non-white (%)
Riverview	14,569	0.33	30,439	0.37	0.31	97.1	2.9
Fraser	14,560	0.33	14,381	0.31	0.20	98.8	1.2
Ecorse	14,447	0.33	20,225	0.12	0.06	57.2	42.8
Grosse Pointe Park	13,639	0.31	35,527	0.73	0.94	98.4	1.6
River Rouge	12,912	0.30	18,618	0.10	0.10	65.6	34.4
Melvindale	12,322	0.28	23,287	0.14	0.09	96.6	3.4
Beverly Hills Village	11,598	0.27	41,923	0.72	1.02	98.0	2.0
Farmington	11,022	0.25	30,006	0.42	0.50	99.1	0.9
Woodhaven	10,902	0.25	29,592	0.26	0.24	97.4	2.6
Grosse Pointe Farms	10,551	0.24	42,252	0.58	1.03	98.8	1.2
Plymouth Township	9,986	0.23	25,848	0.34	0.43	98.7	1.3
Center Line	9,293	0.21	24,034	0.15	0.12	99.3	0.7
Marysville	7,345	0.17	25,216	0.20	0.16	99.2	0.8
Rochester	7,203	0.16	25,118	0.33	0.36	97.6	2.4
Howell	6,976	0.16	21,905	0.17	0.18	98.5	1.5
Huntington Woods	6,937	0.16	36,461	0.50	0.21	98.5	1.5
Flat Rock	6,853	0.16	23,414	0.13	0.11	97.7	2.3
Lapeer	6,198	0.14	17,276	0.13	0.12	96.6	3.4
Grosse Pointe	5,901	0.13	37,864	0.36	0.58	98.8	1.2
Northville	5,698	0.13	32,449	0.24	0.32	98.8	1.2
New Baltimore	5,439	0.12	24,246	0.14	0.09	98.6	1.4
Utica	5,282	0.12	23,211	0.13	0.11	98.0	2.0
South Lyon	5,214	0.12	23,942	0.10	0.10	99.3	0.7
Milford	5,041	0.11	25,916	0.13	0.14	99.1	0.9
Wolverine Lake Village	4,968	0.11	31,323	0.14	0.11	99.5	0.5
Holly Village	4,874	0.11	23,492	0.06	0.05	99.0	1.0
St. Clair	4,780	0.11	22,724	0.12	0.12	99.1	0.9
Walled Lake	4,748	0.11	24,163	0.12	0.08	97.8	2.2
Lathrup Village	4,639	0.11	39,647	0.27	0.33	95.1	4.9
Gibraltar	4,458	0.10	23,489	0.08	0.50	99.0	1.0
Marine City	4,414	0.10	18,790	0.05	0.04	99.4	0.6
Algonac	4,412	0.10	19,727	0.06	0.07	98.3	1.7
Brighton	4,268	0.10	23,429	0.14	0.15	97.3	2.7
Lake Orion Heights	4,087	0.09	25,616	0.09	0.08	98.8	1.2
Bloomfield Hills	3,985	0.09	75,000	0.28	0.47	94.9	5.1
Richmond	3,536	0.09	21,659	0.08	0.09	99.5	0.5

Table 3.9 (*Continued*)

Municipality	Total population	SMSA's population (%)	Median family income ($)	SMSA's professionals (%)	SMSA's college graduate (%)	white (%)	non-white (%)
Romeo	3,509	0.08	25,286	0.07	0.08	92.4	7.6
Rockwood	3,346	0.08	26,789	0.06	0.04	98.3	1.7
Pleasant Ridge	3,217	0.07	29,848	0.17	0.21	98.9	1.1
Grosse Pointe Shores	3,122	0.07	62,819	0.20	0.26	98.4	1.6
Keego Harbor	3,083	0.07	20,833	0.07	0.05	95.5	4.5
Lake Orion	2,907	0.07	24,572	0.56	0.06	98.7	1.3
Franklin	2,864	0.07	53,480	0.22	0.03	98.3	1.7
Oxford	2,746	0.06	23,341	0.06	0.05	98.8	1.2

Source: Computed by the authors from data obtained from the U.S. Department of Commerce, Bureau of the Census, PC80-1-B24, Detroit, Mich., 1980, *Census of Population: General Population Characteristics* (Washington, D.C.: U.S. Government Printing Office, 1982), vol. 1.

The correlation between median family income and occupational status becomes obvious when we consider the fact that Bloomfield Hills also was the municipality with the highest percentage of professional workers (70 percent) in relationship to its employed labor force. On the other hand, only 9 percent of the employed labor force of Hazel Park consisted of professional workers. The remaining municipalities where the majority of the labor force consisted of professional workers were Grosse Pointe Shores (62 percent), Franklin (60 percent), Huntington Woods (53 percent), Beverly Hills Village (54 percent), Grosse Pointe Farms (53 percent), Birmingham (51 percent), and Grosse Pointe (51 percent).

In addition to Hazel Park, other municipalities with 12 percent or less of their employed labor forces classified as professional workers were River Rouge (10 percent), Ecorse (10 percent), Southgate (11 percent), Melvindale (11 percent), and Pontiac, Marine City, Lincoln Park, Garden City, Holly Village, and Hamtramck (12 percent each).

Finally, Bloomfield Hills also had the highest percentage of college graduates (63 percent) in relationship to those members of its population who were 25 years and older. Roseville, Hazel Park, and Ecorse, on the other hand, are suburban municipalities where only 3 percent of the population 25 years and older consisted of college graduates in 1980. Other municipalities where the majority of the population 25 years and older consisted of college graduates were Franklin (58 percent) and Grosse Pointe, Grosse Pointe Farms, and Huntington Woods (51 percent each).

Municipalities where college graduates constituted 5 percent or less of the population 25 years and older were Taylor, River Rouge, Melvindale, and Detroit (4 percent each) and Westland, Warren, St. Clair Shores, and Hamtramck (5 percent each).

In sum, widespread inequality exists between the municipalities within metropolitan Detroit. The wealthiest municipalities seem to cluster primarily in southeastern Oakland County and on the extreme eastern shore of Wayne County. The poorest municipalities are more prevalent in the downriver area. This pattern is consistent with the uneven pattern of economic development. Indeed, some suburban areas had lower socioeconomic status than central-city Detroit. In the next section, changes in income, percentage of professional workers, and percentage of college graduates in the decade from 1970 to 1980 are examined. This examination may indicate a future spatial shift in socioeconomic status.

Socioeconomic Status in Detroit and Its Suburbs and Variations in Growth and Decline, 1970–1980

The municipalities with the highest socioeconomic status in 1980 were not necessarily the fastest growing municipalities in income, percentage of professional workers, or percentage of college graduates. Between 1970 and 1980 Wolverine Lake Village, a suburb in Oakland County, had the greatest amount of growth in median family income. Other areas in the top five in median income growth were Troy, Lake Orion Heights, Novi, and Northville, all located in Oakland County. Areas experiencing the least amount of growth were Highland Park (a municipal enclave surrounded by Detroit), Bloomfield Hills, Detroit, Oak Park, and Ferndale.

Like changes in income, changes in the percentage of professional workers have varied spatially. Municipalities experiencing the greatest amount of growth in percentage of professionals between 1970 and 1980 were Rockwood (308 percent), South Lyon (161 percent), Bloomfield Hills (148 percent), Richmond (94 percent), and Grosse Pointe Shores and Walled Lake (75 percent each).

The municipality experiencing the greatest amount of decline in the percentage of professional workers between 1970 and 1980 was Madison Heights (−67 percent). Other areas experiencing a 20 percent or more decline in professional workers were Mount Clemens (−65 percent), Southgate (−30 percent), Keego Harbor (−27 percent), and Lake Orion (−21 percent).

Finally, growth in the percentage of college graduates over the decade also varied spatially. In Novi and Romeo the percentage of college graduates more than doubled. Other municipalities where the increase in college graduates exceeded 90 percent were River Rouge and Rockwood (99 percent each) and Lincoln Park (96 percent).

College graduates actually left some municipalities over the decade. The municipalities experiencing the greatest decline in the percentage of college graduates were Dearborn Heights (−40 percent), Southfield and Detroit (−38 percent each), Westland (−34 percent), and St. Clair Shores (−31 percent).

In sum, socioeconomic inequality clearly exists between the municipalities within metropolitan Detroit. Furthermore, the inequality, as measured by income, occupational, and educational status, is widespread. Some suburbs have a lower socioeconomic status than that found in Detroit. Among the suburbs with a lower percentage of professional workers and a lower percentage of college graduates than the city of Detroit are the downriver communities of Ecorse, River Rouge, Melvindale, and Taylor and the southern Macomb County suburb of Roseville. This pattern of low professional and educational development is consistent with the pattern of uneven economic development discussed in the previous chapter. Downriver communities are also the least developed economically.

Finally, change in socioeconomic status is not equal among the suburbs. While some suburbs are doubling their median family income, percentage of professional workers, and percentage of college graduates, other suburbs have been experiencing either very slow growth or an absolute decline.

Population and Median Family Income

Although there is an inverse relationship between the population size of municipalities and median family income, the relationship is not significant. Of the 81 municipalities examined in 1980, the correlation between total population and median family income was −.1436.

Population and College Graduates

The spatial distribution of population and college graduates is not even in metropolitan Detroit. Theoretically, one would expect a municipality with

5 percent of the metropolitan area's population to have 5 percent of the college graduates. Such a pattern would reflect an even distribution. In reality, however, the percentage of college graduates is over-represented in some municipalities and under-represented in others. The greatest amount of over- and under-representation is between suburban Southfield and Detroit, two bordering municipalities. In 1980 Southfield had 1.7 percent of the metropolitan area's total population but 4.3 percent of the metropolitan area's college graduates. On the other hand, Detroit had 28 percent of the area's population but only 16 percent of the area's college graduates. Other suburban areas with an extremely high over-representation of college graduates were Troy, with only 1.5 percent of the population but 4 percent of the college graduates, and Birmingham, with .5 percent of the area's population but 2 percent of the college graduates. (See Table 3.9.) For the total Detroit metropolitan area, the index of dissimilarity between total population and college graduates was 26.1 percent.

Population and Professionals

The spatial distribution of population and professionals like that of college graduates, is not even in metropolitan Detroit. Professionals are extremely overconcentrated in Southfield and Troy, two suburban municipalities in Oakland County. In 1980 Southfield had 1.7 percent of the metropolitan area's total population but 3.7 percent of the area's professionals. Troy had 1.5 percent of the population but 3.4 percent of the professionals.

Consistent with the pattern of residence of college graduates, fewer professionals than expected lived in Detroit. Although 28 percent of the metropolitan area's total population lived there in 1980, only 16 percent of its professional workers lived there. The index of dissimilarity between total population and professionals was 21.3 percent in 1980.

Conclusion

This chapter has demonstrated that widespread inequality exists between blacks and whites in metropolitan Detroit. The patterns of racial inequality are related to the uneven spatial distribution of blacks and whites in the metropolitan area. This uneven racial distribution is also related to uneven economic development. Whites are over-represented in economically developing suburban municipalities of Oakland County. Blacks, on the other hand, are over-represented in the central city of Detroit and in Wayne

County. Such residential segregation between the races has had negative consequences for the black population. first, because jobs and amenities generally are more prevalent outside the central city, Detroit's residents have less opportunity for social and economic advancement, and the situation is expected to worsen in the future. Second, central-city residents have less accessibility to mortgage and home-improvement loans, since these loans are distributed unequally according to the racial composition of neighborhoods. Thus, loan application denial for both conventional mortgage loans and home-improvement loans is higher in moderate-to-high-minority neighborhoods.

Such differentially applied lending practices have also had an impact on the racial disparities in the quality of housing and the quantity of home-ownership. Because blacks in metropolitan Detroit are residentially concentrated in the central city, a higher percentage (compared with whites), live in older, overcrowded housing.

Such concentration of blacks in the central city also relates to the higher unemployment rate for blacks compared with whites. The unemployment rate for black males has ranged from 1.5 times to as much as 4 times as high as the rate for white males. Not only is a higher percentage of whites employed, but whites also earn about one-third more than blacks in metropolitan Detroit.

Such inequality on the basis of race is facilitated by metropolitan fragmentation, an effective tool used by white suburbanites to isolate their municipalities from the nonwhite population of the central city.

Such metropolitan fragmentation is also used to deny the poor equal access to certain suburban areas, resulting in class disparity by place of residence.

Like race inequality, class inequality is also widespread in metropolitan Detroit. The high-income, professional college graduates are disproportionately concentrated in the economically developing suburban municipalities of Oakland County and the extreme eastern coast of suburban Wayne County.

Detroit and the downriver municipalities are under-represented in the areas of high income and professionals/college graduates. Not only is the gap wide along race and class lines in metropolitan Detroit but the situation is expected to worsen with time, as population mobility continues to reinforce already unequal patterns of economic and social development. Historically, such patterns of uneven economic and social development have contributed to protracted racial estrangement and conflicts in Detroit —for example, the 1942 Sojourner Truth housing riot, the 1943 riot, and the 1967 rebellion. These social disorders would not have occurred had social and economic development in industrial Detroit been more even and equitable across racial and class lines. In fact, only the countervailing trend of interracial cooperation prevented more frequent and disruptive racial conflicts. Housing offers the best example of uneven economic and social development in Detroit. In addition, it provides an excellent backdrop against which to view the historical tug of war between racial conflict and cooperation.

4

Interracial Conflict and Cooperation

Housing as a Case Study

As we have seen in previous discussions, the spatial logic of auto production over three decades contributed to patterns of disinvestment and deindustrialization in the central city. This historical and structural transformation of the regional economy, in turn, reinforced patterns of racial and class segregation, particularly in housing, education, and employment. The white flight to the suburbs in the 1950s and 1960s in some ways conformed to the spatial logic of auto production; however, the major stimulus behind the flight was the pressure of expanding black neighborhoods. Whites were not alone in the mad dash to the suburbs. When and where they were able, blacks joined the city-to-suburbs migration. As a result of a combination of structural changes in the regional economy and the racial and class responses to these changes, racial and class polarization became permanent features of metropolitan Detroit.

As important as class factors were in the shaping and reshaping of social relations during the period between 1940 and 1980, racial factors exerted far greater influence over both social relations and social policy. Class differences between upriver and downriver communities resulted from structural changes in the regional economy and exclusionary mechanisms and policies instituted by the dominant class. Racism, however, included all these factors and more. As early as the 1920s whites in Detroit felt compelled to control, by lawful and unlawful means, the spatial expansion of the black community. Blacks, on the other hand, felt equally compelled to challenge and resist such means. Racial conflict was the inevitable result. Racial conflict, however, forced progressive blacks and whites to explore ways of bridging the racial chasm and promote racial cooperation, which is one of the central themes of this chapter.

In order to understand the history and nature of racial conflict and cooperation in Detroit, we must first understand the underlying causes of particular types of conflicts that formed the basis for related types of racial cooperation. The spatial direction of black population movement in the search for housing was a major contributing factor to racial conflict in certain city neighborhoods and suburbs.

By examining white responses to black movement into these areas, we will be better able to map out visually the spatial location of racial conflict over housing. Specific case studies of events, city neighborhoods, and suburbs will be presented to help illustrate the social, class, and ethnic dimension of these areas of racial conflict. Racial conflict over housing overshadowed other forms of racial conflict simply because whites perceived housing as their most sacred racial prerogative. Thus, they fought long and hard—and some are still fighting—to maintain racially segregated housing. The major focus of this chapter, then, will be the historical causes and the spatial distribution of racial conflicts over housing. Any study of racial conflict that neglects racial cooperation, however limited such cooperation might be, defeats perhaps the most important reason for studying conflict of any type—namely, to discover ways of resolving that conflict. Therefore, examples of interracial cooperation will also be examined to shed light on the brave and relentless struggle, yet going on, to achieve fair housing in Detroit.

The Emerging Conflict

By the 1940s the expanding black population had generated tremendous resistance from whites who used every means at their disposal to keep blacks out of their neighborhoods. White resistance was strongest in the areas northeast and northwest of Detroit and particularly strong in sections where the populations were largely second-generation European immigrants (a topic discussed further in this chapter). As noted in the preceding chapter, such white resistance was often aided by the courts, the Federal Housing Administration, and the Detroit Housing Commission, which legally supported white resistance because racially restrictive covenants were legal until 1948, when their enforcement was declared unconstitutional by the U.S. Supreme Court.[1]

Some whites, working through neighborhood improvement associations, signed petitions, took blacks to court, and when all else failed, resorted to violence. In situations where black families purchased property in white neighborhoods where restrictive covenants did not run with the land, there was little white petitioners could do legally. In March of 1940 a circuit court judge ruled against whites who had signed a restrictive covenant to bar blacks from occupying a house they had purchased. These legal setbacks rarely discouraged whites determined to keep blacks out of their neighborhoods. Soon after the judge's decision white residents began signing more petitions to prohibit the renting or selling of houses in the neighborhood to blacks.[2]

Later that same year white residents on the northeast side of Detroit signed petitions asking the court to oust a black family from a house because black occupancy violated certain building restrictions based upon agreements that the owners would sell to "pure Caucasians only." The lawyer for the association added that black occupancy was "injurious to the value of the property."[3]

White lawyers who shared prevailing notions that blacks should be restricted to black areas could be extremely helpful in devising effective strategies to keep them out of white neighborhoods. In August of 1940 one such lawyer gave a talk at the luncheon meeting of the Eastern Detroit Realty Association, entitled "Benefits of an Improvement Association." His main theme centered on how to "effect legal restrictions against the influx of colored residents into white communities."[4] Using the widespread allegation that black influx into white communities lowers property values, the lawyer laid out a strategy for his white listeners. He urged them to form improvement associations, obtain competent legal advice regarding restrictions, and then determine the first area to be covered: "Every owner in that area must then be approached with a restrictive or conveyance prepared by the group's legal counsel binding the owners not to sell to Negroes."[5]

He informed his audience that real estate dealers "have been known to cover a district of two miles square in which the owners were not able to sell to anyone but members of the white race." But he cautioned his listeners that such a task was too much for one person. "Organizations are essential for such work and such results," he pointed out. The first step, he advised them, is to pick a community and "block it out by streets or subdivisions or square miles. Select the community most liable to have trouble, or better yet one in which a Negro family is already a resident. The people of that section will be in a most receptive mood."[6] He then pointed out that, under the present law, racially restrictive covenants were not legal unless everyone in a subdivision signed a restrictive contract.[7] Here was white legalized racism at its best. No wonder housing discrimination against blacks proved so intransigent.

Keeping blacks out of white neighborhoods proved especially difficult when white sellers violated restrictive covenants by selling to blacks. In one such case in 1941, a white neighbor not only got an injunction to stop blacks from occupying a house sold to them by a white neighbor but also named the white seller's lawyer as one of the defendants.[8] Restrictive covenants in Michigan, therefore, began losing their legal weight when one white owner's right to sell or rent property was challenged by other whites desiring to keep neighborhoods all white. In June of 1941 the Michigan Supreme Court upheld a decision of a circuit court judge in refusing to grant a temporary restraining injunction to prohibit a white man from renting his apartment to black families.[9]

Some whites did not mind having a black-owned property in their neighborhood, as long as neither the owner nor any other black occupied the premises. In August 1941 a black owner of a house in a white neighborhood rented his house to a black co-worker after his white tenants moved out. A committee of white residents protested to the black owner. He informed them that he had lived in the same house and had raised his family there, moving only because the house was not large enough. He refused to evict his black tenant. The whites then paid the black tenant a visit and told him they did not want blacks in their neighborhood. They ordered him to move or suffer the consequences. He refused and called the police.[10]

Unfortunately, in most cases the police offered little assistance in protecting the rights of blacks buying or renting houses in white neighborhoods. Blacks moving into white neighborhoods were perceived as invaders. And this perception was reinforced by major institutions in the city and the nation, such as the Detroit Housing Commission and the Federal Housing Administration. White police shared this common perception of the black "invader" and often supported or acquiesced to white violence against blacks moving into white neighborhoods.

It is difficult to determine at what stage of the resistance to blacks moving into their neighborhoods whites resorted to violence and at what stage the local authorities chose to intervene to restore order. In cases where local loopholes in restrictive covenants enabled blacks to purchase homes in white neighborhoods resisting blacks, some whites saw violence as the only alternative to keeping blacks out. In March of 1940, in a case representative of others, a black family succeeded in purchasing a home in Ferndale—a white suburb in northwest Detroit—but later was forced to flee, after a group of Ku Klux Klan (KKK) members burned a ten-foot cross close by their house. Later, windows were broken by leaders of the mob that gathered in front of the house.[11]

White Resistance in Ferndale, Hazel Park, and the Sojourner Truth Area: The 1940s

In the 1940s white resistance to black expansion assumed many forms. In the suburbs of Ferndale and Hazel Park, located in Oakland County, white resistance tended to focus on containing blacks already in the area, attempts to rid the area of all blacks, or both. In the Sojourner Truth area in northeast Detroit, first- and second-generation Polish Americans rallied to resist large numbers of black war workers being placed in a housing project adjacent to their neighborhood. The black war workers were supported by a biracial coalition of labor, religious, and civic organizations.

During the 1940s Ferndale employed a range of methods to keep blacks out, including resorting to violence and (in 1941) building a brick wall, eight feet high and a half-mile long, to separate black and white residents in the area. The wall was such a blatant affront to blacks, as well as a glaring symbol of white racism in a northern city, that the Reverend Horace A. White, a local church leader who was both a state representative and a member of the Detroit Housing Commission, said that Ferndale was the only place in the world except Nazi Germany where groups were being segregated into ghettos. The building of the wall, he continued, "is sociologically disgraceful in these times of strain to unify the people."[12]

In the late summer of 1941, 200 whites met in a Ferndale neighborhood bakery to discuss methods of keeping blacks out of their subdivision and getting rid of those already residing there. Blacks were not admitted to the meeting. The discussion included plans to buy out black families who had not yet moved into their houses and to apply pressure on black families already living in the area and if they did not move, "to burn them out."[13]

One black woman, who had lived in Ferndale for 14 years, was warned by hostile whites to move to the black section of the subdivision.[14] During the same period, in the suburb of Hazel Park on the eastern border of Ferndale, the house of a black family that had resided in the area for 18 years and whose sons had played on the Hazel Park High School football team for 11 of those years was stoned by whites several nights in a row. After bricks were thrown through the windows, a family member responded by firing a warning shot. The police arrived and arrested two of the ringleaders, who were later released (one was from Ferndale). Whites had demonstrated in front of the house for four successive nights because the black family had plans to enlarge the house![15]

This black family refused to be intimidated and informed officials of the NAACP that they had no intention of moving out of the area. The NAACP accused the Hazel Park Police Department and the county sheriff's office of allowing the racial disturbance to get out of hand by failing to protect the family adequately. The governor responded by sending Michigan state police to Hazel Park to support the Hazel Park police. Deputies from the county sheriff's office were also ordered into Hazel Park to protect the family.[16] Racial conflicts over housing reached fever pitch during World War II, aggravated by the rapidly increasing population brought on by the labor demands of Detroit's war industries.

Providing housing for these war workers soon became a problem of mammoth proportions. For black war workers the housing problem seemed insoluble simply because they could live only in racially designated areas of the city, while white war workers could live almost anywhere. But some blacks felt relief was in sight. In September 1941 a temporary housing project, named Sojourner Truth after the famous black fugitive slave woman, was financed by the federal government under contract to the Detroit Housing Commission to house black war workers and their families.[17] The project was located in northeast Detroit and segregated in keeping with the declared public policy of both the Federal Housing Administration (FHA) and the Detroit Housing Commission. In fact, the minutes of one of the meetings of the housing commission were explicit concerning this policy:

> The Detroit Housing Commission will in no way change the racial characteristics of any neighborhood in Detroit through occupancy standards of housing projects under its jurisdiction. The importance of housing war workers is recognized by [us] and every effort will be made to accomplish this task. It is [our] opinion . . . that any attempt to change the racial pattern of any area in Detroit will result in violent opposition to the housing program. This could very easily reach a point where war production efforts of this entire community could be endangered.[18]

In the 1930s this policy of segregated public housing had been pushed down the throats of liberal blacks and whites associated with the NAACP and the Urban League, who wanted to see public housing used to destroy racial segregation. The local black leaders were called together and told by one of the white fathers of the city, "Either we have a segregated project, or we won't have any. So make up your minds." And they did.[19] Segregated public housing became the rule.

The Sojourner Truth project was racially segregated, but this policy mattered little to whites (mostly Polish American) who lived nearby. Before long, whites in the neighborhood in which the project was built began objecting not to the housing project but to the blacks who would be living in it. These blacks were a little too close for white comfort. The Reverend C. Dzink wrote the federal coordinator of defense housing and asked him not to allow blacks to occupy the housing project because it would mean utter ruin for many people who had mortgaged their homes to the FHA. Dzink also told the federal coordinator that black occupancy would "jeopardize the safety of many of our white girls, as no colored people live close by [and] it would [also] ruin the neighborhood."[20]

In addition, the newly organized Seven Mile Neighborhood Improvement Association—led by Joseph Buffa, a local real estate man—protested to the Detroit Housing Commission, stating that the housing project would destroy property values in the neighborhood. The housing commission refused to change its policy. Buffa and the Seven Mile Neighborhood Improvement Association then appealed to Michigan's Congressman Rudolph G. Tenerowicz, who succeeded in getting Washington to turn the housing project over to whites.[21]

Working-class ethnic whites were not the only people opposed to black war workers' occupying the project. Middle-class blacks in nearby Conant Gardens were also opposed to these black war workers (most of whom were southern migrants) and for one of the same reasons—namely, the fear of an influx of lower-class black migrants. These middle-class blacks, however, changed their minds when they saw that white opposition was based mainly upon racism. The white opposition, according to August Meier and Elliot Rudwick, reflected the racial attitudes of "a generation of upwardly mobile American-born Poles . . . coming of age, [and] resentful of competing with increasing numbers of blacks in the job market and bitterly opposed to them as neighbors."[22] In 1942 a government investigator's report for the Office of War Information attempted to explain this white opposition:

> The conflict over the Sojourner Truth Housing Project illustrates the changing attitudes of the Poles towards the Negroes. Until the time when the project was to be occupied by Negroes, the Poles and Negroes lived amicably in Hamtramck on the same street and in the same house. The Poles expressed no anxiety over depreciated property values in a mixed neighborhood until real estate agents and the subversive groups involved in the Sojourner Truth fight gave it to them

> when the projects were to be opened. The second generation Poles were the first to take up the battle cry for segregation and discrimination. Like others of foreign descent in Detroit, they were beginning to fear the competition of young and status-conscious Negroes in jobs. The younger Poles are now inducing anti-Negro attitudes among the older generation and the Negroes are being forced out of Hamtramck.[23]

After the project was handed over to whites, blacks and their white allies began mobilizing to have it returned to black workers. Joined by the national office of the NAACP and the Urban League, the local black community dug in for an aggressive campaign. Similar situations were occurring in Buffalo, Baltimore, Indianapolis, and other places where black war workers needed housing. Therefore, Lester B. Granger, head of the national office of the Urban League, wrote John C. Dancy, director of the Detroit Urban League, informing him that they must get "as much pressure organized around the Detroit situation as possible so as to use it in correcting alarming tendencies observed on the national picture."[24]

In its efforts to have the Detroit housing project returned to black war workers, the national office of the Urban League sent telegrams to President Roosevelt, Mrs. Eleanor Roosevelt, and key governmental figures such as Charles F. Palmer, coordinator of defense housing, and Baird Snyder, third acting administrator of the Federal Works Agency. Snyder was one of the Washington bureaucrats responsible for the change from black to white occupancy. The Urban League's telegram to him accused his office of "yielding under the pressure of selfish Detroit groups and reactionary congressmen that seek to bar Negro families from these homes." "We cannot believe," the telegram continued, "that a governmental agency would be guilty of so unworthy an act." The telegram to Mrs. Roosevelt's office, which was responsible for boosting civilian morale, pointed out that such action by the federal government was "impairing the morale of Negroes who [were] being called on for all-out support of a war for democracy." Palmer was told that "facts already produced by [him] show[ed] the need for more, not less, provisions for Negro defense workers." He was asked to bring the full influence of his office into the situation and was warned that Detroit was then "a symbol of what may happen on a wider scale if federal officials retreat under the pressure of local prejudice and reactionary opinions." President Roosevelt was urged to use his office to correct the situation.[25]

Local black leaders began sending telegrams to President Roosevelt and Governor Van Wagoner as soon as the news of the change in occupancy hit the papers. The telegrams said in part that there was no time to raise "the color issue in the arsenal of democracy and rob Negro defense workers of homes." Later that week there was a mass meeting at the Calvary Baptist Church to rally support for a reversal of the decision.[26] Under the direction of local black leader the Reverend Charles A. Hill of the Calvary Baptist Church, blacks prepared to picket the meeting of the Detroit Housing Commission. The meeting was postponed, so the pickets returned the following day. When the commission finally met, a delegation of black leaders asked its members to intervene in the situation. The commission refused, shifting the blame to Washington.

Pressure was slowly building on the side of black war workers. A coalition of groups called the Sojourner Truth Citizens' Committee headed by the Reverend Mr. Hill emerged to challenge those supporting white occupancy of the project. Originally all black, this committee soon became interracial in membership, including Jewish organizations, Protestant liberals in the Detroit Council of Churches, and trade unionists. Perhaps because most of the whites resisting black occupancy were Polish Catholics, few Catholics became involved at this stage.[27]

The citizens' committee started applying pressure by means of nighttime picketing of the offices of city hall and the Detroit Housing Commission. Finally, the mayor and the Detroit Common Council gave in and asked the housing authorities in Washington to reverse their decision and give the housing project back to the black war workers. Realizing that they had to act fast, members of the citizens' committee held an emergency mass meeting to raise money to send an interracial delegation to Washington to help convince the federal housing authorities. Overwhelmed by the militant blacks in the group as well as by the fact that the city fathers endorsed black occupancy, the federal housing officials rescinded their previous decision and returned the housing project to blacks.[28]

Predictably outraged over this new decision of the federal authorities, whites opposing black occupancy protested against the mayor and the common council at the city hall but failed to budge them. The hearings broke up in an uproar, with the protesters threatening to return to demand another audience. Mayor Jeffries told one angry group, "If you can work out a proposition where people can live peacefully and harmoniously, I will send taxicabs for you." He was shouted down.[29]

This latest demonstration by whites opposing black occupancy convinced members of the citizens' committee that they should return to Washington, in case the federal authorities should have second thoughts about giving the project back to blacks. Once again an interracial delegation visited the federal housing officials, who assured the committee representatives that the decision would stand and that the first tenants could move in on February 28, 1942.[30]

At this stage the racial conflict moved to a more volatile level. The night before the move the KKK became involved. One hundred and fifty cheering whites burned a cross near the project. Before dawn the mob had swollen to 1,200, and many were openly armed. That morning as the first black tenants arrived in trucks, they were blocked by lines of white pickets. Tempers flared and before long a riot broke out with blacks and whites on opposite sides of the street throwing bricks at each other. Whites turned over the blacks' furniture vans. Police armed with tear gas and a riot car made frequent runs into the melee. Scores of people, mainly blacks, were injured by the police, who tended to side with the whites by arresting blacks. When news of the riot reached nearby black ghettos, hundreds of black youths rushed to the aid of the black tenants and fought the white mob and the police. Finally, authorities decided to postpone the move.[31]

Later the whites around the housing project, under the leadership of Buffa, president of the Seven Mile Neighborhood Improvement Association, began reorganizing their forces. On March 10, 1942, Buffa led 500 whites in a march on the project. The police broke it up with tear gas. Buffa was jailed but later released because of insufficient evidence. His organization went back to picketing. Circulars passed around in the vicinity of the project said, "Help the white people to keep their district white. Men wanted to keep our line solid."[32]

Racism, however, would not win the day. And interracial cooperation against racial injustice made the difference. The CIO (Congress of Industrial Organizations) unions, particularly the UAW (United Auto Workers), increased their support for black occupancy of the project. And white trade unionists picketed the Detroit City Hall alongside of blacks. The UAW president, R. J. Thomas, backed by the International Executive Board, took a public stand on behalf of the blacks. Polish union members in the vicinity of the housing project denounced his stand, but he and the UAW held firm. Even the Catholics among the UAW leadership "openly endorsed the blacks' side in the housing controversy."[33] At a mass meeting on March 28, 1942, the Polish Women's Division of the International Workers' Order made a $25 donation toward the success of the fight for black occupancy of the project. Two Polish women gave short talks assuring the audience that progressive groups throughout the country were backing the black war workers' occupancy of the Sojourner Truth housing project.[34]

Finally, on April 29, 1942—as a result of the pressing needs of the war and the efforts of a coalition of black organizations; prominent, white members of the Catholic and Protestant clergy; the UAW/CIO leadership; and the black press—black families began moving into the housing project. They were protected by 1,200 state home-guard troops, 300 state police officers, and 800 Detroit police officers. The troops remained on guard in the neighborhood for several weeks, and there was no further violence in the area.[35]

Four years later a picture of black and white children playing together in a field in the Sojourner Truth housing project appeared in *Collier's*, a national magazine. Sadly enough, the photo was part of an article entitled "Housing, Detroit's Time Bomb."[36] Clearly, the Sojourner Truth housing conflict was only the tip of the iceberg. In the summer of 1943 one of the bloodiest race riots in American history exploded on the streets of Detroit. Although the riot was not triggered by racial conflict over housing, housing was one of the underlying causes. No doubt there was yet simmering hatred between blacks and whites as the result of the 1942 housing conflict.

Racial conflict continued as blacks resisted whites' efforts to racially segregate them. As residential segregation emerged as the dominant issue of race relations in Detroit, contributing to the already uneven distribution of the black population, racial cooperation in the struggle for racial justice became more essential.

Dearborn: Orville Hubbard's Racist White Working-Class Utopia

A year before the racial conflicts over the Sojourner Truth housing project, the largely working-class citizenry of Dearborn (a downriver community on Detroit's southwest border) elected a lawyer and former marine, Orville Hubbard, to be mayor of the city. Hubbard had lost his bid for the office in three previous attempts. He succeeded on the fourth try, against the political machine of Harry Bennett, Henry Ford's henchman. From his power base at the Ford Motor Company, Bennett exerted ruthless influence over the political, social, and economic life of Dearborn. He placed his own people in public office, had a direct line to city hall, commanded a secret police force composed mainly of ex-convicts, and supported a profitable system of prostitution and racketeering. Notwithstanding a brief period of reform in the 1930s, Bennett and his cronies maintained control over Dearborn until 1941. That year, first and second generations of working-class immigrants—largely Italian, Polish, Scottish, and Canadian—revolted against the Bennett machine and voted Hubbard into office on a reform ticket.[37]

The first wave of these white ethnic workers came to Dearborn because of Henry Ford's promise of $5 a day. Subsequent waves of these same white groups fled to Dearborn to escape the expanding black population in Detroit, contributing to the overall racial segregation in the metropolitan area. Most times this white flight stemmed from the mass racial hysteria of the white working class that black movement into their neighborhoods would depress property values. Once these people arrived in Dearborn, they felt they were safe from the expanding "black hordes," because Mayor Hubbard was nationally known (and some said internationally known as well) for his policies of keeping blacks out of the city. In return for his protecting them from blacks, who they believed embodied all the growing social ills of Detroit, Dearborn's white ethnic working class kept Hubbard in power for over three decades.[38]

Mayor Hubbard was well aware of the mass racial hysteria of the ethnic working class, who made up the vast majority of his political base. His tenure as mayor of Dearborn was "one of the longest continuous reigns of any U.S. mayor." After all, he not only gave the city what it wanted (which included a range of services unparalleled in the history of any city of comparable size) but perhaps more important, he addressed a deeply felt need —albeit racist—of many white suburbanites: He kept Dearborn virtually free of blacks.[39] During a 1956 interview by a reporter from the *Montgomery Advertiser*, Hubbard explained the tremendous increase in Dearborn's population since 1950 as the result of an influx of prejudiced people of Polish and Italian backgrounds "crowded out of Detroit by the colored people." Hubbard claimed, "These people are so anti-colored, much more so than you in Alabama."[40]

Since Mayor Hubbard relied on such racism to keep him in office, he seized every opportunity to nurture and sustain it. His first opportunity came in 1944. The Detroit metropolitan area was in the throes of a housing shortage crisis. Of all the groups needing housing, blacks were by far the worst off. Between November 1943 and November 1944 over 12,000 blacks were either forced into already overcrowded housing or left totally unserved. The housing problem in turn affected vital war production in the area. The federal Public Housing Administration proposed unrestricted housing projects for all war workers throughout the metropolitan area. But Mayor Hubbard succeeded in marshalling support for a resolution barring any public housing that included blacks. Later he changed the resolution to one opposing all war housing to gain wider political support. But the mayor's original intentions remained intact. In the defense of his original resolution barring blacks, he argued that 400 additional housing units for blacks in Dearborn would not solve the housing problem in the area or the race problem in America and accused officials behind this policy of being "crackpots" interested in interracial marriage of blacks and whites.[41]

Of course, Mayor Hubbard was not the only racist official in the area whose support of racist housing policies burdened blacks and seriously threatened the war effort. Mayor Jeffries of Detroit was at least partly responsible for Detroit's share of the area's black housing problems, which he dumped on Dearborn. Jeffries could not afford to integrate certain Detroit housing sites because of his 1943 campaign promise not to violate the racial characteristics of white neighborhoods. His excuse, not totally unjustified, was that "thousands of Negroes work in Dearborn; therefore, Dearborn ought to help some of them."[42]

As before, in the 1942 Sojourner Truth housing crisis, interracial groups and organizations responded to the blatant racist policy of Mayor Hubbard. One such interracial organization, the Detroit Council of Applied Religion, adopted a resolution criticizing the actions of Mayor Hubbard and Dearborn city officials. The interracial committee of the Detroit Council of Churches also joined in protesting Dearborn's racist policy but to no avail. Mayor Hubbard had the support of most white working-class people in Dearborn.[43] Even white rank and file members of UAW Local 600, even though their union's Housing Executive Committee had endorsed black housing in Dearborn, supported Mayor Hubbard's position. At a meeting called by the mayor, these white workers accused the housing committee of acting without their knowledge or consent. In the end Mayor Hubbard and his supporters won the day. The federal housing project was not built in Dearborn.[44]

Mayor Hubbard's opposition to the government's efforts to build a housing project that would have lodged black workers endeared him to many whites in Dearborn, who saw him as not only a mayor who stood up to the Bennett machine and won but who also faced down what they felt was a government attempt to integrate a rapidly developing whites-only utopia.

Four years later Mayor Hubbard and his cohorts had another occasion to exploit the racial fear of whites in Dearborn. In 1948 the John Hancock Life Insurance Company initiated plans to build a private, 1,000-unit housing development, which (according to some sources) would have included black residents. The project was endorsed by Henry Ford II and was to be built on land purchased from Ford.[45] Hubbard went into action as the suburban white knight protecting Dearborn's white citizens from Detroit's "black hordes," who were sure to arrive *via* the Hancock housing project. He organized meetings to attack the project, which once again evoked the latent mass racial hysteria. Many whites in Dearborn began seeing the Ford Motor Company and the insurance firm as conspiring to bring blacks into white Dearborn. Handbills and stickers were circulated, bearing such racist statements as "Keep Negroes Out of Dearborn. . . . Vote No on the . . . John Hancock Rental Housing Project." One circular printed on official city stationery read, "Wake Up, Dearborn! Wake Up! Open Your Eyes Wide! John Hancock Gives Housing Double-Talk." This circular cautioned whites not to be "lulled into a false sense of security," because John Hancock had 8.5 million policy holders from every racial and religious background; therefore, how could it build a housing project and exclude black families? The message hit home. The Hancock housing project was defeated by the voters, and Mayor Hubbard was reelected "for his achievement in saving the city from the mythical corps of black invaders."[46] To those who might have been upset over the racist mass hysteria of white Dearbornites, Mayor Hubbard had a quick and ready response: "If whites don't want to live with niggers . . . they sure as hell don't have to. Damn it, this is a free country. This is America."[47]

Nowhere was Mayor Hubbard's support so overwhelming as in the older, Polish/Italian neighborhoods of Dearborn—the area closest to the Detroit border, composed of the working-class people Hubbard claimed were crowded out of Detroit by blacks. Constantly on the edge of racial mass hysteria generated in part by their own precarious blue-collar status, on Labor Day in 1963 a mob of these people attacked a house they mistakenly thought was being occupied by blacks. What in fact had happened was that a recent Italian immigrant had rented his upstairs to a white couple, who had hired a black man to help them move. The black mover arrived with his truck and pregnant wife, who came along for company. This was sufficient to incite the white neighbors. When the owner returned home, he came face to face with 250 angry whites, who felt he had betrayed the sacred trust to exclude blacks. For seven hours the hate-filled mob yelled threats and insults and threw bottles and bricks at the owner, his house, and his car. That night he called the Dearborn police 15 times. They arrived but refused to take any action. Later FBI (Federal Bureau of Investigation) agents reported that the police had stood by and allowed the owner's home to be vandalized. Only after the owner showed the title to his house to the mob, indicating that he had not sold the house to blacks, did the mob disperse.[48]

Mayor Hubbard and two of his police officials were indicted for violations of the federal Civil Rights Act of 1870 on two counts of conspiracy and refusal to use their positions to assist the owner of the house. Four Democratic state legislators, three of them black (Senator Basil Brown, Senator Coleman A. Young, and Representative Raymond Hood) and one white (Representative Thomas W. White), began preparing a bill designed to cost Hubbard his job as mayor if convicted of the charges.[49] The four state lawmakers issued a joint statement:

> It is completely unconscionable that any elected official in the state of Michigan, on the local or state level, should be opposed to the ideals contained in the Civil Rights Act of 1870 or its 1964 Amendment. It should be legally unconscionable that any elected official in the state Michigan, of either on the local or state level, should be allowed to be a candidate for or hold public office, if he has been convicted of a violation of these acts.[50]

Mayor Hubbard, however, seemed neither concerned nor repentant. He posted the bill on the city hall bulletin board and during a talk before the East Dearborn Republican Club, remarked that if he did lose his job, one of his three sons could run for mayor and he (Hubbard) could be "hired as adviser to the winner." Assuring Hubbard of its support, the club congratulated the mayor on his fight against what it conveniently labeled as the "encroachment of the federal government on the rights of local government."[51] This interpretation was an ideological and political tactic then in vogue with the southern State rights ideologues. The club then approved a resolution, which passed unanimously, reaffirming its confidence in Hubbard's "integrity as a leader in Dearborn and as a mainstay for human rights." Hubbard also received support from a special defense fund for which money was "quietly and quickly collected."[52]

During the trial several facts surfaced as to the segregationist practices of Hubbard and Dearborn officials. In interviews given by Hubbard to the *Montgomery Advertiser* in 1956, the mayor was asked how he actually kept blacks out of Dearborn:

> A. "We say it's against the law to live here. They say, 'You know what the Supreme Court says.' I tell them we're talking about the law of custom, the law of habit."
> Q. "Do you mean a city law?"
> A. "The unwritten law."

Q. "In other words, all the property owners would have to be in agreement with you?"
A. "Well, that's why I'm still mayor—15 years."
Q. "They just won't sell to Negroes?"
A. "That's the way you do it."

Some blacks, Hubbard pointed out, shopped in Dearborn. "But live there? Not a one," he told his interviewer. He was then asked whether the NAACP had ever called on him. "No," he replied, "we'd chase them to hell out of town." According to Hubbard, politicians like the late Hubert H. Humphrey (then a senator) and G. Mennen Williams (former governor of Michigan) caused racial problems. "The sympathizer with the [race] problem is generally the fellow that doesn't have it, like Humphrey in Minnesota."[53] Notwithstanding such damaging evidence clearly demonstrating his racial views, Mayor Hubbard was acquitted on the more serious charges and settled out of court for $4,500.[54]

To many whites in Dearborn and other suburbs and in certain white neighborhoods in Detroit, Mayor Hubbard seemed invincible in his stand against both blacks and the federal government. In fact, during the 1960s Mayor Hubbard's Dearborn emerged as "a symbol of the deep-rooted racism of the north," and the mayor himself was said to be one who "speaks his city's mind on the subject and the mind of many northern white suburbs as well."[55]

And Mayor Hubbard most certainly spoke his own mind on the subject. When asked by a black person whether he felt that blacks were already in their place, the mayor said, "You're right. I have nothing against the Negro, but don't push us around. Quit pushing the whites around. We've been pretty good to you. We've nursed you along. We've kept you here since the Civil War, put shoes on your feet."[56]

"Concerning integration," Hubbard said, "I just don't believe in integration. When that happens, along comes socializing with the whites, intermarriage and then mongrelization." Yet Hubbard felt his racist views did not mean that he or other whites in Dearborn treated blacks unfairly: "The Negroes who work here are well treated. . . . Go talk to the Negro family who was slipped into the city by some civil rights group ruse. We treat them well."[57]

To contemporary observers, Mayor Hubbard was obsessed with race, displaying little or no hesitation to express his racism on any and all topics. Even when discussing the Vietnam War, Mayor Hubbard could not ignore race: "If they'd end that goddamned war . . . they could take that $30 billion they're spending over there each year and buy every nigger in the country a Cadillac and hire him a chauffeur."[58] But as we have seen, Hubbard did not stop with just expressing his racist views. He also translated them into public policy that kept his supporters equally obsessed with race, thus fueling their mass racial hysteria. One way Mayor Hubbard maintained this mass racial hysteria was by posting antiblack and anti-integration remarks and news clippings in the city hall and the Dearborn Youth Center. Cited in 1965 by the Civil Rights Commission, he was forced to remove the materials.[59] That he would go to such extremes to create and maintain antiblack feelings among whites, especially the white youth in Dearborn, illustrates the sickening depths to which Mayor Hubbard had descended in his use of racial politics.

Not all whites in Dearborn shared Mayor Hubbard's antiblack mania. Yet no movement of white citizens in Dearborn ever effectively challenged the mayor's policy of excluding blacks from the city. And the reason for failure cannot be laid entirely at the doorstep of the ethnic white working class, who by and large shared Hubbard's racial mania. The good liberal whites of Dearborn realized that with all its racism, Dearborn was still a great place to live. As already mentioned, few cities of comparable size delivered such benefits to its citizens: low taxes (in 1967 Ford paid 52 percent of all Dearborn's city taxes), clear streets, a free shoppers' babysitting service, fast snow removal, one of the best-endowed recreation programs in the metropolitan area, a summer camp, a police escort service for New Year's celebrants too drunk to drive, and a senior citizen high-rise located in Florida.[60] Truly, Hubbard had created a white working-class utopia that many white liberals also found satisfying. Therefore, Mayor Hubbard stayed in office, because he satisfied the needs of most, if not all, of the segments of the white community in Dearborn. The price of maintaining this racist white working-class utopia has been long-term mutual racial antagonism between Dearborn whites and Detroit blacks and a racially segregated metropolitan community in which racial conflict rather than cooperation has become the norm.

Building Barricades versus Welcoming the Strangers

While Dearborn was perfecting various methods of maintaining its lily-white working-class utopia, predominantly white neighborhoods in Detroit situated in the paths of expanding black communities braced themselves in anticipation of the unknown. Some white neighborhoods resolved to resist even the slightest change in the racial composition of their communities. Others, perhaps no less apprehensive of the unknowns of initial interracial contact and living, passively acquiesced. Still others welcomed the black strangers.

Three years after the 1943 race riot, both blacks and whites needed housing, but blacks were by far worse off. "With rich and poor, Negro and white alike queued up for a place to live," *Collier's* magazine asked in 1946, "What do you do about the fellow at the end of the line whose needs are so acute that failure to satisfy them will cause a social explosion?"[61] Irrespective of the two race riots, blacks kept the pressure on for better housing. In May 1946 Gloster B. Current, one of the young militants of the local NAACP, told his audience—in a speech called "Challenge to Negro Leadership," delivered in Columbus, Ohio—that "the first challenge to Negroes today is towards a solution of the housing problem in America. Negroes . . . must fight; we must work cooperatively with other groups who are fighting the same battle for adequate housing."[62]

By the 1950s racial segregation in public housing was on the decline. In 1948, when the U.S. Supreme Court ruled against enforcement-restrictive covenants in private housing, racial segregation in public housing ceased being an arguable public policy. Detroit's housing officials, however, continued their segregation policy. Such blatant official intransigence might have led to renewed racial conflicts had blacks not had increased access to the private housing market. After 1948 middle-class blacks broke out of the overcrowded ghettos and began purchasing homes in white neighborhoods. Overcoming the barriers of obtaining mortgage money, blacks increased their home ownership 300 percent between 1940 and 1950. By 1953 the FHA, reflecting the changing racial climate, had begun guaranteeing housing loans without regard to race. But Detroit banks and lending institutions had yet to catch up with the soaring housing demands of blacks.[63]

The 1948 U.S. Supreme Court decision did not deter some whites from violently resisting black advances into their neighborhoods. Several months after the decision a mob of angry whites in southwest Detroit damaged two homes purchased by blacks. In 1950 Detroit veered dangerously close to another race riot, when the common council held a public hearing to discuss a proposal for a cooperative housing project to be built in northwest Detroit, a stronghold of white resistance. Whites in the area wanted no part of the proposed project in their community, because 3 of the project's 54 families would be black. White leaders supporting the project made no headway at the hearing. Blacks became angry, and the mayor fired an important black leader for criticizing what he'd called "the vacillating policy" of the Detroit Housing Commission. The crisis eventually led to the resignation of the director of the city's Interracial Committee.[64]

Between 1954 and 1956 the Commission on Community Relations, formerly the city's Interracial Committee, reported an increase of housing "incidents," where whites were determined to stop blacks from moving into their neighborhoods. Five of these incidents involved serious racial conflicts where large groups of whites demonstrated in front of black homes. Some blacks were forced to move. One brave family stayed on under police protection. Some racial incidents over housing never reached municipal authorities and therefore went unreported. In January 1956 a black man who had recently moved into a predominantly white neighborhood in northeast Detroit was informed by white neighbors that he was not welcome. To impress upon him their seriousness, they burned down his garage. A few months later he found one side of his house soaked in fuel and a fire burning nearby.[65]

The most hard-core resistance to the "Negro tide" centered in the far northwest section of the city. Situated in the 22d ward, in 1956 this bulwark of white racism contained 50 neighborhood improvement associations, which blocked sales of houses to blacks, organized demonstrations in front of black homes, persuaded white brokers not to sell to blacks, and protested against public housing projects.[66]

One of the largest racial demonstrations over housing in the 1950s occurred in this section in February 1957 and according to the city's Commission on Community Relations, "drew nation-wide attention."[67] A white mob of about 300 people gathered in front of the home of Mrs. Ethel Watkins, a black divorcee. A few days earlier whites had noticed the black woman and had begun demonstrating. They objected to the presence of a black person in their all-white neighborhood. As the crowd swelled, police were forced to seal the area off to passing cars and pedestrians. Except for a stone thrown through one of the windows of the house one day and a snowball thrown through the front door glass another day, the mass demonstration was nonviolent. A black reporter on the scene was told by a young member of the mob to take a picture of the "monkey in the cage."[68] Nearly hysterical, Mrs. Watkins felt she could not stand much more of the demonstration. Under police protection she left the house and spent the night at the home of a relative, with the intention of giving up the house rather than facing hostile white neighbors.[69]

The large demonstration surprised the police and other city agencies. The mayor's Commission on Community Relations had made contact with ministers in the neighborhood, and one of them had even visited Mrs.

Watkins in her home to welcome her into the community. Evidently, other white ministers and residents did not share his outlook. The white woman who had sold the house to the black woman was so upset over the reaction that she offered to purchase the house back "to end all this which has affected me as much as it has Mrs. Watkins."[70]

After a few talks with the black realtor who had transacted the sale and representatives of various city agencies, Mrs. Watkins gathered sufficient courage to go back to the house, where she eventually stayed. But the white neighbors persisted in their efforts to get her out of the neighborhood. They sent a delegation to the black realtor to purchase the property for $1,400 more than Mrs. Watkins had paid for it. The realtor refused. Seven hundred residents of the neighborhood held an emergency meeting at a local church, where, with outside assistance, they formed an improvement association and discussed techniques and methods of getting rid of Mrs. Watkins and preventing blacks from entering the neighborhood in the future.[71]

Commenting on this white reaction, the Reverend Horace White, a local black leader, placed his finger on the race, class, and moral aspects of the situation:

> They [the whites] are frightened people. They are frightened by myths about the Negro; they are afraid that if a Negro person moves into their neighborhood, they will lose all thier life's investments. They feel they are protecting themselves against an undesirable neighbor. . . . The funny thing about this mob . . . is that it is led by so-called Christian men and women. These people are members of churches, on trustee boards of churches, members of unions. . . . All of these organizations teach the brotherhood of man. . . . Another ironic thing about the mob . . . is that it uses a church for its meeting place. This church is dedicated to the teaching of Christ. It is supposed to recognize that all people were created by God. Yet these same people deny this fact in their own actions."[72]

The minister was right. These whites were frightened, caught up in the maelstrom of racial changes. They had little preparation for living in a multiracial society. So they fell back on what they knew best: racial myths and stereotypes of invading blacks and declining property values. Although the lack of violence throughout the period of mass demonstrations was of little consolation to Mrs. Watkins, such restraints did suggest that some whites had determined the limits of racial confrontation beyond which they would not proceed. Indeed, several whites in the neighborhood felt the mass protest was at least in the realm of acceptable social protest because it was largely nonviolent.[73]

Some white neighborhoods, instead of protesting, accepted racial change as inevitable. Some even welcomed blacks. This peaceful process of racial change was an encouraging sign to some contemporary scholars and public officials, who felt that far too much emphasis had been placed upon the "inherent drama of conflict and violence accompanying racial change" in urban neighborhoods. These scholars pointed out that, contrary to the then popular belief that housing integration was by its very nature disruptive, many all-white neighborhoods in Detroit had experienced rather peaceful racial change, "differing only slightly from the usual movement of families into and out of a neighborhood."[74]

By the mid-1950s blacks were peacefully moving into such affluent, predominantly white neighborhoods as Arden Park and Russell Woods. Seeking social status as well as social distance from less-affluent blacks, who were then moving into the old black "Gold Coast" south of Hamtramck, some upper-class black families fled this area for the more prestigious neighborhoods of Arden Park. Here they could rub elbows with such rich whites as Samuel Gilbert, the cigar magnate and head of the Detroit Street Railway Commission, and S. S. Kresge of dime store fame.[75] The Arden Park residents, closer to the middle of the city than those in Russell Woods, were proud of their interracial community.[76] But it took white residents in Russell Woods a bit longer to reach a similar positive stage in interracial living. In 1955 the Russell Woods Civic Association responded to one of the first blacks' "invading" their neighborhood, by buying back the house that he had purchased.[77] Before long racial integration proceeded without either "all out resistance or panicky flight."

The most important influence slowing down white flight from racially changing neighborhoods, particularly in Russell Woods, was liberal white residents who placed a high value on housing integration. But even they, liberal as they were, finally succumbed to the more socially attractive suburbs. The gradual flight of white liberals from racially changing neighborhoods seems to have been caused by the declining educational standards of area schools.[78]

The presence of a large number of Orthodox Jews in Russell Woods contributed, at least for a while, to racial integration in housing. Unlike other white groups, the Orthodox Jews (who in 1960 comprised one-third of the Jewish families and 80 percent of all families in Russell Woods) tended to remain in neighborhoods long after most whites had departed.

In the case of these Orthodox Jews, religious custom played as much of a role in their remaining in a racially changing neighborhood as racial liberalism did for other whites. Orthodox Jews in Russell Woods, as elsewhere, looked upon all their nonorthodox neighbors—blacks, whites, Protestants, Catholics, Reformed and Conservative Jews—as outsiders, which is one reason why they were not initially influexced by the gradual white flight out of Russell Woods in the late 1950s.[79] The key factor was that Russell Woods was within walking distance of synagogues, which for Orthodox Jews is crucial, since they are forbidden by religious law to drive to the synagogue on Saturday and religious holidays. Yet the Orthodox Jews soon bowed to the same social pressure, and they too began moving out.[80]

Were these whites, Jews and non-Jews alike, pushed out of Russell Woods and similar neighborhoods by their own racism? One scholar suggests that instead of traditional racism pushing whites out, it was the "American Dream." "For them," he argued, "the arrival of Negroes served as an excuse to invest in that stainless steel, formica, and plywood-paneled dream house and believe at the same time that they were acting wisely from an economic point of view."[81] The pull of the suburbs and the quest for social status was too much for many whites, even those who believed strongly in integration. And in all fairness to those whites who left, many upper- and middle-class blacks, reflecting similar social values, would probably have been right behind them had racism not excluded them from most suburbs.

Certain suburbs attracted particular groups of whites. Jewish families in Russell Woods considered Huntington Woods, Oak Park, Franklin, and Birmingham as desirable places. Non-Jewish whites favored Bloomfield Hills, Birmingham, and Grosse Pointe.[82] Blacks in Detroit, as well as in other large cities, have tended to follow Jews into new housing areas, including suburbs, because of, as one scholar has suggested, "the value placed on non-violence by the Jewish community."[83] But more important, Jews as a group seldom engaged in violent resistance to black expansion and often led the way in welcoming blacks into their neighborhoods.

As middle-class white neighborhoods in Detroit opened up to blacks in the 1950s and 1960s, some after a series of conflicts and others *via* cooperation or at least practical coexistence, they tended to become extensions of the black ghettos rather than long-term biracial communities. Yet this process, described by urban scholars as the racial transition or invasion-succession sequence, was not inevitable but was based upon a combination of social factors. One key factor was the restriction of blacks to limited housing areas, which opened up one by one, resulting in "the familiar invasion and succession patterns." Pressure began to build up in these areas as black housing demands increased as a result of black migration from the South, expansion of a black middle class more able to afford homes in white neighborhoods, and the displacement of blacks caused by urban renewal and the construction of expressways.[84]

Many all-white neighborhoods that became biracial neighborhoods and then black ghettos might have been able to maintain their biracial character much longer, all other factors being equal, had blacks not been restricted to certain housing areas. Yet, however limited the biracial stage of the process of racial transition turned out to be, at least some whites and blacks were exposed to some positive interracial experiences. In some cases, such as Russell Woods, where the initial response of the all-white neighborhood associations to the black "invasion" was to buy out the blacks, an interracial association was later formed, which contributed to the maintenance of both high residential standards and interracial living.[85]

In the 1960s racial conflict over housing in Detroit and its suburbs took place against the larger social and historical backdrop of the Civil Rights Movement. As various local, state, and federal laws were passed and civil rights commissions established to protect the rights of racial minorities, racism became increasingly indefensible and unfashionable in certain white circles. White resistance to black invaders continued all along the fringe areas of the city, but by the early 1960s most whites in these areas knew that they were fighting a losing battle against an expanding black middle class determined to escape the crime and poverty of the ghetto. These black pioneers were subjected to much white harassment, but they persevered, thus paving the way for other black families.

Collective white violence against black families moving into Detroit's white neighborhoods became more and more unacceptable to whites themselves, as they began facing up to the vast social implications of their actions. In late 1961 and early 1962 two attempts were made to burn down the house of a black family in the Seven-Mile-Telegraph neighborhood in northwest Detroit. Before buying the house, the family had informed authorities that they did not want them to intervene. Their reason: "People will accept us when they get to know us." Despite the two fires, the family stayed. Their feelings concerning the two fires were "We needed a little remodeling anyway."[86] Whites in the neighborhood were shocked by the fires. While many of them probably did not want blacks for neighbors, such drastic actions by their fellow whites shamed them into acquiring a more racially tolerant attitude toward other blacks who moved in later.[87]

Building an Interracial Movement for Fair Housing

Racial violence and conflicts throughout this period in the South and in other northern cities alarmed many Detroiters, who feared similar events might occur in their city. Not a few white Detroit suburbanites were ashamed of the 1963 Labor Day mob action in Dearborn. "People living in suburbs," one human relations expert said, "did not want anything like that where they lived." They did not "want that to be the image of their city."[88] White suburbanites who cared enough to do something positive formed human relations groups, modeling them on similar groups in Detroit, particularly the Detroit Commission on Community Relations.[89]

These cooperative efforts emerged out of a growing sensitivity among concerned suburban whites that they were living in an increasingly segregated society (and according to evidence presented in this chapter, they were right). As evidence from the South of the potential for racial conflict within segregated societies mounted day by day, these whites felt compelled to do something positive.

Human relations groups were organized in a dozen or more Detroit suburbs in response to the kinds of racist behavior that occurred in Dearborn. Their purpose was to contribute to an atmosphere of racial tolerance in the event that blacks moved in.[90] Among the suburbs that established human relations organizations were Allen Park, Birmingham, Bloomfield Hills, Dearborn, Inkster, Ecorse, River Rouge, Farmington, Ferndale, the Grosse Pointes, Livonia, Berkley, Royal Oak, Pleasant Ridge, Plymouth Township, Pontiac, Romeo, and Roseville.[91]

The establishment of these human relations groups came in the wake of several major events (besides the embarrassing racist practices of such suburbs as Dearborn), which took place in 1963 and helped galvanize interracial support and cooperation for integrated housing. The first event was the Metropolitan Conference on Open Occupancy held in Detroit in January 1963. The second event was the Martin Luther King "Freedom" March in June of the same year, the spinoffs of which were several Detroit NAACP-sponsored interracial marches into Detroit suburbs to dramatize the need for black housing.

The Metropolitan Conference on Open Occupancy singularly contributed more than any other event during this period to positive change in the white public mind concerning the rights of blacks to buy houses anywhere they could afford. Sponsored by the Detroit Commission on Community Relations, the Catholic Archdiocese of Detroit, the Detroit Jewish Community Council, and the Detroit Council of Churches, the purpose of the conference was to "bring the forces of religious morality behind the concept of equal housing opportunity."[92] This citywide interfaith conference of religious leaders was the first of its kind to "face head-on the problems of racial discrimination in housing in Detroit," and it "heard both a confession of weakness and a united plea to enforce religious brotherhood principles in the neighborhood."[93]

The Reverend Hubert A. Maino, pastor of St. Lucy's Roman Catholic Church in St. Clair Shores, confessed to the conferees that "the people of St. Clair Shores are a long way from [being] ready to accept the policy of unrestricted open occupancy of housing." He and other whites in his area still had "a most formidable task of education" before them. But he promised the conferees that "we shall work at it with unremitting constancy and determination. . . . When we refuse housing or any other necessity of life to a fellow human being, we deny it to the Lord Himself. Christ identifies Himself with the homeless and the disinherited." The Reverend Dr. Allen A. Zarin, president of the Detroit Council of Churches, attacked suburbanites calling their "status-seeking and status-maintaining on the basis of race and color . . . damnable." Rabbi Richard C. Hertz of Temple Beth El, representing the Detroit Jewish Community Council, told the gathering, "Too often we have allowed the voice of fear and bigotry alone to be heard. If men of good will speak out, they will find each other in each neighborhood." By "linking hands and purposes across communities," he explained, "they will allay the fears of the timid and set a new tone of confidence, which will welcome good neighbors and promote standards cherished by all." The Reverend Charles Butler, a black minister of the Metropolitan Baptist Church, condemned what he called the "silent assent" of Detroiters to a slave pattern. He commented on the psychological pressures to control mobility and enforce immobility, which he described as a "refined type of slave control."[94]

Governor George Romney gave the keynote speech at this conference, in which he pledged to use the power of the state to achieve housing equality in Michigan. "I believe discrimination is our most urgent domestic problem," Romney told his listeners. "Ten percent of our citizens are not free to choose where they will work, where they will live, where they will vacation, and often where they will go to school. . . . A free and open housing market is a public responsibility and a public goal. Since property is private, the owner is free to be bigoted. That is why the theme of this conference is so appropriate. Open occupancy is not first of all a challenge to the state; it is a challenge of the conscience and hearts of men and women."[95] Mayor Cavanaugh, who could not attend the conference, sent a message praising the conference for opening the new year by addressing "a basic problem of urban life."[96]

The two-day conference ended on an optimistic note, calling upon all citizens of Detroit to practice brotherhood by accepting the principle of open occupancy in housing. An executive committee was set up to provide the vehicle by which various religious faiths could support an open occupancy ordinance.[97] But much more than pious statements, good intentions, and committees would be needed to break into many white suburbs, which by 1963 were being transformed into the new battle front in the war over open occupancy.

The January conference on open occupancy created a mood of interracial cooperation that would require a constant infusion of optimism and concrete achievements if it were not to become just another well-intended conference of liberal white "do gooders" and frustrated black leaders. That infusion of optimism came on a beautiful Sunday afternoon in June, when "a solid stream of 125,000 persons poured down Woodward Avenue . . . and overflowed a Civic Center rally in the largest civil rights demonstration in the nation's history."[98] This "march to freedom," as it was billed, was to protest racial discrimination throughout the United States. Originally intended to be a black demonstration against racism, several white and biracial organizations began lining up to endorse the march toward the end of the planning stage. The Jewish community, the Wayne County Democratic party, the Seventh (Detroit) Greek Orthodox Archdiocesan District, the Metropolitan Detroit Council of Churches, and the Roman Catholic Archbishop's Committee on Human Relations all issued separate statements endorsing the march.[99] No doubt pleased by the emerging interracial character of the supporters of the march, one of the black weeklies, the *Michigan Chronicle*, announced to its readers, "Bi-racial Groups to Join March Led by Rev. King."[100]

The much-touted biracial character of the march turned out to be misleading, since—except for the group of dignitaries leading the march, which included Martin Luther King flanked by black and white leaders—95 percent of the marchers were black. One local white minister, the Reverend Malcolm Boyd, criticized this lack of white participation in the march. "White participation in the march was noticeably less than it should have been," the minister lamented. "The mighty sea of black faces should have been joined by the presence of more whites committed to the cause of freedom. What some whites may tragically discover too late is that we are not talking essentially about Negro freedom; we are talking about, and concerned with, human freedom."[101] The few whites who did participate in the march were no doubt noticed and appreciated, as exemplified by the picture appearing in a local black weekly of a white youth holding a sign that read, "I'm ashamed I live in Dearborn!"[102]

Whites were more noticeable in the first NAACP-sponsored march in Dearborn to publicize housing discrimination in the suburbs. Held the day before the unprecedented freedom march, this march was composed of whites from both Detroit and Dearborn. Seventeen members of the Dearborn Pastors' Union participated in the march, along with the chairman of the Dearborn Young Democrats and members of the councils on human rights of Dearborn, Inkster, and western Wayne County. Many white bystanders along the route expressed the fear that if blacks moved to Dearborn, they would increase the welfare load. Others shouted to the marchers to "go back to Detroit," and when a leader of the march responded that blacks work in Dearborn but did not live there, the white hecklers shouted, "Then don't bother working in Dearborn."[103]

Although Dearborn officials declined a parade permit to the marchers, the march to the Dearborn City Hall was sufficient to influence some local public opinion on housing in the city many Detroiters called "the Birmingham of the North."[104] After the march the editor of the *Dearborn Independent* reported getting a flurry of letters from Dearborn residents concerned with the possibility of blacks' moving into Dearborn. Most of these residents were fearful that "the wrong type of black" would move into Dearborn's already declining "lower hillbilly" area. Surprisingly, the letters revealed that Dearborn's white citizens were split 50-50 over the issue of housing integration, with some expressing the view that there would be no trouble if middle-class blacks moved into the better sections of Dearborn. The editor, obviously concerned about such a possibility, asked the *Michigan Chronicle* whether the NAACP was planning to move black families into the suburbs. If it was, he wanted to cover the story.[105]

The next couple of NAACP marches into the suburbs were more pleasant. Both Grosse Pointe and Royal Oak Township welcomed the interracial marchers. Close to 500 black and white marchers, including many Grosse Pointers, marched in "the Pointes" that July. Governor George Romney made a surprise appearance in his shirt sleeves and joined the parade leaders. Along the route American flags were flying in response to a request from the *Grosse Pointe News*, which prior to the march took the bold and courageous step of printing a banner headline: "Welcome to Marchers Urged."[106] Oak Park, largely Jewish and destined to become a model multiracial suburb, also extended a welcome to the NAACP marchers. And not only did the mayor, along with city officials and other leaders, encourage Oak Park's citizens to welcome the demonstration but the city also issued the following statement: "The city of Oak Park is proud of its record in the area of civil rights and human relations. We are aware, however, as this meeting dramatizes, that there are unfulfilled tasks and unrealized goals of our Democracy."[107]

The NAACP also marched in several other suburbs, including Redford Township and Livonia. According to the NAACP Housing Committee, the climate was receptive: "Support [was] pledged by citizens, ministers, and organizations to welcome Negroes to all white areas."[108] The marches forced the housing issue to the surface and in the process raised the social consciousness of many white suburbanites. For example, one white owner of a subdivision in Grosse Pointe was sufficiently influenced by the march in his city that he decided to accept a few black families in his subdivision, regardless of pressure from whites in the area.[109] Related actions of other suburban whites during this period reflected significant changes in their racial attitudes on housing, stimulated by the conference on open occupancy, the "march to freedom", the NAACP's march in the suburbs, and most important, the frequent reports in the local press of civil rights demonstrations and racial violence in the South.

Racial conflicts in the South provided Detroit-area fair housing groups with the sense of urgency they needed to prod whites into facing up to racism in their own communities. In the spring of 1965 the predominantly white Greater Detroit Committee for Fair Housing Practices (GDCFHP)—which had already conducted a successful covenant card campaign in metropolitan Detroit to obtain pledges from whites that they would welcome into their communities people of any race or religion—used the bloody demonstrations in Selma, Alabama to further raise white consciousness over housing discrimination: "We believe that since Selma you have sensed, as we have, a growing need for greater personal commitment on the part of many people who want to take an active part in efforts to eliminate discrimination in our northern cities." This "greater personal commitment," initiated by the GDCFHP, was a new campaign for housing aides, which went beyond the earlier campaign for pledges on cards to "the willingness to be available when asked for help."[110]

In addition to campaigns geared to obtaining pledges and commitments from whites to help integrate their communities, the GDCFHP provided a listing service designed for the express purpose of providing "opportunities for people seeking integrated housing in the city and the suburbs." The local NAACP was provided with copies of these listings and asked to bring them to the attention of interested parties.[111]

This interracial cooperation to achieve integrated housing often met with unexpected problems. White officials of GDCFHP complained of "the baffling problem" of finding black buyers to move into homes in white communities. "Frankly, our biggest problem now is getting Negroes to move into homes available in white communities," one white official complained. "We have . . . 50 to 60 listings of homes in such places as Palmer Woods, St. Clair Shores, Livonia, Oak Park, Pleasant Ridge, and other suburbs, but we have been able only to effect about two sales." The official explained why few blacks had looked for homes in the suburbs: "[They] are so sure they are not wanted. As long as they don't go, they will never really know." According to this official, progress would be made when suburban whites saw blacks shopping for houses in their communities: "They will realize that there is no other place for them to go. So, they will have to sit pat." Even more critically important the official claimed, "[President Johnson's new housing Executive Order] won't mean a thing unless Negroes are willing to purchase homes in presently all-white communities." In shifting the responsibility for achieving housing integration to blacks, the official concluded that such black reluctance was the "biggest problem" that would have to be solved before housing integration would be possible.[112]

Such views were not atypical of many liberal whites whose hearts were in the right place but who were yet quite naive about the harsher realities of white racism in Detroit suburbs. The "big problem" was much more complicated than just providing blacks with listings of houses in suburban communities. Even President Johnson's Executive Order on housing meant little in the face of hostile white neighbors. In short, the GDCFHP officials failed to understand that while blacks wanted decent housing anywhere they could obtain it, they also wanted to live in an environment free of racial hostility and harassment. As one middle-class black father explained it, "I'd like to live out in Livonia or Westland, I really would, but it's not worth the physical danger or the long-term psychological damage to my kids."[113] This fear of white suburban hostility was not unfounded. In 1968 Don Bauden of the Michigan Civil Rights Commission reported that nearly all black families that attempted to move to Detroit's suburbs met with racial harassment.[114]

Many blacks in Detroit had not forgotten the ugly incident that occurred in 1956 in Royal Oak Township, when a black secretary working for the school board and living in the city was tied, gagged, and then beaten in her home by three white men wearing masks. The following night someone put a death note on her door.[115] In 1964 blacks purchased a house in Sterling Heights, which was destroyed by fire before they had a chance to move in. In the summer of 1967, soon after a black man and his white wife moved into their new home in Warren, angry whites gathered around the house and for two nights threw stones and broke windows. The Warren police hesitated to arrest members of the mob but finally convinced them to go home.[116]

In 1968 blacks owned no homes in Royal Oak Township, Troy, East Detroit, the Grosse Pointes, Dearborn, Hazel Park, Ferndale, Madison Heights, Sterling Heights, Southfield, Redford Township, Westland, Farmington, Allen Park, Melvindale, or Lincoln Park. There was one black family each in Birmingham, Livonia, and Fraser, and there were four each in Warren (one family was there before World War II, when Warren was a rural township) and Oak Park. During this period the few blacks who lived in St. Clair Shores, Roseville, Ecorse, and Dearborn Heights were concentrated on single all-black streets.[117]

White suburban racial attitudes, and practices fueled antiwhite feelings among blacks in Detroit and undermined interracial efforts to solve the housing problem. Black-power militants began scrapping the Civil Rights Movement's goals of integration and instead began emphasizing black control of black communities. Yet, in the face of this increasing racial polarity, particularly just before and after the 1967 Detroit rebellion, interracial cooperation in the field of housing continued.

The establishment of human relations councils, committees, and discussion groups in some suburban communities was an important first step not only in building and maintaining interracial cooperation in the struggle for integrated housing but also in building bridges between fair housing organizations in the suburbs and Detroit. In 1965 the Dearborn, Inkster, and Western Wayne County human relations councils, in cooperation with the Greater Detroit Committee for Fair Housing Practices and the Commission on Community Relations, held a conference called "The Search for Housing." One of the purposes of the conference was to encourage minority families seeking housing to broaden their search as much as possible. The other purpose was "to encourage the white homeowner to accept without fear or bias all citizens into his neighborhood.[118]

These conferences contributed a great deal to interracial cooperation in the fight for fair housing, but they were too few and infrequent. Human relations councils, like Livonia's Committee for Better Human Relations, and other local institutions and organizations appeared to be more effective in addressing other racial issues. In the late 1960s this committee conducted community seminars and panel discussions on racial problems. Livonia's Holy Cross Lutheran Church was one of the suburban churches that held an informal coffeehouse ministry, where people studied different segments of the Kerner Commission Report that resulted from the 1967 urban disorders. Black leaders were invited to speak to this group. The YMCA (Young Men's Christian Association) assisted in organizing race relations talks at Schoolcraft College in Livonia and sponsoring a recreational interchange between inner-city and suburban children. The YMCA was surprised to discover "how easy it was to get parents [whites] to submit their children to this activity."[119] Some suburban whites held discussion sessions on race in their homes and invited blacks to attend. Discussions, however, tended to be one-way, with whites asking all the questions about blacks and avoiding questions concerning racism.[120] All of these efforts contributed their small share to a climate in which the volatile issue of integrated housing in the suburbs could at least be discussed.

Housing integration and the resolution of racial conflicts might have proceeded with greater dispatch in suburban communities if they had had a municipal organization like the Detroit Commission on Community Relations (DCCR). This organization evolved out of the mayor's Interracial Committee set up after the 1943 race riot. The DCCR's staff played a leading role both in resolving racial conflicts over housing in Detroit neighborhoods and in assisting neighborhoods in the throes of racial change in developing ongoing, cooperative interracial activities and programs. Having honed its skills in racial conflict resolutions in Detroit communities, by the late 1960s the DCCR was assisting suburban human relations councils in establishing fair housing programs to attract black families to their communities.[121]

Functioning in part as a monitor of intergroup conflict in Detroit, the DCCR maintained a close watch over appeals to racial, religious, and ethnic prejudices that could incite tension and hostilities. Yet the DCCR's greatest contribution was in helping black and white residents in changing communities to work out their problems peacefully. For example, in 1962 some whites in a Detroit neighborhood began engaging in panic selling, when black families began arriving in the area. So some residents asked the DCCR to help them set up a community education project to promote peaceful interracial living.[122] In another situation, where a white homeowner sold his home in an all-white Detroit neighborhood to a black family, causing racial tension, a community organization asked the DCCR to intervene. The DCCR notified police to protect the family and then arranged meetings with community agencies and the more responsible white people in the neighborhood. At the meetings a DCCR staff member explained that the purchase was legal and urged everyone to cooperate in preventing racial tension and conflict. Nervous whites present at the meetings were asked not to panic over unfounded rumors of declining property values.[123]

These are only a few representative examples of the countless housing situations in which DCCR intervention contributed to the resolution of racial conflict and the fostering of racial cooperation. The suburbs had nothing comparable to the DCCR. Maybe if they had developed DCCR types of organizations, housing segregation in the suburbs would not have remained so rigidly racist for so long. And maybe the controversy over low-income housing that emerged in the 1970s and 1980s would not have been so explosive. Then again DCCR types of organizations in the suburbs might not have been able to allay the deep fears of relocated white Detroiters who had fled the city to escape blacks.

Suburban Resistance to HUD

The housing conflicts of the 1970s involved many unresolved issues of past decades plus a few more explosive ones, such as the role of federal housing policy in achieving equal housing opportunities in the suburbs. This policy issue heated up long before the simmering racial and class tensions between Detroit and its suburbs. It also placed additional strain on the Detroit/suburban interracial cooperative network that had developed during the peak of the Civil Rights Movement. And it had been tried and tested by the divisive racial hysteria of the 1967 riot.

Essentially, the issue involved the question of whether white suburbs that discriminate against racial minorities should get funding from the federal Department of Housing and Urban Development (HUD). Since the 1964 Civil Rights Act prohibited the use of federal funds to support discrimination of any kind, opponents of housing segregation in white suburbs argued that suburbs that discriminated should not receive federal funding. In August of 1970 the U.S. Civil Rights Commission began gearing up to propose that all federal funds be withdrawn from all suburbs that were all or predominantly white and that adjoined cities containing large black populations. The commission's chairman, the Reverend Father Theodore M. Hesburgh, described the suburban system of racial exclusion as "the apparently hopeless encirclement of black central cities by impenetrable coils of indifferent or hostile white suburbs." The five-member Civil Rights Commission arrived at this position after holding two public hearings on the alleged systematic exclusion of blacks from the suburbs, based on the 1970 census data, which indicated that the suburbs were the nation's major residential area.[124]

White suburbanites, especially the blue-collar working class of industrial suburbs like Warren, were incensed over what they perceived to be government intrusion into their communities or worse, government support of forced integration. Many of these working-class whites had lost money selling their homes in the mad flight to the suburbs and had nowhere else to go nor sufficient funds to run again. Most felt that they had been forced from their east-side Detroit homes by blacks moving in, and they would not run again. In 1970 one former, white east-sider—who started a petition drive in Warren to call a referendum to repeal the city's urban renewal program rather than accept federal guidelines relating to low-income and integrated housing—commented, "I was the last to move out [of east-side Detroit]. . . . [I] fought them [blacks] as long as I could."[125]

White working-class Warren had reasons enough to fear what it called "forced integration." Thirty percent of all workers in Warren in 1970 were black, yet only five black families lived in the city. When Warren's city government went after a $2.8 million grant to be used primarily for low-income housing, HUD held up the funds. In June of 1970, in a city council session, tempers flared as Warren residents and council members battled over the fair housing aspect of the urban renewal program. The conflict over the issue was so intense that it "pitted neighbor against neighbor [and] relative against relative" and necessitated the stationing of uniformed police on opposite sides of the room. One observer claimed that the urban renewal/fair housing issue was the "biggest and angriest" in Warren since its incorporation as a city in 1957.[126] Opponents of the fair housing measure said it would mean giving in to federal control. They also believed that urban renewal was a threat to their homes and "a handout to shiftless people."[127] Those who supported fair housing in Warren, such as the Reverend William McGoldrisk of St. Edmond Catholic Church, called Warren a closed city and accused the opponents of the measure of "trying to keep it so."[128]

All hell broke out a month later when the *Detroit News* printed several articles under the banner captions "U.S. Picks Warren as Prime Target in Move to Integrate all Suburbs" and "How Warren Was Picked for Integration."[129] Supposedly taken from a memorandum on file in the HUD office in Washington, the following quote appeared in the *Detroit News*:

> Detroit suburbs present an unparalleled opportunity for the application of a fair-housing strategy. Nowhere else in the Midwest, perhaps

> nowhere else in the country, is there a combination of a large central city with a substantial black population . . . surrounded by large, white suburbs which may use HUD programs and in which there is extensive black employment and a great deal of middle-class housing. It is proper for HUD to use its resources to [loosen] the "white noose" surrounding the central city.[130]

But why was Warren selected to become the test case? According to HUD's regional office in Chicago, Warren represented "an appropriate occasion for tackling the problem" for the following reasons: In 1964 Warren received $1.3 million in HUD funds, which it desperately needed for neighborhood development. And the city had used the funds effectively. Warren, however, needed more funds and was about to apply for an additional $2.8 million. At this point, according to the article, HUD decided to employ its new strategy. Warren's population of about 180,000 residents was more than 99 percent white, yet 30 percent of all the workers in Warren's auto plants were black and lived in Detroit. Presumably, they could afford to purchase middle-income housing in Warren. Since Warren was using HUD money and wanted more, it should open up its housing market to members of minority groups.

HUD applied the same principle to other Detroit suburbs. Dearborn was also getting HUD money and had large numbers of black workers. Other suburbs getting HUD money were Ferndale, Hazel Park, Madison Heights, Center Line, and Dearborn Heights. Royal Oak Township and Southfield were among still other suburbs considering applying for HUD funds.[131] No doubt they were nervously watching the HUD/Warren drama unfold.

HUD's Chicago office presented a range of suggestions to the city of Warren on ways to achieve fair housing, which included setting up a human relations council and placing housing advertisements in the *Michigan Chronicle*, a local black newspaper in Detroit. Private meetings were held in Chicago and Warren to search for ways to reconcile HUD's demands with Warren's reluctance. Warren's Mayor Ted Bates, who wanted to continue the city's ties with HUD, was in conflict with council members who resented HUD's demands for fair housing. Before long the conflict involved Governor Milliken, U.S. senators Robert P. Griffin and Philip A. Hart, several congressmen, and major labor, church, and business leaders in Detroit. All this involvement, including a meeting between Warren officials and George Romney (the head of HUD in Washington), did little to resolve the conflict.[132]

The *Detroit News* article stimulated great concern among residents of Warren. Mayor Bates accused HUD of wanting to use Warren as a "guinea pig for integration experiments" and warned that he would not tolerate such a policy, even if it meant losing urban renewal funds. Instead, he would meet with leaders of other Detroit suburbs receiving HUD funds to organize support "to fight this forced integration."[133] A few days later Romney issued a statement in which he said, "There is not now, nor will there be, a HUD policy to force integration in the suburbs." He then called a meeting of mayors in Warren, where he again denied the charge. Mayor Bates and several council members raked Romney over the coals, while pickets outside the meeting carried signs saying, "Get rid of the Dud at HUD." The mayors from other suburbs listened to the outcome with obvious interest. During the meeting Romney attacked the *Detroit News* coverage of HUD's policy and argued that a memo from a regional office does not establish policy. The memo, according to Romney, consisted of merely views of and comments between subordinates.[134]

Romney's visit and strained explanation did little to change anyone's mind. Warren remained split and suspicious over the issue. Romney was booed as he left the meeting, and the police had to escort his car out of Warren.[135] Several weeks later Romney told the Senate Select Committee on Equal Educational Opportunity that Warren had an obvious practice of discrimination in the community and that, at the very least, it would have to "establish a genuine human relations commission . . . to qualify for additional urban renewal funds." Warren would not get the money, Romney told the committee, if it did not "comply with that requirement."[136] Mayor Bates retorted, "You show me where anyone in this city administration has withheld the right of anyone to live in this city. Anyone has the right to live anywhere in the city he pleases." Bates then demanded a public apology from Romney.[137]

At this juncture the relationship between HUD and the city of Warren was rapidly deteriorating. Opponents of HUD started a petition drive calling for an election to resolve the issue. And in early November 1970 Warren, the first city in Michigan to qualify for Neighborhood Development Program funds under a new form of urban renewal, became the first community in the nation to vote to drop the program.[138] Warren residents who voted against urban renewal no doubt felt that they had won a great victory against what they perceived to be a government scheme to force integration down their throats.

White working-class Warren was not alone in fearing that its lily-white suburb might be tainted by racial integration. Liberal professional Birmingham, among the first white suburbs in the country to adopt an open housing ordinance in 1968, discovered that it too harbored feelings no less racist than those of its working-class sister suburbs. In 1971 Birmingham failed the first test of its liberal racial philosophy, when it voted down a national program sponsored by Dartmouth College to provide for ten disadvantaged youths to live and attend school in the city. A group of well-meaning white liberals in Birmingham was responsible for bringing the program—called A Better Chance (ABC)—to the city, because they believed Birmingham's fair housing ordinance "implied a willingness of the residents to be realistic [and] implied an ideal."[139] Unfortunately, they were wrong. The uproar over the program at a key commission meeting was described by Ruth McNarmee, then mayor of Birmingham, as "hostile and racist."[140] Birmingham also failed a test of its liberal racial philosophy in 1978, when it voted to reject low-income housing.[141]

As Detroit's white suburbs continued to resist efforts to integrate racial minorities and low-income groups into their communities, in the fall of 1974 civil rights, religious, and civic groups began to organize pressure groups such as the NAACP and the Coalition for Block Grant Compliance. They began applying pressure on HUD to reject applications of those suburbs that did not provide housing plans for minority and other low-income groups that worked but could not live in the suburbs. In March of 1975 the Detroit NAACP charged that 26 Detroit suburbs had submitted federal grant applications that revealed "patterns of systematic racism." The NAACP's charge was backed by the Coalition for Block Grant Compliance, which threatened to challenge the applications unless they were revised before the deadline.[142]

The U.S. Civil Rights Commission did its own prodding in early 1975, by initiating a study to find out whether Michigan cities were using federal block grant funds to further racial discrimination. The commission was concerned that suburbs would use the money for projects, such as purchasing new city hall and firefighting equipment, that were not designed to attract racial minorities and low-income people. Livonia was the first suburb to be investigated by federal investigators and evidently convinced them it would comply with the fair housing component of the grant. But in February 1978 U.S. district court judge Robert E. DeMascio ruled that Livonia could not spend $150,000 in federal housing funds, because it had been receiving grants without complying with the 1974 Fair Housing Act.[143]

In 1982 a U.S. district court judge in Detroit ruled that Birmingham also violated the Fair Housing Act, when it interfered with the efforts of a group of four churches incorporated as Baldwin House to build low-income housing. Two years earlier the Justice Department charged in a lawsuit that Birmingham frustrated efforts to build low-income housing because many of its residents did not want poor blacks living in Birmingham. In the last few years Birmingham has lost the glittering image it once had as a liberal sophisticated community too urbane and civilized to indulge in racist practices. Very much on the defensive, the Birmingham City Commission, in March of 1984, challenged a federal appeals court ruling that its reason for rejecting subsidized housing for senior citizens and low-income groups was racist.[144]

Maintaining the Struggle and the Dream

To a superficial observer, white suburbanites in the 1970s and early 1980s formed a monolith of racist resistance to fair housing and were constantly widening the race and class gap between black Detroit and its white suburbs. Any such scenario sadly underrates the courage and persistence of small liberal and radical white groups working against great odds to effect racial changes in their communities. Such a scenario also ignores the growth in the fair housing field during the years of interracial cooperation.

Notwithstanding the large-scale suburban voter turnout in recent years that rejected low-income housing for minorities and the poor, small groups of progressive whites at least made their views known to the larger public, thus preventing the formation of a racist conscensus around the fair housing issue. While most of the white liberal forces were badly beaten, they still left their mark.

Interracial cooperation in the field of fair housing was and still is best exemplified by the ceaseless efforts of organizations such as the Coalition for Block Grant Compliance, the Michigan Housing Coalition, and predominantly white suburban organizations like the Grosse Pointe Interfaith Center for Racial Justice, which works diligently to keep fair housing issues on the front burner of public attention. For example, in August of 1982, after noting the fact that minorities made up only .012 percent of the total population of the five Grosse Pointes and Harper Woods, the Grosse Pointe Inter-faith Center for Racial Justice addressed the following message to its supporters:

> If we who support the goals, programs, and objectives of the Grosse Pointe Inter-faith Center for Racial Justice truly believe that 1) racial, religious, and ethnic diversity enriches the quality of life in our community, and 2) our children must be prepared to live in a multi-racial,

> multi-cultural world, then must we not ask ourselves why is this percentage so low? Is open housing, which is mandated by law, a reality?[145]

Interracial cooperation in housing has been most effective in the area of fair housing tests, where a black and white team test for housing discrimination. For example, first the black tester asks to see an apartment and if told none is available, then the white tester does likewise. If the white tester is shown an apartment, the manager has obviously discriminated against the black tester. A lawsuit is then filed in court.[146] Testing of this sort has proven invaluable in combating housing discrimination in metropolitan Detroit and would be impossible to implement without interracial cooperation.

The dream of achieving biracial housing patterns in Detroit and its suburbs has encountered countless difficulties. Whites did not resist the dream; they fled from it. Many whites of such limited vision could not see or even appreciate the value of fostering the development of a truly multiracial city, free of racial tension and conflict and conducive to limitless human and societal development. However, at least two Detroit suburbs, Oak Park and Southfield, boasting the two largest black populations, have attempted to realize the dream of a multiracial city. "We are an absolute melting pot," exclaimed Oak Park's Mayor Charlotte Rothstein in 1984. The mayor was referring to the 70 ethnic groups living in harmony in the city. According to official estimates, Jews make up 50 percent of the city's population, followed by blacks at 15 to 18 percent, then Chaldeans at 15 percent. The remaining population includes people of Irish, Polish, Italian, Vietnamese, Chinese, Japanese, Korean, American Indian, and Asian Indian descent.[147]

The racial and ethnic changes in Oak Park's population over the last decade stemmed in part from a housing surplus created by older, white residents who moved into apartments and condominiums. But the housing surplus did not create the spirit and desire that motivated city officials and concerned citizens to work to build and maintain Oak Park as a city for all people. This spirit and desire is best exemplified in the city's 15-member International Festival Task Force, charged with organizing ethnic festivals during Oak Park's annual Fourth of July celebration. Moreover, Mayor Rothstein sees the city library also playing a role in making Oak Park a multiracial and multicultural city by holding "a year-long cultural enrichment program featuring as many of the ethnic groups that we can identify as living in Oak Park.[148]

Oak Park has the potential of becoming a model multiracial and multicultural city. The large Orthodox Jewish community, the largest such community in the Detroit area, has been correctly perceived as one of the key factors in the stability of the larger community. This has been particularly the case in the wake of the flight of younger white families, unnerved by the changing racial and cultural makeup of Oak Park and most especially by the influx of blacks and Chaldeans. So younger white families are fleeing farther north in search of "whiter" suburbs.[149]

In 1973 Oak Park's City Council attempted to control "panic selling and white flight" by outlawing "for sale" signs in residential areas, but in 1976 the U.S. Supreme Court struck down bans on "for sale" signs. Still determined, Oak Park's City Council redrafted the city ordinance so it banned all signs in residential areas in the city except those signs relating to health, safety, and welfare, such as helping hands for children and invalids. This new approach to control panic selling and white flight did not go unchallenged. Some residents resented being ticketed and fined for putting "for sale" signs on their own property. "When the city said I can't put a sign on my lawn," one homeowner complained, "they're infringing on my individual rights."[150] Other homeowners probably shared this view, but most complied with the ordinance. Only one councilman voted against it. He objected to the language of the ordinance, which he argued could also be used to bar seasonal and holiday signs, including "Merry Christmas" and "Happy Hanukah." While agreeing, the pro-ordinance mayor of Oak Park, David Shepherd, pointed out that homeowners were still free to use other seasonal decorations.[151] These measures might seem extreme, but they clearly demonstrated the extent to which Oak Park officials were willing to go to establish a racially and culturally diverse community.

Southfield, west of Oak Park, has also promoted progressive racial policies and along with its sister city, might well become a model multiracial city. According to some observers, "Southfield has managed the stress test of integration and . . . managed it well." Only 102 blacks lived in Southfield in 1970. Ten years later the number increased to almost 7,000 and is steadily moving upward. Southfield also is home to significant numbers of Koreans, Chaldeans, Asian Indians, and Orthodox Jews.[152]

One of the first and truest stress tests of Southfield's commitment to integration occurred in the wake of the 1967 riots in Detroit. Residents of the Magnolia subdivision—just west of the IBM building and St. John's American Church, with its gold dome—were on the verge of being victimized by rumors of white flight and black migration from Detroit. Mass racial hysteria began spreading throughout the subdivision, as people discussed entire blocks' being emptied of white residents fleeing to escape black neighbors. Property values would fall for those who stayed as well as for those who fled. According to the rumor mill, the residents of Magnolia had seen the last of their old world.[153]

Fortunately, the people of the Magnolia subdivision had a progressive neighborhood association, organized in 1939, which decided to resist the mass racial hysteria and instead seek more positive alternatives. The alternative selected was the use of a 1971 city ordinance, which granted residents the right to state that they did not desire to be solicited by real estate agents and which rendered such solicitation or other attempts to persuade residents to sell as illegal. In addition, the neighborhood association persuaded residents who desired to sell to agree not to put up "for sale" signs on their property. The plan worked well. Throughout the 1970s racial integration in the Magnolia subdivision proceeded with quiet dignity. In 1983 blacks comprised 20 percent of the residents in the subdivision and represented the same percentage of the Magnolia Neighborhood Association.[154]

The Magnolia subdivision's peaceful transition to a racially integrated neighborhood would have been far more difficult, if not impossible, had Southfield not seen fit to enact the 1971 Anti-Solicitation Ordinance. As already mentioned, in 1976 the U.S. Supreme Court ruled against the sign ordinance. A month after the court's decision, Southfield officials decided that they needed a strong housing program that would, in part, enable "Southfield to maintain a stable community, to continue to show appreciating housing values, to demonstrate [itself] as an excellent community [in which] to work, live and raise a family and to combat the insidious practices of steering and block busting."[155] In 1981 and 1982 Southfield amended its fair neighborhood practices code several times to render it more effective in combating racial discrimination in housing and steering and blockbusting.[156] In 1980 the city initiated an anti-solicitation card program aimed at prohibiting realtors from soliciting homeowners by "telephone, [by] mail, in person, or [in] any other manner, for the sale of their property." Southfield currently (1985) maintains a list of undated cards, which are made available to realtors on a regular basis. Realtors are then held responsible for obtaining the cards. Realtors who solicit residents on the list can be prosecuted. Several neighborhoods have demonstrated their support for the program by organizing neighborhoodwide "completion" programs to increase residents' involvement.[157]

The anti-solicitation card program is not antirealtor but rather is aimed at a breed of realtors who for decades profited from deliberately inducing mass racial hysteria in racially changing neighborhoods. Many a realtor made his or her fortune by exploiting the racial fears of white homeowners, leaving a trail of racial fear, hatred, and conflict. These realtors destroyed communities when they could have contributed to increasing such communities' racial and cultural understanding.

Not a few Southfield residents had been victimized by such scare tactics while living in northwest Detroit. Those too young to remember the mass racial hysteria of northwest Detroit residents in the late 1950s and early 1960s no doubt had heard their parents discussing how they were forced to flee the area, losing money in the process. And it was clear to many of these Southfielders that realtors had played a major role in causing the white flight. Therefore, they were determined not to let it happen again.

Recognizing the positive role that realtors can play in promoting an open and stable community, Southfield developed a "Preferred Real Estate Sales Agent List" which contains "the names of the sales agents who have successfully completed an extensive orientation and education program, [and] have demonstrated their commitment to promote and maintain Southfield as an open, integrated, well-maintained residential community." After completing the program, the realtor receives a certificate awarding him or her the title of "Southfield Real Estate Designate," certifying that "the above individual has successfully completed an orientation and education program and has demonstrated a commitment to promote a dynamic, exciting Southfield whose housing market reflects equal opportunities and services for all homeseekers."[158]

Southfield also provides a housing service to maintain and stabilize the city's neighborhoods by encouraging whites to remain in the neighborhoods and by bringing whites back into changing neighborhoods or black neighborhoods to keep them from becoming resegregated.[159] Perhaps these efforts will provide the models for other cities interested in positive responses to racial changes. Oak Park and Southfield still have much to achieve in the area of race relations, but they are well on their way to becoming models of the multiracial city.

Conclusion

We have seen how and why housing has been a hornet's nest of racial conflict since 1940. The spatial direction of the black population movement threatened many white neighborhoods, which responded in various racist and violent ways. Racial conflicts were almost inevitable, as the pressure for decent housing built up in the crowded black ghettos. Gradually, blacks began moving into white neighborhoods, and whites, seized by mass racial hysteria, fled to the suburbs. Those who fled to Dearborn were guaranteed protection from the "black hordes" by the unabashed racism of Mayor Orville Hubbard. Other suburbs, such as Warren, exhibited similar racist sentiments, although to a lesser degree.

Racial discrimination and interracial conflicts in housing have all too often overshadowed the valiant efforts of black and white alike to bridge the racial gap and promote interracial cooperation. While some whites were busy fleeing racially changing neighborhoods and some were building barricades to stop blacks from moving into their communities, other whites responded more constructively by welcoming blacks and attempting to build interracial communities.

Still other whites responded constructively by organizing fair housing conferences, inviting blacks to visit and live in their communities, and participating in a range of other efforts to bridge the racial gap. While it is difficult to determine the extent to which these efforts affected the pattern of racial segregation as measured by the index of dissimilarity, it is clear that white racism and black and white racial conflicts do not, in themselves, comprise the entire history of race relations in Detroit. Interracial cooperation, while yet a barely visible trend, kept metropolitan Detroit from becoming even more segregated than it is at present. Southfield and Oak Park are excellent examples. Interracial conflicts, therefore, were never as all-prevailing as some people would have us believe. And we can count ourselves fortunate that such was the case.

When blacks were not struggling to obtain decent housing anywhere they could find it, which often turned out to be in white neighborhoods, they were struggling against the negative consequences of redevelopment policies and programs formulated and implemented by unsympathetic city administrators.

5

City Redevelopment Policies

We move now from housing as a case study of racial conflict and cooperation to city redevelopment policies. As in Chapter 2, we will examine broad aspects of uneven social and economic development, including the role of the political and economic elite in the decision-making process. Race and class factors are still quite salient in this discussion but take their place alongside new aspects of the analysis, such as how and why certain redevelopment decisions were made and what effects they had upon particular segments of the population.

Three aspects of the metropolis have controlled the nature and potential success of city redevelopment efforts: the regional redistribution of resources, the economic decline of the central city, and the ongoing process of race and class alienation and segregation. Changing social, economic, and racial patterns in the Detroit metropolitan area caused many changes in the city of Detroit. As factories and commercial centers shifted to the suburbs, older industrial plants and commercial buildings were left standing empty within the central city. As white, middle-class residents fled the core for suburbs, many city residential areas at first changed from white to black and then, after the black middle class began to exit, depopulated to the point of abandonment. On the whole, growth and development within the region became associated with the perimeters of the metropolis, decay and decline with the core.

As explained earlier in this book, regional economic growth and prosperity, the first trend, steadily shifted commercial nodes of prosperity northwest, northeast, and southwest of the city. Suburban malls attracted commercial venturees, and factories moved to greener suburban locations. Any redevelopment efforts, whether residential, commercial, or industrial, consistently had to compete with attractive and viable suburban alternatives. Although many areas outside the city are not prosperous, such as the older industrial suburbs in the downriver area, many are prosperous enough to reduce metropolitan dependence upon, and even use for, the central city significantly. The very term "redevelopment" is inextricably tied with the central city. Few suburban areas have found it necessary to redevelop, since so much new development or refurbishment has taken place in the nongovernmental marketplace.

The second trend, the economic decline of the central city, has been such a mammoth, inexorable process that at times policy countermeasures have seemed entirely futile. Between 1950 and 1980 the number of city residents employed in manufacturing jobs dropped 68 percent, from 349,000 to 113,000. This loss of manufacturing employment reflected the cumulative effects of plant shutdowns, factory relocation, and work-force reduction in those plants that did remain open. While city population fell 35 percent in those 30 years, the total number of employed residents dropped 48 percent.[1] Such unbalanced loss of employed residents coupled with a real decline in city revenue because of stagnant property values and residential flight added up to serious fiscal problems for the city. These problems limited the resources the city could devote to redevelopment largely to those emanating from federally financed programs, which have been neither large enough nor effective enough to reverse city economic decline.

The third characteristic of the Detroit metropolis that has affected redevelopment efforts has been the persistent racial and class segmentation of the city and region. In particular, the continued high racial polarization within the Detroit metropolitan area, described more fully in previous chapters, has affected redevelopment efforts for decades, as white developers, real estate professionals, and homeowners consistently showed clear preference for the whiter rim over the darker core. As the percentage of blacks within the central city climbed to over half the city population, the tendency of the whiter region to abandon the city became even stronger. Racial alienation and class upward mobility exacerbated decentralizing tendencies, and even within redevelopment projects, the tradition of racial segregation posed several problems.

It was not long after World War II ended that the overall trends of disinvestment and middle-income flight became evident, and it began to appear that the city government was going to have to cope with such changes by taking deliberate steps to halt the decline or mitigate its effects. The city of Detroit defined redevelopment in several ways, and the manifestation of redevelopment changed over the years. In general, early redevelopment involved the massive clearance of residential areas and the sale of razed land to private redevelopers or to hospitals or other local institutions, such as Wayne State University. Redevelopment also focused, in both early and later years, upon the central business district and declining industrial corridors. The term "redevelopment" has also been used to characterize the city's efforts to conserve and rehabilitate sections of residential areas without necessarily clearing out large numbers of structures.

No matter what the particular definition of redevelopment, or the particular moment at which it has taken place, the entire process has generated agony and controversy since its conception. Even today the issue of what should be done with redevelopment money, whether in the form of Community Development Block Grants funds or city revenues, is enough to throw a city council meeting into debate. Many Detroit residents still have negative attitudes about the process of urban renewal and its effects upon former neighborhoods. Others see the cleared areas as slums that needed to be razed, as did the planners who directed the clearance process, but wonder why the program and its spinoffs have not managed to create a livable city. Major redevelopment projects that involve large-scale clearance, such as the Central Industrial Park project of the 1980s (known to many as Poletown), generate as much controversy as if not more controversy than did older projects, such as the West Side Industrial Redevelopment project of the 1950s (known as Corktown). And yet the city continues to lose population, jobs continue to drop, vacant lots proliferate like so many missing teeth in a mouth in serious decline.

The vision of many city professionals has remained brightly optimistic for many years. In an interview published in 1969, former city planning director Charles Blessing commented, "Just a few years ago we had 300,000 people living in the inner city, most of them living miserably. Many have gone. But when we are through, we can have 300,000 people again in the inner city in a creatively planned environment. We needn't settle for less than a great city. Is this unrealistic? I don't think so. Already we have worked 2,000 acres of the inner city into this concept. We've got 7,000 acres to go." While all observers may not agree with Blessing's assessment that redevelopment policies were leading to a great city, or even that 2,000 acres had been creatively planned, they would certainly agree with the existence (if not with his labeling) of the conflicts between the low-income and the "creative": "The main job just ahead," he said, "is to settle the split between the two main groups here—those who want to see renewal creatively approached, and the spokesmen for low-income people who are tired of being pushed around and pushed out. I believe we can work it all out."[2]

In 1979 A. P. DeVito, Detroit planning director and former chief of physical and social planning for the U.S. Department of Housing and Urban Development, displayed much the same optimism. He focused on the positive aspects of central business district and riverfront development in his article "Urban Revitalization: The Case of Detroit" and drew a picture of increasing employment, declining crime, and rebounding citizen optimism in the city as a whole.[3]

Another tireless booster of the city is the charismatic and powerful Mayor Coleman Young, who has single-mindedly pursued his vision of a renewed riverfront and downtown Detroit, studded with shining new buildings and teeming with conventioneers and tourists.

Such optimism surely befits public servants paid to be visionaries and leaders. Even they would admit, however, that the metropolitan context of regional growth and central decline has hampered efforts; that the process of city redevelopment has generated problems as well as successes; and that the city is something less than effectively revitalized. A sports arena and a number of new apartment and office buildings have been built in the downtown area, but no major department store now remains open for business. On the east riverfront, anchored at one end by the shining new Renaissance Center, the current city administration has spurred several promising real estate ventures, but the Renaissance Center itself has experienced severe, sustained financial problems. And the mammoth effort involved in keeping industries in the city has not solved the basic problems of industrial retrenchment and chronic unemployment. Meanwhile many low-income residential areas slowly crumble into decay, abandonment, and social disorder, as palliative programs for community development help only a little.[4] The picture in the 1990s could change, as years of effort gain success, but on the whole, the history of redevelopment in Detroit has been a sad tale of the valiant attempts of a city government to counteract and overcome regional trends that could not be overcome.

In order to understand the current state of city redevelopment, it is important to understand why previous efforts have had only limited success. The first part of this chapter focuses on redevelopment efforts under the Detroit Plan and urban renewal. The Detroit Plan was an ambitious design for clearing and rebuilding the entire city, which was soon superseded by the federal urban renewal program. Close examination of the urban renewal program in Detroit, with special focus on redevelopment at the Gratiot site, demonstrates the early tendency of the city to clear low-income, black residents from central-city land in order to try to attract white, middle-income people back to the city as well as to keep medical and educational institutions. The second portion of the chapter describes the current problem of urban redevelopment efforts in Detroit: It is becoming extremely difficult, if not impossible, to disperse limited redevelopment funds effectively among industries, the central business district, and residential areas. In part because everyone has not been able to benefit from those resources, they have been targeted to the central business district and large institutions and industries, in the hope that the benefits from such investments would trickle down to other parts of the city.

The Detroit Plan and the Problem of Slums

It was in the 1930s that the city of Detroit began serious efforts to address the problem of urban deterioration and slums. At that time, of course, no large-scale federal urban renewal program existed, and the city of Detroit had not yet launched its Detroit Plan, a predecessor of urban renewal. What did exist was a small federal housing and urban renewal program administered by the Public Works Administration (PWA), which funded the city's first public housing program. In November of 1933 the director of the Federal Emergency Housing Corporation of the PWA announced that $3.2 million had been awarded to Detroit for slum clearance and low-income housing in the city. That announcement spurred the creation of the Detroit Housing Commission, an agency to which the Michigan legislature gave further renewal responsibilities in January of 1934. In the spring of 1938, with the earmarking of $25 million for Detroit, a golden era in public housing was launched, characterized by the construction, expansion, or initiation of public housing projects at six major sites over a period of four years: the Brewster-Douglass, Parkside, Charles Terrace, Herman Gardens, John W. Smith, and Jeffries homes. During these years Detroit had the second largest public housing program in the United States, smaller only than that of New York City.

By 1942, when construction halted because of World War II, the city housing commission had completed, or was about to complete, 5,071 dwelling units.[5] The public housing projects themselves were sites of considerable racial strife in their early years, largely because of the desire to exclude blacks from projects in white residential areas (discussed in the previous chapter). Also, in their later years they deteriorated to the point that they became pockmarked eyesores as well as dangerous places to live. But when they were first built, the public housing projects of Detroit were shining examples of the triumph of federal dollars over the dirt of urban slums. Families vied to qualify to get into them, and waiting lists lengthened. Many families who had once lived in ramshackle tenements were able to live in subsidized units with sturdy walls and floors, central heating, and reliable plumbing. Careful screening requirements insured that only stable, working-class families who could afford the rent obtained the units.[6]

In spite of the successes of the program, the problem of slums still existed. Five thousand subsidized units were far from sufficient for a city of over 1.5 million. The master plan of the time showed that greater than one-third of the central business district and industrial areas of the city were blighted, and more than one-fifth of the city's residential areas had declined to the status of slums.[7]

In the fall of 1945 James Sweinhart, a *Detroit News* reporter, argued—in a series of articles entitled "What Detroit's Slums Cost Its Taxpayers"—that slums posed a serious problem not only because they bred crime and disease (a popular image of the time was of slums as breeders of disease) but also because they caused devaluation of taxable property, which led to massive declines in tax revenues collectable by the city. Sweinhart claimed that the lack of civic vision caused slums, and he advocated the adoption of zoning laws, redevelopment plans, and other concerted efforts to eliminate slums.[8]

It was within this context that Mayor Jeffries announced the Detroit Plan in November of 1946. The plan was an attempt to replace slum housing with newly built housing, presumedly for low-income people. According to this plan, the city would declare a district as a redevelopment area, condemn the land, acquire parcels from current owners, clear the sites of all structures, and sell the cleared land to developers at one-fifth to one-fourth of the acquisition costs. In order to finance the program, the mayor proposed that $2 million of the city's $100 million tax budget go into a revolving fund, to be refurbished by increased tax revenues collected from redeveloped land. At this rate the city would clear 100 acres a year, or 10,000 acres in 100 years.[9]

The Detroit Plan and its approach of city subsidization of private enterprise emanated from a year of discussion about the relationship between low-income housing, private enterprise, and slum clearance. In March 1945 a New York builder offered to build low-income housing on cleared blighted land, and Jeffries formed a committee to examine his plan. The committee rejected the plan but continued to consider alternative measures to deal with the problem of slum housing. One alternative it considered was to advise the city to replace all slum housing with public housing projects. The committee chose to reject this option for several reasons: It ruled out the use of private enterprise; it would necessitate turning over vast tracts of city land to public housing; and it would have a depressing effect upon the central business district merchants that the public housing units would surround, since trade based on the income of public housing residents would not be lucrative. The second alternative of relying completely on private enterprise to undertake development was not reasonable, the committee decided, because the cost of privately acquiring and preparing land would be prohibitive. Therefore, the committee suggested a third alternative: that the city acquire and clear the land and provide it to developers at a reasonable cost. In reaching this conclusion, the committee relied not only upon the opinions of its own membership of city officials but also upon the testimony and advice of local real estate and building interests (such as the Construction Industry Council and the Builders' Association of Metropolitan Detroit) and, quite probably, upon ideas generated in contemporary proposals to the federal government by national organizations of realtors. The influence of City Treasurer Albert Cobo, future mayor and champion of the role of private enterprise in urban redevelopment, was also evident. According to authors Robert J. Mowitz and Deil S. Wright, "What is clear is that those with the greatest economic stake in the downtown area's future—the banking, investment, retail-business, real estate, and building interests—took an active part along with city officials in developing this strategy for eliminating slums and stemming the tide of public housing with all of its feared consequences for each of the groups involved in the decision."[10] Thus, the plan to replace slum housing with well-built, low-income housing began to metamorphose into a plan to remove slums and yet prevent public housing.

City officials actively supported the Wagner-Ellender-Taft Bill and other legislation designed to institute a national program of slum clearance. The bill that finally resulted, Title I of the Federal Housing Act of 1949, resembled in several ways the Detroit Plan's approach of condemning and acquiring slum areas for resale to private developers at reduced costs. Detroit Common Council President George Edwards, who had testified in favor of federal redevelopment legislation, informed Congress that 70,000 families were doubled up in the city of Detroit, that only 8,000 houses had been built yearly between 1946 and 1948, and that the number of Negroes in Paradise Valley (the city's worst slum) had risen by 50,000 from 1940 to 1950. Edwards declared that one of the city's priorities had to be the construction of housing for Negroes and asked the federal government to help in the effort.[11]

It is ironic that Edwards testified about the problem of lack of housing for low-income and black residents, because urban renewal as implemented in Detroit actually aggravated this problem. In part this was true because of political transition. Edwards, a liberal Democrat, had been the candidate favored for mayor, but he lost the 1949 election to City Treasurer Albert Cobo, who disliked public housing and actively discouraged the development of more public housing in the city. In part Detroit's urban renewal program aggravated the shortage of low-income housing because of flaws and conceptual contradictions in the legislation that actually passed as Title I of the Federal Housing Act of 1949. Quite simply, Title I's mechanism of clearing slums to help solve the problem of slums was contradictory: Clearance could only reduce the housing supply, and not all residents could be supplied with "decent, safe, and sanitary dwellings," for the legislation itself claimed that such did not exist in sufficient numbers. The language was sufficiently vague that cities could, within conformity of the law, tear down slums to build luxury housing, office buildings, and convention centers.[12] Contradictions within the federal law portended problems in Detroit's urban renewal experience.

Slum Clearance through Urban Renewal

The first site selected under Mayor Jeffries's proposed Detroit Plan, and later picked up by the federal urban renewal program, was a 129-acre portion of Hastings Street just south of Gratiot Avenue. The second site was to include 77 acres between Michigan Avenue and Fort Street, an area known as Corktown. Low-income families occupied both sites.[13] As it happened, the mostly black residents of the Gratiot area moved out with a minimum of protest, while the Corktown planning and relocation process was a protracted battle between the city and organized residents, largely members of white ethnic groups, who had seen what had happened to blacks at Gratiot. It was the Gratiot redevelopment project, however, that more starkly illustrated the inherent contradictions in the city's urban renewal program. Gratiot is an important starting point in an overall assessment of urban renewal in Detroit. (See Map 5.1.)

Gratiot/Lafayette Park

It took from 1946 to 1958 for the city of Detroit to condemn 129 acres at the Gratiot redevelopment site, relocate 1,950 black families, prepare and receive approval for four different sets of plans for reuse of the land, and sell the land to a developer. At the end of this period the developer constructed an impressive 22-story apartment building with rents far above the means of former residents.[14] Other phases of redevelopment, including

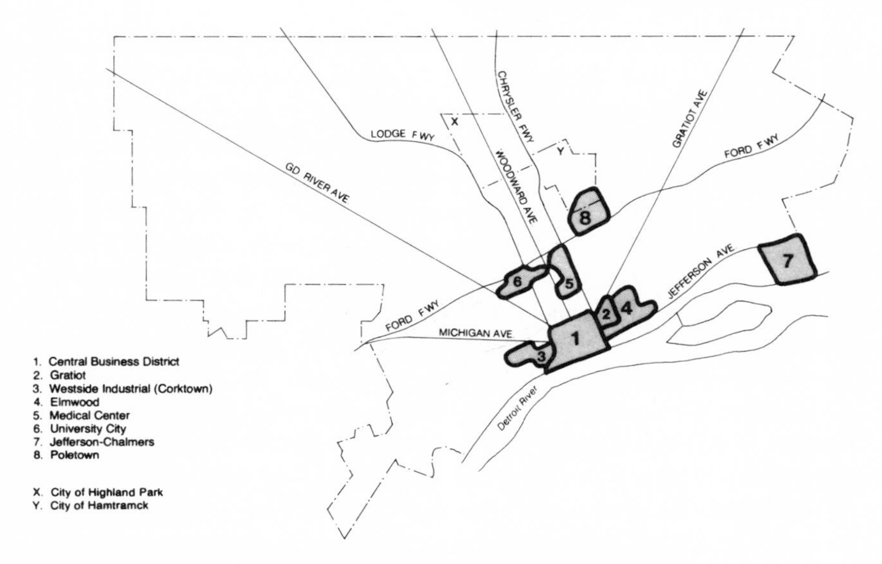

Map 5.1 Selected redevelopment projects in Detroit, 1948–1984

low-rise row houses, were even slower to get underway. Gratiot was not the only urban renewal project to take a long time to implement, but it was certainly one of the most difficult and involved. It is important to examine the experiences at Gratiot in some detail, because precedents set in the case of Gratiot greatly influenced future redevelopment projects in the city. Gratiot and its future extension, Lafayette, together known as Lafayette Park in later years, illustrate early problems with the process of relocation, the procedures for encouraging new uses for the land, and the problem of redeveloping black residential areas in a societal context of racial prejudice and segregation.

Mayor Albert Cobo, who had defeated liberal city council president George Edwards in 1949, was in power in 1951, when the Michigan Supreme Court allowed the city to proceed with the project. Cobo was a conservative fiscal expert, who systematically began to cancel all of the planned public housing projects on vacant sites as soon as he assumed office in 1950. The effect of canceling these sites, which were located in outlying areas of the city, was to concentrate all such projects in the core of the city. Further elimination of projects slated for slum sites meant that the Gratiot redevelopment project held the only possibility for further development of low-income housing, since the Corktown project was intended for industrial development. Cobo pushed for speedy clearance and private redevelopment of the Gratiot land.

Original estimates of the costs of the Gratiot project had been at least $2 million too low, and so city officials were overjoyed with the passage of federal Title I legislation in 1949, which helped to finance the difference between the cost of slum clearance and the price the city would obtain from private developers. Furthermore, the legislation did not mandate the construction of public housing on the cleared site. On the contrary, as a result of a quirk in the law, public housing was difficult to build on renewal sites.[15] This, combined with Cobo's public housing cancellations, significantly slowed the development of low-income housing in the city. Title I did require other conditions, however, and so the money came at a price. The two conditions that posed the most problems for the city were the requirement for an approved city plan for the removal of all displaced families to decent, safe, and sanitary dwellings and the requirement for a redevelopment plan based on permissible reuse of the land.

The federal Housing Act of 1949 had specified that no demolition take place if it would create undue housing hardships and that families be relocated to decent, safe housing within their economic means, but it offered very little guidance as to how this should be done. Detroit faced a severe housing shortage at the time. Furthermore, the Detroit Housing Commission simply did not have the experience necessary to relocate a large number of families in this situation. Its prior relocation experience with residents of sites slated for public housing was far different, because many of those residents were due to move back onto the site when the public housing was constructed and because that relocation experience had taken place before the post–World War II housing shortage. Perhaps the major reason for the difficulty of moving Gratiot residents, however, was racial. The residents were black, and open housing was not even a myth, much less a reality. When housing commission staff interviewed 1,953 families and 989 single persons in May 1950, in preparation for relocation planning, it found that virtually all of the families were black.[16]

Essentially, the only acceptable options for relocated families were three in number: public housing, for those eligible; private home purchase, for those who could afford homes; and rental units in the private market for the remainder. Federal legislation did not require relocation of single persons, so the city did not even bother to keep records of their movements. All three options were inadequate for low-income, black home seekers.

The May 1950 survey showed that over one-half of the families were eligible for public housing, or 1,005 of the 1,953 families. But during the period from July 1950 to December 1951, the housing commission leased 3,175 public housing units to white families and only 648 to black families.

At the beginning of that period the public housing waiting list had 2,247 white families and 5,226 black families. At the end of the period the list had only 574 white families but 7,571 black families. Segregated housing projects meant that there were simply not as many units available for black families as there were for whites. Although the commission claimed in its 1951 relocation plan that it gave high priority to relocated families, only 659 of the Gratiot families were eventually able to get into public housing units, in part because of the segregationist characteristics of the commission's public housing admission practices.

The relocation plan that the commission submitted to the federal government in 1951 showed most concern with the other two housing categories —planned home purchases and planned rentals. Yet here too problems of race and income intervened. Ninety-one of the surveyed Gratiot families planned to buy homes, but the plan noted that prices of new homes were out of reach for many residents, and many of them were not available for black occupancy. The U.S. Supreme Court had declared restrictive covenants unenforceable in 1948, and the plan mentioned this fact as a sign that perhaps housing would soon be available for purchase: "It is submitted that as diminishing segregation makes housing for the first time available to Negroes, it constitutes a provision of housing that meets the requirements."[17] The plan estimated that a two-bedroom house meeting the required standards would require a down payment of $2,000 and monthly expenses of $102. However, of the 20 or so families considering purchases about whom information was available, none had reported being able to afford more than $80 a month. The picture also looked gloomy for the 752 families ineligible for public housing who did not indicate intentions to buy houses. A housing commission survey of 16 apartment buildings, with 11,378 units, found a grand total of three vacancies. In May 1950 the housing commission asked the Detroit Real Estate Brokers' Association, composed of black brokers, to help find rental units for Gratiot relocatees, reasoning that black brokers could find units for black families. The association replied: "The relocation job you have given us is an impossible one. We simply do not have the available vacancies. We not only do not have listings to make available to families displaced by slum clearance, we do not even have listings to take care of our own regular applicants who have been waiting for vacancies for many months."[18]

In spite of these discouraging facts, the relocation plan, displaying a brassy sense of optimism, claimed that acceptable housing could be found to rehouse Gratiot relocatees. And the city did not await either the filing of a relocation plan or the approval of the Federal Home and Housing

Finance Agency (HHFA) before beginning to remove families. The position of Detroit officials was that the Gratiot redevelopment project, announced under the Detroit Plan, had antedated the federal Housing Act of 1949, and therefore, the city could proceed without scrupulous regard for federal regulations. By the time the relocation plan was prepared, in February of 1951, almost 400 families had relocated, many of them because of notification letters implying that demolition was imminent. When the contract was signed with the HHFA in April of 1952, more than 1,000 had moved.

Meanwhile the removal process was causing grave concern among civil rights organizations. The Detroit Urban League issued a report in early 1951 concerning the relocation of the first 258 families. The report charged that the city used high-pressure tactics, failed to notify residents of the commission's responsibilities, and caused considerable hardship among families because of high moving expenses, temporary relocation in unsafe units, and necessary sharing of living quarters. Detroit Housing Commission Director Harry Durbin denied the accusations, but the Detroit Urban League took the report to federal housing officials, who pressured the city to change its notification letter. The new letter seemed to placate federal officials for a while, until the city reported in late 1951 that the locations of 35 percent of the relocated families were unknown. Federal officials asked for a search for the families whose locations were unknown, and in September 1952, after the search proved only partly satisfactory, federal officials asked Detroit to find an impartial, reputable source to undertake a research project designed to answer a number of very specific questions about the relocation process. The city, after preliminary overtures to researchers, refused to contract the study.[19]

By February 1956 the housing commission reported that the site was clear and that only 8 families for whom the commission had responsibility remained on off-site locations. In the final tally of 1,953 families, the status of almost half of the former residents—those who had "refused suitable housing," moved owing rent, or disappeared—was uncertain. In 1959 the urban renewal coordinator estimated that most of the former residents probably still lived within a two-mile radius of the Gratiot site. Since much of this land was slated for further redevelopment, many of the same families would be relocated again.[20]

The problem of how the Gratiot land should be redeveloped was even more difficult than the problem of relocation. At first the city planned to use the cleared Gratiot site for a mixture of uses, including additional public housing. As events developed, the city decided not to build subsidized rental housing, but it had a hard time attracting development projects of any kind. The basic problem was that urban renewal purported to alleviate the problem of slums for low-income people and to encourage redevelopment by private enterprise simultaneously. It was not often possible to do both.

The staff of the Detroit City Plan Commission proposed that the Gratiot land be used for a mixture of low-density, two-story apartment units and high-density, multistory units. But the president of the Builders' Association of Metropolitan Detroit questioned whether builders would be able to build units with rents low enough for low-income tenants. Local and federal officials also expressed concern that the redeveloped area should be open to blacks, who had traditionally faced housing discrimination, yet should become neither a low-income black enclave nor a segregated, high-income white enclave. The mixed plan approved in October of 1951 was a compromise. Aimed primarily at middle-income families, it also included a provision for units affordable to the previous residents of the site.

Local builders dramatically expressed their skepticism about the feasibility of this plan. At the first public auction of Gratiot land, held on July 30, 1952, when the auctioneer called for bids on the property, the 50 builders and brokers simply sat silent, refusing to bid.[21] In public the prospective bidders said that the density standards that the housing commission required were unreasonably low and that building costs would place the housing far above projected rentals. In private the developers expressed doubts about the feasibility of the mixture of low- and middle-income housing that the city requested. Whites, they felt, would simply not move into housing in that area if income levels and races were mixed. Therefore, they claimed they would have to aim the housing toward the "Negro market." A developer would have to increase the density in order to aim for this market and make a profit; not one was optimistic about the chances of selling or renting to both blacks and whites in the same area.[22]

While the Detroit Housing Commission sought bids for the Gratiot property auction, mortgage broker Walter Gessell and city administrator James W. Bell wrote a pamphlet suggesting that local people form a nonprofit corporation to acquire and oversee the development of Lafayette. Mayor Cobo brushed aside their proposal, but Gessell and Bell eventually approached the *Detroit News* with their pamphlet. In immediate response to the newspaper's feature article on the proposal, United Auto Workers President Walter Reuther sent a telegram to the mayor and the common council asking them to set up a citizens' committee. Reuther also pledged $10,000 in UAW money to explore the Gessell and Bell proposal. This placed the mayor in an awkward position. He had already appointed a bloated blue-ribbon board of 230 members to function as the Detroit of Tomorrow Committee and, supposedly, save the core of the city. Cobo, who hated to be pressured into anything, also intensely disliked Reuther. If he were to set up another redevelopment committee, his action would undermine the authority of his own housing director, Harry Durbin.

It is a sign of the desperation Cobo felt that he did name a Citizens' Redevelopment Committee of 11 members, but he made Director Durbin the chairman. He also made sure the committee included adequate corporate representation. He appointed to the "executive" inner group of the larger committee Walter Reuther, proposal coauthor Walter Gessell, Walter Gehrke (board chairman of the First Federal Savings and Loan Association of Detroit), and Foster Winter (vice-president of the J. L. Hudson Company and a trustee of the Urban Land Institute). The mayor also named pamphlet coauthor James Bell as director. Local bankers, merchants, and unions contributed $50,000 to supplement the UAW's contribution. The Citizens' Redevelopment Committee, in its first report of September 13, 1954, proposed the organization of a nonprofit urban renewal corporation empowered to acquire, own, and sell or lease land in the project area. In the meantime the committee, which wanted a single developer for the area, hired several noted architectural firms, including Victor Gruen and Associates, to draw up proposed redevelopment plans. At this stage the committee still made ambiguous references to low-cost housing that was to be included in the project.[23]

The Citizens' Redevelopment Committee became the Citizens' Redevelopment Corporation in April of 1955. Additional funds for the redevelopment corporation came from three auto-making companies ($180,000 from Ford, General Motors, and Chrysler), the UAW ($50,000), the J. L. Hudson Company ($50,000), and other local corporations. By late 1955 the corporation brought in famed architect Ludwig Mies van der Rohe as chief designer. By late 1958 a 22-story apartment tower opened in what was now called the Lafayette Park redevelopment area, and by the early 1960s low-rise units were offered for sale and rent to middle-income families.

In the final analysis, the composition of the group that planned the Lafayette Park project was similar to that of other coalitions and organizations in other cities. The heavy support of local merchants, bankers, and unions and the importance of the automobile industry in funding the project made it no surprise that, at some point in the planning of the project, the proposal for including low-income housing was quietly dropped. Although both blacks and whites subsequently moved into the area, few of low-income did.[24] Prior plans for housing former residents at the site had fallen prey to the desire for middle-income housing.

Only much later, with the advent of federal rent subsidy programs and cooperatives, did developers build low- and moderate-income housing, located mostly in the adjacent Elmwood Park area. Today much of the newer low-income housing in the city is located in areas fairly close to the old Gratiot site, including Elmwood Park and Forest Park. But it was many years before these units were built, and the avowed policy when Lafayette was developed was to build units for middle- and upper-income residents. City officials and developers had already laid the foundation for this trend of displacing the low-income units for the sake of the higher-income units, but they were urged on in its consolidation by a panel of the Urban Land Institute.

During the period between the launching of the Gratiot project and the initiation of the Elmwood Park project, a team of Urban Land Institute affiliates paid a visit to the city to assess the current state of the city's renewal program. In the process of their examination, they legitimized the city's approach to redevelopment.

The Urban Land Institute (ULI) panel members met for only a few days, February 14–18, 1955, but their influence belied the time they spent in the city. The *Detroit News* sponsored the deliberations and report of the ULI Central City Council panel convened to study downtown Detroit. An examination of the list of panel members seems to indicate that neither local people nor academics served on the committee. Rather, membership included prominent business people and professionals from around the country, representing banking, realty, and transit firms. The panel made a number of comments, but some of the most influential were its recommendations on Lafayette Park, then known as the "Gratiot tract." In a supplemental report to its recommendations on the downtown area, the panel attempted to steer city officials away from the already faint notion that the only people who would occupy the central city were those of restricted income. According to the panel, city renewal should be directed toward those at the middle rather than the bottom of the income ladder, with special targeting toward the large number of workers able to pay market prices for housing. Walter S. Schmidt, founder and first president of the ULI and member of the panel, elaborated:

> It is the feeling of the panel that as slums are wiped out, as they should be in increasing degree in your city, the land thus recovered should be put to its best use for the best benefit of the future city. We

> feel that such residential construction should not be in the form of the lowest-rent property, because that may become a slum again. . . . We feel that this close-in construction should be attractive to persons who are able to pay an economic rent for modern apartments or for homes that would normally be constructed elsewhere in the region for your better paid workers.[25]

Much of the panel's recommendation made sense. Panelist Cyrus Hackstaff, of Denver's Frederick R. Ross Investment Company, was absolutely correct in his comment that it cost a lot of money to build new housing and that a more economical approach might be to upgrade existing residences for use by the low-income population. As he pointed out, "They [the low-income population] would not only have cheaper rent, but would get away from the ghetto living that public housing encourages."[26] The problem was that the panel's recommendation, and the city's subsequent actions, did not take into full account the reality of the situation for low-income families. Former residents of the Gratiot site had disappeared into a surrounding black ghetto that was already overcrowded. At that point in time no rehabilitation programs existed that could begin to match the funds available in the 1930s for public housing or in the 1950s for urban renewal, although in 1953 the city did launch a small housing conservation program with federal funds. Even with six public housing projects, waiting lists for available public housing units ran exceptionally long. Furthermore, while the ideal of integrating lower-income families into the general population may have seemed reasonable, those familiar with the problem at hand surely realized that housing segregation practices made such dispersion all but impossible for black residents, the very residents removed from the Gratiot site and later from the Elmwood Park site. Public housing, with all its flaws, was simply the only practical way of quickly housing a population in great need of at least as many housing units as had been cleared out.

The panel, like the mayor, evidently had a great antipathy toward public housing. The earliest plan for the reuse of the Gratiot land had specified the construction of 3,600 units of public housing. By the time the ULI panel convened in 1955, the number of planned public housing units had dropped to 900. Panel members opposed even this many public housing units, although the chairman commented that this might not be too many "if they were separated from the rest." In the end no public housing went into the Gratiot/Lafayette Park area. By 1955 the city had built 8,155 public housing units, and it built virtually no more until the 1970s.[27]

The *Detroit News* gave extensive coverage to the ULI report and drilled its findings and recommendations into newspaper readers. The report was a significant factor in subsequent changes in the Gratiot/Lafayette plan. The report was issued two months before the incorporation of the Citizens' Redevelopment Corporation.[28] The report undoubtedly also influenced plans for subsequent renewal projects in the city, largely because it legitimized the existing biases of city officials: that redevelopment should remove slums and the low-income people who occupied those slums and replace them with housing for middle- and upper-income people.

Urban Renewal in the City

By the middle of the 1960s the city of Detroit had six major renewal projects either in the process of completion or under contract. These included the original Gratiot site, the Lafayette extension, and the West Side Industrial Redevelopment project (Corktown)—all near completion—and the Elmwood Park, Medical Center, and Central Business District projects. (See Map 5.1.) With the possible exception of the Medical Center project, all of these first urban renewal projects were located in areas near the central business district of the city of Detroit. All six lay within the ring formed by the semicircular Grand Boulevard, referred to in city documents as the old city or inner city, an area that city planners have consistently targeted for reclamation by renewal. Elmwood Park, a three-stage, 474-acre project, lay to the east of Gratiot and Lafayette; in total, the size of the conterminous projects established the area south of Gratiot as a primary district for clearance and redevelopment. The Medical Center, later joined by the University City projects near Wayne State University, extended the reach of urban renewal between the critical downtown areas and the major institutions of Wayne State University and its neighboring hospitals.

In general, redevelopment projects under urban renewal managed to increase the value of tax revenues coming into the city from redeveloped areas, a goal of the original Detroit Plan. However, urban renewal in Detroit never quite managed to overcome the administrative problems that led to the delays, duplication of effort, cost overruns, and long periods of vacancy that characterized the projects of other cities in the country as well. Official relocation practices improved over the years, but the concerted effort to remove slums and attract revenue succeeded in only a limited fashion, and the cost of that effort for the original residents of the areas was high.

In the early years of the program, city officials fully expected urban renewal to provide increased tax revenues. In a report issued in the mid-1960s, *Urban Renewal and Tax Revenue: Detroit's Success Story*, the Detroit Housing Commission claimed that the old assessed value of the properties on the Gratiot site was $2,844,000, while the new assessed value of the apartment towers and cooperative apartment units totaled about $15 million.[29] Another report by the Detroit City Plan Commission, *Renewal and Revenue*, offered similar findings for Gratiot and other projects.[30] The high estimated tax assessment of postredevelopment land did not take into account the fact that cleared land remained vacant for years, offering absolutely no tax revenues, while the city wooed developers and overcame administrative delays.

If one separately enumerates the phases of major projects and additional minor urban renewal and conservation projects, the number of projects that the city of Detroit began between 1949 and 1971 totals at least 27. Into those 27 projects the city poured $116.1 million in federal grants and $174.2 million of its own funds. Of those projects, only 4 had been "closed out" (because of completion or lack of additional federal funding) during that 22-year period: Gratiot/Lafayette Park, Medical Center Phase 1, University City Phase 1, and the neighborhood conservation project in the Mack-Concord areas.[31]

The projects dragged on for years, in large part because over 20 government and nongovernment groups had to approve or develop some aspect of urban renewal projects and various agencies and officials seldom agreed.[32] Initial redevelopment of the Gratiot site lasted from 1946 to 1958, and the total amount of time from the beginning to the end, or close out, of that project was 15 years. At other sites the process was slow even when a buyer was assured. In January of 1961 the city announced the initiation of University City Phase 1, the first phase of redevelopment specifically initiated for the purpose of Wayne State University expansion. But the first structure, a parking garage planned for the site, was not begun until March of 1969. Elmwood Park, originally intended as a site for public housing but eventually developed as town houses for several different income classes, received initial council approval in 1960 and sold the first four tracts in 1965. Phase 2 of Elmwood Park required in excess of 10 years and Phase 4 in excess of 12 years. In April of 1971 residents of undeveloped areas of Elmwood Park filed suit because of the delay in land acquisition, demanding payment for the deterioration of property values they were suffering as a result of the long delay in the purchasing process. Carl Levin, member of the Detroit Common Council, was so upset that he claimed he didn't know whether the city should act as plaintiff or defendant in the case; the council, too, was distressed by the long delay.[33] Logjams in the Detroit administrative process greatly reduced the speed and therefore the effectiveness of urban renewal in Detroit. Land lay barren for years, posing clear danger for passers-by, who sometimes fell prey to thieves or muggers hiding in the tall weeds. Wild dog packs freely roamed the Elmwood Park site and lived in its vacant houses. Homeowners hung on to houses only to see property values decline because of delays. It was this situation, coupled with the uneven relocation record of the city, that caused widespread disenchantment with the city's urban renewal process.

Tallies of official revenue increases rarely included the costs of administrative delays, and neither did they include the human costs of the redevelopment process. Procedures for relocation assistance and benefits gradually improved over the years, in part because of 1970 federal legislation that set minimum requirements for relocation benefits. During the active years of the urban renewal program, however, the city never could overcome the basic problem of urban renewal: Residents of settled areas had to be removed, and they were not likely, at least in the short run, to be able to afford housing in the redeveloped area. Sometimes the redeveloped area did not even include new housing. While not all suffered from the process, many did. It was this basic problem that the city has had to face even in more recent projects, such as the Central Industrial Park (Poletown).

Reliable information about the experience of relocation and displacement in the urban renewal program is available only because the city's Community Renewal Program eventually contracted with Wayne State University social scientists Eleanor P. Wolf and Charles Lebeaux to conduct an assessment of relocation in urban renewal project areas.[34] The research team recorded, two years after the fact, the relocation experiences of former residents and business owners of the Elmwood Park Phase 1 and Medical Center Phase 1 projects. Their findings did much to document the social costs of urban renewal.

The team found that 95 percent of the Elmwood Park Phase 1 and Medical Center Phase 1 relocatees were black and that the former residents also tended to be elderly and of low income: One-fourth of the former residents were 65 years of age or older, and one-fourth of the households received relief payments of some kind. One-third of the relocatees expressed hostile feelings toward the process of urban renewal, and 44 percent said they would move back into their former neighborhoods if that were possible. Almost all of the respondents expressed dismay over the danger they had felt because of the decline of their old neighborhoods during the long period between site designation and physical relocation.

Many felt that they had not received adequate assistance from the city in their search for new housing: Thirty percent had to search on foot, 20 percent by public bus, and one by wheelchair. Only 3 percent reported that they moved into a house that the city helped find for them. Also, in spite of the fact that 60 percent of the relocatees felt their current housing was better than their former housing, the majority preferred their old neighborhoods. Longing for the old neighborhood was closely related to emotional ties with former neighbors and neighborhood institutions. Of the 80 percent who perceived relocation as having a negative impact on their lives, half felt that their sense of loss had never been completely eliminated. "A few even felt that relocation marked the end of meaningful life," the researchers noted.[35]

The experiences of local business owners were also traumatic. Of those businesses that the city removed from the Elmwood Park Phase 1 site, only about half survived. The business owners who managed to stay in business and who sometimes benefited from relocation had clientele drawn from the entire city rather than from the neighborhood. The effect on most businesses, however, was devastating; 69 percent of the 64 businesses in Elmwood Park Phase 1 were small, neighborhood convenience stores, mainly operated by owners who depended on surrounding residents for customers. Half of the businesses were owned by blacks, and all but two black businesses were local convenience stores. Fifty-seven percent of the businesses owned by blacks did not survive relocation. The small, black-owned barbershops, grocery stores, and pool halls, which were so unlikely to survive relocation, were also important community institutions. The majority performed noneconomic functions that greatly helped neighborhood cohesion: They extended credit, supervised juveniles, and served as centers of communication and contact. Many of these businesses simply could not survive as neighborhood establishments once their neighborhoods were destroyed. Some former proprietors remained bitter years after their relocation.[36] Urban renewal had killed a large pocket of viable minority enterprises.

Institutions and Citizen Protest

While people in targeted residential areas often suffered because of urban renewal, major institutions benefited. The two major institutions that benefited from the redevelopment process, largely under the urban renewal program, were the Detroit Medical Center and Wayne State University. Each was able to pay prices far below market value for land that the city, rather than the institutions themselves, condemned and cleared, using city and federal urban renewal money.

The Detroit Medical Center project began in 1954, when the directors of Grace, Harper, Women's, and Children's hospitals met with the director of the City Plan Commission to discuss the problems of surrounding blight and their inability to expand the institutions' facilities. As a result of this meeting, the four hospitals formed a "citizens' committee" composed of the dean of the College of Medicine of Wayne State University and the directors and selected trustees of the hospitals. The committee retained a planning consultant to develop and implement an overall plan for the area, with the "blessings and cooperation of the city government," which gave not only staff assistance but also office space for the hospitals' planning consultant.[37] The plan, essentially completed in 1956, provided for a "fully self-contained urban complex": a public medical-service center; a cultural center for medical research and training; and a residential area with its own shopping and service centers, schools, and parks. The site was to encompass 307 acres.[38] The problem was, of course, that much of the site was already occupied by low-income residents. Therefore, the committee presented the plan to the city in the form of a proposal for an urban renewal site, which the hospitals would purchase when cleared.

Most of the dollars for land purchase and construction were to come from foundations and wealthy individuals identifiable as members of the city's elite. By 1968, $12 million had been donated to the Harper-Webber Medical Center Fund (chaired by Joseph L. Hudson, Jr., of the Hudson Department Store), with major donations coming from the Webber Foundation ($3 million), the Kresge Foundation ($1.5 million), and local wealthy people, such as Mrs. Edsel Ford ($750,000). The U.S. Department of Health, Education, and Welfare provided $15.5 million for grants for hospital construction. The total costs of the Medical Center exceeded $300 million in federal, state, city, and private funds.[39]

The Detroit Medical Center, once completed, was composed of six corporation members, including Children's, Detroit General, the consolidated Harper-Grace, and Hutzel hospitals, the Rehabilitation Institute, and Wayne State University medical school. Over 10,000 people are now employed by the member institutions, compared with about 3,500 at the old site. Because of the Medical Center construction, the city managed to retain institutions that might have otherwise left.[40] But the redevelopment project had the same problems and delays as other urban renewal projects. Although the project was announced by the city in September 1959, only two of the four planned phases had been accomplished ten years later.[41]

Community opposition to the original plans for the Medical Center focused not on the right of the city to proceed with the project, but rather on the issues of relocation of black churches and discrimination against blacks in the hospitals. Early plans for the Medical Center removed all churches from the site except white churches, an action that outraged the predominantly black residents of the site. The black ministers formed an alliance in 1961, the Detroit Fellowship of Urban Renewal Churches, specifically for the purpose of protecting their interests in the renewal project. Several churches filed suit to gain the right to buy land within the Medical Center complex. At the same time other groups, such as the Urban League, vociferously protested the use of public funds to assist hospitals that had well-documented policies of discrimination against black health professionals and patients. They used persistent lobbying techniques to threaten the project's urban renewal funds.

In the end the groups obtained important concessions. They were, in fact, the first opposition groups in the city to gain any changes in proposed urban renewal projects. A few black churches were allowed to buy land and rebuild within the new complex. Although these churches could not convince the city to develop low-income housing to allow relocated residents to live in the area, some of the churches, such as Friendship Baptist Church, were able to sponsor their own income-assisted housing in the area, with the assistance of federal housing programs. Likewise, the antidiscrimination forces succeeded in gaining pledges of nondiscrimination from the hospitals. Although the hospitals did not entirely change their policies, monitoring over the next few months recorded discernible improvements.[42]

University City projects are another example of institutional projects causing great sacrifice on the part of surrounding neighborhoods. After the city declared the area near Wayne State University an urban renewal site in 1960, the neighborhood changed rapidly from a residential area of old but sturdy homes to a blighted slum. According to one newspaper reporter writing in 1970, Don Tschirhard, "For ten years, residents in an eight-block area near Wayne State University have been watching their neighbors' homes burn down. . . . They want the city to buy their homes . . . so that they can move away from an area which was once a Detroit beauty spot, but which is now a habitat for thugs and vandals."[43] Eight years lapsed between the city's announcement of University City Phase 1 in January 1961 and its sale of the land to the university in 1969. Most of the project area was used for an athletic campus, a fact that led to emotional disputes between the university and a neighborhood that resented being relocated for the sake of a football field. Other phases of the project remained in process even longer.[44] The University City projects, while not an unqualified success, certainly allowed the university to save money: During the five-year period before the 1961 declaration of an urban renewal project area, the university had spent $7 million on acquiring land and clearing surrounding residences.[45]

Protest groups in the University City area were more aggressive than those in the Medical Center area. The fiery West Central Organization picketed, arranged meetings with state officials, distributed newsletters, nd peppered the city council and the local media with statements of protest.[46] Another group, the governing board of the Model Cities project, won a court decision to halt the project until the city clarified and improved relocation plans, reduced the size of the project area, and adopted rehabilitation projects in lieu of some of the planned clearance.[47]

When the Medical Center and University City projects were first initiated, federal laws did not require a great deal of citizen participation. By the time the first phase of the Medical Center was closed out in 1972, however, citizen protest against the Corktown project, the Medical Center relocation activities, and the nearby University City projects had generated a state law requiring organized citizen district councils (CDCs) at redevelopment sites. Spurred in particular by the activities of several vocal organizations in the University City area, this state legislation, implemented in 1968, led to the establishment of CDCs in 14 city urban renewal areas, including the Medical Center and the two University City areas. Organized citizen protest had accomplished organized citizen input in geographic areas far beyond those covered under new Model Cities legislation and long before federally required citizen groups under the Community Development Block Grants program.[48]

The official citizen district council for the University City area, however, virtually watched from the sidelines as various groups, such as the Model Cities board, the Committee of Concerned Property Owners, and the People Concerned about Urban Renewal, jockeyed for power. The CDC board, with 10 of its 25 members appointed by the mayor, obtained no major concessions that met the concerns of these disparate groups.[49]

The citizen protest movements of the 1960s and 1970s, while partially effective, also had significant shortcomings. Protests against the Medical Center obtained land for black churches and positions for black physicians, but they did little or nothing to alleviate the relocation problems of the former residents of the site, at least not in the short run. Residents relocated from the project site suffered extreme financial and emotional distress. Although in time some low-income people were able to move into the vicinity of the project, the time lag was extensive, as these church-sponsored projects did not begin to appear until well into the 1960s. In the meantime, in great part because of time delays in the project, surrounding residential areas declined, as residents moved out and remaining housing deteriorated. By the time University City neighborhood groups won concessions, project delays had already depopulated much of the surrounding neighborhood. Competition among groups that varied widely in size and militancy reduced overall effectiveness, and none of the groups succeeded in sponsoring low-income housing similar to that developed by churches in the Medical Center area. These problems were different from the narrow-focus problem of protest groups in the Medical Center area but just as important.

Overall, urban renewal in Detroit involved administrative ineffectiveness, long delays, and painful relocation of former residents. The effort was supposed to stimulate the rise and expansion of crucial institutions and industries and the revitalization of residential neighborhoods. Urban renewal, however, allowed the city to make only limited progress in these areas. A part of the problem was the conflict in goals and means: Who was supposed to benefit from urban renewal? Although the city used the program to clear slums, the beneficiaries of the rebuilding process were not slum dwellers. The people who had the most influence in defining redevelopment were citizens of powerful position: members of the Gratiot Redevelopment Committee, panelists from the Urban Land Institute, hospital administrators on the "citizens' committee" of the Medical Center, and administrators from Wayne State University. Groups of neighborhood residents in the Medical Center and University Center areas had some influence but mainly as reactors to the process. The group that author Lynda Ann Ewen has referred to as Detroit's "ruling class" influenced redevelopment but did so in a disjointed fashion.[50] During the urban renewal years, the closest thing to an effective "growth coalition" was the Medical Center Committee, which had the very specific goal of rebuilding hospitals and their surroundings, a much more modest vision than that of many other growth coalitions in other cities.[51] The narrow goals of the several redevelopment groups were met: Gratiot did turn into a higher-income enclave, the Medical Center was built, and Wayne State University did expand. These successes, however, were not sufficient to reverse decay, and their negative effects may have actually damaged the city's vitality.

Balancing Redevelopment Resources

After the late 1960s the focus of city redevelopment policy shifted, as did federal policy, away from the wholesale slum-clearance characteristic of urban renewal. Several events in the city of Detroit had made new policy directions necessary: the increasingly strident citizen protests against urban renewal projects; the new directions in federal policy, as embodied in the War on Poverty and Model Cities programs; and the Detroit rebellion of 1967. Specifically because of the devastating impact of the rebellion, the city's business elite created New Detroit, Inc., a nonprofit organization designed to placate the city's rebellious masses.[52] New Detroit's programs, along with those of the War on Poverty and Model Cities, provided assistance in the growing problem areas of unemployment and poverty, education and health. However, after it became obvious that the antipoverty and Model Cities approaches to attacking both physical and social problems would give way to the physical development strategy embodied in the Community Development Block Grants program of 1974, the city moved away from human services. It focused instead on continued central business district refurbishment, residential rehabilitation, and economic development policies designed to keep institutions and industries from leaving the central city.

Official economic development plans and master plans since that time have consistently ranked neighborhood development as a high priority, just as they have ranked industrialization and renewal of the central business district. The bitter tradeoff facing the city, however, is that it has not always been possible to support, simultaneously, neighborhood residential areas, industries, and the central business district to the extent necessary. A closer look at the history of recent industrial, neighborhood, and central business district development illustrates these trends.

Keeping Industry: A Poletown Strategy

In the city of Detroit industrial obsolescence and loss had been evident as early as the 1950s. A 1954 study of industrial areas showed that as much as 67.3 percent of the industrial acreage, or 4,785 acres, lay in varying states of decline, ranging from severe to mild obsolescence, and only 32.7 percent earned a relatively problem-free, "Class 1" designation.[53] Industries began to leave the city, assisted in no small part by the extensive highway network, which allowed easy flight as well as easy access. Between 1950 and 1980 the population of the city dropped 35 percent, from 1,849,568 to

1,203,339. But the number of manufacturing jobs fell 68 percent from 349,000 to 113,000, a 236,000 job drop that was only feebly counterbalanced by the 40,000 increase in health, education, and other professional service jobs. During the same period the number of manufacturing jobs within the entire SMSA remained fairly steady.[54]

Mayor Coleman Young, elected in 1973, was very aware of the loss of employment and industry and its effects on the city, and he developed policies to counter that loss. Encouraged by the Carter administration, in 1976 Young presented the federal government with a $2.5 billion economic development plan, which included ten projects costing a total of $526 million in its industrial development component.[55] Although the federal government did not give Detroit money for much of the plan, it did channel important resources to Detroit, and the city used federal grants to bolster industrial development. The request for $56.3 million for the 1978–1979 Community Development Block Grants allocation, for example, included a $5 million request to acquire property for Riverside Industrial Park, where the city hoped that John DeLorean would build a sports car assembly plant. In fact, Detroit made an offer of a $38.4 million package to DeLorean, in an international competition for the firm that Northern Ireland won.[56]

The loss of the DeLorean plant, the steady decline of the Chrysler Corporation, and the loss of other automobile firms combined to create a crisis for economic development in the city. As both city and corporation officials in Washington, D.C., argued for loan guarantees for the virtually bankrupt Chrysler, an internal city administration document spoke of the need to "bulwark Chrysler at home." It chronicled the implications of Chrysler retrenchment for employment in the city and projected that "unless something is done," 23,951 Detroit residents would lose jobs by 1985 as a result of Chrysler's current planning.[57] Although the city's resources were obviously limited, the mayor publicly announced in November of 1979 that Detroit would give tax breaks and loans totaling $30 to $40 million to the Jefferson Avenue plant. Mayor Young also told the Senate Banking Committee that the city was considering building a new plant for Chrysler, costing $150 million.[58]

In its 1979 Overall Economic Development Plan, the city declared that one of its industrial development strategies was to prepare a large industrial site for a single large industry. The city actually proceeded to develop Delray as a mammoth industrial site, a 375-acre parcel in southwest Detroit, even though it had obtained no commitment from any large industry to use the site.[59]

Then two events intervened to turn attention from Delray to Poletown and from Chrysler to General Motors. First Chrysler closed the huge Dodge Main plant on January 4, 1980, idling thousands of workers and leaving an abandoned hulk of a factory. Second General Motors issued a May 1980 challenge to the city to find a site big enough for a modern plant, clear it within a year, and deliver it to General Motors.[60]

Poletown, known officially as the Central Industrial Park project (CIPP), was to become one of the largest industrial redevelopment projects ever attempted.[61] Poletown required concentrated investment in one large project that would provide thousands of jobs in one stroke. All the city had to do was provide an area of between 500 and 600 acres, rectangular in shape, with access to both a freeway and a mainline railroad, all cleared and ready for development within a year.

That General Motors expected the city to clear an entire site of that size within a year was phenomenal. But Mayor Young made it quite clear to his staff, to General Motors, and to the public that the Poletown project was one of the top priorities of his administration. He selected a task force, which after screening nine potential sites, selected one of 465 acres, which spanned the boundary between Detroit and the smaller city of Hamtramck. The site held 1,176 residential, commercial, and industrial structures; 996 families; and 634 individuals: All would have to be cleared in a matter of months. General Motors would buy the cleared site for $8 million, but in the meantime the governmental costs incurred would exceed $200 million.[62]

In return, the city of Detroit expected to gain reuse of a site, Dodge Main, which had once employed over 35,000 people. The new plant that General Motors planned would provide a maximum of only 6,000 direct jobs, but 20,000 jobs would potentially be created indirectly through related industries and businesses. Detroit also would receive a 4.5 percent increase in its property tax base, assuming an estimated assessed value of $274 million for the plant. After 12 years, when the city-granted 50 percent tax rebate expired, Detroit and Hamtramck would receive a net property tax revenue of about $21 million a year.[63]

The benefits were long-term, but the costs were not. The city was going to have to pay in order to meet its side of the bargain. Somehow Detroit would have to raise $200 million. One of the first financing tactics that the city used was to borrow $100 million from the HUD Section 108 loan program. The city would have to repay the loan within nine years, or HUD could tap the city's annual Community Development Block Grants allocation for repayment. City officials also decided to spend $65 million from Community Development Block Grants projects that had not yet been started, money that would have to be repaid once those projects began. In addition to borrowing money from its housing and community development program, Detroit applied for and received money from the federal Economic Development Administration, the Urban Mass Transportation Administration, and two state agencies. The city topped off this money, and other revenue received from property sales, with the company's 12-year tax rebate.

In answer to the question of whether or not it was wise for the city to spend so much money for the project, and in addition grant a rebate that would cost the city over $60 million in lost tax revenue over 12 years, GM officials replied that tax relief was an important factor in their overall expenditure of $500 million for a new plant. They also said that they owed it to their stockholders to ask for all the benefits the company could get. The city of Detroit, for its part, took no chances and gave General Motors all that it asked for. Detroit attorney Ronald Reosti, the lawyer who handled the Poletown Neighborhood Council's case against the city, bewailed the situation: "Cities and communities have to surrender their constitutions if necessary to get private development. In essence, private development is so essential [that] the only way the city can compete and make greener pastures is to keep giving the city away. It's a nothing strategy."[64]

Detroit, like other cities, counties, and states across the country, had decided that if it was necessary to spend money and make tax concessions in order to keep industry, then it would spend the money and make the concessions. The fact that this is, in sum, a no-win situation for the nation's localities did not change the hard realities of the moment.

If the cities involved were to receive a new plant and future tax revenues and if the corporation was to receive a new plant, then the only real losers in the whole project would be the residents of the area, who would have to move out. Even among these residents, losses were not always evident. Some residents publicly expressed relief at having the city buy their property, thus allowing them to move out of a declining area. Some of these residents formed the core of the Citizen District Council, the official citizen advisory body for the city's project. For others, principally the older Polish residents, the CIPP was a tragedy that threatened to disrupt their lives severely. Residents had begun efforts to revitalize their neighborhood in the late 1970s and had formed a task force, the Revitalization Task Force, which had received a small grant to renovate a local shopping area just before the city announced its Central Industrial Park plans. The task force leaders, who protested that the city had misled them by encouraging their redevelopment efforts, formed the nucleus of the organized opposition group the Poletown Neighborhood Council (PNC).

The PNC brought suit against the city and led protests that gained nationwide media attention. The group was largely Polish, although the entire residential area was not. More than half the area residents were black, and they also included Albanians, Yemenis, and Filipinos. Older Polish residents, some of whom had lived in the area for 40 to 50 years, formed the core of the protest group. Many had grown dependent on the convenient location of their neighborhood, which was within walking distance of bus stops and convenience grocery stores. Many had previously resisted moving to the suburbs, as had their children, and opted to stay near friends that they had known for decades.

The PNC had many of the resources that conventional wisdom suggests are necessary for successful community organization.[65] Although many groups lack administrative expertise, the PNC had good leadership with skills in administration as well as community politics. The group also had political support, but Mayor Young's administration strongly opposed the PNC. Several block clubs, Polish organizations, and other groups supported the PNC. Its most important support came from Ralph Nader, a well-known national leader in the consumer movement. Nader has a long history of organized opposition to faulty automobile products as well as an extensive legal staff. The PNC's financial resources, some of which came from Nader's organization, allowed it to pursue several court cases that could possibly have halted the project. Its media campaign, which led to a spate of sympathetic articles, television interviews, and films, took full advantage of public sympathies.[66]

But throughout the process of protest, the officially sanctioned vehicle for citizen participation, the Citizen District Council (CDC), supported the city. Only a few members of the CDC were PNC members. Like most citizen councils formed under the Community Development Block Grants, its powers were only advisory. This official organization simply had no power to set or influence policy, even if the majority of its membership had supported the PNC, which it did not. The CDC organized counter-rallies in support of the Poletown redevelopment project.[67]

When the Poletown Neighborhood Council sued to stop the project, the potential for success was already slim. In a 1954 case the U.S. Supreme Court had ruled that the legislature clearly has the right to declare the public interest—a decision that implied that if the Detroit City Council and the Michigan legislature decided it was in the public interest to condemn land and sell it for the private use of General Motors, then it was indeed in the public interest to do so. The Michigan Supreme Court upheld the city's right to proceed with the Poletown condemnation. In a long, passionate dissenting opinion, Justice James Ryan argued that the majority opinion was motivated by circumstances rather than law. He said that the law clearly states that eminent domain is supposed to be used only for land taken for public *use*, not for land taken for public benefit such as job creation. By the time Ryan issued his dissenting opinion, the project was already well underway. The city of Detroit had proceeded quickly because of the Michigan "quick take" law, which the city of Detroit had requested in anticipation of such a project. The legislature had passed the "quick take" law a mere two months before General Motors issued its original challenge to the city. According to the law, a city could undertake rapid condemnation and clearance of a site even while litigation over condemnation awards was pending.[68]

The city moved steadily toward its General Motors–imposed deadline of one year. It gained the backing of the archdiocese to destroy the area's Catholic churches. It bought and proceeded to raze homes, businesses, and institutions. It quickly relocated the former residents of the area, helped no doubt by almost 30 years of experience in relocating redevelopment project residents.

Even as the PNC fought its last legal battles, residents began to move out. Many welcomed the chance to move. By this time relocation allowances given were generous. Federal law allowed homeowners to receive up to $15,000 above the market value of their houses as relocation compensation. Citizen participation, in the form of the Citizen District Council, at least gave the semblance of democracy, and at no time did the city enter into serious dialogue with the PNC. Soon there was little neighborhood left to defend.[69]

In spite of the rush to clear the land, however, General Motors did not complete and open the plant until 1985. It was in May 1980 that General Motors issued the challenge to Detroit to find, within one year, a site big enough for a modern plant.

In the meantime the city experienced continued budgetary problems and had difficulty meeting expenses generated by the Poletown project. In the fall of 1983, for example, the city killed nine neighborhood projects approved earlier in the year by city council, because it needed the money for CIPP bills. The council had allocated $64,325 in Neighborhood Opportunity Funds for the nine organizations, but Young planned to use $3 million in Neighborhood Opportunity Funds to pay legal debts incurred from the Poletown projects. While this did not consume the entire Neighborhood Opportunity Funds budget for that year, it did serve to remind observers of the costs of a project such as Poletown.[70]

The overall effects of the project are not clear and will not be until some years after the plant is opened. What is clear is that what might be called a "Poletown strategy" is very expensive. The tremendous amount of money that the city had gathered from various sources to pay for Poletown had a depressing effect on the dollars that it could accumulate for further industrial development. Litigation with property holders drove the cost of the Poletown project tens of millions of dollars above the original estimate of $200 million in local, state, and federal government funds. At the beginning of the 1983 fiscal year, the city intended to spend only slightly more than $3 million for its priority projects in industrial development.[71]

It is also clear that the project, even with its optimal estimates of 6,000 direct jobs and 20,000 indirect jobs, is not sufficiently large to offset the mammoth losses of jobs that the city of Detroit has suffered in the past few decades. Chrysler Corporation retrenchment alone cost the city 11,700 direct jobs in the three years from 1980 to 1983. The net job loss during that short period, according to a tally of all reported business openings, expansions, and closings, reached 14,915 direct jobs.[72]

By 1986 it became obvious that Coleman Young intended to repeat the Poletown strategy. The city announced a new project to refurbish Chrysler's Jefferson Avenue plant, which lies just on the border of the Jefferson-Chalmers area (area 7 on Map 5.1). This project would be partially funded by a $50 million Urban Development Action Grant, announced in September 1986. At the same time, Young announced his intent to rebuild housing in the immediate vicinity of the plant and to likewise refurbish and rebuild housing around a number of other plants, a strategy that would be an improvement over Poletown's approach of ignoring housing (except to tear it down).[73] This possibility especially excited observers because one of the most intractable problems in Detroit city has been the decline and abandonment of many of its residential neighborhoods.

Neighborhoods

Many of the city's residential areas have experienced marked decline in recent years. This is not true of all areas. Detroit has sectors of relatively stable areas with good housing stock, few vacancy and abandonment problems, and steady or rising housing values. Some examples are the Indian Village area, a small, historic district close to the central business district; several northwest subdivisions; working-class sections of southwest Detroit; and Elmwood Park, a redevelopment area launched under the old urban renewal program. In the Elmwood Park area, because of federal housing construction programs, the city and private developers were able to construct housing for a wider range of income groups than was the case in early phases of the Gratiot redevelopment project, and until federal cutbacks in new housing construction funds, lower-income families were moving into assisted housing in significant numbers. Yet in spite of these solid areas, in vast stretches of the city of Detroit, residential decay has prevailed. Entire streets have lost over half of their houses to fires, abandonment, and demolition. After the loss of the first few houses, the process becomes a vicious circle. Remaining residents find that their homes are no longer marketable. They then abandon them, which leads to more blight and more abandonment.

Some abandonment has developed because of flawed government policies. The urban renewal program caused decline in some residential areas. More recently, the U.S. Department of Housing and Urban Development (HUD) became the owner of thousands of vacant homes almost overnight after the large-scale abandonment caused by the Detroit "HUD scandal." Local contractors had bribed HUD inspectors to overlook the woefully inadequate repairs that the contractors had made on Federal Housing Administration homes, and home buyers' incomes were too low to undertake the substantial repairs the houses really needed. As frozen plumbing burst and shoddy furnaces exploded, the new owners rapidly defaulted on their loans, HUD acquired the properties, and vacant houses blighted entire neighborhoods. The scandal led to over 200 convictions and indictments, but the damage to Detroit's residential areas is taking years to overcome.[74]

Certainly other trends beyond the reach of local government policy have led to neighborhood decline. Population loss has been massive, and the population lost to the city has consisted largely of middle-income people. Those remaining have had lower incomes and could not necessarily afford home upkeep or homeownership. Between 1970 and 1977 the real income (in constant 1970 dollars) of central-city homeowners in Detroit fell by 4.26 percent, while the real income of suburban-ring homeowners rose by 4.27 percent. Even worse, among central-city renters, real income fell between 1970 and 1977 by 23.3 percent, compared with only a 9.89 percent income decrease among suburban renters. Such a large income decline among central-city renters did not bode well for residential areas in which a large proportion of dwellers rented their housing.[75]

The area known as Jefferson-Chalmers is a cluster of neighborhoods on the city's southeast side, where the effects of the cumulative problems of neighborhood decline are evident. Although its population increased until 1960, by 1970 the Jefferson-Chalmers population began to decrease. In 1977 approximately 4,559 housing units remained, a decline of 3,000 units since the peak year of 1960. Thirty percent of the housing stock had been demolished between 1970 and 1977, mostly near the Chrysler plant, the area with the longest history of continued black residence. In 1980 Jefferson-Chalmers had approximately 15,000 residents remaining; 76 percent were black.

Jefferson-Chalmers is bounded on four sides by the Detroit River, the Chrysler Corporation's Jefferson Avenue plant, Jefferson Avenue, and the boundary between the city of Detroit and the suburb of Grosse Pointe. An area of great contrasts, it once had mansions bordering the Detroit River, complete with family boathouses, as well as housing built for working-class factory employees. At one time Greyhaven Island, one of four Jefferson-Chalmers islands, was home to millionaires. Only the Fisher mansion, now transformed by the International Society for Krishna Consciousness into an amalgamated place of worship, restaurant, and museum, survives fairly intact from that era.[76] Plans are fairly advanced for a housing development to be built on Greyhaven Island, largely supported by state housing development funds.

Jefferson-Chalmers offers a good example of the effects of industrial decline upon industrial neighborhoods. For many years three plants—Chrysler's Jefferson Avenue assembly plant, the Hudson Motor Company, and Continental Motors—dominated the area. In the boom years workers could buy housing close to the plant where they worked and raise a family in a stable, wholesome environment. In the bad years Hudson Motor Company and Continental Motors closed their doors, Chrysler employment declined, and the entire area experienced a recession.

In the late 1970s the automobile industry remained dominant. Researcher Rory Bolger found in 1977 that 35 percent of all workers in his survey of the area received either paychecks, unemployment compensation, or pensions from one of the big three automakers (Ford, Chrysler, and General Motors). Fully 26 percent of all workers were affiliated with Chrysler. Forty percent of the households included a union worker.[77] According to the 1980 census, 30 percent of the area labor force worked in the manufacturing sector.[78] The fortunes of the area have clearly risen and fallen as has the automobile industry. As unemployment has risen, so has population loss.

Detroit has poured millions of redevelopment dollars into Jefferson-Chalmers. By 1976, $16 million in federal, state, and local dollars had been spent.[79] In that year, with the dollars that were left after administration, community residents and planners decided to tear down the worst houses, preserve the best, and clear ten acres of marginal housing. Then the loans and grants program fell prey to poorly monitored contractors who did shoddy work. Relocation efforts led to more people moving out than staying. Soon, in large part because of HUD defaults, people abandoned housing *en masse*, wiping out many of the benefits of the rehabilitation program. Of 455 houses rehabilited by December 1976, one-third had already been either demolished or slated for demolition.

By the early 1980s some positive results of redevelopment were visible, largely in Jefferson Square, a modest complex of about 200 town houses for low- and moderate-income families, which had been constructed by black developer Henry Hagood. Some site improvements of the Jefferson Avenue commercial strip were also evident: new planters, trees, street lighting, and sidewalks (although the new sidewalks often fronted abandoned storefronts). The school board built two new schools in Jefferson-Chalmers. The city used community development funds to acquire and clear sites next to the schools for playgrounds and outdoor recreation. At least $22 million in community development money was spent in the Jefferson-Chalmers area. The city spent most of that money demolishing housing, improving sidewalks and streets, and relocating residents.[80] It became evident that redevelopment in Jefferson-Chalmers, like redevelopment in earlier urban renewal projects, was at best a slow process.

A combination of political and institutional factors have slowed redevelopment in Jefferson-Chalmers. The millions of dollars poured into the area have had only limited success, because they were not sufficient to counter the negative effects of other trends taking place in the community, such as redlining, urban renewal and clearance, HUD defaults, and continued white flight. These have combined with marked cuts in federal resources to play havoc with redevelopment plans.[81]

For years most of the residents of the west end of Jefferson-Chalmers were black and those of the east end white. Relatively few houses inhabited by white families were demolished during the early 1970s, but urban renewal and Community Development Block Grants demolition of the black housing stock in the community's west end led to an increase in black home seekers in the community's east end. This phenomenon, combined with the closing of the primarily white parochial school and white flight, led to a rapid shift in the ethnic makeup of the area.[82] In many cases fleeing whites rented their former homes to poorer black tenants, who could not afford to maintain the properties. This caused rapid deterioration in some sections of Jefferson-Chalmers. White flight combined with other problems, including the collapse of HUD's low-income home mortgage program, and caused increased residential turnover and abandonment. The city spent even more money demolishing abandoned homes, using precious, limited city resources in what many perceived as a destructive process. As one resident commented in 1980, "Demolition, demolition, and more demolition—that's all we've seen here." Another said that the community looked as if it had been "hit by a tornado."[83]

Some residents expressed suspicions that the process of demolition and slow redevelopment was a deliberate attempt to reclaim the area for future, higher-income residents. Jefferson-Chalmers lies in the eastern portion of the area that the city has targeted for riverfront development. Rory Bolger, who conducted numerous interviews in the area for his dissertation research, reported that many residents saw the destruction of so much housing as a purposeful attempt to reclaim the area as part of the city's riverfront strategy. Bolger noted that much of the Community Development Block Grants budget not consumed by demolition was used for infrastructural improvements, such as parks, sidewalks, and streets, rather than housing, a policy that may have favored future lenders rather than existing residents. If this strategy fails to spur gentrification, or return of middle class residents to the city, he suggested, "Jefferson-Chalmers will have a lot of tumbleweed and unused sidewalk on its hands, while those who have been dislocated make do with their new quarters and watch their old land values rise in wait for a new speculator to enter."[84]

The fears expressed by Bolger are shared by other neighborhood activists in Detroit. His charge that much of Detroit's redevelopment planning focuses on the arch formed by the Grand Boulevard has been heard before. Others agree with his claim that "beyond Grand Boulevard neighborhoods anxious to maintain their housing stock find virtually no monies and city assistance to do so. Saving the city has been translated by City Hall as saving the area around downtown. It is difficult to discern in the mass of delays and red tape involved with 'redevelopment' if the city is guilty of gross inefficiency—as the *Detroit Free Press* suggests—or planned neglect."[85]

In many ways Jefferson-Chalmers is favored among neighborhoods. Few other areas have had nearly as much redevelopment money available. The discontent that exists is a reflection of the resentment neighborhood activists feel in a city where it is clear that the administration highly values downtown redevelopment. As resources decline, the battle over those resources will take on ever more desperate tones.

The Battle for Resources

The city of Detroit can no longer hope that federal dollars will save the city from decline and disinvestment. As federal programs have declined, the city has turned to more innovative sources for redevelopment projects. For example, Mayor Coleman Young has encouraged the creation of organizations such as the Detroit Economic Growth Corporation and its two spinoffs, the Economic Development Corporation, which can issue revenue bonds, and the Downtown Development Authority, which taxes all central business district (CBD) businesses in order to levy money for development activities.[86] In recent years the city has initiated a regional hotel sales tax to pay for expanded convention facilities and economic development.[87]

While corporate leaders and developers have worked in organizations and coalitions designed to promote the city's CBD, they have continued to invest in the new suburban downtowns in Dearborn, Southfield, and Troy. Meanwhile, until at least the early 1980s, the city's retail function declined drastically. In late 1983 Corinne Gilb, then city planning director, reported that an independent survey of 38 major cities ranked Detroit's downtown in the bottom one-third of all the downtowns surveyed in economic growth and retail strength. Detroit was one of six cities with no new downtown office space under construction (although downtown office space has since been built). In addition, 35 percent of available first- and second-floor retail space in the Detroit downtown was reported vacant. In 1980 CBD sales were half their 1967 level. In 1967 the CBD had 675 retail or service establishments with $308 million in sales. In 1980, 367 establishments generated only $122 million in sales. More than half of Detroit's city residents surveyed said that they were more likely to shop at suburban malls than within the city. The 1985 opening of a small specialty mall in the Greektown section of the CBD provided small hope that these retail trends might reverse.[88]

In Detroit's 1979 *Downtown Detroit Development* the city included five "Short Range Development Strategies": The Renaissance Center (including spinoffs such as the Millender Center), Riverfront West, Washington Boulevard, the Cadillac Center, and the downtown People Mover (Control Automated Transit System, or CATS). By the mid-1980s progress had been made on all of these projects except the Cadillac Center. The city also initiated a large east-side riverfront development project to beautify several miles of riverfront land sweeping east and north of the civic center and create links with the CBD riverfront development. Investors Max Fisher and Al Taubman have developed Riverfront West, the high-rise, high-income apartment complex described in an earlier chapter, and it appears to be a market success. Construction has begun on the People Mover, although cost overruns have been chronic. After years of effort the city has spurred construction of the Millender Center, an imaginative apartment/hotel/retail facility designed to link the isolated Renaissance Center with the City-County Building and the rest of the downtown. That construction came after the city provided developers with $17 million in tax abatements, $29 million in Urban Development Action Grants (UDAG) and other HUD funds, and a loan of $33 million from the state employee pension fund. The Cadillac Center project, a planned shopping mall with three major department stores, 100 smaller shops, and pedestrian plazas and skywalks, would have required $108 million in public funds out of a total cost of $235 million. This project died after the city failed to find three major department stores willing to move into the CBD.[89]

The city's proposed riverfront strategy may be successful. In 1980 almost 150 persons or organizations owned the four-mile stretch of riverfront land on either side of the CBD, between the Ambassador and MacArthur bridges. By 1985 that stretch had fewer than a dozen owners, including the city of Detroit and developers or corporations dedicated to riverfront redevelopment for residential, commercial, and tourist use.[90]

Yet it is not possible to support both expensive downtown/riverfront development and extensive neighborhood redevelopment. In this context, the city has chosen to target many of its resources to certain select areas, specifically the central business district, the riverfront on either side of the CBD, and the corridor between the CBD and the Wayne State University/Medical Center area (known in current documents as the Central Functions area). Even targeted neighborhoods within this area, such as Jefferson-Chalmers, are not assured that projects will be speedy enough to prevent continuing decay and blight. Neighborhoods outside of these areas are even less likely to have successful redevelopment projects. The debate continues over how to spend economic development funds. At times the debate has developed into wholesale confrontations between the major and the city council and between neighborhood organizations and the city.

Examination of city plans for economic development indicate some of the reasons for the debate. In 1983 an appointed program committee wrote a report that identified six major priority areas for economic development activity:

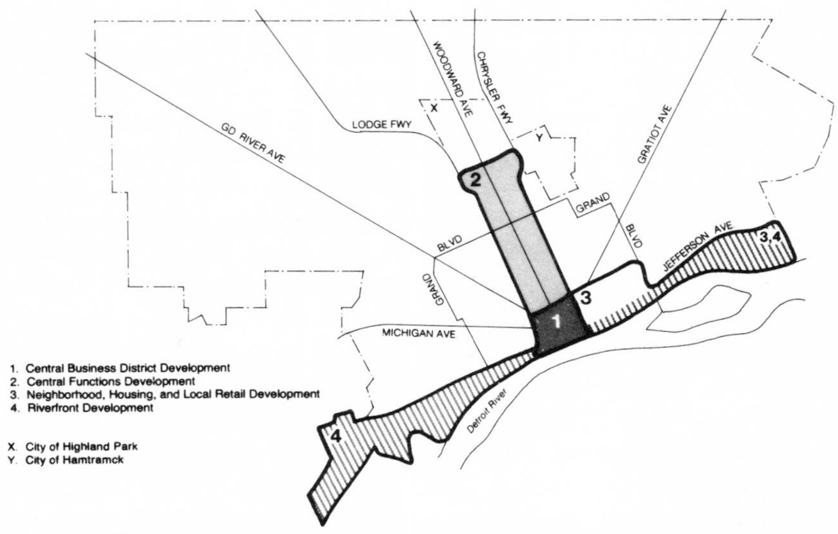

Map 5.2 Targeted areas for Detroit Overall Economic Development Plans

1. Industrial corridor development
2. Central business district development
3. Riverfront development
4. Central Functions area development
5. Neighborhood and housing and local retail development
6. Freight transport development

Map 5.2 shows the location of four of these development areas within the city and shows how these four areas overlap. The riverfront development area includes the central business district, which is adjoined by the Central Functions area. The city has included neighborhood and housing development within its economic development plan, but a large part of that development is located in the riverfront area and the Elmwood Park project, immediately east of the central business district.

Overall Economic Development Plans are usually written because they are required for federal economic development funds and should be viewed with caution. The city of Detroit publishes an economic development plan, for example, only when it is likely that the federal Economic Development Administration will provide grants or loans and uses it as only a rough guideline to city actions. Recently announced projects, such as the new Jefferson Avenue plant, were not included in the 1983 plan. But the plan still offers interesting insight into city administration priorities. Although spending patterns subsequently shifted, the plan stated where, in 1983, the

Table 5.1 Detroit Overall Economic Development Plan, priority projects, 1983–1985

Projects	Projected cost[a]	Portion of cost to be paid with city funds	Percent-age of cost to be paid with city funds	Percent-age of city economic develop-ment funds allo-cation
1. Industrial Corridors	$ 3,270,988	$ 551,197	16.9	0.9
2. Central Business District	2,434,152,590	47,434,000	1.9	74.2
People Mover and Rapid Transit	(2,037,000,000)	0	0	0
Other CBD projects	(397,152,590)	(47,434,000)	(1.9)	(74.2)
3. Riverfront	180,375,344	8,229,800	4.6	12.9
4. Central Functions Area	12,797,500	2,895,000	22.6	4.5
5. Neighborhood Development and Housing[b]	70,624,950	4,619,950	6.5	7.2
Greyhaven Estates	(24,830,000)	0	0[b]	0
Elmwood Park III	(33,850,000)	(500,000)	(7.4)	(3.9)
All others	(11,944,950)	(2,119,950)	(17.8)	(3.3)
6. Freight Transport	11,455,500	175,100	1.5	0.3
Total[c]	$2,712,676,872	$63,905,047		100.0

Source: Compiled from City of Detroit, *Annual Overall Economic Development Program Report and Program Projection*, June 30, 1983, pp. V-37 to V-61.

a. Includes costs that would be covered by federal, state, private, and local funds.

b. Additional funds for neighborhood development would be provided through CDBG federal funds.

c. Numbers in parentheses pertain to subprojects and are not be included in totals.

city intended to target its resources for the 1983–84 and 1984–85 fiscal years, including which projects would receive funds, how much those projects would cost, and how much of the money would come from city, state, federal, and private sources, respectively. A portion of that information is included in Table 5.1.

By the time the city issued the 1983 plan, the funding for the Central Industrial Park project (Poletown) and the Riverside Industrial Park, near Jefferson-Chalmers, had been secured. The enormous costs of Poletown had diminished the overall industrial development effort to $3 million for several modest projects. The city intended to target most redevelopment money in the near future for the riverfront and the central business district. It later proceeded to construct Chene Park, part of the city's east-side riverfront project, and to encourage auxiliary riverfront development activities, such as River Place on the property of Stroh's Brewery. Other riverfront undertakings were to include housing projects and the refurbishment of historic Fort Wayne as a tourist attraction, with total costs of $180 million, slightly over $9 million of which would come from city funds, $7 million from federal funds, and the remainder from private sources.

Although the city projected spending $12 million on the Central Functions area, which included continued expenditures for the Detroit Medical Center and the technology crescent it proposed for the area surrounding a new Metropolitan Center for High Technology, downtown redevelopment prevailed. The city claimed that the central business district serves as the "financial and convention center for Southeast Michigan" and the "symbolic retail center for the City and the region".[91] Some of these claims were clearly wishful thinking. The regional economy had long been multicentric, and retail activity had become very weak in the city CBD. Yet in the summer of 1983 Detroit hoped to generate spending of close to $400 million on the central business district for nontransportation projects in the immediate future. This amount included funding for some projects that have since been abandoned, such as the Cadillac Center. In addition, the city planned to use state and federal funding to build the downtown People Mover and a Rapid Transit Light Rail system, which together would cost over $2 billion.[92]

These projects vastly overshadowed the $70 million planned, at the time of the 1983 report, for neighborhood development projects. In addition, much of that $70 million was to be used in direct support of the riverfront development strategy. For example, the city planned to generate $25 million in funding for Greyhaven Estates, a housing development on Greyhaven Island in the Jefferson-Chalmers area. Of the remainder, $34 million was slated for further residential development at Elmwood Park III, the large former urban renewal site. Both of these projects were to rely heavily upon private funding. Only minor sums remained for projects such as the Jefferson-Chalmers shopping area ($750,000), other commercial projects outside of the riverfront/Central Functions area corridor, and public housing rehabilitation ($3.7 million, including $3 million in federal funds). It should be noted, however, that much neighborhood and housing development activity is financed by Community Development Block Grants rather than by economic development funds.

As Table 5.1 illustrates, the city projected that a total of $2,712,676,872 would be spent on economic development projects, primarily during the 1983–84 and 1984–85 fiscal years. Of this total, the city would contribute only $63,905,047 in city funds, because many of the projects would use federal, state, or private funds. But of the funds that the city planned to contribute, the largest proportion by far was to go to the central business district, 74.2 percent, and another large portion was to go to the riverfront, 12.9 percent. In total, the city planned to channel over 87 percent of the funds it planned to spend on priority economic development projects to the CBD or to the riverfront area.

In general, the city's economic development planning document indicated the city's intent to concentrate city, federal, state, and private resources on the central business district, the riverfront, and neighborhood projects in the CBD and riverfront areas. The total amounts involved in economic development activities, to be funded in great part by private development funds, were much greater than the amounts that the city receives regularly for its entitlement grant under the Community Development Block Grants (CDBG) program. In fiscal year 1983–84, the annual amount the city received from that program was only $58 million, a modest sum by economic development standards. Nevertheless, the fact that many economic development resources have been, and continue to be, targeted to the CBD and the riverfront, even those project funds supposedly directed to "neighborhoods," meant that the scramble for CDBG funds was certain to be ferocious.

Community Development Block Grants are the major resource for neighborhood development funds. Some limited private reinvestment has taken place in historic preservation districts such as Indian Village (an area near Elmwood Park) and in New Center (a project designed by the General Motors Corporation to upgrade a residential area near its headquarters).[93] But these minor attempts at spearheading a gentrification movement have not succeeded to any significant degree. They have not changed the basic conditions of most of Detroit's neighborhoods. Neither have they replaced the dependence of those neighborhoods on the Community Development Block Grants program.

Unfortunately, many priorities have competed for the use of CDBG funds. As a result, those funds have been used to help finance large public and industrial development projects, to finance large-scale demolition of housing abandoned because of the failures of HUD's low-income mortgage program, and to support the CBD strategy. All of this has directed resources away from residential areas outside of the CBD.

In Poletown the city administration used CDBG not only to make infrastructure investments in the site and not only as a source of temporary loan monies for mammoth industrial development but also to help pay legal bills associated with citizen suits against the project. The Poletown project was not the first time the city had borrowed against future CDBG allocations to help finance other projects. Such usage, permitted by Section

108 of the CDBG legislation, did not comfort those who feared that the city could not pay back the loans and would lose future allocations. In 1979, for example, city council members vocally objected to Young's plan to finance a downtown sports facility, the Joe Louis Arena, in part by using $38 million borrowed with the use of future CDBG monies as collateral. As Councilman Kenneth Cockrel protested, "I don't believe that money that is targeted pursuant to federal regulations to benefit moderate and low income people should be used for arena construction." His more conservative colleague Jack Kelley agreed: "It's very dangerous. . . . The block grants were really not intended for that use. But I know . . . we've got to find some money somewhere."[94] The mayor argued that if the arena was not built, other plans for the central business district would be jeopardized because developers would reexamine their planned investments. In the end the council approved the loan and the arena was built. Since that time the city has made other uses of the Section 108 program.[95]

City council members, pressured by neighborhood organizations protesting what they saw as an overemphasis on the CBD, have frequently wrangled with the administration over the use of funds. At one point the council withheld a token $1 million because of concern over unusually high administrative costs. At other times it has called on the administration to shift more of the program into human services, an area that is allowable but discouraged under federal regulations. The council altered the city's planned use of funds, reducing demolition budgets, increasing the urban homesteading and home rehabilitation budgets, and slashing Young's planned expenditures for crime prevention and community development planning. In 1983 the city's own planning commission issued an advisory report asking the city to spend less on Poletown loan repayment and more on neighborhood improvements.[96]

It is difficult to determine exactly how the city administration has ordered its community development priorities. A 1979 city report claimed that for the period from May, 1975 to June, 1980 the CDBG program had allocated 78 percent of its funds to neighborhood and housing development and 22 percent to economic development.[97] Like the performance reports of most cities with CDBG entitlement funds, Detroit's reports do not readily reveal the spending patterns of the city over time. It is also difficult to tell how much money has benefited low- and moderate-income people, because city data collected on this issue are unreliable in Detroit as well as nationwide.[98]

But it is possible to tell the approximate geographic location of allocations by subcommunities. During the period from 1975 to 1982, funds the

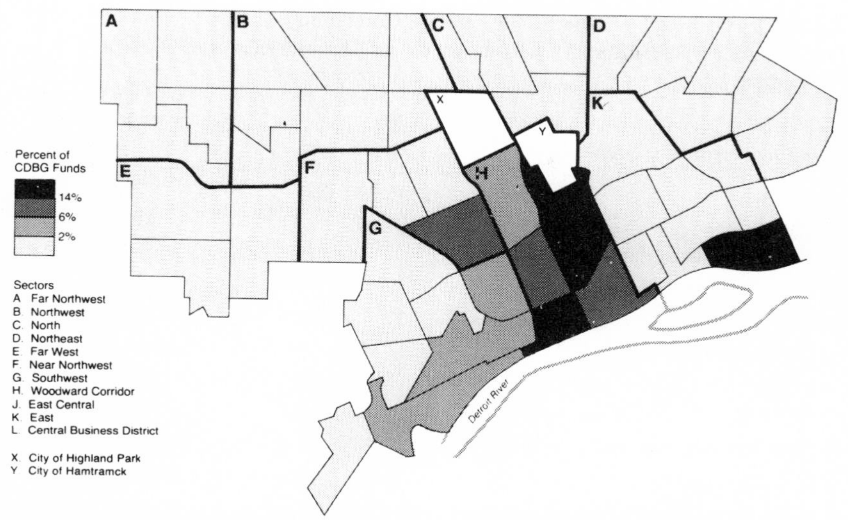

Map 5.3 Approximate allocation of targeted Community Development Block Grants funds by subcommunity and sector, 1975–1982

city spent in specific, identifiable areas constituted approximately 45 percent of all the city's CDBG expenditures.[99] By locating these projects in their appropriate subcommunities—fairly small community areas that contain anywhere from 10,000 to 50,000 people for which the city collects demographic data—it is possible to discern broad patterns of expenditures for identifiable areas. As Map 5.3 illustrates, the city targeted many of the CDBG funds to the central business district, the riverfront, and the Central Functions area (Woodward Corridor), just as it proposed to do with economic development money. For example, Table 5.2 shows that the city of Detroit spent at least $25 million, or 16.2 percent of targeted funds, in the central business district. Additional funds, which were not specifically identifiable as targeted to the central business district, may have been diverted there also. In addition, the city spent large amounts in the East Riverside subcommunity of the east sector, an area only slightly larger than the Jefferson-Chalmers neighborhood, and in the Lafayette subcommunity east of the central business district. The Woodward Corridor, immediately northwest of the CBD, site of the urban renewal projects for the Medical Center and Wayne State University, received at least $18 million in CDBG funds.

Map 5.3 shows some exceptions to the generalization that the city of Detroit centralized its CDBG expenditures. The city spent at least 13.4 percent of its targeted CDBG funds in the Virginia Park area of the Rosa

Table 5.2 Geographic dispersion of selected Community Development Block Grants Expenditures, city of Detroit, 1975–1982[a]

Planning sector or subsector	Expenditure	Percentage of funds targeted to specific sector or subsector
East central	$ 36,390,128	23.5
Chene only		(16.1)
Area on official riverfront only		(6.3)
Remainder of section		(1.1)
East	27,140,432	17.5
East Riverside (on official riverfront) only		(14.7)
Remainder of sector		(2.8)
Central business district	25,129,048	16.2
Near northwest	22,353,444	14.4
Rosa Parks only		(13.4)
Remainder of sector		(1.0)
Woodward Corridor	18,141,781	11.7
Southwest	17,987,324	11.6
Delray (on river) only		(2.9)
Remainder of sector		(8.7)
Northwest	5,588,030	3.6
North	1,760,332	1.1
Far northwest	212,000	0.1
Northeast	203,000	0.1
Total[b]	$154,905,519	100.0[c]

Source: Calculated from City of Detroit, Planning Department, "Community Development Entitlement Grant Program: Program and Project Descriptions," January 1982, pp. 4–32.

a. Includes only those funds geographically identifiable as spent on housing and community development in a particular sector or subcommunity. Does not include CDBG administration or planning, Neighborhood Opportunity Funds, public and social services, and other categories. When projects fell on the border between two subcommunities or were listed in areas that crossed the boundaries of anywhere from two to four subcommunities, money was divided evenly into two to four parts.

b. Numbers in parentheses pertain to subprojects and are not be included in totals.

c. This column actually does not add up to 100 percent due to rounding.

Parks subcommunity located in the near northwest sector. Between 1975 and 1982 Virginia Park received over $14 million in general neighborhood improvement funds for its Neighborhood Strategy Area, $3 million for a community center, and over $1 million each for a fire station and a shop-

Map 5.4 Percentage of poverty in Detroit subcommunities, 1978–1979

ping center. Residents of the Virginia Park area have independently made great strides in community economic development. Neighborhood residents have bought shares to help fund the shopping center, while city community development funds helped provide a much needed boost for this project. The Virginia Park expenditures are the only significant exception, during that 1975–1982 period, to the centralized strategy of concentrating on the CBD, the Woodward Corridor, and the riverfront.

The Chene subcommunity, east of the Woodward Corridor in the east central sector, might at first appear to be an exception, but it really is not. Although Chene received $25 million in targeted funds during the study period, almost as much as the CBD, more than $3 million of that went to the Poletown project, and over $15 million went to a Neighborhood Strategy Area that is separated from the Medical Center complex in the Woodward Corridor only by an expressway.

To an extent, the city's pattern of dispersing community development monies makes sense. Several residential areas northwest and northeast of the city of Detroit have relatively higher-income residents and fewer housing problems than the central portions of the city. Map 5.4 shows poverty rates for the city's subcommunities from 1978 to 1979. The northwest and northeast sections of the city are more prosperous. A comparison of Maps 5.3 and 5.4 reveals a number of subcommunities with fairly high poverty rates that received little or no targeted community development funds.[100]

Table 5.3 Community Development Block Grants expenditures, city of Detroit, 1975–1982

Sector or project	Expenditures	Percentage of total funds
Identifiable areas [a]	$154,905,519	44.9
Community development administration —general	37,158,090	10.8
Neighborhood strategy areas —public and social services	31,444,210	9.1
City-wide demolition	28,656,400	8.3
Neighborhood Opportunity Funds	24,055,725	7.0
Community development planning	19,564,900	5.7
Community development property acquisition	9,160,000	2.7
Senior citizen/low-income housing repair	8,260,000	2.4
Community development administration —citizen district councils	7,339,000	2.1
Urban renewal closeout	4,681,083	1.4
Other Miscellaneous projects and categories [b]	19,669,014	5.7
Total	$344,893,941	100.0 [c]

Source: Calculated from City of Detroit, Planning Department, "Community Development Entitlement Grant Program: Program and Project Descriptions," January 1982, pp 4–32.

a. From table 5.2.

b. Includes some Model Cities allocations, numerous categories of mostly under $1 million (such as the rehabilitation of commercial areas, the purchase of fire-fighting equipment, and the rehabilitation of historic buildings, which city documents did not identify as falling within any one area.

c. This column actually does not add up to 100 percent due to rounding.

Several areas in the east sector suffer from high poverty rates, but only the Jefferson-Chalmers area (East Riverside subcommunity) obtained more than 2 percent of targeted funds. Several distressed areas in the southwest and near northwest received few or no funds. The correlation of targeted CDBG funds and poverty rates of the various subcommunities yields a correlation ratio of .375 with a sample size of 49 subcommunities, significant at a level of .01. This is not a particularly high level of correlation. While poverty rates should not be the only criteria for dispersion, the federal government has consistently stressed targeting the low-income people in CDBG legislation. Poverty rates make up an important component of both formulas in allocating CDBG funds to entitlement cities. In one of the two CDBG formulas, the percentage of housing built before 1945 was a significant component. In Detroit subcommunities the correlation between targeted CDBG funds and the percentage of pre-1945 housing is .36 (with a sample size of 51 subcommunities, significant at a level of .01).

But spatial allocations do not tell the complete story. Some funds, though relatively modest, were used to refurbish streets and sidewalks in residential areas. In addition, funds distributed through the Neighborhood Opportunity Fund program included grants, usually in the $100,000 range, directly to community-based organizations for home repair and community services.[101] Demolition costs consumed over $28 million in a seven-year period, as Table 5.3 shows.[102] In precisely which neighborhoods the city spent $31 million in public and social service funds and where it spent $8 million for senior citizen/low-income housing is not clear. Nor is the overall breakdown of home rehabilitation, economic development, and community development activities clear.

In response to charges that the neighborhoods have not received their share of CDBG monies, the city has argued that most of the targeted money goes neither to the CBD nor to the riverfront. Yet targeted CDBG money that went to the CBD and to what the city technically defines as the riverfront—including the CBD and those parts of the southwest, east, and east central sectors that border the riverfront—totaled 40.1 percent of geographically identifiable CDBG allocations from 1975–1982, or $62 million. When the Woodward Corridor expenditures are added in, the total is 51.8 percent, or $80 million. (See Table 5.2.)

City administration officials correctly note that many of these centralized areas include "neighborhoods," or residential areas. In the Woodward Corridor, for example, CDBG funds have supported residential projects in the Cass Corridor, Medical Center, and GM-sponsored New Center areas. The controversy appears to center not so much on this point as on the fact that residential projects in the CBD, Woodward Corridor, or riverfront have a higher likelihood of funding than those elsewhere.

City officials say it is more difficult to fund low-income rehabilitation projects than to spend the money on CBD projects. According to redevelopment officials, money spent on the CBD and riverfront can be used as leverage to attract private development resources and federal programs such as Urban Development Action Grants. Money spent on housing rehabilitation must be financed almost completely by the city. Officials logically claim that housing rehabilitation, which must be spread over a city that is close to 130 square miles and which may not even be visible if it focuses on home interiors, appears to be less rewarding than CBD, riverfront, and economic development projects.[103]

At various times community groups have vocally protested the fact that redevelopment was skewed to the downtown and riverfront. One of the most vocal, formed in 1974, has been the Michigan Avenue Community

Organization (MACO), an omnibus organization composed of some 70 smaller civic, church, and block clubs and known as "the largest and perhaps best-organized of Detroit's increasingly vocal community associations."[104] MACO leaders have traditionally used flamboyant, publicity-seeking tactics closely identified with the style of social activist Saul Alinsky.

To draw attention to houses abandoned under the HUD program, the organization tried, unsuccessfully, to deliver to former HUD secretary Carla Hills an Easter basket filled with 51 charred eggs representing 51 HUD houses it wanted demolished. In 1980, while the city administration prepared to fete conventioneers attending the national convention of the Republican Party, MACO sent the conventioneers invitations to room in any of the city's 4,000 abandoned HUD houses. At one point in 1978 representatives of MACO poured soft drinks over a man costumed as the "Spirit of Detroit" to protest the millions of dollars going into downtown development instead of neighborhoods.[105]

Many politicians and journalists have criticized MACO for its confrontationist style. Some residents within MACO's boundaries have disagreed with the approaches of its leaders, and at least a few neighborhood groups have withdrawn from the organization. But many, including its critics, grudgingly admire MACO. Councilman David Eberhard, speaking about former MACO Board President Virgina Davidson, said that she "understands confrontation politics and the limits of it. Publicity gets a following; she knows that and uses it widely." Over the years, however, MACO has quieted both its tactics and its protests, as have a number of other neighborhood groups. Part of the reason for this is the city's Neighborhood Opportunity Fund, which has given implementation funds directly to organizations and simultaneously, perhaps, helped quiet them.

MACO has been especially successful in receiving money, approximately $500,000 a year in CDBG funds beginning in 1981. MACO used some of its funding to complete a professional revitalization plan for the area it covers, a large swath of southwest Detroit that lost 21 percent of its population from 1970 to 1980, largely because of auto plant closings and cutbacks.[106]

As such organizations have met the challenge to spend CDBG money wisely, their attention has been somewhat diverted from the protest mode of thought. In addition, community leaders have come to realize the limitations of redevelopment funds: If the funds continue to shrink, as the city's tax receipts and CDBG allocations have shrunk, to focus only upon fighting over those shrinking resources is to fight a zero-sum game. Community groups cannot continue to ask city hall for money it does not have or services it cannot provide.[107]

The battles over community development resources merely reiterate the crucial problem: The city does not have enough resources to meet all of its redevelopment needs. It has been able to obtain only limited dollars from federal and state grants and the private sector and has chosen to spend those dollars where it can get the most leverage. City officials have to select projects to support, necessitating a process that is by definition inequitable.

Conclusion

Urban redevelopment as a public initiative is a slow, arduous, and expensive process, one that takes many years, many plans, and many dollars. Urban renewal projects in Detroit, as in other cities around the country, dragged on for decades yet reduced the stock of low-income housing and in some cases increased neighborhood blight. More recent community development efforts have been confronted by the same problems and have not managed to halt residential decline and abandonment. In some areas the city had to tear down housing almost as fast as it rehabilitated it. Limited success is apparent in some sections of the city, but other sections look pretty much the way they did before redevelopment efforts began, or worse, because of private market forces.

Those who have shaped redevelopment decisions have been those with the political and economic clout necessary to make an impact. In the early years of the Detroit Plan and urban renewal, the real estate industry and downtown business owners were influential lobbyists. The Urban Land Institute panel was an example of nonlocal business owners recommending that the city de-emphasize public housing and select committees of prominent local business owners and professionals to guide future actions. The directors of major institutions, such as Wayne State University and large medical center hospitals, managed to divert urban renewal funds to the benefit and profit of their institutions. And the city made great sacrifices to maintain the health, well-being, and visible presence of the Chrysler Corporation and General Motors.

In the process someone had to lose, or at the very least someone did not receive the resources that were directed to major businesses, institutions, and corporations. Urban renewal programs were infamous for their negative effects upon relocated businesses and residents. In the 1970s blatantly inept and insidious relocation practices faded, in part because of protective legislation. But in the decade of the 1980s, with the examples of Poletown and the CBD, it became evident that such enormous resources could not be channeled to one constituency without sacrifices on the part of the other constituencies. Money used for downtown development would not be used for neighborhood housing. Those neighborhoods with the most sophisticated organizational support, such as MACO, and with the most advantageous locations, such as Jefferson-Chalmers on the riverfront, received proportionately more funds than did other neighborhoods.

City officials today clearly believe it is best to centralize and focus redevelopment efforts for the city of Detroit. For example, Mayor Coleman Young pushed the Poletown project as a necessary antidote to the steady losses the city has suffered as jobs and industries have moved out. No alternative seemed possible at the time. Similar sentiments (that is, when the CBD improves, so does the city) have fueled efforts to revitalize the central business district. This approach may in fact be correct; it is too early to tell, especially since the precise nature of the city's redevelopment strategy changes over time, revealed piecemeal as the mayor announces new components of his vision. Yet surely a central-city government cannot completely reverse city and regional trends that negatively affect that central city. Industrial and commercial disinvestment counterbalance central-city efforts to bolster industry and commerce and spur neighborhood redevelopment. To make real progress in the face of mass exodus is extremely difficult.

The old problems continue to haunt efforts. Although racial conflict has not directly tainted post-1970 redevelopment projects as it did earlier urban renewal projects, it continues to play a role. Polls have consistently shown voters in the city sharply polarized for or against Mayor Young, depending on race. As the city proportion of blacks increases, whites unwilling to remain as minorities continue to move out, with serious repercussions for neighborhood housing. Class polarization increases as middle-class blacks exit. Regional antagonism grows as suburbanites become ever more estranged from the city center. All of these trends influence redevelopment.

In the final analysis, centralized public investment has not yet managed to save the city, because in the context of the region total investment has been decentralized, not centralized. Private developers have been drawn to suburban nodes of growth like nails to a magnet. Only a regional strategy could save the central city, and yet the concept of regionalism in government or in the economy has never been realized.

6

Politics and Policy in Metropolitan Detroit

All of the issues discussed thus far—the economy of the region, patterns of race and class, race relations, redevelopment strategies—relate in some sense to politics. Although the political environment has not always determined the course of events in the Detroit metropolis, it has certainly helped shape them. The political fragmentation of the region is the single variable that best explains why certain areas of the region suffer the most from the effects of the massive extremes in regional economic development.

If, as had happened in metropolitan regions in the southern United States, the city of Detroit had been able merely to annex the developing region instead of watch helplessly as outlying areas incorporated, it would have mattered little to the tax base of the city whether development decentralized. The political fragmentation that did occur exacerbated race and class conflicts that had already begun to take place within the central city. Soon it became fairly easy for whites to escape diversity, merely by moving to one of many suburbs surrounding the city. Redevelopment policies constantly intertwined with politics within the city, especially as mayors used redevelopment to try to gain political favor with voters. They failed to address problems of race and income discrimination or inequity because of the political environment on national and local levels.

This chapter examines three aspects of politics and policy in Detroit. Rather than recite a litany of mayors and councils within the city throughout the years, it is more instructive to look specifically at politics in the region, as related to race and regional conflict and cooperation.

The first part of the chapter offers a history of the ascendency of black political power within the central city and the region. Beginning in the era when even one black political candidacy was a victory, it explains how blacks eventually succeeded in electing many blacks to political office, including the present mayor. Throughout this era the natural tension between the black moderate coalition builders and the black radicals, or nationalists, influenced the contours of black political power.

The second section examines a policy case study that illustrates the conflicts over school desegregation. The issue of whether schools should be substantially integrated by race offers a microcosm of the conflicts between cities and suburbs that spilled over into the judicial as well as the political arena.

The last section picks up on an earlier chapter's discussion of racial and income inequality between municipalities within the region. It also reviews the efforts that have been made to reduce inequities and to institutionalize regional governance and cooperation.

As a whole, the chapter suggests that the rise of black political power has been a victory for those concerned with creating a democratic society. But the current inequities between the municipalities of the region have given black political ascendency a hollow ring. Proposals for increased metropolitan cooperation have failed, because so many people within the region gain from political fragmentation. Because of the importance of black political power in Detroit, little interest exists—even in Detroit, one of the most disadvantaged municipalities—in instituting meaningful metropolitan reorganization.

Black Political Power in Detroit

One of the most remarkable stories in the constellation of potential narratives about politics in the Detroit region is the story of the growth and development of black political power.

This story actually begins with the black migration during and after World War I that paved the way for black political power in Detroit. By the mid-1930s blacks had begun to shift from the Republican party, the party of Abraham Lincoln and Henry Ford (bestowers of freedom and jobs, respectively), to the Democratic party. Charles C. Diggs, Sr., the first black Democrat to be elected to a state office, represented a political coalition of blacks and of labor-based, ethnic, and liberal white Democrats.[1] He was reelected several times after his first victory in 1938, but he fell from power when he was convicted of accepting bribes in 1944. He was jailed from 1948 to 1950. Because of that conviction, the state senate refused to seat him after his reelection in 1950. Between 1946 and 1962 eight blacks, including several black women, won election to the Michigan legislature. One of these was Charles C. Diggs, Jr., who in 1951 won election to the seat that had been refused his father.[2] The steady stream of black lawmakers from Detroit reflected the expanding black population in districts where blacks were rapidly becoming the majority.

Throughout the 1950s a coalition of black, labor, and liberal organizations worked to elect blacks to state and city political and judicial positions. One crucial election was that of William T. Patrick, Jr., a former assistant prosecuting attorney, who became the first black in the city's history to win a seat on the Detroit Common Council.[3]

The liberal coalition that had elected other blacks exercised caution in choosing Patrick. Patrick's education, moderate speech, and action—in short, his overall cultivation as an acceptable member of the black upper class—rendered him sufficiently suitable for upper-class whites' political taste. Patrick's election reflected the period in the history of black political development in Detroit when black, upper-class professionals were becoming increasingly interested in liberal politics. Patrick believed in the politics of the liberal coalition and demonstrated this belief by campaigning with Councilman Ed Carey, a UAW official and minority leader in the Michigan House of Representatives, and with another candidate of Polish descent, taking both of them into black precincts. They, in turn, took Patrick into their precincts. Because he was the candidate of the liberal coalition, Patrick stayed away from racial appeals to black voters. However, he still ran four-to-one ahead of the nearer whites in black areas and four-to-one behind Polish candidates in Polish areas.[4] Regardless of the liberal coalition's nonracial political posture, race still dominated politics in Detroit elections.

As important as the liberal coalition had been and would still be to the election of blacks to political office in Detroit, the growth, expansion, and increasing politicalization of the black population were rapidly becoming the dominant factors in the black community's political development. Liberal coalition politics of necessity placed ideological constraints on independent black political development. Not unlike other ethnic and nationality groups in Detroit and other cities, blacks in Detroit and elsewhere were straining at the political leash for their turn to lead big city politics. It would only be a matter of time before liberal coalition politics would collide with the movement for increased black political independence. But in the late 1950s liberal coalition politics continued to benefit black political development in Detroit.

Of all the blacks elected to public office in Detroit in the 1950s, Congressman Charles C. Diggs, Jr., best symbolized black political progress during the decade. Diggs lost a race for the Detroit Common Council in

1953, but the close results strongly suggested the possibility of victory in the 13th U.S. Congressional District, which corresponded to the 3d Senatorial District, which Diggs represented in the state senate. He challenged and defeated the white 14-year incumbent, Democratic congressman George D. O'Brien, in the 1954 Democratic primary. He then went against three opponents—including Republican Landon Knight, son of John S. Knight, the newspaper publisher—and won. It was a great victory! Diggs had not only polled more than two-thirds of all the votes cast, but had accomplished this political feat in an area 55 percent white, made up of Greek, Jewish, Mexican, Chinese, Lebanese, Maltese, Irish, and Italian ethnic minorities. Diggs became Michigan's first black congressman. When he traveled to Washington for the swearing in ceremonies, 400 blacks went along with him on a special train. The gallery was so crowded that the late Sam Rayburn had to conduct two swearing in ceremonies so all the visitors could witness this historic occasion.[5]

Once in Washington, Diggs wasted no time in making his political views known and refused to be restrained by his party's politics. Though not as independent and outspoken as New York's black congressman Adam Clayton Powell, he was much more so than Chicago's black congressman William L. Dawson. During his first month as a congressman, Diggs introduced 11 civil rights bills and attacked the Veterans Administration for racial discrimination. He considered himself a "fighter against injustice" and put his own party on notice that he would not be their "tool" where black interests were involved. He challenged his party's views on civil rights and in 1956 threatened to bolt the party if it did not "stop pussyfooting on civil rights views."[6]

When Diggs won reelection in the fall of 1958 for a third term, he had become one of the major black political figures in the nation and the symbol of the decade of black political development in the Motor City.[7]

Black Consciousness and the Road to Black Political Independence

Black political consciousness and power in Detroit quickened in the tumultuous 1960s. Early in the decade blacks rallied against the excessive police power of Mayor Louis C. Miriani and succeeded in throwing him out of office. Black radicals, unimpressed with the incremental political progress of the past, rejected the idols of black and white liberalism as "false gods" used to maintain and perpetuate black political subservience to "the white establishment." Black rebellion punctuated the decade, placing in question the efficacy of an entire tradition of liberal coalition politics in Detroit. Just before the end of the decade, Detroit came close to electing its first black mayor.

In 1961 blacks comprised about one-third of the total population in Detroit. This percentage would expand as whites left for the suburbs. Black political awareness was moving apace with the expanding black population, as white politicians nervously eyed their districts' rapidly changing complexions. The most pressing issue to politically aware blacks in 1960 was to get rid of Mayor Miriani, who had instituted a police crackdown that translated into wholesale arrests of black citizens. Not everyone was dissatisfied with Miriani. The white power structure in Detroit, including members of the liberal coalition such as the UAW, gave Miriani strong support. This was perhaps the first sign of divergence of blacks and key white segments of the liberal coalition. Blacks rallied behind Jerome P. Cavanaugh, who was challenging Miriani for the office. The Trade Union Leadership Council (TULC), a black labor organization with a history of conflicts with the white leadership of the UAW, mobilized the black community behind Cavanaugh, giving him the votes necessary to win the election.[8] By demonstrating their political power in this mayoral campaign, called "the biggest political upset in Michigan politics in 32 years," blacks also demonstrated that they would no longer let the liberal coalition determine their political direction.[9] Consequently, this election widened the gap between liberal whites and blacks in the coalition.[10]

In response to the groundswell of black activism, some blacks in Detroit abandoned liberal coalition politics for a more nationalistic approach to black political development. In 1962 blacks of this political persuasion started a campaign to elect blacks to replace white congressmen in predominantly black districts. While this effort received some black support, the entrenched black political leadership, still tied to the liberal coalition, rejected such appeals to race.[11]

By the early 1960s the Freedom-Now party was sufficiently organized in Detroit to put forward a slate of candidates for local public offices as well as for Congress. The Freedom-Now party's attempts failed, but the mood of black political independence remained strong and persistent.[12] When William Patrick resigned from the Common Council in 1964, some black leaders mobilized to fill his seat and two other seats with three blacks in the 1965 council elections. "Crime-in-the-streets" for whites and "black support for black candidates" soon became the only issues of the campaign.[13]

Just before the primary, pandemonium ensued when the *Detroit News* published an article questioning the credentials of Jackie Vaughn, one of the black candidates. The Wayne County AFL-CIO (American Federation of Labor and Congress of Industrial Organizations) sided with the *Detroit News* and endorsed ex-mayor Miriani. Black groups, led by the TULC, accused the white political elite of trying to impose white candidates on the black community. Some community support for Vaughn took on the appearance of a crusade.[14]

As if this were not enough excitement for one election campaign, the *Detroit News* triggered another round of conflict when it published statistics revealing that whites supported only white candidates. In contrast, blacks supported both black and white candidates. In response, a group of black ministers, the Interdenominational Ministries Alliance (IMA), threatened to call a boycott of all white candidates if whites did not show more respect for black candidates. A similar campaign, organized by black nationalist the Reverend Albert B. Cleage, Jr., urged blacks to support only the four black candidates. This group's rallying cry was "four and no more."[15]

The IMA threat attracted much white media attention but in the process turned off moderate black organizations like the TULC, which opposed the boycott. The threat did stimulate some liberal white religious and labor organizations to action. Concerned that white liberal candidates could not defeat white conservative candidates without black votes, they began a modest push for white support of black candidates. Moderate black politicians rejected the radical approach of the IMA, but benefited from such approaches. For example, the IMA boycott threat opened doors in white areas to such moderate candidates as Nicholas Hood, who normally would not have been acceptable to many whites.[16] Whites perceived the Nicholas Hoods of the black community as "safe" alternatives to the more radical political activists. Obviously bowing to the black political moderates, IMA decided to withdraw its boycott threat. Other black organizations, however, continued supporting only black candidates. These organizations included the Inner-City Voters' League, the League of Negro Women Voters, and the National Organization on Negro Education. Out of the four black candidates, only Nicholas Hood, who came in eighth, won a seat on the Detroit Common Council.[17]

In the 1960s the threat of radical black politics—or at least black politics to the left of black moderates in the liberal coalition—posed problems for the established black politicians, but the threat never materialized into any substantial challenge. The Freedom-Now party vaporized before it even registered in the consciousness of the average black voter. Political indifference among many blacks in Detroit was due to preoccupation with the countless problems associated with surviving in a harsh urban environment. In Wayne County in 1964 only 175,000 of 300,000 potential black voters were registered. Since only about one-third of those registered actually voted, black political activists faced a problem of black political apathy.[18]

Black radicals did help redefine black political independence in Detroit. This meant more than just a redistribution of political power within a coalition under the perpetual control of the white political and business elite. In 1968 the Reverend Albert Cleage, Jr., a major leader of the Group on Advanced Leadership (GOAL), one of several black nationalist groups in Detroit, stressed the importance of black political power in areas where blacks were in the majority: "We can vote black and we can control political structures in any area in which we are a majority. This is a reality, and it's exactly the same thing that whites would do if they were black." Blacks would soon be a majority in Detroit, the Reverend Mr. Cleage stated, and "by voting black we can elect a black mayor, a black council and a black school board." A black candidate's only necessary qualification, according to Cleage, was that he be "devoted to the black nation, putting his dedication to black people first."[19] Clearly, this political philosophy had no room or patience for traditional liberal coalition politics.

What role would whites play in the black political community as envisioned by Cleage? "We would appreciate it . . . if people in the suburbs [whites] would stay in the suburbs, if they would stop trying to live in the suburbs and run our black community, if they would stop living in the suburbs while holding . . . political offices in the cities."[20] According to Cleage's views of black political independence, therefore, white suburbanites, even those within the liberal coalition, had little or no role to play in the future of black politics in Detroit. With regard to whites who still lived in a black-majority city, one could only speculate that black nationalists such as Cleage would see them accepting, reluctantly or otherwise, black majority rule in the city.

This black political scenario, however, did not materialize in quite the way that some black nationalists desired. Several black moderate activists, no less "nationalistic" than Cleage and other black radicals, pursued the same political goals but without the rhetoric and fanfare.

The "King Maker"

The late Robert Millender was one such moderate political activist. A brilliant political strategist, Millender contributed more to black political development in Detroit between 1964 and 1973 than all the black radicals and moderate political activists combined. He first became involved in politics in the late 1940s while studying law at the Detroit College of Law. There he met fellow student Zolton Ferency, the future chairman of the Michigan Democratic party, who introduced him to politics. Ferency started what the law students called a Democratic Study Club, in which Millender participated. Millender's first big opportunity to become involved in a political campaign came in 1948 when he worked for the election of "Soapy" Williams for governor. He joined the TULC soon after it was organized in 1957, as one of the two nonlabor members. John Conyers, the current congressman, was the other nonlabor member. Millender also played an active role in the 1957 campaign to elect William T. Patrick, Jr., to the Detroit Common Council.[21]

The remarkable skills in political strategy that Millender would use to foster black political development in Detroit were honed in 1960 when he became co-manager of Zolton Ferency's campaign to defeat Prosecuting Attorney Samuel Olsen. Unfortunately, Ferency lost the election, but in the process Millender earned the respect of political observers for his skills in managing the campaign. Here was a man, according to predictions, destined to become "one of the most outstanding political strategists in the city and the state."[22]

Beginning in 1964 Millender began using the considerable political skills that would earn him the title of "King Maker." Soon after Michigan realigned its congressional districts, Millender devised a plan that not only protected Diggs's district as a black district but also made it possible for another black person to be elected from the first district in Detroit. Incidentally, his plan also helped out-state Republican incumbents to hold on to their districts and pitted five incumbent Democrats against one another. Millender came up with the master stroke to get his plan adopted. He convinced black Democratic legislators to vote with their political rivals, the Republicans, to reapportion the state.[23] After reapportionment Millender successfully managed the congressional campaign of John Conyers, Jr., in a close and bitter race with Richard Austin, also black. Conyers's victory made him the second black congressman from Michigan and made Detroit "the first city to be represented by two black congressmen."[24]

This black political advance came at great cost to the larger black community: It split the black leadership. When the first district was newly reapportioned, a group of concerned citizens sent Millender to ask TULC labor leader Horace Sheffield to run for congressman from the district. He refused, telling Millender that if a black could win, which he doubted, his candidate would be Richard Austin. Millender informed Sheffield that he was their first choice, and if he did not accept, the group would support Conyers. Millender and his group went on to campaign for Conyers. Sheffield and other major black labor leaders, along with the Democratic party's white leadership, rallied behind Austin. The wounds of this campaign between two prominent blacks took years to heal.[25]

Millender's efforts to get George Crockett elected to the Detroit Common Council in 1965 failed, but a year later Crockett won election to the Detroit Recorder's Court. In 1968 Millender scored again by quarterbacking Robert Tindal's election to the council. Overcoming the rift caused by the Conyers and Austin campaigns, in 1969 Millender worked on behalf of Richard Austin for mayor in the closest race in the history of Detroit. Roman Gribbs edged Austin by a margin of only 6,194 votes. Three years later Millender added another impressive black political victory to his record by masterminding the election of Erma Henderson to the council to replace Tindal, who had died in office. Millender's biggest political success came in 1973 when he managed Young's campaign to become the city's first black mayor. By then he had overcome his bitterness against Coleman Young for allegedly failing to marshal votes for Austin.[26]

Richard Austin: First Black Bid for Mayor of Detroit

Richard Austin's bid for mayor in 1969 was a momentous occasion for the city. Although eclipsed by Young after the 1973 election, Austin became the first black in Detroit to win a mayoral primary. He lost the final election in what went down in Detroit's annals as the closest political contest in the city's history, but his campaign lingered in the hearts and minds of both black and white Detroiters for many years.

Richard Austin was a black moderate who not only believed in the liberal coalition but also understood the pragmatism of biracial politics as one means to achieve black political ends. Like other blacks of his generation, he had achieved several black "firsts." He was the first black in Michigan to become a certified public accountant (CPA), the first black to achieve membership in the American Institute of CPAs, the first black to serve on the board of directors of the Certified Public Accountant Association, the first black financial advisor to the U.S. Commission of Internal Revenue, and the first black to be elected Wayne County auditor.[27] By any objective standard of merit, Austin had the experience and background to become the first black mayor of Detroit. That he did not was testimony both to the irrational racism of whites, who two years after the black rebellion were still trapped in their self-imposed phobias and fantasies of blacks taking over the city, and to the yet underdeveloped political consciousness of significant segments of the black community.

Some blacks believed that 1969 was not the year to elect a black mayor. But Congressman John Conyers ignited a spark in the black community earlier in the year by pushing hard for a black mayoral candidate. While the choice of his old political rival, Austin, for this historic achievement did not initially excite Conyers, he rallied behind him. Austin came in first in the primary election with 45,856 of the votes, and Wayne County's Sheriff Roman S. Gribbs came in second with 34,650. The white vote was largely split between Gribbs and Mary Beck, a white conservative, who placed third and received 26,480 of the total votes.[28]

The primary clearly demonstrated the influence of race on local politics. Austin received most of his votes from the black community. He hoped to get 15 percent of the white vote but received less than 10 percent. Gribbs and Beck received tremendous support from the white community for their emphasis on "law and order." Gribbs, a moderate who believed in integration, had antagonized many black leaders when, as assistant Wayne County prosecutor in 1963, he aggressively prosecuted black protesters who participated in the sit-in at the First Federal Savings and Loan Association. As Wayne County sheriff, Gribbs also alienated many people, particularly blacks, when he attempted to get approval for his officers to use Mace, a controversial form of gas. He decided to be a candidate for mayor 24 hours before the filing deadline to save the city from a field of what he considered less than acceptable candidates.[29]

Almost overnight Gribbs received financial backing from executives at major banking, business, and legal establishments in the city, including General Motors. Ninety percent of Gribbs's support during the primary came from managers, executives, and lawyers; and most of his financial support was centered in the suburbs. Austin's support came mainly from Detroiters, most of whom were doctors, dentists, and small business owners.[30]

As the two top runners prepared for the November election, everyone knew that race would be the determining factor in the outcome. As the *Detroit Free Press* stated in September, "Although he finished first in the primary, Austin must woo many white voters to win in November. . . . On the surface it looks like a tough assignment, given the racial polarization shown by Tuesday's overall voting patterns."[31] Austin refused to believe that whites would not vote for a black to be mayor of Detroit, but he had no illusion that race was not a key issue. Attacking Gribbs, who had denied that race was a factor, Austin told a group of students in northwest Detroit, "I wish to God he was right. Race is relevant to too many people in this election."[32]

Race seemed far more important to whites in the city than to blacks. For example, following a racial voting pattern much like that of the 1965 city election, black voters voted for both black and white candidates, while white voters tended to vote only for white candidates. A citizen research group, the Citizen's Committee for Equal Opportunity, discovered that in the primary election "white voters in appalling numbers simply did not vote for black candidates at all, or in instances where they did so, gave them such low consideration as to virtually exclude them from serious consideration." The committee reported that, unlike many black voters, white voters were not demonstrating a belief "in the bi-racial future of the city and in bi-racial representation in city government."[33]

A white reader's letter to the editor of the *Detroit Free Press* asked the question, "Will whites help elect the best council candidates?" Pointing out that the November election would be a crucial test in race relations, the writer lamented the fact that the "best qualified candidate for mayor might not be elected because he is black," considering the fact that "two-thirds of the white voters have acknowledged his superiority in a poll—but only half of that group indicated that they would support him."[34]

A *Detroit Free Press* survey of voter attitudes during the year revealed that white voters were mainly concerned about welfare, crime, and "the colored taking over."[35] Yet the primary election also revealed that while whites supported blacks for seats on the Detroit Common Council, they held back on supporting a black for the top office of mayor. A case in point was that one white west-side residential area gave black Councilman Nicholas Hood 35 percent of the vote but gave Austin only 10 percent of the vote. No wonder a group of white leaders supporting Austin put full-page advertisements in local newspapers asking white voters, "Can you vote for a black mayor?"[36] For many whites the answer was a resounding no. A northeast Detroit paper, reflecting the views of many white home-owners in that section of Detroit, informed its readers that if Austin was elected as Detroit's first black mayor, it would mean the beginning of the end "for the white, tax-paying homeowner." Another paper in the same area, considered the official voice of the Northeast Council of Homeowners Association, warned its readers, "Unless the white conservative voting element of this city exhibits a sudden wave of political intelligence, the election of Negro candidate Richard Austin as Detroit's first black mayor is a foregone conclusion."[37]

Surveys repeatedly indicated that the vast majority of white voters in Detroit rejected Austin solely on the basis of race.[38] This fact greatly disturbed the quiet black moderate who sincerely wanted to bridge the racial gap in Detroit. Realizing that he needed white votes, Austin campaigned in white communities as he had done before. But many of his black supporters—those who had marshalled the black vote that won him first place in the primary—were becoming increasingly frustrated by white voters' reluctance to vote on merit instead of race. The Reverend Albert B. Cleage, Jr., of past black nationalist fame, wrote in his column published in the local black newspaper: "I support Dick Austin and I feel that he should receive the total black vote, but inasmuch as his election is dependent upon a large white vote, I see no possibility of his election. . . . [We] could elect Dick Austin mayor and . . . could elect a majority of the city council [but] we probably won't do either because we won't try hard enough." After criticizing the fact that blacks had not registered enough blacks, Cleage said, "The white racist syndrome will wipe out white support for black candidates by election day."[39]

Another writer for the same newspaper put white liberals on notice that if blacks did not come out of the November election "with a healthy victory," there would not be any more black/white coalitions. Complaining that in past elections black/white coalitions had mainly benefited white politicians, the writer warned, "The black community is not going to accept the short end or the blind, lame or dead horse in the trade this time."[40]

Black leaders supporting Austin knew all too well that white liberals were not working hard enough to get white votes for black candidates. At a meeting of the black and white liberal politicians and labor leaders, the black leaders informed their white allies: "The records will show we in the black community can deliver votes better than the white community. We are sick and tired of delivering votes for white folks and listening to their excuses later. We are going to stop delivering if you don't deliver for Dick Austin and other black candidates we have selected."[41]

Black political activists and strategists had reached the point where they realized that they could call the shots in coalition politics. Liberal whites in the coalition, now reduced to a minority faction, had to face up to the fact that, as blacks became a numerical majority in Detroit, they would be less responsive to the dictates of the liberal coalition. But that time was surely not in 1969. Dick Austin badly needed the coalition in order to win. The coalition, however, could not deliver sufficient white votes to give Austin the lead. Austin lost the election but left his indelible mark on the political history of black and white Detroit.[42] Subsequently, Austin was elected to the office of secretary of state of Michigan and became an even more visible presence for state residents than he would have as mayor of Detroit.

Coleman Young: Detroit's First Black Mayor

Blacks lost a major political battle in the 1969 mayoral election, but they were winning the protracted political war in the city. As one very perceptive white reporter observed after Austin's defeat, "After years of fitful and sometimes explosive growth, a new politics has emerged in Detroit. It belongs not to the left or the right, but to the steadily growing black community. . . . Within a very few years, most of the burdens and benefits of local political power will rest with blacks."[43] Most whites knew that it would only be a matter of time before blacks would have enough votes to elect a black mayor and a predominately black common council without heavy reliance on white votes. Black political activists and strategists also knew this. Coleman Young, sitting in the state senate, bided his time, foreseeing that he was destined to play a major role in the "new politics" of Detroit.

Senator Coleman Young was a striking contrast to Richard Austin. Unlike Austin, with his quiet and accommodating political demeanor and style, developed through the process of being the "first black" in countless white-only situations, Young evolved a more combative political demeanor and style so evident in the black radical tradition of the late 1930s and early 1940s. Young's father had been forced to flee Tuscaloosa, Alabama, where Young was born, because he was considered an "uppity nigger." As a young man working at Ford, Young hit a racist white foreman in the head with a steel bar and as a result lost his job. He became involved in the UAW-CIO (United Auto Workers and Congress of Industrial Organizations) union drives in Detroit and later won election as the Wayne County CIO's first black organizational secretary. But he was ousted, along with other radicals, after Walter Reuther became UAW president. Always disturbed by racial discrimination, Young, as a second lieutenant in the famous Tuskegee Airmen, found himself constantly at odds with the U.S. Army's Jim-Crow regulations. He was arrested along with 100 other black officers for attempting to integrate an officers' club at Freeman Field, Indiana. In 1948 Young assumed the Michigan chair of Henry Wallace's Progressive party presidential campaign.[44]

In 1951 Young contributed to the formation of the National Negro Labor Council (NNLC), the most radical black labor organization of that period, and became its executive director. The redbaiting witch hunts of the early

1950s, led by Senator Joseph McCarthy, soon began focusing on the NNLC. The House Committee on Un-American Activities investigated the Detroit chapter of the NNLC, in which Young was involved. In February 1952 Young stood his ground and defiantly told the members of the committee: "I am part of the Negro people. I am now in process of fighting against what I consider to be attacks and discrimination against my people. I am fighting against un-American activities such as lynchings and denial of the vote. I am dedicated to that fight, and I don't think I have to apologize or explain it to anybody."[45]

Young was one of the first radicals, black or white, to stand up to the committee. Informing them that he would not be a "stool pigeon," Young proceeded to lecture the southern congressional representatives and staff members on the correct pronunciation of "Negro." Such brash and bold behavior elevated Young to the status of a local hero in the black community. Soon phonograph records of his testimony were circulating throughout the black community.[46]

Coleman Young began his political career in 1960 as an elected delegate to the state constitutional convention. He drafted the first version of the Civil Rights Commission Act. In 1964 he was elected to the state senate and moved to the position of Democratic leader in the senate. And in 1968 he was elected the new Democratic national committeeman from Michigan amidst the upheavals of the Chicago Democratic Convention. Young became the first black in the nation to be elected to that position. To Young, his election proved that racial attitudes were changing and that whites were beginning to vote regardless of the candidate's color. At this point in his political career, Young still believed in the efficacy of the liberal coalition for black political development but with qualifications: "I am a Negro first and a Democrat second."[47] At the height of the black nationalist period in the nation and Detroit when separatists talked about carving out their own country in the South, Young said they were "just smoking marijuana." To Young, coalition with liberal whites was "the only way."[48]

Senator Coleman Young seriously considered becoming a candidate for mayor of Detroit in 1969 but was prevented from doing so by a Michigan Supreme Court ruling that barred a state legislator from running for another office before the expiration of his current term. Young, then a three-term senator, had wanted to run because Austin, according to Young, had not caught on and had failed to give "the people anything to sink their teeth into as far as what he would do as mayor." Austin's biggest shortcoming, Young felt, centered on his failure to commit himself publicly to such issues as civilian control of the police department.[49]

In 1973, four years later, Young was ready not only to run for mayor but also to make control of the police a central part of his campaign. He filed early enough to provide himself ample time to appeal a Wayne County Circuit Court ruling against his running. When the Michigan Supreme Court ruled in his favor and Austin, then secretary of state, announced that he was not in the running, Young became a serious mayoral candidate.[50] In a speech kicking off his primary campaign, Young put the police department and Police Commissioner John Nichols on notice:

> Detroit today is a racially polarized city, and now is the time we need to have a black mayor. One of the problems is that the police run the city. . . . STRESS [a controversial undercover police operation] is responsible for the explosive polarization that now exists; STRESS is an execution squad rather than a law enforcement squad. As mayor, I will get rid of STRESS. . . . The whole attitude of the whole Detroit Police Department, historically, has been one of intimidation and that citizens can be kept in line with clubs and guns rather than respect. The present department under Nichols is following the old blackjack rule by terror. If elected, I would fire Nichols.[51]

The white police responded by endorsing Nichols.[52]

In the primary Nichols and Young came in first and second, respectively, with Nichols getting 33.8 percent of the vote and Young getting 21.1 percent. The remaining votes went to the other three candidates. The voting patterns revealed that each candidate would have to appeal to both black and white voters in order to have a chance of winning in November.[53]

Young's broad political experience in local, state, and national politics gave him an edge over the single-issue Nichols. Yet Nichols did have the advantage that exploiting white fears of black crime in the street gave him. Young knew better than to ignore crime, but his appeal to white voters emphasized economic development for the city. Young promised to lead a "business resurgence" that would produce thousands of jobs and would include "new park facilities, a stadium, rapid transit, recreational facilities, and housing." Speaking at the Economic Club of Detroit, Young advised the assembled cream of the Detroit business class to invest in the city instead of the suburbs. Nichols could do little better than accuse Young of being a professional politician compared with himself, a practical man heading one of the city's largest departments. Predictably, Nichols fell back on crime in the street, which he argued was the most important issue in the city.[54] In the end, Young—with the support of many business groups, the support of the Urban Alliance (a nonprofit, interfaith, nonpartisan voter information organization), and significant financial support—won the election and became Detroit's first black mayor.

The victory did not blind Mayor Young to the need to bring the races together in a city half black and half white. Soon after his victory he proclaimed to his supporters, "I didn't win; we won. All of Detroit won."[55] Although he emphasized racial unity in his inaugural address, saying, "What is good for the black people in this city is good for the white people in this city," Young and his black and white supporters surely knew that the "new politics" was emerging in full bloom. This was a black political victory, plain and simple. On the morning before the inaugural luncheon, some of Young's followers held a prayer meeting, and the Reverend Charles Butler of the New Calvary Baptist Church, referring to Young, cited the biblical phrase "Behold this man." Although the power elite were present, "for the first time in Detroit the street people who knew 'Coleman' when he was down and struggling were in on things, watching from the edges of the crowd, smiling as if they had been graced by greatness."[56]

At the Cobo Hall inaugural luncheon, world corporate leaders such as Henry Ford II (chairman of the Ford Motor Company) and labor leaders such as Leonard Woodcock (UAW president) gathered around a smiling, former radical, now the mayor of one of the world's largest industrial cities. Henry Ford got up and explained what the new day really meant: "We, here in this room, represent the beginning of a new coalition of business and labor, brought together by our mutual desire to pledge our support to the newly inaugurated mayor."[57] Black political power in Detroit personified by Mayor Young would still need powerful and willing white allies to rebuild the city. While some of Young's black followers might have been too drunk with the wine of victory to see or want it, of necessity the "new politics" would include the liberal coalition.

The greatest evidence of black political power in Detroit during Young's first term of office was the radical change in the racial makeup of the police department. This was not an easy task because of the resistance of white police officers and their union. After several years of power struggles and countless bouts of negotiations, Young made some progress in changing a predominantly white police department into one that was at least in the process of becoming more racially integrated. By the end of 1976 Detroit boasted its first black police chief and a top command structure that was half black and half white. One hundred black officers had been hired since Young's election, increasing black representation from 17 percent to 22 percent.[58] The "old boys network," which had perpetuated and maintained white, male privilege in promotions for decades, had to give way to Young's aggressive affirmative action program. As this program began to take hold, blacks went from 5 percent of all officers holding the rank of sergeant to 15 percent.[59] Young would continue to have problems with the police department, but never again would it be the symbol of white, official oppression.

Mayor Young ended his first term in office by helping to put Jimmy Carter into the White House. As a major black figure in national Democratic politics and in labor and business circles, Young had both the power and credibility to deliver powerful black voting blocks to Carter. Young possessed such influence that when Carter slipped during the 1976 presidential campaign, saying that he saw nothing wrong with "ethnic purity," a statement many interpreted as advocating racial purity, Young defended the Democratic candidate, explaining that he had been misunderstood. Carter was still apologizing when he met Mayor Young at the Detroit airport. As soon as Young boarded Carter's plane, he told Carter, "Get up off your knees and keep on walking."[60]

When Carter became president Mayor Young's political power multiplied by virtue of the leverage he now had in the White House. Carter's urban policies reflected the influence of the mayor of Detroit. Young's appointees ended up in the Carter administration, channeling federal money to Detroit. All during the Carter administration, Young could be seen operating in the country's highest councils.[61]

Mayor Young ran for reelection against black councilman Ernest Browne in 1977. Young was supported by Henry Ford II (chairman of the Ford Motor Company), Douglas Fraser (president of the UAW), and President Carter. This was the first general election in a major city in which both mayoral candidates were black. Black voters rejected Browne both in the primary and in the general election, so Browne hoped for a winning coalition of a majority of white voters and a minority of black voters. It did not work. Young won handily. The campaign turned bitter when Young accused Browne of selling out blacks for political gain and Browne retorted that Young used racist tactics.[62]

The mayor faced even tougher times during his second term, the worst of which was a budget crisis in 1981 that forced Detroit voters to approve an income tax hike and city officials to sell $125 million in emergency bonds.[63] Young not only had to persuade city voters to go along with his plan to save the city from bankruptcy but he also had to convince the state legislature and twist the arms of municipal workers to accept a two-year wage freeze. Black unemployment in the city remained a problem and stood at 25 percent as Young prepared to run for his third term. Even the impressive Renaissance Center complex could not lift the gloom. Times were tough in the Motor City and getting tougher, especially for many blacks who still saw Young as the "big daddy," a symbol of their power and success.[64]

The loss of Carter as president hurt Detroit and cut the ties that had once provided so much financial lifeblood to the struggling city. But that did not prevent Mayor Young from calling President Reagan "pruneface" and accusing him of "lacking any compassion for urban residents and the poor." In his third inaugural address, he told Detroiters to "circle the wagon" and to "close ranks and send a message to the President. . . . [This country] can't go forward if its cities are sinkholes of poverty and starvation."[65]

Now that Detroit has had a black mayor for more than a decade and boasts a predominantly black city council, has Detroit become a hollow prize? If political observers have learned nothing else about the long history of black political development in Detroit and other cities, they have learned this: Black political development alone cannot solve the basic economic problems affecting the black urban masses in the major cities of the nations.

William Lucas: A New Breed

For close to a decade Mayor Young was the premier black politician in the metropolitan community. But even as his political star continued to rise, dimmed only slightly by the ignominious fall of Jimmy Carter in 1980 and the spectacular victory of Ronald Reagan, another local political star also rose. Democrat William Lucas's political career represents a sharp break in the historical patterns of black political development.

Lucas first became involved in Wayne County politics in 1968 when he was appointed undersheriff by then Wayne County sheriff, Roman Gribbs. Gribbs had convinced Lucas to leave the FBI to take the job. After Gribbs became mayor of Detroit in 1969, Lucas was appointed Wayne County sheriff. He won reelection to the office three times. After 14 years as Wayne County sheriff, Lucas won election to the newly created office of Wayne County executive, with strong support from the Black Slate, the most powerful black political organization in the metropolitan area and in the state. This organization had played a key role in Coleman Young's first victory and since then had been successful in electing other black candidates to office. Mayor Young, however, did not endorse Lucas for the office of county executive.[66]

Soon after Lucas took office, he not only hired a prominent, white Republican as an advisor but also sharply reduced the county budget, which included curtailing services essential to the poor, most of whom were blacks living in Detroit. These decisions enraged the Black Slate: "[Lucas's] political decisions and associations are fraught with evidence of a lack of sensitivity and a lack of concern for the effects of the political process on the lives of black and poor people." The organization attempted to recall Lucas but failed. While Mayor Young shared the concerns of the Black Slate, he did not support its recall movement, even though some of his strongest supporters were behind it. Instead, Young expressed the view, "To the degree that Lucas is not living up to his promise . . . we ought to speak out loudly and make it be known. . . . We ought to let Lucas know that those of us who elected him are disappointed with what he is doing and we will see him at the next election." Young's decision not to support the recall movement disappointed the Black Slate. Lucas, however, commented that Young's decision not to join the recall movement was what he had expected: "He's a straight-forward individual."[67]

In less than three years as Wayne County executive, Lucas transformed many aspects of county government, ruffling many feathers on the way, including those of his own party. Often called "Cool Hand Luke," he took on established labor leaders, abolished the powerful Wayne County Road Commission, greatly reduced the county's work force, and set up a blue-ribbon commission to push for additional prison space in the county. Observers in Washington, D.C., first noticed Lucas when he initiated a trade mission to Japan. To some political observers, Lucas had "given Wayne County a badly needed dose of respect."[68]

After years of fighting with members of the Democratic party, in May 1985 Lucas switched to the Republican party and invited other blacks to join him. Meeting with President Reagan at the White House soon after his switch, Lucas said, "I am not here to say they [blacks] all have to rush and join in, but just think. Just think about the value of your vote. Just think about attaching some degree of importance to the political process and not just following blindly everyone's lead."[69]

Leading Democrats were not surprised by Lucas's switch. Lieutenant Governor Martha Griffiths, among others, had already accused Lucas of openly flirting with Republicans, who, Griffiths claimed, were "trying to lure him out of the Democratic Party to cut up the black vote."[70] A month before Lucas switched to the Republicans, Mayor Young called the anticipated move "desperate" and commented, "There's a hell of a lot wrong with the Democratic Party. I've often said I'm a Democrat, not because they are perfect. They have a lot of bastards in the Democratic Party, but I think there are more in the Republican party, and that explains my party preference."[71]

By mid-1985 the Republicans in Michigan were busy showboating their newest black convert, who they hoped to run for governor against the Democratic party's Governor Blanchard. Leading white Republicans, such as former governor George Romney and Richard DeVos (president of Amway Corporation and one of the major financial contributors to the Republican party) seemed eager to dump longtime party regulars who were in line to run on the Republican ticket for governor of Michigan to support Lucas instead. Many white Michigan Republicans felt Lucas would not offend white voters. "He [Lucas] is not a [Jesse] Jackson or a Coleman Young," explained Romney. "Jackson tends to turn a lot of white people off. Coleman has clearly conducted a racist administration in the city of Detroit."[72] Lucas ran and lost the race for governor.

It certainly was one of the most intriguing dramas in the political history of the state. A black politician had gained the top political office in the county, governing an area much larger than the majority-black city, yet had thereafter distanced himself from the Democratic party and, some claimed, from his black constituency. Nevertheless, the possibility existed that he would be catapulted to state office.

All of this offered amazing possibilities, considering that two decades before, the likelihood of having even a black city mayor had seemed remote. Blacks had come far in the political realm, not only because of population shifts in the city and region but also because of the special talents and efforts of politicians and political organizers. In the process they had moved from fragile coalition predicated on the acceptability of black candidates to white sensibilities, to black political power supportive of the most outspoken ethnic politicians. The steady ascendency of black political prowess, however, had not bridged racial chasms in the region.

Metropolitan School Desegregation: A Policy Issue

Although school desegregation policy is not always thought of as a political issue, school district boundaries have become as important as (or more important than) political jurisdictional boundaries in many regions of the country. In the previous section of this chapter it became obvious that over the years blacks gained great political power and influence in the city of Detroit and, to a more limited extent, in the region. This portion of the chapter suggests that one reaction of white citizens to increasing black visibility and political power was first to retreat to whiter areas of the city of Detroit and then to retreat even farther to whiter school districts.

Schools and housing have been the most contested areas in the racial struggle that has taken place in Detroit. Schools, like houses, represented racial territory and social status. More important, schools have always been among the most central institutions in any community. Like the neighborhood church, the neighborhood school often embodies the collective values of the surrounding community. One reason why Detroit whites resisted blacks' moving into their neighborhoods was that they knew residential integration would lead to school integration. This would further challenge their claim to what they perceived as their exclusive right to their racial space.

By 1953 black students attended two-thirds of the schools in the city of Detroit. However, many white teachers and principals and a few white administrators seemed completely oblivious and insensitive to the racial changes occurring in their midst. Some schools responded to these racial changes by lowering curriculum standards to accommodate prevalent white stereotypes of blacks as a class of people unable to learn as fast as whites. Black teachers were still largely confined to predominantly black schools and were becoming frustrated over being forced to teach in schools considered inferior. White teachers in these mostly black schools shared their frustration.[73]

Racial conflicts in the school system punctuated the decade of the 1960s setting the stage for the protracted bussing controversy that tested the racial tolerance of blacks and whites in metropolitan Detroit. Many school-related racial conflicts seemed inevitable, originating as they did from unpredictable and largely uncontrollable changes in the racial demography of Detroit. But some school-related racial conflicts could have been foreseen and perhaps controlled, if not prevented. These conflicts erupted as a direct result of urban renewal policies of the 1940s and 1950s that forced the relocation of thousands of blacks from one overcrowded ghetto to another equally overcrowded ghetto, overloading already seriously handicapped schools.

Racial Segregation in the Schools

In 1960, as ghetto schools strained to accommodate more students, the Detroit Board of Education opted to bus black students from the overcrowded center-district schools to the closest schools with sufficient student capacity. Predominantly white schools located on the extreme northwest side of Detroit and in surrounding neighborhoods were extremely hostile to this bussing plan because they perceived it to be an invasion of their community by vastly inferior black students. As soon as the bussing plan was made public, whites on the far northwest side of Detroit organized a meeting of some 500 people. They circulated petitions to recall the members of the Detroit Board of Education and encouraged parents to boycott classes for three days. When school opened, 30 percent of the children boycotted classes at one school and 67 percent at another. Some parents who participated in the boycott did so only because they feared violence.[74]

Anticipating the possibility of racial conflict, the Detroit Commission on Community Relations set up meetings with the press, police officials, the Catholic Archdiocese of Detroit, representatives of the Council of Churches, and the religious leaders in the neighborhood to discuss the racial problems associated with the bussing plan. They condemned the actions of the people who organized the boycott and circulated the petitions.[75] But the fear of bussing ran deep, and even liberal whites who chose to live in integrated neighborhoods began to worry about the declining quality of their schools as black students were bussed in from overcrowded ghetto schools. A common statement at the time was "I'll stay until the school declines." As more black students arrived, white teachers began asking for transfers.

Meanwhile black parents were up in arms over inadequate and segregated schools in black neighborhoods. Their protests were justified, based as they were on charges of racial discrimination in the school system, and confirmed in 1962 by the Citizens Advisory Committee on Equal Educational Opportunities. The Detroit Board of Education had directed this committee to identify "the factors which affect equality of educational opportunities in the Detroit Public Schools and to recommend to the Board of Education ways which would increase equality of opportunities for all pupils."[76] The committee boldly acknowledged the presence of racism in the Detroit school system and recommended bussing as one solution for ending segregation. The committee also censured the historical practice of segregated teacher placement: "While the Detroit Public School system has employed a large number of Negro teachers in recent years, the committee found a clear-cut pattern of racial discrimination in the assignment of teachers and principals to schools throughout the city."[77] This practice, the committee stated, "of assigning teachers, principals, and other school employees on the basis of race is educationally, legally, and morally unsound and weakens the democratic opportunities of children in the Detroit

Public Schools. We urge that immediate action be taken to remedy this situation."[78]

The main responsibility for implementing the committee's recommendations was correctly placed upon the Detroit Board of Education, but support from the community at large was needed for the successful implementation of the recommendations. The school system could not be expected to carry the entire burden of uprooting racism and ending discrimination.

Black parents began to organize. They were encouraged by leaders such as radical black minister the Reverend Mr. Cleage, who said, "It is deplorable that years of protests by a generation of parents has not sufficiently impressed the board with the fact that the administrators were busy as beavers establishing Jim Crow districts, Jim Crow curricula, and Jim Crow schools. Now that the facts are known, now that the board sees the patterns of segregation and second rate facilities foisted on Negro children, the course of necessary action is obvious."[79] The committee report came on the heels of a groundswell of black community protest against segregated schools, sparked in part by a race discrimination suit filed in federal court against the school board by a group of black parents from Sherill School. The Sherill School Parents Committee was soon joined by other interested organizations.

Two months before the school committee report came out, these protest organizations formed a citywide group called Parents Committee for School Integration. They agreed to concentrate their efforts on combating racial discrimination in the school system, leaving nonracial school problems to the Parent-Teacher Association (PTA).[80] The parent group proved so effective that a local black newspaper commented: "The school report would already be as dead as a dinosaur if it were not for the Sherill School Parents' bias suit."[81] Essentially a grass-roots movement of concerned black parents, the Sherill School Parents Committee put the local NAACP in the embarrassing position of trying to catch up with a school desegregation struggle in Detroit that had been initiated without its support or guidance. As one writer put it, "The NAACP . . . must understand that any action it may wish to take at this time must be taken in cooperation with the Sherill School Parents Committee."[82]

The committee report paved the way for as much racial cooperation as racial conflict. Its recommendations exposed previously contested aspects of racism in the school system and provided official sanctions for the continuation of bussing, which angered many whites. The report also increased the expectations of black parents for a speedy and significant change.

In 1964, two years after the report was issued, Detroit's liberal groups received a long-awaited opportunity to effect further change in Detroit's school system. When three school board members decided not to run for reelection, the liberal groups saw their chance to install a liberal majority on the school board. They formed a coalition, rounded up candidates, organized a campaign, and won the victory, a high point in the history of interracial political cooperation in Detroit. In the following years the liberal-dominated school board altered school boundaries to promote racial integration, increased the number of black teachers and administrators, and pressured publishers to produce textbooks that provided a more accurate picture of the races. "Every decision, every appointment, every statement," one observer commented, "reflected the board's overriding commitment to the goal of racial integration."[83]

For all their good intentions, guided by the visions of an integrated school system, the liberals on the board were soon swept into the unpredictable crosscurrents of racial change. The 1967 rebellion polarized blacks and whites all over the country and especially in Detroit. The death of Martin Luther King in 1968 mortally wounded the spirit of interracial cooperation, which had so inspired the liberal school board members after their election victory and subsequent successes. "Black power" was becoming increasingly more popular within the black community. In March of 1968 the *Michigan Chronicle* newspaper reported, "The crisis in Detroit's inner-city schools is fast approaching the dimensions of a forest fire."[84] The "forest fire" was the outbreak of racial conflicts that swept through Detroit schools. Black students became enraged at their fellow white students at Pershing High School when they refused to accept the elected black student government. On Detroit's east side black parents at the Marcy and Stephen schools were organizing efforts to eliminate white administrators. Black community control organizations and black parent groups were springing up all over the city, demanding black community control over their schools. A month earlier white parents at Finney High School had threatened to keep their kids at home if any more black students were transferred to the school.[85] The school board was caught between the proverbial rock and a hard place. And although it was for different reasons, a significant number of blacks and whites opposed racial integration in the schools.

In 1969 the Michigan legislature passed a law that required the decentralization of Detroit's public school system. In the Detroit school board's view, decentralization, or "increased community involvement," would help bridge the gap between them and the black community, but integration remained the board's primary goal. Decentralization was only a means to that goal. The goal, however, seemed to be rapidly slipping away. As A. L. Zwerdling, president of the school board, sadly informed a group of school administrators in Washington, D.C., in 1969, "No one who came to our public meetings on decentralization was interested in integration. Everyone wanted segregation so they would be assured a little piece of control; you cannot have both integration and community control."[86] Zwerdling made it clear that if he had to choose between the two, he would choose integration. He had not become the president of the Detroit Board of Education, he later informed the League of Women Voters, "to preside over the liquidation of integrated school systems."[87]

The School Board Recall and the Roth Decision

Events in 1970 and 1971 illustrated the extent to which school desegregation had become a political issue. In 1970 a plan for desegregation of the Detroit school system spurred a bitter school board recall election. This in turn led to a series of events that culminated in a court-ordered plan for the desegregation of the school systems of the entire metropolitan area.

The recall came about because of a modest proposal to desegregate city high schools. On April 7, 1970, the Detroit Board of Education voluntarily adopted a plan to effect a more balanced distribution of black and white students in 12 of 21 Detroit high schools. The so-called April 7 Plan was to take effect over a three-year period, applying initially to those students entering the 10th grade in September 1970. For the 11th grade, the plan was to be instituted at the opening of the 1971–1972 school year and for the 12th grade, at the beginning of the 1972–1973 school year. The plan was designed to reduce segregation in a school system that then was 63.6 percent black.

On July 7, 1970, however, the governor of Michigan signed into law Act 48, Public Acts of 1970. Section 12 of that act had the effect of delaying and ultimately blocking the implementation of Detroit's April 7 high school desegregation plan.

In the meantime predominantly white groups from the northwest and northeast neighborhoods in Detroit spearheaded a recall drive that succeeded in removing four members of the board who supported the April 7 Plan. According to the *Free Press* education writer, the recall election "was the only successful recall election in the history of the school system . . . and . . . left the city's liberals and its civil rights groups reeling from the shock."[88]

After the recall, the governor of Michigan appointed four new board members. These four members, together with the incumbents who had originally opposed the April 7 action, rescinded the plan. This decision generated a complaint, filed by the parents of individual black and white school children and the Detroit branch of the NAACP, against the board of education of the city of Detroit and its members, the superintendent of schools, the governor, the attorney general, and the superintendent of public instruction of the state of Michigan.

The complaint alleged that the Detroit public school system was segregated on the basis of race, as the result of actions and policies of the Detroit Board of Education and the state of Michigan. The complaint specifically challenged the constitutionality of Act 48 of the Public Acts of 1970 of the state of Michigan.

In an opinion announced October 13, 1970, the U.S. Court of Appeals for the Sixth Circuit held that Section 12 of Michigan's Public Act 48, and hence the blocking of the April 7 desegregation plan, was unconstitutional.[89] In addition, the court of appeals ordered the district court to hear the case involving school segregation in Detroit on its merits. The trial of the case began April 6, 1971, and continued until July 22, 1971.

After extensive hearings U.S. District Court Judge Stephen J. Roth ruled that *de jure* segregation existed in the Detroit public schools. Roth indicated that the principal causes were population movement and housing patterns, but state and local governmental actions, including school board actions, played a substantial role in promoting segregation. Roth also blamed federal, state, and local governmental officers and agencies, lending institutions, and real estate firms for establishing and maintaining the segregated residential patterns that led to school segregation.

According to Judge Roth, school districts were accountable for the natural, probable, and foreseeable consequences of their policies and practices, and where racially identifiable schools were the result of these policies, the school authorities bore the burden of showing that the policies were based on educationally required, nonracial considerations.

The court case uncovered a number of discriminatory policies practiced by the Detroit school board. For example, beginning in 1950 the board created and maintained optional attendance zones within neighborhoods undergoing racial transition and between high school areas of opposite predominant racial compositions. In 1959 there were eight basic optional attendance areas affecting 21 schools. Optional attendance areas provided pupils living within certain elementary school neighborhoods a choice of attendance at 1 of 2 high schools. At least one optional area existed in 1960 between 2 junior high schools of opposite predominant racial components.[90] All of the optional high school areas except 2 were in neighborhoods undergoing racial transition, from white to black, during the 1950s. The effect of these optional zone policies was to allow white youngsters to escape identifiably black schools.[91] The school board also had a policy, supposedly to relieve overcrowding, that included the bussing of black students past or away from closer white schools with available space to more distant black schools. This practice continued until the late 1960s. In addition, the board had created and altered attendance zones, maintained and altered grade structures, and altered feeder school patterns in a manner that had the effect of continuing black and white students in racially segregated schools. Until 1970 the board separated school attendance zones of opposite racial compositions by north–south boundary lines despite the board's awareness (since at least 1962) that drawing boundary lines in an east–west direction would result in significant racial integration. The effect of the board's actions or its failure to act was to perpetuate school segregation. Finally, the board constructed schools on sites that guaranteed racially identifiable schools. Of the 14 schools that opened in 1970–1971, 11 opened with 90 percent black students, and 1 opened with over 90 percent white students.[92]

In summary, most of the evidence suggested that the state and its agencies, such as the school board, acted directly to control and maintain the pattern of racial segregation in the Detroit schools. Until 1970 the state refused to provide authorization of funds for the transportation of pupils within Detroit, regardless of their poverty or distance from the school to which they were assigned. On the other hand, the state willingly provided funds for transportation to adjacent, mostly white suburban districts. This action, along with other differences imposed on Detroit *vis-à-vis* the suburbs, created and perpetuated systematic educational inequalities.

After his findings of *de jure* segregation, Judge Roth grappled with the problem of fashioning a remedy in accordance with *Swan v. Board of Education*, *Monroe v. Board of Commissioners*, *Green v. County School Board*, and *Brown v. Board of Education*.[93] Initially, he contemplated a "Detroit only" solution. Judge Roth required the school board defendants, Detroit and state, to develop and submit plans of desegregation "designed to achieve the greatest possible degree of actual desegregation, taking into account the practicalities of the situation."[94] Three "Detroit only" desegregation plans were submitted by the plaintiffs and by the Detroit Board of Education.

Judge Roth found that none of the plans would result in the desegregation of the public schools of the Detroit school district and that desegregation could not be accomplished within the corporate geographical limits of the city.[95] Judge Roth concluded that he had the duty to look beyond the limits of the Detroit School District for a solution to the illegal segregation in the Detroit public schools. Any desegregation plan involving only the city of Detroit would lead directly to a single segregated school district overwhelmingly black in all of its schools, surrounded by a ring of suburbs and suburban school districts overwhelmingly white. This seemed uncalled for in a state in which the racial composition was 87 percent white and 13 percent black.[96] Accordingly, the court ruled that it had to consider a metropolitan remedy for segregation. Judge Roth proceeded to request that each party submit plans for metropolitan desegregation. The parties submitted a number of plans, including one by the Michigan Board of Education, but Roth rejected all of them. The proposals submitted by the plaintiffs were all good-faith efforts to accomplish desegregation in the Detroit metropolitan area. All would have incorporated geographically most, if not all, of the three county areas of Wayne, Oakland, and Macomb. However, none of the proposals represented a complete plan for the effective and equitable desegregation of the metropolitan area.

Judge Roth appointed a nine-member panel to prepare and submit an effective metropolitan desegregation plan. The court identified the 54 metropolitan-area school districts that the plan was to include. It also directed that transportation and pupil assignment were to be a two-way process, with both black and white pupils sharing the responsibility for transportation requirements at all grade levels. In all, there were 780,000 students in the affected area, about a third of all public school students in the state. At the time of the ruling, the Detroit public school system was 65 percent black, and the suburban schools were less than 10 percent black.

City/Suburban Reaction to the Roth Decision

Suburban reaction indicated deep-seated and widespread opposition to the cross-district desegregation decision. A sampling of the opinions of suburban Detroit officials, teachers, parents, and students showed nearly unanimous disapproval. Many said they had no objection to blacks' being bussed into the suburbs, but they opposed suburban children's being bussed to Detroit schools.[97] Suburban school officials almost overwhelmingly opposed the metropolitan desegregation decision.

Opposition also came from some suburban mayors and municipal officials. The city commissioners of Royal Oak, for example, proposed an ordinance to make cross-district desegregation difficult and expensive. Some of the provisions of the ordinance were that all busses have speed governors to keep them traveling at less than 25 miles per hour and have seat belts and that all drivers have three years of college and three months of driver training.[98]

Opposition to metropolitan desegregation in Detroit impacted every level of the political arena. One day after the court decision, President Nixon phoned Michigan's Governor Milliken to stress that the decision clearly demonstrated the need for a moratorium against bussing until 1973. Instead of a moratorium, the U.S. House and Senate passed a bill that sought to prohibit the carrying out of any court-ordered bussing until all appeals of a case had been heard by the U.S. Supreme Court. This bill was supported by the five Democratic members of the Michigan congressional delegation. The five—John Dingell, William Ford, Martha Griffiths, James O'Hara, and Lucien Nedzi—voted for the bill with the hope that it would prevent bussing in Detroit.[99]

Among many suburban residents, Judge Roth became known as the "bussing judge." His name appeared on bumper stickers throughout metropolitan Detroit with such comments as "Roth is a four letter word" and "Roth is a child molester." Hatred for Judge Roth descended to such depths that in July of 1974, when he lay dying in his hospital bed, many suburban Detroit residents called to express their joy that he was near death.[100]

Although a minority, some civic and religious groups spoke out in support of the metropolitan school desegregation decision. The League of Women Voters of Metropolitan Detroit urged peaceful and thoughtful compliance with the desegregation order. The league asked the citizens of metropolitan Detroit to devote their best energies to making the desegregation process peaceful and constructive for the education of all the children in the area.[101]

Also, nine Detroit-area religious leaders urged the community to unite behind the federal court order. The joint statement, stressing the urgency of the goals behind the court order, said, "We must put aside differences. . . . We have an opportunity to make the classrooms of the metropolitan area a living lesson in American pluralism, and this great lesson can go beyond the classroom and renew the spirit of our country."[102] The statement released by the Metropolitan Detroit Council of Churches was signed by representatives of several denominations and faiths. Despite the support by some civic and religious groups, the widespread suburban opposition to metropolitan desegregation speeded up the appeal of the decision.

Before the panel appointed by Judge Roth could make a report on the specifics of metropolitan school desegregation in Detroit, the Court of Appeals for the Sixth Circuit remanded the case to the district court for the taking of additional evidence, because several of the suburban school districts had not been heard or had had no opportunity to be heard. In other words, as a prerequisite to the implementation of a desegregation plan affecting any school district, "the affected district must be made a party to the litigation and afforded an opportunity to be heard."[103]

The U.S. Supreme Court reversed the decision of the court of appeals, holding that no remedy involving any school district other than Detroit would be within the equitable power of the district court without evidence that the suburban district or districts had committed acts of *de jure* segregation.[104]

There were no findings that the differing racial composition between schools in the city and in the outlying suburbs was caused by official activity or collusion between the central city and suburban school districts. Thus, the decision to include in the desegregation plan pupils from school districts outside Detroit was not predicated upon any constitutional violation involving those school districts. According to *Swan v. Charlotte Mecklenburg Board of Education*, the nature of the violation determines the scope of the remedy.[105] Therefore, the court of appeals approval of a remedy that would reach beyond the limits of the city of Detroit to correct a constitutional violation found to have occurred solely within that city went beyond the governing equitable principles established by the U.S. Supreme Court.[106] Despite Judge Roth's conclusion that school desegregation could not be accomplished within the corporate geographical limits of the city, future school desegregation plans were based on Detroit only. Detroit was to remain a very racially segregated school system.

Suburban School Desegregation

The Roth cross-district plan was not the only generator of controversy over bussing. For example, Pontiac, Michigan—an industrial suburb 25 miles northwest of Detroit—was outside the scope of Roth's cross-district plan yet had its own court case. Appalachian whites and southern blacks in Pontiac shared a history of racial conflict. As one observer put it, "Racial clashes are endless here." At one time black and white neighborhoods fought over the location of a new $15 million high school, "turning one school board meeting into a chair-throwing melee."[107] The bussing controversy emerged in Pontiac in 1969, as a result of the local NAACP's charge that the Pontiac school board was perpetuating segregationist practices. District Judge Damon J. Keith, a black man from Detroit, ruled that the school board had maintained a segregated school system by planned site selection and teacher placement. In fact, the district had changed its boundaries six different times since 1948 to maintain segregated schools.

Judge Keith ordered the school district to come up with a desegregation plan. The plan that eventually evolved required only that 37 percent of the student population be bussed to 36 predominantly white schools, which worked out to a black mix of 20 to 36 percent. The plan was relatively modest, but it was still too much for the school board. The board appealed Judge Keith's decision and lost. Immediately, a group of irate white mothers set about organizing an antibussing group called the National Action Group (NAG) to frustrate compliance with the court order. Irene McCabe, the housewife who led the group, claimed NAG's opposition to bussing was not racially motivated. Yet the organization's first public act was sponsorship of a stadium rally attended by 5,000 people and featuring George Wallace, famed opponent of Alabama school desegregation and champion of white rights.

A week before school opened, ten Pontiac school busses were blown up, at a loss of $50,000. NAG leaders repudiated the bombing but carried on a campaign that created more racial conflict and violence. On the first day of school five women chained themselves to the bus yard gates to prevent the busses from moving, and other women sat down in front of the gates. As the first black children arrived, the NAG pickets joined the white bystanders in yelling "nigger, nigger" at the black children filing into school.[108]

Massive demonstrations continued for three days. Police responsible for providing security "idled on the sidewalk," which was understandable given that the Pontiac Police Officer Association had contributed $300 to NAG. Neither local union leadership nor General Motors intervened to resolve the racial conflict. In the end the Parent-Teacher Association and many students labored to bring forth some semblance of racial peace. When school opened again in the fall of 1972, a racial trouble-shooter commented that it was "the quietest school opening since '63; it's even hard for us to understand."[109] Twelve years later in 1984, Pontiac's school superintendent, Odell Noils, made an even more positive evaluation of the racial climate in the school system: "Pontiac has worked itself out of the confusion. Not everybody likes it. But the great majority have accepted it and are cooperating."[110]

Desegregation gradually took place in other suburbs but with much less racial conflict and fanfare. The Department of Health, Education and Welfare (HEW) withheld funds from Ferndale in 1969 for illegally segregating black elementary students in a single school. The school district also maintained racially segregated school faculties and student populations within easy walking distance of each other. Segregation persisted and in 1972 funds were cut off. In 1980 the Court of Appeals for the Sixth Circuit ordered Ferndale to come up with a plan to end racial segregation in its elementary schools. In 1981 the city came up with a voluntary desegregation plan.[111]

When the Ecorse school board voted for a voluntary desegregation plan in 1976, board members who voted for it were recalled. Five years later the new school board finally got rid of the plan. And the NAACP responded with a lawsuit, charging both the school system and the state board of education with *de jure* segregation. The suit claimed that Ecorse built an elementary school in 1939 to deliberately segregate black and white students. When the black student population increased, the suit maintained, white officials expanded the school rather than allow black students to attend white schools. The school system was found guilty and ordered by a federal judge to take all the necessary steps to desegregate the system. In 1981 a desegregation plan went into effect.[112]

In rare cases blacks and whites were able to achieve desegregation without court orders. Southfield is one of the best examples in Michigan, and probably the nation, of a suburb whose school system was integrated without a court order, thanks in part to a history of integrated housing. Such a positive interracial history obviously influenced race relations at Southfield High. According to one writer, "Racial integration is not merely an anomaly . . . but a deeply held matter of faith." Between 1977 and 1984 black enrollment in the school increased from 7 percent to 43 percent without any major racial conflicts.

The most impressive feature of this racial transformation is the existence of interracial friendship outside the school. Southfield High does have its special problems, such as not enough black staff and a fear among both blacks and whites that the school might become segregated, but for now it is a positive model of racial cooperation.[113]

In general, however, the reactions of suburban whites to bussing raised grave questions about the possibilities for metropolitan political cooperation. Their reactions to bussing were not unlike the responses of the white

South during the Civil Rights Movement in the 1960s. During the 1970s white, northern suburbanites suddenly discovered that they had a serious racial problem, which many had denied existed. Many were surprised by their responses, which, however benign they appeared, were no less racist than those of their southern counterparts. Surely southern whites must have savored the moments when they, long maligned by northern whites for their rude and vicious form of race relations, could witness white, northern racist antics on the six o'clock news.

Antibussing sentiments became so intense in the Detroit metro area during the 1970s that advocates organized seven major antibussing groups: Roseville Action Group, Citizens Against Busing, National Action Group (NAG), Save Our Children, Concerned Citizens for Quality Education (CCQE), Tri-county Citizens for Intervention in Federal School Actions (TCIFSA), and Kids Attend Their Schools (KATS).[114]

While these groups shared basically the same aims, they varied in size and strategies of resistance. NAG, described in the infamous Pontiac case, had about 20 operating chapters in 20 Detroit suburbs. TCIFSA had a membership of close to 48,000 people, each of whom contributed one dollar to finance the fight against the Roth decision. KATS had supporters mainly in Warren and in Berkley and the rest of Oakland County. They wanted freedom of choice and preferred private to integrated schools. CCQE boasted 1,800 members in Grosse Pointe and had members who threatened to go to jail rather than send their children to schools in Detroit.

White suburbanites' reaction to cross-district bussing revealed a wide range of racist feelings toward blacks in Detroit, feelings similar to the mass racial hysteria that had driven many of them out of Detroit. Many white suburbanites perceived bussing as an assault upon the last bastion of white society and culture. As one observer pointed out, "Bussing threaten[s] the whole way of life for hundreds of thousands of white people whose culture, whose options, whose ambitions all point away from the city."[115] In order to protect his way of life, one white suburbanite threatened to "go out and get a gun." "I've never done anything like that before," he said, "but this is one thing I'd go to war for." Another said, "I'd throw myself in front of a bus before I'd let them take my children to Detroit. . . . My kids will never go to Detroit; I will move to the Upper Peninsula."[116]

White suburbanites who could see no way out of the bussing situation contemplated relocating to their former home states, West Virginia, Virginia, Georgia, and elsewhere. In 1971 a group of whites in Warren, seeking a way to evade racial integration by establishing a private school system, was given permission by the city's consolidated school board to use its public building after regular school hours. Warren's residents also signed pledges protesting bussing:

> We __________ , residents of the City of Warren, do hereby pledge that we shall not allow our children to attend school if bussing is ordered by the courts, whether it is our child or our neighbors' child that is chosen to be bussed.[117]

While some white suburbanites accepted one-way bussing of black students to suburban schools as opposed to having their children bussed into Detroit, many whites wanted to avoid all contact with blacks, particularly those whites who had moved to the suburbs to get away from blacks in Detroit.

A small yet significant minority of suburban whites accepted school desegregation. They believed that black and white children should get to know one another and that white parents were doing a disservice to their children by not letting them know any black children: "Children should learn to appreciate differences," asserted proponents of this view. "Too many children [are] growing up in unrealistic settings. If youngsters are going to live and work successfully in a world that's getting smaller all the time, they're going to have to be in contact with people who are not just like themselves." The most progressive of these whites believed in racial integration even if it meant cross-district bussing: "I believe in integration and I don't know how else we're going to achieve it, because no one will sell their house to a black person here in Wyandotte. In order to change things that aren't right, you're going to have to make sacrifices." From this perspective, antibussing whites seemed pathetic: "They are so afraid and the sad thing is they really don't know what they are afraid of."[118]

White suburban attitudes toward school desegregation were just a pale reflection of their negative attitudes toward the city of Detroit and its citizens. And black parental attitudes, while far milder, suggested that the level of estrangement was deep, for many of those blacks had moved to a philosophy of community self-control. Education had become a battlefield.

Toward Metropolitan Cooperation

Neither the regional experience concerning racial politics in the city nor the record of school desegregation battles bode well for regional governmental cooperation in the Detroit area. Nevertheless, over the years some individuals and groups have made efforts to increase metropolitan cooperation within the region. These have ranged from nonprofit corporations devoted to good government and greater efficiency to politicians sincerely concerned about the increasing isolation of municipalities in the region.

The following portion of the chapter reviews some of the major efforts made to promote regionalism. It starts with a description of the great political fragmentation that exists within the region, and then it describes the movement toward voluntary metropolitan cooperation supported in the mid-1960s, efforts initiated by the state of Michigan to equalize school financing, subsequent proposals for a strong metropolitan authority supported by state representative William Ryan, and recent changes in the functions and powers of Wayne County (the county that includes the city of Detroit and other municipalities). The overall assessment of the chapter is that, in spite of numerous efforts to decrease political isolationism and increase cooperation, the region remains severely fragmented and that this fragmentation has a number of deleterious effects on the poorest of the municipalities, including Detroit. Yet little evidence suggests that this situation will change, in part because Detroit politicians now jealously guard their black political base and in part because the largely white suburban municipalities feel perfectly content with their political isolation.

Separation and Cooperation

As Maps 2.1 to 2.5 illustrate, the number and size of suburban municipalities greatly increased during the years from 1940 to 1980. Much of this expansion took place by the 1960s. By 1980 the region was very much fragmented, isolated, and in some sense antagonistic. A report issued by the Metropolitan Fund, Inc. in 1965 documented the extent to which such fragmentation had taken place by the mid-1960s.[119]

In 1965 the southeast area of the state—including Wayne, Oakland, Macomb, Monroe, St. Clair, and Washtenaw counties—contained a total of 404 units of government, including the 6 counties, 67 cities, 39 villages, 109 townships, 165 school districts, and other districts and authorities dealing with services such as sanitation, water, hospitals, and incinerators. Wayne County alone contained 94 of these units of government, Oakland County had 98, and Macomb had 54. By 1982 the number of units of government in Wayne County had dropped only slightly to 91, and the number in Oakland to 93. In Macomb County the number remained at 54. Between 1945 and 1964, 41 new municipalities (cities and villages) had incorporated in the 6 counties, although during that time period only 3 municipalities in the area had annexed land exceeding a quarter of a square mile. No such annexation occurred in the 3 central counties of the region: Wayne, Oakland, and Macomb.[120] As in many other northern states, communities have defensively incorporated to prevent absorption by larger municipalities, and state laws have made such incorporation much easier and quicker than annexation.

Nevertheless, examples of regional cooperation do exist, mainly in the form of authorities, special districts, and cooperative agreements. For example, the Huron-Clinton Metropolitan Authority has existed since 1940, and it developed and maintained parks and recreational areas for the residents of five counties. Although not without conflict—central-city mayors constantly complained that the authority provided more services for suburbanites than for their constituencies—it did offer an example of longstanding, albeit single-purpose, cooperation.

Other authorities and special districts have included single-purpose agencies that sometimes served a portion of a county, such as the People's Community Hospital Authority in western Wayne County, the Southeast Oakland County Water Authority, and the South Macomb Sanitary District. Cooperative agreements between municipalities proliferated in the region, including service contracts under which one unit of government would pay another to supervise its tax assessing activities or to provide police, fire protection, utility, park, public health, or planning services. The premier example of such agreements was the city of Detroit's provision of water for dozens of local units of government in southeast Michigan. Municipalities have also entered into joint service agreements to provide mutual assistance for library facilities, refuse disposal, fire fighting in times of need, and other services.[121]

Some forms of regionwide planning and program development also existed in early years in the southeast Michigan region. The Detroit Metropolitan Area Regional Planning Commission, established in 1947, included Wayne, Oakland, and Macomb counties as consistent members, with Monroe and Washtenaw counties as members for part of its history. Financed by county contributions, this agency undertook comprehensive planning research throughout the 1950s and 1960s. Another regional organization was the Supervisors' Inter-county Committee (SICC), formed by the members of the boards of supervisors of first five and then six southeast Michigan counties—the same counties involved in the regional planning commission, plus St. Clair County. This voluntary cooperative council, granted legal status in 1957, provided a forum for discussions of mutual concerns and for setting up and managing cooperative agreements. SICC also established a research arm that eventually became the Metropolitan Fund, Inc., a leader in promoting regional thought and fact gathering.

However, all of these agreements, authorities, and organizations did not add up to meaningful political cooperation. The SICC, for example, only included county levels of government, and the Metropolitan Area Regional Planning Commission did not link planning and governance. In the mid-1960s discussion began about the possibility of increasing the level of regional cooperation in the southeast Michigan area.

In 1964 the Metropolitan Fund asked the Citizens Research Council of Michigan to write several papers assessing the status of regional cooperation and suggesting improved structures. The council's report encouraged the Metropolitan Fund to establish a small policy committee in 1965. The policy committee concluded that two primary options existed: A metropolitan government with areawide authority and jurisdiction could be established, (an option that the policy committee said was not feasible politically) or the existing framework of local government and interlocal cooperation could be strengthened in several ways, including by the establishment of a voluntary Council of Governments (COG). The policy committee favored the second option and suggested that SICC and the Metropolitan Area Regional Planning Commission merge into a new council of governments. The chairman of the Metropolitan Fund appointed a new multimember body, the Committee of 100, to develop a specific proposal for a COG to include governments in six counties—a proposal that delegates to a prospective council approved in substance in 1967. The new council, the Southeast Michigan Council of Governments (SEMCOG), was formally created on January 1, 1968.[122]

The state of the region today would have been vastly different if the Metropolitan Fund's policy committee had chosen to press for a stronger metropolitan governance system. About the same time that these deliberations were taking place, in the mid-1960s, citizens in other regions of the country—such as Nashville, Tennessee; Jacksonville, Florida; and Indianapolis, Indiana—were approving new governmental structures that combined cities with their surrounding counties. In those cases, of course, only one county was involved, but the new structures did provide broader territory and thus broader taxing powers for the cities.[123] And it was about the same time that Minnesota's Twin Cities, Minneapolis and St. Paul, were developing a structure of regionalism that eventually led to a pioneering tax base-sharing agreement for that region.[124]

Southeast Michigan, however, was apparently ready for nothing stronger than a voluntary council, SEMCOG. While this council in its early years made great strides in promoting regional cooperation, it has always operated within strong limitations. With its establishment the membership abolished SICC, and the Metropolitan Area Regional Planning Commission was absorbed into SEMCOG as its planning unit, thus reducing the possibility of duplication. But at first only slightly more than 100 of the 400 eligible units of government joined. As a COG the organization functioned well, undertaking comprehensive land use planning as well as eventually supervising comprehensive planning of regional criminal justice, waste treatment, public health, and other services.[125] The COG structure, however, is by definition weak. SEMCOG, for example, could not force membership, which remains voluntary, or undertake activities as ambitious as tax base sharing. Though many metropolitan-area political leaders opposed any greater degree of regional cooperation in governance, the financial situations of the central city of Detroit and several other urban municipalities in the region were becoming so acute that it was obvious that some larger unit of government would have to help.

In the early 1970s that unit appeared to be the state government. Although metropolitan governance in the Detroit region did not succeed greatly, the state stepped in to assist redistribution of financial resources in some small fashion. This is apparent in several program areas, but we would like to focus on the issue of equitable financing for school districts, an issue of importance beyond the Detroit region but one pushed to the fore because of the crisis of the Detroit public school system.

Fiscal Crisis in the Detroit Public School System

The fiscal crisis of the public schools of Detroit offered an example of the effects of fiscal inequity in the region. In November 1972 the nation's fourth largest school system, responsible for instructing one in seven students in the state, was bankrupt.

The basis of the problem was escalating school costs in the face of declining revenues. The rising costs were due to inflation, rising expenditures for the special service needs of poor children, and increasing labor costs.[126] At the same time property taxes, which accounted for 85 percent of Detroit's locally raised school revenues, became insufficient as property values declined and voters refused millage increases.[127] Detroit's total property value actually declined by $865 million between the 1960–1961 and 1967–1968 school years. By 1971–1972 the city of Detroit was finally worth on

Table 6.1 Relationship of school district to tax rates, local revenue per pupil, and total expenditures per pupil for the 86 school districts in the Detroit metropolitan area, 1970–1971 school year

School districts (in deciles)	Average state equalized vaulation per pupil	Average equalized millage rates	Local revenue per pupil	Total operation expenditure per pupil[a]
Poorest tenth ($n = 9$)	$ 9,339	35.2	$ 311	$ 756
Next tenth ($n = 9$)	11,803	32.1	337	772
Next tenth ($n = 9$)	13,152	34.3	398	766
Next tenth ($n = 8$)	14,730	34.4	446	797
Next tenth ($n = 8$)	16,034	34.4	517	803
Next tenth ($n = 8$)	18,063	32.4	545	865
Next tenth ($n = 8$)	20,581	32.1	605	869
Next tenth ($n = 9$)	23,994	30.8	652	917
Next tenth ($n = 9$)	29,433	32.4	865	1013
Richest tenth ($n = 9$)	47,035	24.5	1055	1085
Detroit	18,325	22.9	441	895

Source: Calculated from raw data provided in (1) Michigan Education Association, Research Division, *Michigan Public School District Data 1970–71*, East Lansing, Mich. and (2) Michigan Department of Education, *Local School District Results, the Fourth Report of the 1971–72 Michigan Educational Assessment Program*, Lansing, Mich. September 1972.

a. Total expenditure by local, state, and federal governments.

the market what it had been in 1960–1961. But by then the Detroit school system had lost over $91 million in taxes.[128]

Detroit faced a contradiction. The city could try to tax itself at a higher rate to provide the services needed by an ever poorer population. To follow that path was to risk driving more firms and well-off families out of the city to the suburbs and to bring on tougher tax resistance among those who stayed in town.[129] Or the city could keep taxes steady and cut services, thus decreasing the quality of life not just in the city but in the whole region.

Central cities must provide services that more affluent communities can avoid, such as redevelopment projects and welfare. Central cities also provide services that suburbanites use but do not pay for, such as libraries, museums, and water and sewage systems. This kind of central-city overburden explains why Detroit's school millage rate fell well below that of most of its suburbs in the early 1970s, while its municipal tax rate ranged from two to five times that of its neighbors.[130] Detroit could not focus its financial energy on its school system the way many suburbs could, yet the

Table 6.2 Distribution of taxable property and pupil enrollment among the 86 school districts in the Detroit metropolitan area, 1970–1971 school year

School districts (in deciles)	(*A*) Percentage of total taxable property in metropolitan area	(*B*) Percentage of total public school pupils in metropolitan area	*A*/*B*
Poorest tenth ($n = 9$)	3.0	6.2	.48
Next tenth ($n = 9$)	4.5	7.5	.60
Next tenth ($n = 9$)	4.9	7.1	.69
Next tenth ($n = 8$)	3.7	4.8	.77
Next tenth ($n = 8$)	4.4	5.2	.85
Next tenth ($n = 8$)	34.2	39.9	.86
Next tenth ($n = 8$)	10.5	10.2	1.03
Next tenth ($n = 9$)	7.5	5.9	1.27
Next tenth ($n = 9$)	13.9	9.0	1.54
Richest tenth ($n = 9$)	13.1	4.2	3.12
Total ($n = 86$)	99.7	100.0	
Detroit	27.5	29.2	.94

Source: Calculated from raw data provided in (1) Michigan Education Association, Research Division, *Michigan Public School District Data 1970–71*, East Lansing, Mich. and (2) Michigan Department of Education, *Local School District Results, the Fourth Report of the 1971–72 Michigan Educational Assessment Program*, Lansing, Mich., September 1972.

city was subsidizing the suburbs to the tune of tens of millions of dollars each year.[131]

Because the distribution of the tax base among local governments bore no relationship to the educational requirements of the metropolitan population, fiscal revenues were divorced from social needs, and this perpetuated race and class inequality in the Detroit region. In 1970–1971, the average property value per pupil among the wealthiest tenth of Detroit-area school districts ($47,035) was over five times that of the average property value of the poorest tenth ($9,339). (See Table 6.1.) So poorer school districts had to impose higher tax rates than their wealthier neighbors if they wanted to raise equivalent resources for their students. For example, the tax base in Dearborn, the home of Ford Motor Company, was $45,339 per pupil. Next door was Dearborn Heights with a tax base of $9,206 per pupil. At that time Dearborn Heights would have had to levy a 5 percent property tax to come up with the same school revenues that Dearborn could raise with a 1 percent tax. Obviously, Detroit was not the only school district suffering from fiscal inequity.

As Table 6.1 illustrates, while the property tax rates among the wealthiest tenth of school districts in the Detroit metropolitan area averaged only 70 percent that of the poorest tenth, per-pupil expenditures among the wealthiest tenth exceeded those of the poorest tenth by an average of 44 percent. And while the poorest tenth of school districts instructed 6.2 percent of the area's students with 3 percent of the metropolitan area's property wealth, the wealthiest tenth of school districts instructed only 4.2 percent of the area's student population with 13.1 percent of the area's taxable wealth (see Table 6.2).[132]

The primary emergency of the early 1970s, however, was the status of the Detroit school system. How difficult it would be to find genuine solutions to the fiscal crisis of education in the city of Detroit was clearly revealed in the events of 1972–1973. After lengthy debate, the Michigan legislature responded to the school district's financial collapse by authorizing special loans to pay off the debt. The legislature then passed a law requiring the Detroit school board to impose a 1 percent income tax to remain in effect until Detroit voters passed a millage renewal. The education income tax would automatically come into force whenever the school millage fell below the state mandated operating level.[133] Detroit residents were left with a choice: They could pass a millage renewal or they could continue to pay the state-imposed income tax. On September 11, 1973, Detroit voters passed a seven-mill tax increase by a two-to-one margin, and the income tax was rescinded.[134]

The Michigan legislature's decision to disenfranchise Detroit residents and impose a solution was an emergency measure. A more durable policy was clearly called for. The fiscal crisis was easily solved in theory. All that was necessary was to shift fiscal responsibility to a higher level of government—to a regional government, the state, or Washington, D.C. The higher government could collect taxes and distribute the money to local school districts according to a formula based on the number of students and educational need. Most national planning bodies, including the President's Commission on School Finance Reform, were then recommending state or federal financing of schools.[135] State or federal financing, supporters argued, would remove local incentives for fiscal zoning, curb regressive features of the local tax system, tie growth in local tax revenues to growth in the national economy, and help increase educational productivity by circumventing the duplication that comes from the fragmented system of local school districts.

William Milliken, Michigan's Republican governor in the early 1970s, was a national leader in the movement for state financing of public education. Milliken was one of the first U.S. governors to attack inequities in school finance. In his alternative plan, he argued that every school system in Michigan should get the same financial return from each mill of tax it raised, and the extent to which wealthy districts could outspend poorer ones should be limited.[136] When his proposal took a bad beating in the state legislature, the governor sponsored a petition drive to get the financial reform measure on a referendum ballot for the elections in November 1972. The Michigan Education Association pledged $250,000 to the campaign, and the successful petition drive was also backed by civic and business groups like the League of Women Voters and the Michigan Chamber of Commerce.[137]

Milliken's proposal placed low constitutional ceilings on property taxes for public schools and instructed the state legislature to make up the difference in revenue from other, unspecified, sources. It was known that the governor favored raising the state income tax and creating a new value-added tax to fund the schools.[138]

Michigan voters soundly defeated Milliken's proposal.[139] Shifting from local to state financing would bring large increases in educational costs and in taxes. Recent court cases, in Michigan and elsewhere, implied that a shift to state financing would require reducing expenditure disparities among districts within the state. Reducing expenditures in wealthy districts was out of the question, so expenditures in less-affluent communities would have to rise nearer to those of the big spenders. Governor Milliken estimated a shift to state financing would cost an added $45 million in Michigan. But the head of the Michigan Senate Taxation Committee put the figure between $114 million and $1.3 billion, depending upon the norm toward which all districts would be raised.[140] Tax resistance was already palpable in Michigan, so the prospect of further tax hikes virtually killed the reform proposals.

Suburbanites opposed the state financing of education because it would mean a decline in the autonomy and power of local districts. This concern was intertwined with suburban fears about metropolitanwide bussing and with out-state sentiments that the reform proposals were designed to benefit Detroit's schools and not their own.[141]

The Michigan legislature finally managed to reach a compromise agreement, after a turbulent period of many months. The state came up with a new allocation formula that encouraged local school districts to raise their taxes, by tying the amount of state aid to the local tax rate. The state also made a modest effort to equalize spending among school districts by guaranteeing a floor below which local expenditures would not be allowed to fall. And Michigan implemented a property tax relief plan designed to help the elderly and low-income groups. These reforms combined incentives to increase the local tax effort with measures to blunt some of the harsher features of the fiscal system, and they brought Michigan a national reputation for progressive school finance.[142] Yet these reforms didn't really address the causes of the fiscal plight of Detroit, nor did they challenge the unequal structure of education in Michigan.

Metropolitan Governance

The school finance battle was just one attempt to try to equalize the financial status of local units of government. A far more ambitious—though unsuccessful—effort took place in the mid-1970s with the introduction of regional governance legislation into the Michigan House of Representatives. This did not succeed, but other crises in the region forced politicians to look at other options, most notably the reorganization of the Wayne County governmental structure. At the end of this period of proposals and reorganizations, the region's municipalities remained practically as isolationist as they had at the beginning.

William Ryan, chairman of the House Urban Affairs Committee, introduced legislation (HB 5527) establishing regional governance in southeast Michigan. Metropolitan Fund President Kent Mathewson had designed the proposal, which was backed by "good government" advocates within the state. Ryan's introduction of the bill, staff of the Metropolitan Fund later wrote, was "easily metro Detroit's most significant . . . regional event in the mid-1970's."[143] The proposal called for the wholesale restructuring of the relatively weak SEMCOG, a voluntary association of local governments, into an agency responsible for both planning and implementation at the regional level. Designed to cover the entire seven-county SEMCOG area, the new agency would have been supported by mandatory dues levied upon all the municipalities in the region. Half of the representatives to the policy body would have been elected by direct vote and half indirectly by local governments, with a highly visible chairperson to be elected directly by the public. A bold proposal, it generated swift reaction. Although media editors, business leaders, and labor representatives endorsed the legislation, local government officials opposed. Members of SEMCOG were particularly vocal in their opposition.[144]

Although the legislation did not pass, a survey conducted by the Metropolitan Fund before the bill's introduction revealed opposition to increased regional cooperation was not as great as casual observers may have thought. The Metropolitan Fund commissioned a political science professor to supervise structured interviews of regional leaders. A total of 51 leaders interviewed in 1974 included 18 party officials, 8 county officials, 8 city or township officials, and 17 civic, business, and union leaders from a cross section of southeast Michigan counties. Examination of the leaders' reactions to the proposal revealed possibilities for cooperation as well as likely reasons that the legislation did not eventually pass.

Almost one-half of the respondents were in favor of a strong, central regional governance system. Although 11 thought that any form of regional government was "a mistake" and 16 said that a voluntary association like SEMCOG was adequate, 24 were much bolder in their assessment, selecting the option of regional government as a "real answer to area problems [that] should be developed." The proponents of strong regional government generally gave one of two reasons for their position: that the growing urban area had generated the need for widespread pooling of resources and coordinated action or that the population was not evenly distributed across geographic space by age or income and that it would be better to deal with the region as a whole.

About half of the 51 leaders interviewed opposed regional governance. Their opinions clustered around three basic arguments. First the "prolocal government" group complained about big government and protested that regional government would destroy the power base of local politicians. Second the "no benefits" group, mainly from outlying counties, thought that regional government would give their communities few if any benefits. Third the "suspicious" group, largely from suburbs and outlying areas, feared that regional government would be a wing of Detroit city government and that the city's problems would be dumped upon the outlying areas. Although the interviewers reported that race was seldom mentioned as a factor by opponents, some respondents did specifically mention the widespread fear of bussing and of losing control of local schools, even though the proposal did not involve the educational system.

Interviewers also asked the 51 leaders about specific aspects of the proposal, such as the suggested funding system, election of delegates, district plan, and compulsory participation. Although polarization in responses to these questions was not as great as polarization over the whole question of regional governance, strong disagreement did arise over whether the system should be compulsory or voluntary, whether the elections to the assembly should be partisan, and which district plan should be chosen. Twenty-eight respondents opposed the popular election of the chairperson. If a chairperson had been elected, he or she would have been a powerful figure in state as well as regional politics, a fact not lost on respondents. Opponents thought the plan would lead to "name" candidates, chosen with powerful political or economic backing. Comments from both opponents and proponents are revealing: "A 'name' isn't a qualification and with a big area we would get 'name' candidates." "Election would give him an independent political club. He would dominate the assembly as he should. He [would be able to] communicate with the people as the governor would." "It [popular election] would . . . create a chief executive, probably more powerful than the governor."[145]

After HB 5527 was introduced, the *Detroit Free Press* analyzed its chances of success. It claimed that the plan was "feared and despised" by white political suburban leaders, who would have to provide more support to the hub city of Detroit, as well as by Detroit's black political power structure, whose power base would be diluted. Mayor Coleman Young had freely commented in several interviews that he did not believe his white suburban colleagues would cooperate in such an effort, so neither would he. "Those people who fled to the suburbs to escape Detroit's problems in the first place aren't going to help support Detroit now," he said. "I might feel differently if there were some way we [Detroit] could get in on the tax base of the whole region."

At a seminar held on regionalism at Wayne State University, where many of these opinions were expressed, one black critic said that the measure had been "spoon-fed" to him by the influential white leadership of the Metropolitan Fund. Young enumerated for the seminar audience a long list of grievances, including the fact that the Detroit Zoo, the Detroit Art Institute, and the Detroit Free Library had been supported largely with Detroit money, even though the primary users were non-Detroiters. He noted that the city furnished half of the water in the state of Michigan, but others wanted to take control of the service. He said that Detroit's bus system was used and financed primarily by Detroit residents but was threatened with takeover by a regional body, the Southeast Michigan

Transportation Authority (SEMTA). Young proclaimed, "Detroit's current fiscal problems stem from the fact that we furnish services to people who don't pay for them because of an unequal tax structure. We must achieve some equity before we'd be willing to go further or exchange any power. I'll tell you up front [that] I'm not willing to deal with people who have refused to deal fairly with me. I'm going to turn over my autonomy to people like that? I have to look askance at this whole proposal."[146]

The ironic thing about Young's statement is that he was presenting arguments that could be used for regional governance. Detroit had indeed carried an unfair burden; the plan proposed to remedy that. Metropolitan Fund's Kent Mathewson suggested that Young wanted equity in the financing of regional facilities and institutions but did not want commensurate equity on the boards that oversaw those facilities and institutions. In sum, Young wanted other municipalities' money, but he wanted to keep control in the hands of the city.

Young, of course, was not the only reluctant party; suburban leaders also balked. This was true even though other municipalities in the region, such as suburbs in the downriver area, also suffered from financial problems and low socioeconomic status. At no time did a viable coalition of poorer municipalities rise to press strongly for regionalism, in large part no doubt because of racial politics. When the proposed legislation failed, it had been the region's one big chance at meaningful regional governance.

Other efforts continued. SEMCOG survived and gained skill and influence as a regional planning agency. SEMTA, the regional transportation authority created in 1967, survived several structural changes to become a fairly powerful agency supported by federal transportation dollars, although conflicts between SEMTA and the city of Detroit's Department of Transportation continued well into the 1980s. Occasionally new proposals arose, such as Governor William Milliken's proposed tax-growth sharing plan, based on the Minneapolis/St. Paul, Minnesota program. The tax proposal fell before the wrath of suburban Detroit communities. By the early 1980s what had been a growing public awareness of regional issues had declined considerably.[147]

Regionalist thought plummeted to such depths that in 1980 the Citizens Research Council of Michigan wrote a report considering the policy implications of an actual separation of the city of Detroit and Wayne County, a proposal that certainly moved in the opposite direction from consolidation. Apparently inspired by the rising fiscal crisis of Wayne County, which ran an illegal deficit between $20 million and $22 million in fiscal year 1980, the proposal would have relieved Wayne County of the costs of serving the citizens of Detroit. Authors of the report indicated that Detroit residents provided $102 million in revenues for 1980 but required $148 million in county expenditures. Out-county residents more than paid their way with $179 million in revenue contributions and only $133 million required in expenditures.[148] Although this proposal died an early death, it illustrated the fact that those concerned with the declining economic status of Detroit's parent county were desperate for some changes in county governance.

The change that was finally chosen was simply to reorganize Wayne County's government. The Citizens Research Council of Michigan, which in past years had sponsored many regionalist proposals in cooperation with the Metropolitan Fund, spent much of the later part of 1981 refining proposals for a new Wayne County charter. The charter provision had many positive features and refined the governance of what had become an unwieldy, almost comically inept county government. The charter separated the powers of the executive and legislative branches. It reduced the awkwardly large county commission to a manageable size, cutting it from 27 members to 15. It required improved financial management. Most important, perhaps, it provided for the election of a chief executive officer, who would be able to appoint several executive branch officials and veto decisions of the commission.[149]

Wayne County voters eventually adopted the new charter but only after an extended battle over its terms. The charter commission, that body of citizens who had been charged with writing the new charter, was itself split between those who wanted drastic change and those who wanted to keep the *status quo*. A strong racial split developed on the charter commission as black members united in opposition to reducing the size of the 27-member board, fearing that Detroit's power would be reduced. The black members were outvoted at the charter commission's adoption of the provision, and all 9 of them promised to work against the charter's ratification by county voters. Prominent local interracial and black organizations, including the 13th Congressional District Organization, the Detroit Urban League, and the interracial New Detroit, Inc., also expressed misgivings about the new county charter. Detroit's Mayor Young, who chose not to fight the charter revision, publicly expressed distaste for it, both because of the representation issue and because a county executive could emerge as a powerful rival to the mayor of the central city. In spite of these misgivings, county voters did adopt the new charter in November of 1981. Soon thereafter many of the fears of black politicians were calmed, after a county reapportionment committee—whose 5 members included at least 1 staunch political ally of Coleman Young—adopted a redistricting plan for the county commission that gave Detroit candidates from predominantly black districts a good chance to win 6 or 7 of the 15 seats. The redistricting would end the historic dominance of the Board of Commissioners by suburban white Democrats.[150]

When the voters elected Wayne County Sheriff William Lucas as the new Wayne County chief executive, they sent a strong signal about the future direction of the county. An elected chief executive could be much stronger than one appointed by the commission, since an appointed executive could hardly be expected to show strong opposition to any commission decisions. William Lucas had already earned a reputation in his position as Wayne County sheriff as a strong-headed, effective individual who did not hesitate to oppose, even defy, the Board of Commissioners. For example, when the commission, in an economy move, had ordered the sheriff to eliminate the road patrol, Lucas filed a suit to block the move and ordered his deputies to keep working. Lucas effectively doubled the costs of running the sheriff's office (in real dollars) during his tenure, yet this only gained him a strong law-and-order aura that doubtless increased his acceptability as a black candidate in conservative white voters' opinions.[151]

The decision to restructure Wayne County's government also meant that, for the time being, other regional governance proposals would not be practical. Those citizens in the region who might have pushed for stronger cooperation, as they had in 1975 for the seven-county governance plan, had put all of their efforts into either supporting or revising the new county charter and its reapportionment. In the process they created a stronger county government and placed at its helm a leader whom the press quickly dubbed the "governor of a small state," a man clearly unafraid to exercise power even in the gray areas of the new charter, where such power was not particularly clear.[152] It was hardly the time to discuss multicounty, multipurpose authorities.

By 1981 the regionalist Metropolitan Fund, Inc., had become the Metropolitan Affairs Corporation. For a few years it issued reports suggesting intergovernmental cooperative arrangements and regional economic development, but later it focused on improving local governmental performance.[153] Rather than promote regional thought and action, central-city and area county officials are seriously talking about dismantling one of the two primary regional organizations, the transportation authority, SEMTA. In mid-1985 the state legislature's passage of a regional hotel tax provided a mechanism for funding expansion of Detroit's Cobo Hall, but little else provided evidence of increased metropolitan cooperation.

Conclusion

In the final analysis, both suburbanites and central-city residents have been content to keep the council of governments, SEMCOG, as the primary vehicle for intergovernmental cooperation above the county level. SEMCOG's beneficial functions include regional economic development, promoting a successful ride-sharing program (to encourage commuters to share work trips), and regional planning data analysis. The annual budget of $3.5 million (fiscal year 1983) limits the activities of the agency, as do its bylaws, which state clearly that the purpose of SEMCOG is to foster "cooperative efforts to resolve problems, and to formulate policies and plans that are common and regional."[154]

Previous attempts to strengthen or replace this agency have failed because of the fears of both suburbanites and central-city residents. Suburbanites have been afraid of taking on the burden of a declining city with seemingly endless problems. Many central-city residents have been afraid of losing control to the very people who abandoned the city, thereby creating many central-city problems. Racial hostilities in the region, as evidenced by housing and school desegregation controversies, have made matters more difficult.

Given the history of black political development in the central city, the turf mentality of Detroit's black politicians is understandable. As the first part of this chapter explains, black political power did not come easily in the city. Many qualified black candidates lost elections over the years simply because white voters would not support them. Only careful coalition building and aggressive political organization enabled blacks to obtain local offices, and many black politicians, notably Coleman Young, overcame great personal obstacles to obtain political success. Even after Young's election and reelection, not many black candidates could draw a significant number of white votes. William Lucas accomplished this in Wayne County only by becoming a political conservative. Blacks more comfortable with the labor/liberal/black coalition feared that very liberal black candidates would not stand a chance in a district or region with no black majority. In this assessment they were probably right.

Likewise, given the history of racial flight and school desegregation battles, the turf mentality of suburbanites is also understandable. Racial and income segregation still exist to the extent that racial and class isolationism are accepted as a matter of course. It's barely conceivable that suburban politicians would actively work to promote true regionalist cooperation and responsibility, in spite of the fact that many might believe this is a viable option. To take the initiative to promote it could be political suicide.

Though Detroit's financial status remains uncertain and its school system has neared collapse, no regional tax base plan on anything other than a token scale has ever succeeded. It just never seemed to be the right time to implement regional governance schemes.

7

What Future for Detroit?

What does the future hold for the Motor City? Forecasting much beyond the present is a risky business. But based upon our findings from this study, we can venture a few concluding prognostications.

Uneven Development

To a significant degree, the economic future of the Detroit region is still tied to the future of the auto industry. If Michigan's localities are to thrive in the face of stiff international economic competition, they must carve out a competitive economic advantage. A competitive advantage comes from well-integrated clusters of firms, suppliers, skilled laborers, and supporting government institutions. Michigan's economic development specialists seem to agree that the state's best hope for the economic future continues to be founded upon durable goods manufacturing, especially in the metal-bending industries: auto, steel, machine tools, and industrial chemicals. Metropolitan Detroit has sizable clusters of manufacturing skilled labor, industrial infrastructure, networks of suppliers and complementary industries, and universities strong in industrial technology.

State economic policy analysts also argue, however, that Michigan is in deep economic trouble because it no longer employs its manufacturing resources in the most innovative, productive, and competitive ways. What is required is a reorganization of the state's metal-bending economy from standardized, mass production to a more flexible, targeted system of production.[1] At least this is the argument forwarded in Michigan's new *Path to Prosperity* policy report, which outlines a long-term economic strategy for the state. Put out by the Governor's Cabinet Council on Jobs and Economic Development, the report bluntly asks, "How can Michigan survive in a competitive environment that has changed radically since its industrial heyday?" And the report concludes that Michigan has three choices: "It can 'get poor,' it can 'get out,' or it can 'get smart.'"[2]

If Michigan businesses continue the same kind of standardized, metal-bending work they have promoted in the past, the state is bound to get poor. Poor people in poor countries can do the same work just as efficiently and at far lower wages. Michigan could get out of heavy manufacturing altogether by trying to attract electronics and computer firms. But states like California and Massachusetts are already far ahead in that race. So Michigan's best bet, the report suggests, is to get smart by specializing in advanced, heavy manufactured products that poor nations can't make and by performing high-skilled industrial work that people in poor nations are not trained to do.

In short, Michigan should shift to a more highly valued position in the new international division of labor by specializing in the "factory of the future." In the auto industry that means replacing the conventional production of cars and parts with computer- and robot-assisted manufacturing and precision engineering and incorporating new materials—graphite, ceramics, and plastics—into the production process. In the steel industry it means replacing basic steel production with custom-cast, specialty steel and applying advanced manufacturing techniques—continuous casting, computerized controls, automated inspection—to the organization of work.[3]

General Motors's new Saturn project fits Michigan's "get smart" strategy like a glove. And although Michigan didn't land Saturn, that project is an excellent example of what is at stake in Michigan's attempt to shift to the factory of the future.[4] General Motors has recently bought into robotics, machine vision, artificial intelligence, information processing, and advanced microelectronics companies in an effort to become the leading manufacturer of automated factory equipment for the future. GM's Saturn is a new corporate subsidiary charged with making a new car with new methods to boost the company's share of the small-car market. Saturn adds up to as much as $5 billion worth of new plant and equipment, and the project will create perhaps 6,000 new production jobs and 14,000 more spinoff jobs with parts and service suppliers. Tennessee, the state that landed it, hopes Saturn will just become a magnet for other industrial innovators and a linchpin in a new high-tech industrial economy.

What's really new about Saturn, though, is the way GM proposes to make the car. Saturn will have a computer for a heart; robots will perform most tasks; work stations will be linked by computer-guided vehicles; and fancy software of all sorts will guide the design, engineering, production, and distribution of the vehicle. But since the inner workings of this electronic factory are fragile and easily turned awry, workers have to be committed to the enterprise to make it all work.

The Saturn project therefore calls for a big change in GM's style of management and work organization. In the automated factory, technical expertise will be more widely distributed, reducing distinctions between blue- and white-collar work. Work will be organized by production teams. Teams will share in Saturn's successes and failures, because wages will be tied to team productivity and corporate profitability. Saturn will probably have less of a hierarchy, less inequality, and less separation between mental and manual work and more worker access to corporate information, more worker participation in decision making, and more social benefits, including child-care and recreation facilities, than any previous method of organizing manufacturing in the United States.[5]

Where GM goes Detroit's other car companies are sure to follow. Ford is now ballyhooing its Saturn-like Alpha project. Chrysler too has its Saturnesque claim to fame, by the name of Liberty. GM executives are looking beyond the auto industry and are touting Saturn as a model for all of manufacturing. Should that come to pass, the implications for industrial work seem profound indeed.

That's Saturn's sunnier side. But there's a gloomier side too. Saturn's mission, after all, is to increase productivity and corporate profits in great measure, by producing as many cars as are now being produced but with less than half the work-force and plant space. The Saturn model applied to most of manufacturing forecasts a massive decline in industrial employment and a job market that will likely expand most in the direction of temporary, part-time, and low-wage service work. Saturn also forecasts a society where the biggest social divisions may lie between those workers who manage to become attached to a big corporation and those left on the other side of the corporate divide.

The authors of Michigan's *Path to Prosperity* report are straightforward about the down side of their "get smart" strategy. This is what they have to say about it:

> To prosper, Michigan's economy must change. Change can create new opportunities for many people and places, but it can also disrupt them. The transition to a more technology intensive, high skill manufacturing economy that creates a job for a recent community college graduate with computer programming skills may also end up laying off a middle-aged unskilled steel worker somewhere down the line. Such a transition may contribute to the prosperity of Ann Arbor, Troy, and Grand Rapids while deepening the economic despair in Detroit, Flint, and Jackson. Transitions can be both painful and uneven.[6]

So the urban policy issues connected with the shift from standardized- to flexible-system manufacturing seem to sort into two critical areas: employment and uneven development.

Michigan's industry is most concentrated in the Detroit metropolitan area, and the Detroit region is the hardest hit by the economic transition. Between 1970 and 1983 the state of Michigan lost 210,000 manufacturing jobs; 70 percent of those jobs disappeared from metropolitan Detroit. Between 1970 and 1983 Michigan gained 331,100 jobs overall, but the Detroit region actually lost employment during the same period.[7]

Victims of industrial crisis and reorganization include unskilled workers who often suffer long-term unemployment and downward mobility into low-paying service work. But many skilled workers—welders, painters, tool and die makers—are also displaced by computers and robots. Victims too are new entrants into the labor force for whom opportunities for gainful employment have dried up. Between 1973 and 1982, for example, metropolitan Detroit lost 108,000 jobs, but the area's labor force grew by 105,100.[8] This is the structural foundation for a permanent underclass.

More ominous yet, the Motor City is unlikely to get its share of the new jobs that come out of the industrial reorganization now underway. The city of Detroit has more unemployment, more poverty, and less wealth than its suburban neighbors, and the gap is widening.[9] Older industrial suburbs, like those downriver, are falling by the industrial wayside too. Less income means less tax revenue to fund the kinds of infrastructure and public services that attract new business investments like Saturn, so the already afflicted fall even farther behind.

Patterns of Race and Class

If present trends continue, racial polarization between Detroit and its suburbs is likely to increase along with the class gap between the poor in the central city and the affluent in the suburbs. Central-city financial problems are likely to worsen, and the city's political influence in the region will continue to decline.

The Detroit Planning Department estimates that the Motor City's population declined 3.6 percent between 1980 and 1982. If that trend continues, population loss will be 215,000, or 18 percent, by 1990, and that would reduce Detroit's population to below 1 million.[10] At that rate, by the year 2000 Detroit would no longer number among the top 20 cities in the United States. Most who leave Detroit will continue to be white and affluent. But a sizable number of middle-class blacks will also migrate to the suburbs. The geographical line between black and white will still be rigidly drawn. Those remaining in the central city will be mostly black and mostly poor.

Detroit's racial pattern could be altered should the city attract more white, middle-income residents. Although it would be difficult, it may be possible to draw in younger families who cannot afford comparable housing in the suburbs or who wish to live closer to their places of work. Over 65 percent of Detroit's residential structures are for single families, and 58 percent of the city's housing units are owner occupied. However, much of Detroit's housing is old and dilapidated: Seventy-five percent of the city's housing stock is at least 40 years old, and 30 percent is substandard.[11] Detroit will have to continue to wrestle with aging housing stock, a poor correlation between types of housing available and types of housing needed, and a reduction in federal housing assistance. Rising energy costs will also delay needed repairs, especially in neighborhoods where the elderly and other families on fixed incomes live. Households with female heads, as a percentage of the city's total population, are likely to increase too.

If Detroit continues to lose jobs to the suburbs, the poor and the underclass will continue to concentrate in the central city, and the gap between the poor and the rich within the central city and between Detroit and its suburbs will rise. The number of jobs held by Detroit residents dropped 30 percent between 1970 and 1980. Detroit's black unemployment rate reached 34 percent during the early 1980s. And Detroit's 22 percent poverty rate way outdistanced the 12.5 percent national figure. In 1970 Detroit's median family income was 83 percent of the region's; by 1980 it had fallen to 71 percent. If present trends continue, Detroit's median family income will add up to only 47 percent of the region's by the year 2000.[12]

With the drastic reduction in manufacturing employment, the need to retrain workers becomes ever more critical. However, the city of Detroit's level of education is low compared with the national average. Only 54 percent of Detroit's population has completed high school, compared with 66 percent of the nation. Only 8 percent are college graduates as compared with 17 percent for the United States.[13]

Knowledge and skill levels will have to go up if Detroiters are to secure good jobs in the future. Good schools are essential. Improvement of the city's schools has been slow and difficult, but student scores on standardized tests did reach an all-time Detroit high in 1985. During the past decade the percentage of Detroit fourth graders who mastered the state's reading objectives rose from 24 to 58.1 percent; in math the percentage increased from 48.6 to 73.6 percent. Seventh graders and tenth graders achieved similar gains.[14] But if improvement is to continue, Detroit will have to work more effectively on the problems of teenage pregnancy and high dropout rates. Nearly half of all Detroit high school students still fail to graduate.

Redevelopment Policies

As the economic functions of the region continue to fragment and new investment concentrates in suburban nodes, Detroit's redevelopment activities will continue to undergo redefinition. Political leaders acknowledge this. Governor Blanchard agrees with the assessment that several centers of economic activity are likely in the metropolis of the future. As for the city of Detroit, he stated, "Detroit itself has to be realistic on what it can or cannot offer at this point. Some industrial parks are locating in the northwest part of the region because it is near all of the freeways, and you can get to the airport quickly. . . . Detroit can't compete with that. But no one can compete with the potential beauty of working on the riverfront in a nice office building overlooking the water. So, Detroit has its comparative advantages, too."[15] The governor's vision of a multinucleus "Los Angeles" future for Detroit seems to relinquish the now near-dead retail role the city once played, but it also relinquishes the industrial role the city still apparently hopes to play.

The riverfront's role in city-sponsored redevelopment will expand, as will investment in the Central Functions area. This matches the policy inclinations of the mayor and other civic leaders, and as such projects gain success, market demand in those areas will likely grow. According to Thomasina Brown, the deputy director of the Detroit Community and Economic Development Department (CEDD), city-sponsored redevelopment is easier on the riverfront and in the central business district (CBD) than elsewhere because developers are interested in these areas. Backed by developer contributions, the city can get more leverage from the money it invests with funding from federal programs and from local authorities such as the Economic Growth Corporation. This stretches city dollars farther and is a prime incentive for the city to concentrate its efforts on the CBD and the riverfront.[16]

From the CEDD's perspective, neighborhood redevelopment is more difficult and less rewarding. Neighborhood redevelopment efforts are less visible, since many repairs are made inside buildings, and resources must be spread over some 130 square miles, in contrast to the 1 square mile of the CBD. It's also hard to raise money for neighborhood redevelopment, since developers aren't as interested. Little wonder, then, that city officials are noticeably less committed to neighborhood redevelopment.[17]

The battle between downtown and the neighborhoods will continue, however, because Detroit's legislative branch, the city council, is sensitive to vocal neighborhood demands for greater redevelopment resources. So city council members will continue to press the mayor and the CEDD for more investment in neighborhoods, and they will continue to instruct the advisory body for the legislative branch, the Detroit Planning Commission, to help promote neighborhood-directed efforts. If the executive branch, served by the CEDD and the Detroit Planning Department, continues to push for centralized investment, the groundwork will be laid for future warfare in city hall.

What will happen to the broad stretches of Detroit that are not in the centralized investment area? Much depends on trends in state and federal assistance. The city's latest master plan, released in 1985, suggests that some residential areas have suffered so grievous a decline that they should be cleared and replaced with new projects. The nature of such projects is still unclear, however. The mayor has proposed an Atlantic City–style casino gambling complex.[18] Another solution would be housing construction that improves the quality of rental units available to low- and moderate-income city residents. But money for that kind of strategy has dried up as the federal government has reduced housing subsidies. The cold truth is that many of these areas are likely to continue to decline, becoming empty prairies or ghost neighborhoods.

If Detroit's forsaken areas are to be turned around, other uses must be found, such as casinos or Poletown-style industrial projects. An upsurge in middle-class demand for central-city residential locations is unlikely in Detroit. But Detroit's now stable neighborhoods can continue to be stable with help. One important source of support, many observers agree, could be a more active promotion of neighborhood organization and economic development by the current, or by a future, administration. Neighborhood promotion need not necessarily require more redevelopment dollars. What's most needed is better local planning, more decentralization of decision making, and greater use of residents as resources for development.[19]

But the central city can do only so much. The problems of uneven urban development can be fully addressed only by lessening the balkanization and competition among the region's cities, and that means considerably more regional political cooperation and planning and perhaps even total metropolitan restructuring. As the postwar history of race relations and regional politics in metropolitan Detroit demonstrated, that won't be easy. To try to accomplish those goals, however, would facilitate interracial cooperation. To do nothing would guarantee interracial conflict.

Interracial Conflict and Cooperation

From the 1940s to the early 1970s, racial conflicts over housing, jobs, and education dominated the social landscape. Since then, however, race relations have undergone radical changes with the emergence of black political power in Detroit and the further entrenchment of white political and economic power in the surrounding suburbs.

As Detroit became predominantly black and poor, white suburbanites tended to put down the city, especially to new, white arrivals. "It took me one week out here to find out what terrible feelings were expressed by suburbanites for the city," commented Robert McCabe, president of Detroit Renaissance. "I'd find people who had their tremendous sense of pride that they haven't been in downtown Detroit in 15 years and don't intend to go."[20]

Similarly, many blacks in Detroit who long ago abandoned their vision of an integrated society now perceive white suburbanites as incorrigible racists. In their view the city is finally under the political control of blacks, who can now shape their own future. Their main concern is to consolidate black political and economic power in the space that they control. Yet there are black leaders like Mayor Young and Superintendent of Schools Arthur Jefferson who recognize the need for suburban/city cooperation, yet understand the persistent nature of white racism in the suburbs. "[Race] is an issue that prevents us from moving forward on many fronts," Jefferson argues. "In education, we have some of the finest technical facilities in Southeastern Michigan. How come there isn't more collaborative effort with surrounding communities? . . . I suggest to you that if the colorations were different in this city and more compatible with the demographics and ethnic and racial majority in the suburban communities, there would be efforts."[21]

Unfortunately, Jefferson is correct. Far too many suburban whites are still clinging to racial stereotypes. For example, a *Detroit News* poll conducted in 1985 revealed that while blacks in Detroit rated blacks and whites almost identically on a favorable-to-unfavorable scale, whites in

Detroit "rated whites three times as positively as they did blacks, and suburban whites rated whites twice as positively as they did blacks." Likewise, suburbanites rated themselves "three times more favorably than they did Detroiters, and blacks living in Detroit . . . rated Detroiters twice as positively as they did suburbanites." Whites living in Detroit "apparently exhibiting a frustration over racial issues rated suburbanites 25 percent more favorably than they did Detroiters." What do these ratings tell us about present racial attitudes in the metropolitan Detroit area and their relationship to future race relations? First they tell us that "blacks or Detroiters are still not regarded as highly as whites or suburbanites, except by blacks themselves" and second that major segments of the black and white communities in Detroit and its suburbs are moving in opposite directions.[22] This again suggests a scenario of increasing racial polarization.

The emergence and consolidation of black political power also has contributed to racial polarization in the Detroit metropolitan area. Realizing that many whites did not value racial integration, black political leaders embarked upon a strategy of developing and consolidating black political power within the city. Contrary to popular white belief that blacks had some driving desire to be near whites, racial integration was merely the only way blacks could obtain the necessities for decent living. Had blacks not protested racial segregation in housing, education, and jobs as well as seized the reins of political power in the city, they would have been far worse off than they are at present. But in seizing and consolidating political power, they had to depend increasingly upon racial solidarity as their primary ideology. Integration and interracial cooperation were not scrapped but rather became ideologically subservient to the objectives of black political development.

This shift from a social change strategy dominated by the ideology and visions of a racially integrated society to one emphasizing black racial solidarity is fueled by infusions of black political rhetoric calculated to call forth the troops to close ranks against the common enemy, whites. As a black psychologist pointed out in response to Mayor Young's habit of engaging in racial rhetoric for political ends, "If your Mayor invokes racism for political purposes, it has the effect on those who don't understand the political behavior paradigm of serving as another vicarious communication of experienced racism. As this is communicated through the media, it heightens the level of mistrust of whites among blacks in the community—even though it might be that no actual racism has been experienced by anyone in that particular case."[23] However, given the still pervasive racism of whites in Detroit and the suburbs, one wonders if Mayor Young's political racial "rhetoric" is the cause or the effect of present racial polarization. "I see that the white people are getting tired of me talking about race," Mayor Young commented. "Well, I'm sorry about that; it just happens to be a fact of life."[24]

Whites who are honest about racial issues in Detroit readily concede that race is on everybody's mind. "Everybody talks about the race issues, but not for public consumption," according to Wayne State University President David Adamany. "You can't go anywhere in the metropolitan area without having the issue of race relations opened up. It's worse now than when I came here two summers ago."[25] Clearly, from this perspective the future of black/white relations does not look good.

But there are other equally valid perspectives that hold some promise for creating a racially harmonious metropolitan community. The multiracial, cooperative perspective so evident in the efforts of New Detroit, Focus Hope, the suburbs of Southfield and Oak Park, plus a host of human relations organizations and people of good will all point to a reservoir of hope remaining in the metropolitan community. These efforts embody a vision of what the Detroit metropolitan community can become if hope is not abandoned in favor of fashionable skepticism.

Regional Politics

Economically, the lines separating the central city from its suburbs aren't very relevant, but those lines still mean a lot politically, in large part because of racial estrangement in the region. Lasting solutions to regional inequities will require some rethinking of political alignments. One possibility is for Detroit to become more allied with other economically troubled municipalities in the region, like those downriver. Another possibility is to build upon the valiant organizations mentioned above, which are still struggling to promote racial justice and cooperation.[26] Alliances like these can raise issues but can't reallocate resources. Strategies to achieve greater regional equity have been advanced before; none have succeeded thus far, but that doesn't mean a comparable plan won't succeed in the future. Much will depend upon support from the state government.

In the meantime the best the city can probably do is continue to cooperate with its neighbors in limited-purpose human relations organizations and regional agencies, like SEMCOG and SEMTA. Summit meetings between the region's Big Four—Detroit's mayor and the chief executives of Macomb, Oakland, and Wayne counties—are a step forward too. But population loss is eroding central Detroit's political clout. Between 1960 and 1980 Detroit's share of the state's population dropped from 21 percent to 13 percent. As a result, Detroit's share of the seats in the U.S. House of Representatives declined from 4.1 percent to 2.3 percent, and the city's share of the seats in the Michigan legislature was actually cut in half.[27] Detroit's representation on regional policy-making boards isn't in line with its share of the region's population. Detroit has only 3 of the 153 votes in the Southeast Michigan Council of Governments (SEMCOG), although the central city has over 25 percent of the region's population.[28] If Detroit is to have a brighter future, the city will have to gain greater influence in regional and state political forums.

But within the city of Detroit blacks will continue to have great political power. As the black proportion of the city grows, the likelihood of the election of a black mayor after Coleman Young seems certain. It also seems likely that black central-city politicians will continue to focus on keeping their political turf safe and white suburban politicians will continue to resist having to contribute resources to "save" Detroit.

The image of the future that comes out of this analysis seems incentive enough to try for more regional equity and cooperation. Otherwise the future Detroit will be a region segregated by race and divided by class into affluent cities competing for even more new capital and new-class residents cheek by jowl with inner- and outer-city slums inhabited by the unemployed and the workers who provide low-cost services for low wages to the business and professional technocrats at work and at play.

Guideposts for the Future

The picture drawn by our ruminations on Detroit's future is not particularly optimistic, and the findings presented have been connected only modestly with suggestions for action. Yet the reader has the right to expect more from the authors. Where are the visions, the recommendations for those who have a sincere desire to improve the city and the metropolis and to bring about greater economic equity and more racial cooperation?

We have spent some time discussing these issues. It is easy to describe the situations, not at all hard to criticize current directions, yet excruciatingly difficult to make reasonable, achievable suggestions for resolving the complex problems facing the city of Detroit and the region's other distressed municipalities. In addition, the purveyor of recommendations is obligated to offer sensible ideas for their implementation.

We can't lay out a blueprint for solving all problems. Past attempts to do so have caused numerous credibility problems for both the designers of the blueprints, who often sincerely believed they could accomplish such a daunting task, and for those who tried to follow their lead, quite often practical people who soon confronted the real-world flaws of the ideal-world designs. Implicit in this final chapter, however, are three requirements that any effort to make substantive gains would have to address: strengthening of the economy, improvement of race relations, and reduction of regional inequity.

1. Weak areas in the Detroit metropolitan economy must be strengthened by improving the labor force and increasing the number of jobs.

Improving the labor force is easier done at the state and local levels. The labor market is moving away from heavy manufacturing and its attendant low-skilled mass labor requirements. Different areas may become leaders in different aspects of manufacturing, the business of high technology or various products and services may ascend or descend, but the fundamental truth is that the old industrial way of life is doomed. These economic changes are causing the most serious problems for declining industrial cities and suburbs.

A sensible response to these changes is to revolutionize the way we train the work force. Not able to respond to the demands of the economy by radically improving the functional quality of the work force, school systems in the most distressed areas are instead struggling to keep their heads above water. Yet the most effective way to insure that Detroit youngsters will have a role in the future economy of the region is to make them extraordinary leaders in reading, mathematics, logic, human relations, and other skills that will become indispensable. This is, of course, nothing new; educators have been saying the same thing for generations and have always placed a (perhaps unduly) high value on education as the key to upward mobility. We do not see education as a panacea but feel it should certainly warrant as much attention as other efforts to improve economic development in distressed areas.

Boston provides one kind of model for change. There private industry formulated an agreement with the public school district that guarantees college financial assistance to every public school student who graduates with a C average and is admitted to a college or university. A job is also guaranteed for those who graduate from college. Simultaneously, the existing work force cannot be shunted. A massive attempt to reeducate the work force could begin most effectively with a sane, comprehensive approach to retraining workers displaced by plant closings. This could be expanded to link future economic development projects with simultaneous education programs for current workers.

An education strategy attempts to change workers but does not increase the supply of work. Some effort will also have to be made to expand the availability of jobs. This can be done most effectively by full employment policies at the federal level. States now attempt to maximize their share of existing jobs by assisting in plant retention and expansion. Plant retention is important, but the push to automate, or make Michigan "get smart," may actually reduce the number of industrial jobs. It will be necessary to create jobs that replace those lost by industrial decline and automation. Encouraging individual entrepreneurship or community economic development are possible ways to create new jobs, but these options will have to be carefully examined. Pilot programs should be launched to test the theory that training individuals or communities to become entrepreneurs can lead to significant job creation.

2. Race relations must be improved Racial issues have greatly influenced the development of Detroit and have contributed to social estrangement in the region. This has been true throughout the twentieth century, but the fragmenting effects of racial hostility have scarcely lessened in the past 20 years, with devastating results. Yet when confronted with the challenge of closing the rift, one stops short; how could this be accomplished?

It is important to build upon successes that already exist. Earlier chapters have described several groups that have managed to open housing or otherwise help to rebuild an urban society torn apart by racial strife. Other traditional civil rights groups have been contributing to these efforts as well. Certainly these organizations should be supported and strengthened, and those seeking a route to the improvement of regional fragmentation might do well to consider participation in their diverse efforts.

Current efforts to protect civil rights, attain open housing and fair employment, and promote interracial cooperation are laudable, but there needs to be an even more concerted attempt to mix the metropolis racially and promote interracial unity. This problem too may have to be solved largely through education. It will become necessary to educate the populace to live in a new society, one not truncated by lines of wealth or color. Perhaps the best attempts to foster this sort of world-mindedness are taking place in those school systems that have managed to attain some semblance of racial balance and economic diversity. Adults too become educated over time, as efforts to desegregate schools and neighborhoods gain success.

The pragmatic effects of greater interracial unity would be to make it easier to make improvements in other areas, such as the necessary dissolution of political and economic boundaries that truncate the metropolis.

3. Regional inequity must be reduced. Improvement of the economy and promotion of greater interracial unity could well take decades. The guidepost most likely to produce results in the short term may be the solution of removing some of the political barriers that hem in existing municipalities.

Two kinds of action are possible: modified and sweeping. Both require some degree of courage, but the modified route would be easier. That route would be to implement stopgap devices that have been effective in other metropolitan areas and even to a limited extent in the Detroit metropolis. For example, legislation set up to tax hotel and motel rooms in the three counties bordering the city of Detroit helped pay for the reconstruction of Cobo Hall; a precedent now exists that could perhaps be used as the basis of a regional tax base–sharing scheme. Strong land-use control policies initiated by the state would go a long way toward halting the unchecked sprawl of the region. These kinds of steps require at least two kinds of support: a strong and committed leadership at the state level and a political coalition at the local level. Yet too little effort to develop this leadership and these coalitions has been exerted.

The sweeping approach would be to go back to the ideas promoted by the Metropolitan Fund in the 1960s and develop a strong system of metropolitan governance. We are well aware of the barriers to such a system, from both the suburban and city perspectives, but feel strongly that regional governance is the only sure way to overcome gargantuan problems of regional economic inequity. Such a government would have to include more than one county, as many have learned from the example of Dade County, Florida (where fleeing whites and wealth have merely moved north to Broward County), and would have to implement in some form a sharing of regional economic growth and revenue.

As our chapter on metropolitan politics demonstrated, this is not a totally unrealistic idea. Political leaders surveyed by the Metropolitan Fund were, in general, supportive of the concept although skeptical of the details. The initial problems would be to start up such efforts after the momentum previously generated has died and to overcome opposition by

Mayor Young and prominent county executives. A more difficult requirement would be to gain the support of the citizens of the metropolis.

Our suggestions for the above guideposts—improvement of the economy, betterment of race relations, lessening of regional inequity—have been addressed to no one in particular, yet certain levels of responsibility are clear. The federal government is an important actor in improving the economy. It is becoming obvious, however, that the federal government cannot be relied upon today to solve the problems of the economy as they affect older industrial cities. The state of Michigan is just beginning to try to address the dissolution of the old industrial economy. Our book has highlighted certain problems that should be attacked in a state economic development strategy; the current strategy, as far as we can tell, needs further development in its proposed remedies for distressed urban areas, displaced workers, and young workers ill prepared for the new economy. We also feel that the state can play a stronger role in facilitating necessary changes in Detroit's regional structure or in other related areas, such as metropolitan land use.

At the local level municipal governments, school systems, and counties will all have to participate in rebuilding for the future. On the whole, although we may disagree with the exact approach that the city of Detroit is taking to improve its future economy and redevelop its territory, we feel that it is doing about as well as can reasonably be expected given the limitations of its resources and the narrowness of its options. About the same can be said for the school system. It is time for other, more well-to-do municipalities to shoulder more responsibilities.

In the final analysis, of course, it is up to individuals to do whatever is possible to help build a more equitable metropolitan society.

Notes

Chapter 1

1. Robert Sinclair and Bryan Thompson, *Metropolitan Detroit: An Anatomy of Social Change* (Cambridge, Mass.: Ballinger Publishing Company, 1977), pp. 10–11.

2. *Ibid.*, p. 30; U.S. Department of Commerce, Bureau of the Census, *Census of Population and Housing*, 1940, 1960, and 1980 (Washington, D.C.: U.S. Government Printing Office), p. 198.

3. The proportion of those poor in the Standard Metropolitan Statistical Area (SMSA) who lived in the city was about the same in 1969 and 1979. Data from U.S. Bureau of the Census, *Census of Population*, 1970 and 1980 (Washington, D.C.: U.S. Government Printing Office).

4. John H. Mollenkopf, *The Contested City* (Princeton, N.J.: Princeton University Press, 1983), p. 40.

Chapter 2

1. Daniel Fusfeld, *The Basic Economics of the Urban Racial Crisis* (New York: Holt, Rhinehart and Winston, 1973), p. 32.

2. Sheldon Friedman and Leon Potock, "Detroit and the Auto Industry: An Historical Overview" (paper delivered at an international conference on "Economic Crisis and Political Response in the Auto City," sponsored by the Harvard Center for European Studies, Detroit, Mich., 1981).

3. Neal P. Hurley, "The Automotive Industry: A Study in Industrial Location," *Land Economics* 35, no. 1 (February 1959), pp. 2–3.

4. Servet Mutlu, "Interregional and International Mobility of Industrial Capital: The Case of the American Automobile and Electronics Companies" (Ph.D. diss., University of California, City and Regional Planning, Berkeley, Ca., 1979).

5. *Ibid.*, pp. 85–93.

6. *Ibid.*, p. 97.

7. *Ibid.*, p. 111.

8. James Jacobs, "Suburbs and Disinvestment" (manuscript, Macomb Community College, Detroit, Mich., 1981).

9. William Serrin, "Detroit Grows Lean While Suburbia Fattens," *Detroit Free Press*, November 1, 1971.

10. Robert Sinclair, *The Face of Detroit: A Spatial Synthesis* (Detroit, Mich.: Wayne State University, Department of Geography, 1972), pp. 38–39.

11. The 1950 figures come from Melvin G. Holli (ed.), *Detroit* (New York: New Viewpoints, 1976), p. 269.

12. Marilyn Morehead, "Industrial Disinvestment," *DARE City Life Task Force Report*, Detroit, Mich., 1981.

13. The J. L. Hudson Company was founded in 1881 by Joseph Lowthian Hudson. He had been a fruit picker and then a clerk in his father's general store in Ionia, Michigan before coming to Detroit. Hudson first opened a men's clothing store on the main floor of the old Detroit Opera House. Within a few years he had put together a chain of shops across the Midwest. In 1891 he moved across Woodward Avenue and built the block-square, four-acre emporium, Hudson's.

Joe Hudson, Jr., lives in Grosse Pointe Farms and has been one of Detroit's most powerful people for two decades. Apart from being chief executive at J. L. Hudson's, Joe Hudson has been chair of New Detroit, Inc., chair of the United Fund, president of the Detroit Arts Commission, and director of Detroit Renaissance. Joe Hudson was replaced as chief executive of the Hudson Division of the Dayton-Hudson Corporation on January 5, 1981.

14. Hudson's parent, the Dayton-Hudson Corporation, owns Diamond's and John A. Brown's department stores, the Target and Merwyn's retail chains, the B. Dalton bookstore chain, and Lechmere, a New England retailer.

15. Quote from Bruce Alpert, "Hudson's Accused of Deserting City," *Detroit News*, March 21, 1984. The preceding profile of the J. L. Hudson Company was drawn from David Snyder, "Commercial Disinvestment," *DARE City Life Task Force Report*, Detroit, Mich., 1981; David McNaughton and Bob Luke, "Downtown Hudson Sale Expected," *Detroit News*, August 23, 1983; "Hudson's to Relocate Main Office," *Detroit News*, March 20, 1984; Alpert, "Hudson's Accused of Deserting City."

16. The reorganization of commercial capital in the metropolis is neatly reflected in changing census definitions. In preparation for the 1954 census, the U.S. Bureau of the Census asked all large cities to chart the boundaries of their central business districts (CBDs). The CBD was defined as an area of "very high land valuation . . . characterized by a high concentration of retail businesses, offices, theaters, hotels and service businesses, and . . . high traffic flow."

In preparation for the 1958 Census of Business, the Bureau of the Census created a new category, major retail centers (MRCs). MRCs were defined as "those concentrations of retail stores [located inside the Standard Metropolitan Statistical Areas in which the CBD cities are located but outside of CBD's themselves] which include a major general merchandise store—usually a department store." MRCs included planned suburban shopping centers, but the older string street and neighborhood commercial developments still met the definition.

But in 1967 another requirement was added to the MRC concept: It had to have "concentrations of retail stores having at least $5 million in retail sales and at least 10 retail establishments, one of which [had to be] classified as a department store."

So by now the regional reorganization of commercial capital was complete enough to have become institutionalized in the U.S. census. See Snyder, "Commercial Disinvestment."

17. Lewis Mandell, *Industrial Location Decisions: Detroit Compared with Atlanta and Chicago* (New York: Praeger, 1975).

18. Richard Child Hill, "Transnational Capitalism and Urban Crisis: The Case of the Auto Industry and Detroit," in Ivan Szeleyni (ed.), *Cities in Recession* (London: Sage Publishers, 1984).

19. Harvey Brazer (ed.), *Michigan's Fiscal and Economic Structure* (Ann Arbor, Mich.: University of Michigan Press, 1982).

20. Dan Luria, "Deindustrialization and Public Policy: Labor" (paper presented at the Midwest Sociology Society meetings, Chicago, Ill., April 20, 1984).

21. See Richard Child Hill, "Global Factory and Company Town: The Changing Division of Labor in the International Automobile Industry," in J. Henderson and M. Castells (eds.), *Global Restructuring and Territorial Development* (London: Sage Publishers, 1987).

22. Steve Lohr, "The Company that Stopped Detroit," *New York Times*, March 21, 1982.

23. *Ibid.*

24. See Richard Child Hill, "Race, Class, and the State: The Metropolitan Enclave System in the United States," *Insurgent Sociologist* 10, no. 2 (Fall 1980), pp. 45–59.

25. Sixty-two percent of the payroll dealt out by Macomb employers comes from manufacturing, as compared with 49 percent in Wayne County and 34 percent in Oakland County. See James Jacobs, "Small Business and Economic Development in Macomb County," Macomb Community College, Center for Community Studies, Detroit, Mich., June 1983, table 7.

26. A. R. Jazowski, "Statement Before the Michigan Congressional Budget Impact Hearing," Lansing, Mich. May 22, 1981.

27. Cases in point are the 1973 closing of the Briggs Bathtub facility in Sterling Heights (the company moved to rural Tennessee and Macomb lost 250 jobs) and the overseas relocation of the E. H. Gross Corporation of Fraser (the company established machine-making facilities in England, Germany, and Japan). See James Jacobs, "The Urbanization of Macomb County," Macomb Community College, Detroit, Mich., 1981.

28. *Ibid.*, table 11.

29. Jacobs, "Small Business and Economic Development."

30. Jazowski, "Michigan Congressional Budget Impact Hearing."

31. *Ibid.*

32. Liz Twardon and David Markiewicz, "Warren—Striving for Maturity," *Detroit News*, December 9, 1984.

33. As cited in *ibid.*

34. Roger Martin, "Construction Sparks More Suburban Growth," *Detroit News*, March 18, 1984.

35. Robert E. Roach, "Myth Exploded: Birmingham Wealth Exaggerated, Study Finds," *Detroit News*, March 22, 1984. According to Roach, Oakland County's top ten cities in per capita income are (1) Bloomfield Hills ($36,698), (2) Franklin ($25,406), (3) Bingham Farms ($23,791), (4) Bloomfield Township ($19,910), (5) Orchard Lake ($18,621), (6) Lake Angelus ($17,312), (7) Beverly Hills ($16,126), (8) Huntington Woods ($15,419), (9) West Bloomfield Township ($15,165), and (10) Lathrup Village ($14,693).

36. Robert Benson, "The Southfield Strip," *Detroit News*, August 16, 1983.

37. Marcia Biggs, "The Northwest Passage: Hot Route to Romance," *Detroit News*, August 24, 1983.

38. Compare the Oakland County population figures in Figure 2.1 with the county's assessed valuation figures in Figure 2.2.

39. Robert E. Roach, "Southfield Paces Oakland Surge as Business Center," *Detroit News*, May 24, 1984.

40. Douglas Ilka, "Southfield 2001: The City Matures But Still Finds Much to Congratulate Itself About," *Detroit Free Press*, August 1, 1983.

41. Jack Woerpel, "Northwestern Highway Building Booms," *Detroit News*, July 1, 1984.

42. Marney Rich, "Troy: Is the Boom Over?" *Monthly Detroit*, August 1984, pp. 94–95.

43. Rebecca Powers, "Golden Corridor Glows for Troy," *Detroit News*, July 23, 1982.

44. Rich, "Troy: Is the Boom Over?", p. 95. Many developers see M-59—a heavily traveled, 63-mile state trunk line running east to west across the far northern suburbs of Macomb and Oakland counties—as replacing the Troy corridor in commercial importance in the decade ahead. Already in place on M-59 are (1) the Oakland-Pontiac Airport, home to 120 corporate airplanes, (2) the Pontiac Silverdome (the largest roofed stadium in the United States), the 40-acre Silverdome industrial park across the way, and a $100 million Silverdome convention center/arena/hotel complex in the works, (3) Oakland Technology Park, (4) Lakeside Mall, the second largest shopping mall in Michigan, owned by the Al Taubman Company, (5) the center campus of Macomb Community College, and (6) the Henry Ford Health Care Corporation's medical complex.

M-59 and Oakland County also seem to be benefiting from the "just in time" Japanese style kanban system adopted by the auto companies. The Big Three now want their suppliers located near their factories or along readily accessible freeways to provide easy access for deliveries. Many supply firms seem to be drawing lines between various auto plants in the northern region and are coming up with a map that looks like spokes of a wheel with the hub on Oakland Technology Park. See Robert E. Roach, "M-59—Mapping 'Golden Corridor' for Year 2000," *Detroit News*, November 18, 1984.

45. Robert E. Roach, "Execs' Job Is to Sell Oakland First, Then Area," *Detroit News*, February 19, 1984.

46. Robert E. Roach, "Oakland Park Goal 20,000 Jobs," *Detroit News*, March 8, 1984.

47. Robert E. Roach, "New GM Unit Spreads Out in Oakland County," *Detroit News*, November 12, 1984.

48. Robert E. Roach, "Robotics Firm Eyes Area Site," *Detroit News*, November 23, 1984.

49. James Higgins and Robert E. Roach, "Oakland Gets Hi-Tech Plum," *Detroit News*, December 14, 1984.

50. Roach, "M-59—Mapping 'Golden Corridor.'"

51. David Anderson, "Fairlane, Michigan's Newest City," *Detroit Free Press*, April 25, 1975.

52. Ann Lange, "Fairlane: The $750 Million Super Community that Ford's Building in Dearborn," *Detroit Magazine*, June 23, 1974.

53. Anderson, "Fairlane, Michigan's Newest City."

54. Detroit's Mayor Coleman Young charged that the Fairlane development was hurting Detroit by luring tenants away from downtown office buildings. Ford Motor Land Development Corporation head, Wayne Doran, denied the charge. But a number of downtown tenants were in fact solicited to move to Fairlane, including the

Central Business District Association, a downtown booster association! See Anderson, *ibid.*

55. *Ibid.*

56. For a fuller portrait of the Downriver story, one upon which this analysis is based, see Richard Child Hill and Michael Indergaard, "Downriver: Deindustrialization in Southwest Detroit" (paper presented at the annual meeting of the Society for the Study of Social Problems, San Antonio, Tex., August 26, 1984).

57. One, Woodhaven, even ranked number two on Michigan's fastest growing city index. See David I. Verway (ed.), *Michigan Statistical Abstracts, 1980*, 15th ed. (East Lansing, Mich.: Michigan State University, Graduate School of Business Administration, 1980).

58. Hill and Indergaard, "Downriver," table 2.

59. Louis Schorsch, "The Abdication of Big Steel," *Challenge*, March–April 1984, p. 36.

60. Hill and Indergaard, "Downriver," table 5.

61. U.S. Senate, Committee on Labor and Human Resources, Subcommittee on Employment and Productivity, *Examination of the Automotive Industry's Problems of Unemployed Workers and What Alternative Measures Might Be Adopted to Improve Overall Employment* (Washington, D.C.: U.S. Government Printing Office, January 11–12, 1982).

62. Prior to the late 1970s the strongest intergovernmental link among Downriver's communities was the 1967 Mutual Aid Pact, through which fire and police services were organized and distributed on a regional basis.

63. Downriver Community Conference, "Downriver Comprehensive Jobs and Economic Development Programs," Southgate, Mich., April 1, 1983; Joe Hoshaw, "Business Venture: DCC Incubator Nurtures Budding Companies Along," *Mellus Newspapers*, March 14, 1984.

64. Donald Riegle, "Senator Riegle Speaking on the Downriver Community Conference Job Center," *Congressional Record*, vol. 128, no. 3 (May 1982).

65. "The Dislocated Worker: There Are Answers," *Showcase* 5, no. 3 (April 1984).

66. For example, the DCC hopes its Michigan Investment Fund project will generate 2,300 new jobs over the next 5 years and bring a return of $15 million in 12 years.

On November 30, 1984, Mazda Motor Corporation announced it would build a new auto assembly plant downriver, next to the abandoned Ford casting plant in Flat Rock. The new Mazda plant may employ as many as 4,000 workers and should mean a boost for the downriver economy. But the state and local financial subsidies put together to lure Mazda to Flat Rock will likely total $120 million. See James Higgins, "State Lures Mazda to Flat Rock Site," *Detroit News*, November 30, 1984.

67. Antoine de la Mothe Cadillac founded Fort Pontachartrain d'Etroit in 1701. The fort, a fur-trading depot overlooking the narrowest part of the river, stood just west of today's Renaissance Center. During the eighteenth century the site was virgin forest, and then it was a source of lumber during the early nineteenth century. Land along the river was later cleared for ribbon farms and became the first permanent agricultural settlement in Michigan.

68. Linda Brenners-Stulberg, "Rivertown Gamblers," *Monthly Detroit*, June 1984, p. 78.

69. *Ibid.*, p. 79.
70. *Ibid.*, p. 80.
71. Andrew McGill and Barbara Young, "One Man Shakes a City—Ford Has the Power," *Detroit News*, October 8, 1978.
72. David Zurawick, "Power Politics on the Riverfront," *Monthly Detroit*, October 1982, p. 61.
73. *Ibid.*, p. 63.
74. Al Stark, "Renaissance Center: How a Team of Businessmen Put It All Together," *Detroit News*, June 24, 1973.
75. *Ibid.*
76. *Ibid.*
77. *Ibid.*
78. Renaissance Center, *News Release*, Detroit, Mich., August 1975.
79. Another six investors were banks and insurance companies, all of whom did substantial business with Ford and General Motors. The seven remaining partners were AMOCO, which sells gasoline; the Automobile Club of Michigan, which sells auto insurance; Parke-Davis Company, which sells large quantities of pharmaceuticals to automaker-operated and -supported clinics and hospitals; and Western International Hotels, which was slated to operate the RenCen hotel. The *Detroit News* and the *Detroit Free Press* also depended upon a healthy Motor City economy, as did the retail conglomerate K-Mart, the last investor on the list. *Source*: Arvid Jouppi, auto analyst for John Muir and Company, as reported in the *Detroit News*, September 8, 1978.
80. McGill and Young, "One Man Shakes a City."
81. This finding supports Ewen's conclusions about the central place of banks in Detroit's interlocking corporate structure. See Lynda Ann Ewen, *Corporate Power and the Urban Crisis in Detroit* (Princeton, N.J.: Princeton University Press, 1978). See Kirk Tabbey, "The Renaissance Center Team" (unpublished manuscript, Michigan State University, Department of Sociology, East Lansing, MI, 1977).
82. Roger Williams, "Facelift for Detroit," *Saturday Review*, May 1977.
83. William Bulkeley, "Developers Call Detroit Complex the Renaissance But There Is Skepticism that It Signals a Rebirth," *Wall Street Journal*, April 15, 1977.

The city functions brought under the RenCen roof, it merits noting, are mainly service functions. For example, the RenCen Plaza Hotel initially provided 1,800 new jobs. This included 1,400 service and 100 clerical jobs for file clerks, typists, telephone operators, reservationists, chefs, room attendants, bartenders, waiters and waitresses, and maintenance personnel. Most of these jobs are low-wage, and they provide an informative contrast to the kinds of jobs lost in the auto industry in recent years. Western International Hotels, a UAL, Inc. subsidiary, runs the hotel at RenCen, and it manages 50 hotels in 14 countries. See Renaissance Center, *Progress Report*, Detroit, Mich., September 1976.

84. RenCen, *News Release*, 1975.
85. Nancy Cutter, "Everything You Ever Wanted to Know About Renaissance Center," *Detroit Magazine*, April 4, 1976. The original plans also called for a second and a third phase, to include a residential complex of apartments and condominiums for the area between the podium structure and the Detroit River and ten additional 19-story office towers. Had the original design come to fruition, RenCen would have

contained 5 million square feet of office space and over 300,000 square feet of retail space.

86. Robert Benson, "What's Wrong with RenCen? Just About Everything," *Detroit News*, January 11, 1983.

87. Williams, "Facelift for Detroit"; Bulkeley, "Developers Call Detroit Complex the Renaissance But There Is Skepticism."

88. Benson, "What's Wrong with RenCen?"

89. Thirteen thousand tenants and employees go in and out of the RenCen every day, not counting hotel guests and visitors. See Brenda Ingersoll, "Views Vary on RenCen's Safety Status," *Detroit News*, April 29, 1984.

90. RenCen, *Progress Report*, 1976.

91. William G. Conway, "The Case Against Urban Dinosaurs," *Saturday Review*, May 14, 1977.

92. Bruce G. Knecht, "Renaissance Center: Ford's Costly and Failing Bid to Revive Detroit," *New York Times*, July 3, 1983.

93. Billy Bowles and Sandra J. White, "Ford Triples RenCen, Will Lease an Entire Tower," *Detroit Free Press*, January 28, 1977.

94. Laura Berman, "The Downtown Experience—Bad Mixes with Good," *Detroit Free Press*, February 9, 1977.

95. Bob Luke and David McNaughton, "RenCen Loses $33.5 Million; Behind on Debt," *Detroit News*, October 25, 1981.

96. It lost $3 billion between 1980 and 1982.

97. Luke and McNaughton, "RenCen Loses $33.5 Million."

98. Ken Fireman, Luther Jackson, and Dorothy Weddell, "RenCen Sold at Loss to Investor Group," *Detroit Free Press*, April 29, 1982.

99. The default was by the Renaissance Center partnership that owned Phase I of the complex—the hotel, four office towers, and associated retail area.

100. David McNaughton, "Renaissance Center in Default on Mortgage," *Detroit News*, January 12, 1983.

101. David McNaughton, "RenCen Sales Drop $200 Million in Less than a Year," *Detroit News*, January 19, 1983.

102. David McNaughton, "Latest RenCen Deal Doesn't Rule Out Future Sale," *Detroit News*, February 27, 1983.

103. The fate of RenCen II—the $70 million, 21-story twin office buildings adjacent to RenCen I, owned jointly by Ford Motor Land Development Corporation and the Rockefeller Group—is also in question. Until recently, one tower was vacant, the other 80 percent leased. It is now 90 percent filled, after American Natural Resources decided to lease 19 floors of the vacant tower by vacating 250,000 square feet of office space in the Guardian Building. So musical chairs is still being played in downtown Detroit. See David McNaughton, "New Partnership Shores Up RenCen," *Detroit News*, November 4, 1983.

104. Bulkeley, "Developers Call Detroit Complex the Renaissance But There Is Skepticism."

105. Luke and McNaughton, "RenCen Loses $33.5 Million."

106. Knecht, "Renaissance Center."

107. Bob Luke and David McNaughton, "RenCen Near New Phase II Lease," *Detroit News*, October 14, 1983.

108. Zurawick, "Power Politics on the Riverfront," p. 64.

109. Laura Berman and Betsy Hansell, "The Maestro of the Malls," *Detroit Free Press*, August 7, 1983.

110. Kirk Cheyfitz, "The Power Broker," *Monthly Detroit*, July 1980, p. 121.

111. Berman and Hansell, "The Maestro of the Malls." Taubman's private art collection may be the most valuable part of his fortune, but no one knows, since it is veiled in secrecy. An artist himself, he started collecting art early, buying works by Frank Stella and Robert Rauschenberg. Then he collected masterpieces by French impressionists like Degas and Monet; sculptures by Brancusi, Arp, and Giacometti; and modern works by American painters as diverse as Jackson Pollock, Andy Warhol, and Morris Louis.

112. *Ibid.*

113. *Ibid.*

114. Max Fisher and Al Taubman together have donated a park across from the King David Hotel in Jerusalem in their parents names. See Zurawick, "Power Politics on the Riverfront," p. 62.

115. Cheyfitz, "The Power Broker," p. 122.

116. *Ibid.*, p. 128.

117. Michael Schroeder, "First Federal Suitors Woo Ex–Wall Flower," *Detroit News*, May 19, 1985.

118. Shelley Eichenhorn, "For Max Fisher Money Is a Way of Life and a Responsibility," *Detroit Free Press*, January 11, 1976. Fisher became chair of United Brands in 1975. His predecessor had committed suicide by jumping out of a window. At the time, there were Securities and Exchange Commission charges pending against the company for failing to report a bribe of $1.25 million to an official in the Honduran government in exchange for a reduction in the country's export tax on bananas. Fisher was a big stockholder in United Brands, and after he took the chair, he bought a substantial amount of additional stock.

119. *Ibid.*

120. Cheyfitz, "The Power Broker," p. 121.

121. *Ibid.*

122. *Ibid.*, p. 188.

123. Eichenhorn, "For Max Fisher Money Is a Way of Life."

124. Max Fisher's friends don't appear to stretch very far into the labor camp, however. Mary Fisher, Max's socialite daughter, recently began a new business, Mary Fisher Associates, dealing in "designer yarn goods" like knitted placemats, napkins, baby clothes, and quilts. Fisher's product line is targeted for shops like Hattie's Boutique in Birmingham, Bergdorf Goodman's in New York, and Bonwit Teller in California. In a recent interview Ms. Fisher argued that her latest project aims to boost American textiles and to help the unemployed. All of her products are made at home by a crew of 50 to 100 women, who are paid by the piece at rates averaging $3.50 to $6.00 an hour. "It's a cottage industry," Mary Fisher told a Detroit reporter. "There's a huge work force out there that can't work the hours or the places that the unions or whoever say they must. A lot of the ladies who work for me have children, and they sew in the middle of the night. . . . Unemployment is so high in Detroit. I wanted to help because, as you know, our family has always felt very keenly about building up Detroit. So I've made it a policy to use American fabrics to do this in

Detroit instead of Taiwan." See Anemona Hartocollis, "Friendly Yarn: Pal's Suit Complicates Debut of Mary Fisher's Knit Goods," *Detroit News*, September 8, 1983.

125. Jack Woerpel, "Towering Over the Detroit Riverfront," *Detroit News*, September 25, 1983.

126. Zurawick, "Power Politics on the Riverfront," p. 63.

127. Brenners-Stulberg, "Rivertown Gamblers."

128. Robert Benson, "Chene Park: Success in the City." *Detroit News*, October 2, 1984.

129. Jack Woerpel, "River Place Is a Garden Spot in Old Industrial District," *Detroit News*, July 15, 1984.

130. Robert Benson, "River Place—Stroh's Dream for Detroit," *Detroit News*, July 24, 1984.

131. Bruce Alpert, "Stroh Unveils Greektown by the River," *Detroit News*, July 13, 1984.

132. Rick Ratliff, "Big Plans for Downtown," *Detroit News*, May 7, 1985. The city is also touting other potential projects in the Warehouse District. Among them is the old Uniroyal building on a 50-acre site just west of Belle Isle Bridge. The city is hoping to turn this location into a mixed-use development, containing a high-tech production facility, housing, and a theme park. MoTown Records has already expressed interest in the theme park idea. And the former Federal Marine Terminal site on the riverfront east of the RenCen has been purchased by Beta West Properties, Inc., reputedly for a high-rise retail and commercial development. See John Holusha, "Detroit Embarks on the Greening of the Riverfront," *New York Times*, April 29, 1985.

133. See Richard Child Hill, "Crisis in the Motor City: The Politics of Economic Development in Detroit," in Susan S. Fainstein *et al.*, *Restructuring the City* (New York: Longman Publishers, 1983), pp. 104–106.

134. George White, "ANR to Buy, Then Resell RenCen II Office Towers," *Detroit News*, September 25, 1984.

135. Mark Ivey and Maralyn Edid, "The Oil Patch's Slickest Takeover Yet," *Business Week*, April 1, 1985.

Chapter 3

1. *Detroit News*, January 6, 1985.

2. August Meier and Elliot Rudwick, *Black Detroit and the Rise of the UAW* (New York: Oxford University Press, 1979), p. 214.

3. Robert Shogan and Tom Craig, *The Detroit Race Riot: A Study in Violence* (Philadelphia; New York: Chilton Books, 1964) p. 32.

4. *Michigan Chronicle*, March 7, 1953.

5. *U.S. News and World Report*, May 11, 1956, pp. 30–37.

6. Walter P. Reuther, *Statement to the Senate Labor and Public Welfare Committee in Support of an Effective Federal FECP*, March 2, 1954, Michigan American Federation of Labor and Congress of Industrial Organizations Collection, Box 51, Archives of Labor History and Urban Affairs, Wayne State University (hereafter cited as ALUA-WSU), Detroit, MI.

7. *Michigan Chronicle*, March 7, 1953.
8. *Ibid.*
9. *Ibid.*
10. *Ibid.*
11. *U.S. News and World Report*, May 11, 1956; *Detroit Courier*, November 23, 1963.
12. City of Detroit, Civil Service and Community Relations Commission, *Annual Report*, 1962.
13. *Michigan Chronicle*, March 17, 1962.
14. *Detroit Courier*, November 23, 1963.
15. Phillip S. Foner, *Organized Labor and the Black Worker, 1619–1981* (New York: International Publishers, 1981), p. 296.
16. Albert A. Blum and Charles T. Schmidt, Jr., "Job Training Through Adult Education: A Second Chance for the Negro and the Community," in Arthur M. Ross and Herbert Hill (eds.), *Employment, Race, and Poverty* (New York: Harcourt, Brace and World, Inc., 1967), p. 466.
17. *Detroit Courier*, October 12, 1963 and May 23, 1964.
18. *Detroit Courier*, May 23, 1964.
19. *Michigan Chronicle*, August 31, 1962; *Detroit Courier*, August 10, 1963.
20. *Detroit Tribune*, August 8, 1964.
21. *Detroit Courier*, June 15, 1963.
22. *Ibid.*
23. *Detroit Free Press*, February 4, 1970.
24. *Detroit Free Press*, March 17, 1974.
25. *National Advisory Committee Report on Civil Disorders* (New York: Bantam Books, 1968), p. 84; B. J. Widick, *Detroit: City of Race and Class Violence* (Chicago: Quadrangle Books, 1972), pp. 166–167.
26. Widick, *Detroit*, p. 183.
27. *National Advisory Committee Report on Civil Disorders*, p. 107.
28. *Ibid.*, p. 110.
29. *Ibid.*, p. 111.
30. *Ibid.*
31. *Ibid.*, p. 112.
32. *Ibid.*
33. Widick, *Detroit*, p. 189.
34. Quoted in *Ibid.*
35. *Ibid.*, pp. 200–205.
36. Jack Kresnak, "City Police: A Past of Racism," *Blacks in Detroit* (Detroit, Mich.: *Detroit Free Press*, December 1980) p. 74.
37. *Ibid.*, p. 70.
38. *New York Times*, May 15, 1975.
39. *Detroit News*, June 13, 1984.
40. *Detroit News*, January 8, 1985.
41. *Ibid.*
42. *Ibid.*
43. Allen E. Radtke, "Political Fragmentation and Inequality Among Municipali-

ties in Detroit" (Master's thesis, Michigan State University, Department of Sociology, East Lansing, Mich., 1975), p. 2.

44. The index of dissimilarity measures the amount of unevenness in the spatial distribution of two population groups. The index is simple to compute and easy to understand, and it's the most widely used measure of residential segregation. It can be stated mathematically as

$$D = 100\left(\tfrac{1}{2} \left| \sum_{i=0}^{k} x_i - y_i \right|\right)$$

where

x_i = the percentage of the city's white population living in a given census tract;
y_i = the percentage of the city's black population living in the same census tract;
D = the index of dissimilarity, or one-half the sum of the absolute differences (positive and negative) between the percentage distributions of blacks and whites in the city. A similar analysis was done for the suburbs and the entire Standard Metropolitan Statistical Area.

The index value may range from 0, indicating no segregation, to 100, indicating total segregation. Whatever the value of the index, it reflects the minimum percentage of either race (white or black) that would have to relocate from one census tract to another to achieve an even spatial distribution throughout the city. The index of dissimilarity is not influenced by the percentage of blacks in the total population. Thus, it is capable of mathematically reflecting a high degree of segregation, even though the area in which it is being applied has a low percentage of blacks in its population. See Joe T. Darden and Arthur Tabachneck, "Algorithm 8: Graphic and Mathematical Descriptions of Inequality, Dissimilarity, Segregation, or Concentration," *Environment and Planning A* 12 (1980), pp. 227–234; Dudley Poston and Jeffrey Passel, "Texas Population in 1970: Racial Segregation in Cities," *Texas Business Review* 46 (July 1972), p. 1.

45. William H. Frey, "Lifecourse Migration of Metropolitan Whites and Blacks and the Structure of Demographic Change in Large Central Cities," *American Sociological Review* 49 (December 1984) p. 805.

46. *Ibid.*

47. William H. Frey, "Mover Destination Selectivity and the Changing Suburbanization of Metropolitan Whites and Blacks," *The University of Michigan, Population Studies Center: Research Report No. 83–84*, 1983.

48. Reynolds Farley, "Components of Suburban Population Growth," in Barry Schwartz (ed.), *The Changing Face of the Suburbs* (Chicago: University of Chicago Press, 1976), pp. 3–38; William H. Frey, "Black Movement to the Suburbs: Potential and Prospects for Metropolitan-wide Integration," in Frank D. Bean and W. Parker Frisbie (eds.), *The Demography of Racial and Ethnic Groups* (New York: Academic Press, 1978), pp. 79–117; Kathryn Nelson, "Recent Suburbanization of Blacks: How Much, Who and Where?" *Journal of the American Planning Association* 46 (1980), pp. 287–300.

49. Frey, "Lifecourse Migration and Demographic Change," p. 805; Donald Foley, "Institutional and Contextual Factors Affecting the Housing Choices of Minority Residents," in Amos H. Hawley and Vincent P. Rock (eds.), *Segregation in Residential*

Areas (Washington, D.C.: National Academy of Sciences, 1973), pp. 85–147; Karl E. Taeuber, "Racial Segregation: The Persisting Dilemma," *Annals of the American Academy of Political and Social Science* 442 (1975), pp. 87–96; Thomas A. Clark, *Blacks in the Suburbs: A National Perspective* (New Brunswick, N.J.: Rutgers University, Center for Urban Policy Research, 1979).

50. Gary Orfield, *Must We Bus?* (Washington, D.C.: Brookings Institution, 1978), p. 80.

51. Rose Helper, *Racial Practices of Real Estate Brokers* (Minneapolis, Minn.: University of Minnesota Press, 1969), p. 202.

52. A. P. DeVito, "Urban Revitalization: The Case of Detroit," *Urban Concerns*, May–June 1979, p. 3.

53. Robert Lake, *The New Suburbanites: Race and Housing in the Suburbs* (New Brunswick, N.J.: Rutgers University, Center for Urban Policy Research, 1981), pp. 49–53; Harold M. Rose, *Black Suburbanization: Access to Improved Quality of Life or Maintenance of the Status Quo?* (Cambridge, Mass.: Ballinger Publishing Company, 1976); Reynolds Farley, "The Changing Distribution of Negroes within Metropolitan Areas: The Emergence of Black Suburbs," *American Journal of Sociology* 75 (January 1970), pp. 512–529.

54. Joe T. Darden, "Residential Segregation of Blacks in the Suburbs: The Michigan Example," *Geographical Survey* 5 (July 1976), p. 10. Harold X. Connally, "Black Movement into the Suburbs: Suburbs Doubling Their Black Population During the Sixties," *Urban Affairs Quarterly* 9 (September 1973), pp. 91–111.

55. Phillip L. Clay, "The Process of Black Suburbanization," *Urban Affairs Quarterly* 14 (1979), p. 419.

56. Gary Sands, "Ghetto Development in Detroit," in Joe T. Darden (ed.), *The Ghetto: Readings with Interpretations* (Port Washington, N.Y.: Kennikat Press, 1981), 89–107.

57. *Ibid.*

58. Low value was defined as housing value below the median for the Standard Metropolitan Statistical Area (SMSA) as a whole and low rent as rent below the median for the SMSA as a whole. Value is the amount for which the owner estimates that the property, including any land that belongs with it, would sell. The value data are limited to owner-occupied, one-family houses on less than ten acres, without a commercial establishment or medical office on the property. Owner-occupied cooperatives, condominiums, mobile homes, and trailers are excluded from the value tabulations. Rent refers to gross monthly rent for 1960 and contract monthly rent for 1970 and 1980. Gross rent is the contract rent plus the average monthly cost of utilities. Contract rent, on the other hand, is monthly rent agreed to, or contracted for, even if the furnishings, utilities, or services are included. For 1960, 1970, and 1980 the median value of housing for the Detroit SMSA was $13,300, $19,600, and $42,500 respectively. Its median rent was $79, $92, and $201 respectively. See U.S. Department of Commerce, Bureau of the Census, Detroit, Mich., *Census of Population and Housing*, 1960, 1970, 1980 census tracts (Washington, D.C.: U.S. Government Printing Office).

59. Joe T. Darden, *Afro-Americans in Pittsburgh: The Residential Segregation of a People* (Lexington, Mass.: D. C. Heath and Co., 1973), p. 6.

60. Karl E. Taeuber, "Residential Segregation," *Scientific American* 213 (1965), pp. 12–19.

61. Michigan Department of Commerce, Financial Institutions Bureau, *Mortgage and Home-Improvement Lending in Michigan Pursuant to the Anti-Redlining Act*, Annual Report, 1983 (a report of the Financial Institutions Bureau, Lansing, Mich., January 1985).

62. *Ibid.*, p. 32.

63. *Ibid.*

64. *Ibid.*

65. *Ibid.*

66. U.S. Department of Commerce, Bureau of the Census, Detroit, Mich., *1980 Census of Housing—General Housing Characteristics for Michigan*, (Washington, D.C.: U.S. Government Printing Office), vol. 1, pt. 24.

67. *Ibid.*

68. John F. Kain, "Racial Discrimination in Urban Housing Markets and Goals for Public Policy" (paper presented at the Conference on Blacks, Presidential Politics and Public Policy, Howard University, Washington, D.C., October 25–27, 1979), p. 18.

69. U.S. Congressional Budget Office, *The Budget of the United States, Fiscal Year 1980* (Washington, D.C.: U.S. Government Printing Office, January 1979), p. 17.

70. *Detroit Free Press*, February 4, 1970.

Chapter 4

1. Harold Black, "Restrictive Covenants in Relation to Segregated Negro Housing in Detroit" (unpublished master's thesis, Wayne State University, Detroit, MI, 1947); Bette Smith Jenkins, "The *Racial* Policies of the Detroit Housing Commission and Their Administration" (master's thesis, Wayne State University, Detroit, MI, 1950); Clement E. Vose, *Caucasians Only: The Supreme Court, the NAACP, and the Restrictive Covenant Case* (Berkeley and Los Angeles: University of California Press, 1967), pp. 122–123.

2. *Detroit Tribune*, March 23, 1940.

3. *Detroit Tribune*, August 17, 1940.

4. *Detroit Tribune*, August 10, 1940.

5. *Ibid.*

6. *Ibid.*

7. *Ibid.*

8. *Detroit Tribune*, August 17, 1941.

9. *Detroit Tribune*, June 14, 1941.

10. *Detroit Tribune*, August 9, 1941.

11. *Detroit Tribune*, March 23, 1940.

12. *Detroit Tribune*, July 4, 1941.

13. *Detroit Tribune*, August 2, 1941.

14. *Detroit Tribune*, August 31, 1940.

15. *Ibid.*

16. *Ibid.*

17. *Michigan Chronicle*, February 7, 1942.

18. Jenkins, "*Racial* Policies," p. 21.

19. Robert Conot, *American Odyssey* (New York: William Morrow, 1974), p. 465.

20. *Michigan Chronicle*, February 7, 1942.

21. *Detroit Free Press*, January 16, 1942.

22. August Meier and Elliot Rudwick, *Black Detroit and the Rise of the UAW* (New York: Oxford University Press, 1979), p. 178.

23. Quoted in *Ibid.*, p. 178.

24. Lester B. Granger to John C. Dancy, letter, January 13, 1942, Michigan Historical Collection, Detroit Urban League Papers (hereafter cited as MHC-Dulp), Executive Secretary General Files, Folder January–March 1942, Box 4, Ann Arbor, Mich.

25. Lester B. Granger to Baird Snyder, telegram, January 14, 1942; Lester B. Granger to Mrs. Franklin D. Roosevelt, telegram, January 14, 1942; Lester B. Granger to Charles F. Palmer, telegram, January 14, 1942; Lester B. Granger to the Honorable Franklin D. Roosevelt, telegram, January 14, 1942. MHC-Dulp, Executive Secretary General Files, Folder January–March 1942, Box 4, Ann Arbor, Mich.

26. *Detroit Free Press*, January 18, 1942.

27. *Detroit Free Press*, January 19–21, 26, 28, 1942; *Michigan Chronicle*, January 31, 1942; Meier and Rudwick, *Black Detroit*, pp. 180–181.

28. Meier and Rudwick, *Black Detroit*, p. 181.

29. *Detroit Free Press*, February 3–4, 1942; *Michigan Chronicle*, February 7, 1942.

30. Meier and Rudwick, *Black Detroit*, p. 181.

31. B. J. Widick, *Detroit: City of Race and Class Violence* (Chicago: Quadrangle Books, 1972), pp. 95–96.

32. *Michigan Chronicle*, March 13, 1942.

33. Meier and Rudwick, *Black Detroit*, p. 183.

34. *Michigan Chronicle*, March 28, 1942.

35. Ulysses W. Boykin, *A Handbook on the Detroit Negro* (Detroit, Mich.: Minority Study Associate, 1943), p. 57.

36. Lester Velie, "Housing, Detroit's Time Bomb," *Collier's*, November 23, 1946.

37. *Detroit Free Press*, December 19, 1982.

38. William Serrin, "Mayor Hubbard Gives Dearborn What It Wants—and Then Some," *New York Times Magazine*, January 12, 1969, p. 26.

39. *Detroit Free Press*, December 17, 1982.

40. Quoted in *Detroit Free News*, June 11, 1965.

41. *Michigan Chronicle*, November 25, 1944.

42. *Michigan Chronicle*, December 9, 1944.

43. *Ibid.*

44. *Michigan Chronicle*, November 25, 1944.

45. There has been some disagreement as to whether the housing development was open to blacks. In *Forbidden Neighbors* Charles Abrams, foremost expert on national housing, said, "The company had no intentions of housing Negroes." But other sources, such as William Serrin's articles, claimed that the John Hancock project was to be integrated. A *Detroit Free Press* article also claimed the housing project would have rented to blacks. See Charles Abrams, *Forbidden Neighbors* (New York: Harper and Brothers, 1955), pp. 100–101; William Serrin, *Detroit Free Press*, December 11, 1982, p. 32.

46. Abrams, *Forbidden Neighbors*, pp. 100–101.

47. *Detroit Free Press*, December 17, 1982.

48. Serrin, *Detroit Free Press*, p. 32; *Detroit Free Press*, December 17, 1982.
49. *Detroit Free Press*, June 6, 1965; *Dearborn Press*, February 23, 1965.
50. *Ibid.*
51. *Ibid.*
52. *Ibid.*
53. *Detroit News*, June 11, 1965.
54. *Detroit Free Press*, December 17, 1982.
55. Serrin, *Detroit Free Press*, p. 26.
56. *Detroit News*, June 11, 1965.
57. *Detroit News Magazine*, June 28, 1967.
58. Serrin, *Detroit Free Press*, p. 27.
59. *Detroit News Magazine*, June 28, 1967.
60. *Ibid.*; *Detroit Free Press*, December 19, 1982.
61. Velie, "Housing, Detroit's Time Bomb."
62. Gloster B. Current, executive secretary Detroit Branch National Association for the Advancement of Colored People (NAACP), speech, Seventeenth Annual National Pan Hellenic Council Meeting, Columbus, Ohio, May 10–11, 1946, Folder, Reports, NAACP Detroit Branch Collection, Box 1, Archives of Labor and Urban Affairs, Wayne State University, Detroit, Mich. (hereafter cited as ALUA-WSU).
63. *Michigan Chronicle*, February 28, 1953.
64. Widick, *Detroit*, p. 124.
65. "A Northern City 'Sitting on a Lid' of Racial Trouble," *U.S. News and World Report*, May 11, 1956, p. 38.
66. *Ibid.*
67. City of Detroit, Commission on Community Relations, *Annual Report*, 1957.
68. *Michigan Chronicle*, February 16, 1957.
69. *Ibid.*
70. *Ibid.*
71. *Michigan Chronicle*, February 23, 1957.
72. *Ibid.*
73. *Ibid.*
74. Albert J. Mayer, "Russell Woods: Change without Conflict," in Nathan Glazer and Davis McEntire, *Studies in Housing and Minority Groups* (Berkeley and Los Angeles: University of California Press, 1960), p. 198.
75. *Colliers*, November 23, 1946, p. 77; Mayer, "Russell Woods," p. 204.
76. The Arden Park area includes the "Boston-Edison" area mentioned in Mayer, "Russell Woods."
77. Mayer, "Russell Woods," p. 203.
78. *Ibid.*, p. 212.
79. *Ibid.*
80. *Ibid.*
81. *Ibid.*, p. 213.
82. *Ibid.*, p. 214.
83. Eleanor Caplan and Eleanor P. Wolf, "Factors Affecting Racial Change in Two Middle Income Housing Areas," *Phylon* 21 (Fall 1960), p. 231.
84. Eleanor P. Wolf, "The Baxter Area, 1960–1962: A New Trend in Neighborhood Change?" *Phylon* 26 (Winter 1965), p. 334.

85. Caplan and Wolf, "Factors Affecting Racial Change," p. 231.
86. *Detroit News*, March 22, 1964.
87. *Ibid.*
88. *Ibid.*
89. *Ibid.*
90. *Ibid.*
91. Detroit Commission on Community Relations, *Annual Report*, 1963, p. 5.
92. *Detroit Free Press*, January 3, 1963.
93. *Ibid.*
94. *Detroit Free Press*, January 4, 1963.
95. *Detroit Free Press*, January 3, 1963.
96. *Ibid.*
97. Detroit Commission on Community Relations, *Annual Report*, 1963, p. 1.
98. *Detroit Free Press*, June 24, 1963.
99. *Detroit Free Press*, June 16, 1963.
100. *Michigan Chronicle*, June 22, 1963.
101. *Michigan Chronicle*, June 29, 1963.
102. *Ibid.*
103. *Ibid.*
104. *Ibid.*
105. *Michigan Chronicle*, August 3, 1963.
106. *Michigan Chronicle*, July 13, 1963.
107. *Michigan Chronicle*, July 27, 1963.
108. "Suggestions for Speakers of NAACP Housing Committee," memo, NAACP Detroit Branch Collection, Box 22, Folder, Housing Committee, 1963, ALUA-WSU, Detroit, Mich.
109. *Michigan Chronicle*, July 20, 1963.
110. Greater Detroit Committee for Fair Housing Practices to Dear Friend, letter, April 30, 1965, NAACP Detroit Branch Collection, Box 29, Folder, Housing Committee, 1965, ALUA-WSU, Detroit, Mich.
111. Rose P. Kleinman, chairperson Fair Housing Listing Service, to Robert H. Tindal, executive secretary, letter, NAACP Detroit Branch Collection, Box 29, Folder, Housing Committee, 1965, ALUA-WSU, Detroit, Mich.
112. *Michigan Chronicle*, July 2, 1963.
113. Tony Zimeski and Michael Kenyon, "Where the Racism Really Is—in the Suburbs," *Detroit Scope Magazine*, August 31, 1968, p. 6.
114. *Ibid.*
115. "A Northern City 'Sitting on a Lid' of Racial Trouble," p. 40.
116. *Ibid.*, p. 4.
117. Zimeski and Kenyon, "Where the Racism Really Is," p. 6.
118. "The Search for Housing," leaflet, NAACP Detroit Branch Collection, Collection Box 29, Folder, Housing Committee, 1965, ALUA-WSU, Detroit, Mich.
119. Zimeski and Kenyon, "Where the Racism Really Is," p. 10.
120. *Ibid.*
121. Detroit Commission on Community Relations, *Annual Report*, 1967, p. 4.
122. Detroit Commission on Community Relations, *Annual Report*, 1962, p. 9.
123. Detroit Commission on Community Relations, *Annual Report*, 1960, p. 9.

124. *Detroit Free Press*, August 29, 1970.
125. *Ibid.*
126. *Detroit Free Press*, June 1, 1970.
127. *Ibid.*
128. *Ibid.*
129. *Detroit News*, July 21, 1970.
130. *Ibid.*
131. *Ibid.*
132. *Ibid.*
133. *Detroit News*, August 22, 1970.
134. *Detroit Free Press*, July 28, 1970.
135. *Ibid.*; *New York Times*, August 17, 1970.
136. U.S. Senate Select Committee on Equal Educational Opportunity, *Statement of Hon. George Romney, Secretary of Housing and Urban Development*, 91st Congress, 2d Session, 1970, p. 2,786.
137. *Ibid.*
138. *Detroit Free Press*, August 27, 1970.
139. *Detroit Free Press*, January 4, 1971.
140. *Ibid.*
141. *Detroit Free Press*, April 6, 1978.
142. *Detroit News*, March 22, 1975; *Royal Oak Tribune*, March 22, 1975.
143. *State Journal*, March 5, 1978.
144. *Detroit Free Press*, March 22, 1984.
145. *Key-Note*, August 1982.
146. *Fair Housing News*, March–April 1984.
147. *Detroit News*, February 9, 1984.
148. *Ibid.*
149. *New York Times*, December 20, 1983.
150. *Detroit News*, August 24, 1977.
151. *Ibid.*
152. David Zurawick and Cris Stoehr, "A Suburb Grows Up," *Monthly Detroit*, April 1983, p. 126.
153. *Ibid.*, p. 97.
154. *Ibid.*
155. City of Southfield, "Implementation of Housing Program," *Clerk Records*, July 11, 1977.
156. City of Southfield, *Ordinance No. 1051*; City of Southfield, *Ordinance No. 1088*.
157. *Southfielder* 17, no. 1 (January–February 1985), p. 3.
158. City of Southfield, interview, Director of Community Relations, March 3, 1985; "To Build a Better Southfield" (brochure), p. 55.
159. "To Build a Better Southfield," p. 37.

Chapter 5

1. City of Detroit, *Annual Overall Economic Development Program Report and Program Projection*, June 30, 1983, pp. III-2, III-10.

2. Leo Adde, *Nine Cities: The Anatomy of Downtown Renewal* (Washington, D.C.: Urban Land Institute, 1969), pp. 233–234.

3. A. P. DeVito, "Urban Revitalization: The Case of Detroit," *Urban Concerns*, May–June 1979, pp. 3–13. DeVito, in Detroit because of a program that allowed contractual interchange of employees between federal and local governments, has since returned to HUD in Washington, D.C.

4. Some of the problems may be due to the shortcomings of a "centralized investment" strategy. See Dennis McGarth, "Who Must Leave?: Alternative Images of Urban Revitalization," *Journal of the American Planning Association* 48 (Spring 1982), pp. 197–198.

5. Harold Black, "Urban Renewal: A Program Involving a Multiplicity of Participants" (Ph.D. diss., The University of Michigan, Ann Arbor, 1973), pp. 39–42.

6. *Detroit Free Press*, November 11, 1983, p. 1b.

7. *Ibid.*, pp. 5–6; Robert Conot, *American Odyssey* (New York: William Morrow, 1974), p. 516.

8. James Sweinhart, "What Detroit's Slums Cost Its Taxpayers," *Detroit News Reprints*, 1946 (reprint of articles from November 26, to December 1, 1945).

9. Conot, *American Odyssey*, pp. 516–17.

10. Robert J. Mowitz and Deil S. Wright, *Profile of a Metropolis: A Case Book* (Detroit, Mich.: Wayne State University Press, 1962), pp. 15–16.

11. Conot, *American Odyssey*, p. 517.

12. Mark Gelfand, *A Nation of Cities: The Federal Government and Urban America, 1933–1965* (New York: Oxford University Press, 1975), pp. 153–155.

13. Conot, *American Odyssey*, pp. 516–17.

14. Mowitz and Wright, *Profile of a Metropolis*, pp. 18–19.

15. Gelfand, *A Nation of Cities*, p. 209. Cities could include public housing on the sites but would thereby have to pay a larger portion of the project costs. Mowitz and Wright, *Profile of a Metropolis*, p. 23.

16. Mowitz and Wright, *Profile of a Metropolis*, pp. 27–29.

17. *Ibid.*, p. 31.

18. *Ibid.*, p. 32.

19. *Ibid.*, pp. 33–35, 40–44. At first, the city went through the motions of soliciting the study. Durbin's assistant contacted the dean of the School of Social Work at Detroit's Wayne State University, who arranged a meeting with several interested faculty members. After several meetings the faculty sent a letter to Durbin with the specific proposal for a study of the relocation process; the Federal Home and Housing Finance Agency approved the planned expenditure; and a contract was drawn up, with a clause giving the university faculty full publication rights to their findings. The faculty left a final meeting expecting that a formal signed copy would be mailed, but they waited months in vain for a contract that never arrived. The city gave no official explanation, but it was obvious that some city officials balked at having a study done and the results made public. Almost a decade passed before an impartial university study of urban renewal relocation was done. That study, which focused on the Elmwood Park project, was by Eleanor P. Wolf and Charles Lebeaux, *Change and Renewal in an Urban Community: Five Case Studies* (New York: Praeger, 1969).

20. Mowitz and Wright, *Profile of a Metropolis*, pp. 45–46. The tally of 1,950 families included 483 who had "refused suitable housing," thus absolving the city of

responsibility; 775 who had rented permanent public or private housing; 226 who had purchased homes; and 279 who could not be traced after "diligent search." The other 187 had moved owing rent money, presumedly absolving the agency of any obligation to discern their whereabouts. Mowitz and Wright do not explain the difference of 3 between the 1,953 families interviewed (see above text) and the 1,950 families included in these figures.

21. *Ibid.*, pp. 46–56.

22. Adde, *Nine Cities*, p. 227; Mowitz and Wright, *Profile of a Metropolis*, pp. 56–61.

23. Detroit Community Renewal Program, *Detroit: The New City*, summary report, 1966, p. 102; Adde, *Nine Cities*, pp. 230–231.

24. A study conducted in 1963, a continuation of a 1960 study, found that 10 percent of the residents of the high-rise Lafayette Pavilion were nonwhite and 58 percent had a family head with at least a college degree. Prices for the low-rise cooperative ranged between $21,000 and $34,000, and 19 percent of the families in those cooperatives were nonwhite. Fully 75 percent of the nonwhite household heads (and 66 percent of white household heads) had earned a college degree, and at least 62 percent of the nonwhites had previously lived in housing less expensive than Lafayette, compared with only 45 percent of whites. Some of the 344 respondents indicated that they moved to Lafayette in part because of its racial mixture, although a few whites said they did not like that mixture and would not recommend the development to friends. Wolf and Lebeaux, *Change and Renewal*, pp. 133, 138, 145, 151–155.

25. Adde, *Nine Cities*, p. 224.

26. *Ibid.*, p. 225.

27. *Ibid.*, pp. 224–225.

28. *Ibid.*, p. 222.

29. City of Detroit, Detroit Housing Commission, *Urban Renewal and Tax Revenue: Detroit's Success Story*, n.d. (probably 1964–1965), p. 3.

30. City of Detroit, City Plan Commission, *Renewal and Revenue: An Evaluation of the Urban Renewal Program in Detroit*, 1962, p. 38. See also Detroit Housing Commission, *Urban Renewal and Tax Revenue*, pp. 6–8, 9–11.

31. Black, *Urban Renewal*, pp. 45–46.

32. *Ibid.*, pp. 50–65, 90.

33. *Ibid.*, pp. 102–104.

34. Wolf and Lebeaux, *Change and Renewal.*

35. *Ibid.*, ch. 20, pp. 433–437.

36. *Ibid.*, pp. 491–494.

37. Detroit Community Renewal Program, *Detroit*, p. 102.

38. The Detroit Medical Center Citizens' Committee, *The Detroit Medical Center: A Proposal for the Re-use of Land Cleared Under the Federal and City Urban Renewal Program*, Detroit, Mich., 1958, p. 8.

39. Detroit Alliance for a Rational Economy (DARE), *City Life in the 80's: Tour Guide Book*, August 1980, p. 12; Black, *Urban Renewal*, p. 110.

40. The Detroit Medical Center Citizens' Committee, *The Detroit Medical Center*, p. 8 and "Facts About Detroit's Medical Center," a brochure available in *Central Business District Association Billion Dollar-Plus Bus Tour: Mid-town, Riverfront, and the Central Business District* (a loose-leaf notebook), 1980.

41. Black, *Urban Renewal*, p. 108.

42. The Reverend Louis Johnson, Friendship Baptist Church, interview, June 29, 1984; Clarence C. White, "Community Organization, Participation and Interaction in Renewal Areas of Detroit" (master's thesis, Wayne State University, Detroit, Mich., 1964), pp. 23–24, 51–69.

43. Quoted in Black, *Urban Renewal*, p. 108; *Detroit News*, January 5, 1970.

44. Black, *Urban Renewal*, p. 107.

45. Norbert H. Gorwick, "University City: A University Renewal Project" (a summary of a report prepared for the conference on "The University and the City—Planning and Urban Renewal," held at Detroit, Mich. January 29–31, 1961), p. 2, 10. Gorwick was project director of the Master Plan Committee led by the Campus Planning staff of the Department of Urban Planning, Wayne State University, Detroit, Mich.

46. The West Central Organization, a client of Saul Alinsky, was perhaps the most vocal of the protest groups, but it only lasted from approximately 1965–1967. See files in Walter Reuther Library. See also *Detroit Free Press*, March 1, 1970, and August 22, 1965; and Robert Sinclair and Bryan Thompson, *Metropolitan Detroit: An Anatomy of Social Change* (Cambridge, Mass.: Ballinger Publishing Company, 1977), pp. 35–44.

47. *Detroit Free Press*, December 16, 1971 and March 1, 1970.

48. *W.C.O. Action Booklet*, July 1966 (Walter Reuther Library); City of Detroit, News Release, November 12, 1968. Coincidentally, in Michigan these were called citizen district councils, a term that later referred to citizen groups formed for Community Development Block Grants project areas.

49. *Detroit Free Press*, March 1, 1970, pp. 1b, 4b.

50. Lynda Ann Ewen, *Corporate Power and the Urban Crisis in Detroit* (Princeton, N.J.: Princeton University Press, 1978).

51. John H. Mollenkopf, *The Contested City* (Princeton, N.J.: Princeton University Press, 1983).

52. New Detroit, Inc., "New Detroit: What Has It Done?" pamphlet, 1975.

53. Detroit, City Plan Commission, *Master Plan Technical Report: Industrial Renewal: A Comparative Study of the Tendency Toward Obsolescence and Deterioration in Major Industrial Areas*, March 1956, p. 19.

54. The population within the SMSA, however, almost doubled. City of Detroit, *Annual Overall Economic Development Program Report and Program Projection*, June 30, 1983, pp. III-2, III-10, III-11.

55. City of Detroit, Mayor's Office, *Moving Detroit Forward: A Plan for Urban Economic Revitalization*, April 1975, p. 21a. The ten industrial programs listed include the Detroit General Hospital at the Detroit Medical Center and expansion of the city's airport.

56. *Detroit Free Press*, April 20, 1978, p. 13a and June 14, 1978, p. 3a. Of course, DeLorean's firm reached heights of international infamy after its founder was arrested on a drug-related charge.

57. City of Detroit, Mayor's Office, *Economic Diversification and Revitalization Plan*, vol. 1, pp. 1–4, 8–10. This document, which appears to be in draft form, includes no cover letter, date (probably 1979 or 1980), or permanent binding.

58. *Detroit Free Press*, November 21, 1979, p. 5c, 6 and December 23, 1979, p. 1a.

59. City of Detroit, *Overall Economic Development Plan*, 1979; *Detroit Free Press*, May 5, 1979, p. 3a and February 25, 1980, pp. 3a, 17a.

60. *Detroit Free Press*, November 18, 1979, p. 3a and December 8, 1979, p. 1a; Katherine Warner, John Ehrmann, Luther Jackson, and Jerry Lax, "Detroit's Renaissance Includes Factories," *Urban Land* 41, no. 6 (June 1982), p. 4.

61. The name Poletown had been used to refer to another neighborhood before the GM project.

62. Gary Blonston, "Poletown: The Profits, the Loss," *Detroit Free Press Magazine*, November 22, 1981, p. 8.

63. Warner *et al.*, "Detroit's Renaissance," p. 6.

64. Blonston, "Poletown," p. 50.

65. Norman Fainstein and Susan Fainstein, *Urban Political Movements: The Search for Power by Minority Groups in American Cities* (Englewood Cliffs, N.J.: Prentice Hall, 1974), pp. 185–209.

66. Carter Wilson, "A Study of Organized Neighborhood Opposition to the General Motors Plant Redevelopment Project in Poletown" (Ph.D. diss., Wayne State University, Detroit, Mich., 1982), pp. 150–197. See also *Detroit Free Press*, February 1, 1981, pp. 3a, 7a.

67. Wilson, "Neighborhood Opposition," p. 88; *Detroit Free Press*, March 15, 1981, p. 1a and April 17, 1981, pp. 3a, 11a.

68. Blonston, "Poletown," pp. 53–55.

69. Leon Pastalan, "A Study of Relocation of Elderly Residents: The Detroit Central Industrial Park Project" (undated report available in the Detroit Municipal Library vertical file), pp. 1–3. Pastalan reported that relocation proceeded fairly efficiently, with a minimum of trauma for the elderly. See also "Poletown," special issue of *Detroit Free Press Magazine*, September 8, 1985.

70. *Detroit Free Press*, November 28, 1983, pp. 3a, 10a.

71. Cost overruns of $46 million over the original $200 million had developed by mid 1984, according to *Detroit Free Press*, September 23, 1984, pp. 1, 6. For estimates of 1983 planned expenditures, see City of Detroit, *Annual Overall Economic Development Program*, 1983.

72. Calculated from "Detroit Report of Business Openings, Expansions, and Closings from July, 1980 through June, 1983"; City of Detroit, *Annual Overall Economic Development Program*, 1983, pp. B1–B11.

73. *Detroit Free Press*, September 24, 1986, p. 1a.

74. *Detroit Free Press*, June 13, 1979, p. 11a.

75. Annual Housing Survey, 1977, quoted in David Rasmussen and Raymond J. Struyk, *A Housing Strategy for the City of Detroit: Policy Perspectives Based on Economic Analysis* (Washington, D.C.: Urban Institute, 1981), pp. 12, 43.

76. Rory Bolger, "Recession in Detroit: Strategies of a Plantside Community and the Corporate Elite" (Ph.D. diss., Wayne State University, Detroit, Mich., 1979), pp. 23–28, 42–48, 178.

77. *Ibid.*, pp. 36, 46–49, 55–57.

78. U.S. Bureau of the Census, *1980 Census of Population and Housing* (Washington, D.C.: U.S. Government Printing Office).

79. *Detroit Free Press*, December 13, 1976, pp. 3a, 10a.

80. *Detroit Free Press*, February 3, 1980, p. 15a; Bolger, "Recession in Detroit", p. 109.

81. Bolger also suggests that redlining may have been a problem. From 1975 to 1977 Jefferson-Chalmers and Roseville, both blue-collar suburbs, each had about 15,000 residents. Roseville home buyers received a total of 1,006 mortgage loans from six major Detroit lenders; Jefferson-Chalmers and the surrounding area with the zip code 48215 received only 59. As in many inner-city areas, the loans available came from the FHA or the VA, which backed 37.3 percent of the loans in the Jefferson-Chalmers census tracts from 1975 to 1977 and only 11.1 percent of the loans in Roseville. Bolger, "Recession in Detroit," pp. 186–191.

82. *Ibid.*, p. 178.

83. *Detroit Free Press*, February 3, 1980, p. 15a.

84. Bolger, "Recession in Detroit," pp. 109, 175.

85. *Ibid.*, p. 183.

86. Nansi Rowe, consulting attorney, Detroit Economic Growth Corporation, interviews, April 17, 1984.

87. *Detroit News*, January 20, 1985, p. 12a.

88. *Detroit Free Press*, May 11, 1983. The $20 million Greektown retail center, Trappers Alley, is located only a few blocks from the Renaissance Center. Greektown and a companion area, Bricktown, began gaining in popularity in the mid-1980s because of their small, attractive restaurants and retail shops. See *Detroit Free Press*, May 6, 1985.

89. *Detroit Free Press*, September 30, 1983. Alfred Taubman, promoter of the project, blamed its demise on the shortage of central business district housing, which led to a failure to attract major retailers. When the city could not package the project within a reasonable time, the Department of Housing and Urban Development withdrew a $12 million Urban Development Action Grant.

90. Facts taken from a talk given by Emmett Moten, head of Detroit's Community and Economic Development Department, at Michigan State University, East Lansing, Mich., March 6, 1985.

91. City of Detroit, *Annual Overall Economic Development Program*, 1983, pp. V-23, V-40, V-44 to V-66.

92. *Ibid.*, pp. V-44, V-45. By mid-1985 the costs of the People Mover had exceeded $200 million and threatened the Rapid Transit Light Rail system. It also appeared that the city would have to pick up cost overruns.

93. *Lansing State Journal*, November 24, 1983, p. 13b. See also *Detroit Free Press*, February 10, 1983, p. 3a; and January 20, 1984, p. 3a.

94. *Detroit Free Press*, November 25, 1979, p. 3a.

95. *Detroit Free Press*, December 4, 1979, pp. 3a, 14a and December 13, 1979, p. 3a.

96. *Detroit Free Press*, April 13, 1983, p. 2a. See also Thomasina White, "Monitoring Evaluation of Detroit's CDBG Program," Unpublished report to the U.S. Department of Housing and Urban Development, 1982; and *Detroit Free Press*, January 9, 1983, pp. 1a, 8a.

97. *Detroit Free Press*, February 19, 1981, p. 1a. Allocation percentages in City of

Detroit, Planning Department, "Community Development Entitlement Grant Program and Project Descriptions," October 1979, p. 3.

98. General Accounting Office, *HUD Needs to Better Determine Extent of Community Block Grants' Lower Income Benefits*, November 1982, pp. 5–25. Detroit claimed that all of the more than $25 million in Community Development Block Grants (CDBG) funds it planned to spend on the central business district from 1979 to 1982 would benefit low- and moderate-income residents, a difficult claim to believe. See City of Detroit, Planning Department, *CDBG Application*, 1979–1980.

99. City of Detroit, Planning Department, "Community Development Block Grant Program: Program and Project Descriptions," January 1982. Identification of project locations made by the author, not the city, does not include CDBG administration, planning, public and social services, Neighborhood Opportunity Funds, and small amounts of Model Cities funds. When projects fell on the border between two subcommunities or were listed as falling into areas that crossed the boundaries of subcommunities, the author divided the money evenly between the subcommunities.

100. Poverty rates were obtained from City of Detroit, Planning Department, Data Coordination Division, "Profile Package for Sectors and UCS Subcommunities," Fall 1981, pp. 1–7 of table 4. Cities are not required to use poverty rates in dispersing funds, although the federal government uses the poverty rate as a component of its dispersement formulas. Cities are required under CDBG legislation to expend money primarily for the benefit of low- and moderate-income residents.

101. The pattern of expenditures of Neighborhood Opportunity Funds (NOF) requires further study. Under NOF, the city disperses a portion of the development money directly to community groups and institutions that are distressed. There appears to be little monitoring of how these funds are spent. The amount of these funds that goes to any one neighborhood is so small that its likely impact is modest, although it appears in Table 5.3 that the city spent $24 million in this category, or 7 percent of its total CDBG allocation. The city's 1982 "Community Development Entitlement" report indicates that almost $17 million of that amount was unallocated, which presumedly means unspent, between 1978 and 1982 (see p. 27 of the report). The Neighborhood Opportunity Funds are also subject to raids, in times of economic crisis, as happened when Poletown expenditures exceeded expectations.

102. More demolition activity took place in the neighborhood strategy areas. City of Detroit, Planning Department, *Community Development Entitlement Grant Program: Program and Project Descriptions*, October 1979, pp. 8–87. Categories from City of Detroit, Planning Department, *1979–80 CDBG Application*, pp. 267–272.

103. Thomasina Brown, deputy director, and Ron Flies, Detroit Community Economic Development Department, interviews, May 3, 1985.

104. Suzanne Dolezal, "The Squeaky Wheel Gets the Grease," *Detroit Free Press Magazine*, August 2, 1981, p. 7.

105. *Ibid.*; *Detroit Free Press*, May 27, 1978, p. 3a.

106. Michigan Avenue Community Organization, *Revitalization Plan*, October 1982.

107. Tom Holler, executive director, Michigan Avenue Community Organization, interview, December 1984.

Chapter 6

1. August Meier and Elliot Rudwick, *Black Detroit and the Rise of the UAW* (New York: Oxford University Press, 1979), pp. 32–33.

2. *Detroit Free Press*, April 26, 1969; Wade H. McCree, Jr., "The Negro Renaissance in Michigan Politics," *Negro History Bulletin* 26 (October 1962), pp. 7–8; "Women in Politics: Negro Women Hold Ten Positions," *Ebony*, August 1956, p. 82.

3. McCree, "The Negro Renaissance," p. 8.

4. David Greenstone, *Report on the Politics of Detroit*, p. V-30.

5. Edward T. Clayton, *The Negro Politician* (Chicago: Johnson Publishing Company, Inc., 1964), pp. 86, 89.

6. *Ibid.*

7. McCree, "The Negro Renaissance," p. 8.

8. B. J. Widick, *Detroit: City of Race and Class Violence* (Chicago: Quadrangle Books, 1972), p. 155.

9. *Ibid.*

10. *Ibid.*

11. Denise J. Lewis, "Black Consciousness and the Voting Behavior of Blacks in Detroit: 1961–1968" (master's thesis, Wayne State University, Detroit, Mich., 1969), p. 29.

12. *Ibid.*

13. *Ibid.*, p. 88.

14. *Ibid.*

15. *Ibid.*

16. *Ibid.*, pp. 88–89.

17. *Ibid.*, p. 92.

18. *Michigan Chronicle*, October 31, 1934.

19. Albert B. Cleage, Jr., "Black Power—An Advocate Defines It," *Public Relations Journal* 24 (July 1968), p. 18.

20. *Ibid.*

21. *Michigan Chronicle*, November 22, 1969.

22. *Ibid.*

23. Remer Tyson, "Long Struggle Led to Firm Power Base," *Blacks in Detroit*, a reprint of articles from the *Detroit Free Press*, December, 1980, p. 40.

24. *Ibid.*

25. *Michigan Chronicle*, November 22, 1969; Tyson, "Long Struggle," p. 40; Widick, *Detroit*, p. 160.

26. Tyson, "Long Struggle," p. 40.

27. *Michigan Chronicle*, September 6, 1969.

28. *Detroit Free Press*, September 10, 1969.

29. *Ibid.*; *Detroit Free Press*, August 17, 1969; *Michigan Chronicle*, September 6, 1969.

30. *Detroit Free Press*, September 28, 1969.

31. *Detroit Free Press*, September 10, 1969.

32. *Michigan Chronicle*, September 20, 1969 and October 18, 1969.

33. *Michigan Chronicle*, November 1, 1969.

34. *Detroit Free Press*, November 1, 1969.

35. *Detroit Free Press*, September 11, 1969.
36. *Detroit Free Press*, November 2, 1969.
37. Quoted in *Detroit Free Press*, October 21, 1969.
38. *Detroit Free Press*, September 11, 1969 and September 19, 1969.
39. *Michigan Chronicle*, August 23, 1969.
40. *Michigan Chronicle*, September 23, 1969.
41. *Ibid.*
42. *Detroit Free Press*, November 5, 1969.
43. *Detroit Free Press*, November 9, 1969.
44. *Detroit Free Press*, January 4, 1976; Tyson, "Long Struggle," p. 39.
45. Philip S. Foner, *Organized Labor and the Black Worker, 1619–1981* (New York: International Publishers, 1981), p. 295.
46. *Detroit Free Press*, January 4, 1976.
47. *Ibid.*; *State Journal*, September 26, 1968.
48. *Detroit Free Press*, September 22, 1968.
49. *Detroit Free Press*, July 3, 1969.
50. Patrick James Ashton, "Race, Class and Black Politics: The Implications of the Election of a Black Mayor for the Police and Policing in Detroit" (Ph.D. diss., Michigan State University, East Lansing, Mich., 1981), p. 301.
51. *Detroit Free Press*, May 11, 1973.
52. Ashton, "Race, Class and Black Politics," p. 30.
53. *Ibid.*, p. 313.
54. *Ibid.*, pp. 3–4.
55. *Detroit Free Press*, November 8, 1973.
56. *Detroit Free Press*, January 3, 1974.
57. *Detroit Free Press*, January 4, 1974.
58. Ashton, "Race, Class and Black Politics," p. 369.
59. *Ibid.*, p. 368.
60. Tyson, "Long Struggle," p. 38.
61. *Ibid.*
62. *Detroit Free Press*, November 7, 1977.
63. *Detroit Free Press*, January 5, 1978.
64. *Lansing State Journal*, November 2, 1981; *Detroit Free Press*, January 1, 1984.
65. *Detroit Free Press*, January 1, 1984.
66. *Detroit Free Press*, January 7, 1984.
67. *Detroit Free Press*, January 2, 1984.
68. *Detroit News*, January 6, 1985.
69. *Detroit Free Press*, May 16, 1985.
70. *Detroit Free Press*, January 31, 1985.
71. *Detroit Free Press*, April 27, 1985.
72. *Detroit Free Press*, June 1, 1985.
73. *Michigan Chronicle*, March 14, 1953.
74. City of Detroit, Commission on Community Relations, *Annual Report*, 1960, p. 11; *Michigan Chronicle*, October 29, 1960.
75. Detroit Commission on Community Relations, *Annual Report*, 1960, p. 12.
76. Citizens Advisory Committee on Equal Educational Opportunities, *Findings and Recommendations* (Detroit, Mich.: Detroit Board of Education, 1962), p. v.

77. *Ibid.*, p. ix.
78. *Ibid.*
79. *Illustrated News*, March 19, 1962.
80. *Illustrated News*, February 5, 1962.
81. *Illustrated News*, March 19, 1962.
82. *Illustrated News*, February 26, 1962.
83. William R. Grant, "Community Control vs. School Integration in Detroit," *Public Interest*, Summer 1971, p. 63.
84. *Michigan Chronicle*, March 23, 1968.
85. *Michigan Chronicle*, February 24, 1968.
86. Grant, "Community Control," p. 63.
87. *Ibid.*
88. *Ibid.*
89. *Bradley v. Milliken* 433 F. Supp. 2d 897 (6th Circuit, 1970).
90. *Bradley v. Milliken* 338 F. Supp. 582 (1971).
91. *Ibid.*, p. 587.
92. *Ibid.*, pp. 588, 589.
93. *Swan v. Board of Education* 402 U.S. 1 (1971); *Monroe v. Board of Commissioners* 391 U.S. 450 (1968); *Green v. County School Board* 349 U.S. 294 (1955); *Brown v. Board of Education*, 347 U.S. 483 (1954).
94. *Bradley v. Milliken* 345 F. Supp. 914 (1972), p. 916.
95. *Ibid.*
96. *Bradley v. Milliken* 484 F. Supp. 2d 215 (1973), p. 249.
97. *Detroit Free Press*, June 15, 1972, p. 3a.
98. *Detroit Free Press*, June 21, 1972.
99. *Detroit Free Press*, June 16, 1972, p. 1a.
100. Marianne R. Zepka and Stephen Franklin, "Races Are Still Apart in Detroit Schools," *Blacks in Detroit*, a reprint of articles from the *Detroit Free Press*, December, 1980, p. 52.
101. *Detroit Free Press*, June 24, 1972.
102. *Detroit Free Press*, June 17, 1972.
103. *Bradley v. Milliken* 484 F. Supp. 2d 215 (1973), pp. 250–251.
104. *Bradley v. Milliken* U.S. 418 (1974).
105. *Swan v. Charlotte Mecklenburg Board of Education* 402 U.S. 1 (1971).
106. *Bradley v. Milliken* U.S. 418 (1974), p. 757.
107. William R. Grant, "The Detroit School Case: An Historical Overview," *Wayne Farm Review*, October 1970, pp. 857–863.
108. *Detroit Free Press*, March 9, 1976.
109. George Metcalf, *From Little Rock to Boston: The History of School Desegregation* (Westport, Conn.: Greenwood Press, 1983), p. 131.
110. *Ibid.*
111. *Detroit Free Press*, May 13, 1984.
112. Metcalf, *From Little Rock to Boston*, p. 132.
113. *Detroit Free Press*, May 13, 1984.
114. *Detroit Free Press*, November 10, 1971 and July 23, 1972.
115. *Detroit Free Press*, November 21, 1971.

116. *Detroit Free Press*, November 21, 1971, July 23, 1972, and June 15, 1972.

117. *Detroit Free Press*, July 18, 1972.

118. *Detroit Free Press*, July 23, 1972.

119. Metropolitan Fund, Inc., *Regional Organization: Part One*, (summary of staff papers by the Citizens Research Council of Michigan, May 1965).

120. The 1965 data is from *Ibid.*; the 1982 data is from the U.S. Bureau of the Census, *1982 Census of Government* (Washington, D.C.: U.S. Government Printing Office).

121. Metropolitan Fund, Inc., *Regional Organization*, pp. 17, 35–50.

122. Citizens Research Council of Michigan, "Southeast Michigan Regionalism" (May 1972), in Kent Mathewson (ed.), *The Regionalist Papers*, 2d ed. (Southfield, Mich.: Metropolitan Fund, Inc., 1978), pp. 85–89.

123. York Wilbern, "Local Government Reorganization in Indianapolis," in Kent Mathewson (ed.), *The Regionalist Papers*, 2d ed. (Southfield, Mich.: Metropolitan Fund, Inc., 1978), pp. 48–49.

124. Ted Kolderie, "Regionalism in the Twin Cities of Minnesota," in Kent Mathewson (ed.), *The Regionalist Papers*, 2d ed. (Southfield, Mich.: Metropolitan Fund, Inc., 1978), pp. 26–47.

125. Citizens Research Council of Michigan, "Southeast Michigan" (1977 update), pp. 91–92.

126. See Citizens Research Council of Michigan, *Financial Problems in the Detroit School District*, Memorandum No. 222, Lansing, Mich., February 1972, pp. 7–9; Robert Reischauer and Robert Hartman, *Reforming School Finance* (Washington, D.C.: Brookings Institution, 1973), pp. 62–64; *Detroit Free Press*, July 2, 1974.

127. Citizens Research Council of Michigan, *Financial Problems in the Detroit School District*, Memorandum No. 222, Lansing, Mich., February 1972, pp. 3–4, 6; Detroit Board of Education, *Facts About Detroit Schools* Detroit, Mich., February 1, 1974, p. 14.

128. Detroit Board of Education, *Facts About Detroit Schools*, p. 3.

129. George Peterson (ed.), *Property Tax Reform* (Washington, D.C.: Urban Institute, 1973), p. 9. According to Peterson's research, suburban tax rates averaged 50 percent less than those in central cities in the early 1970s.

130. James Guthrie *et al.*, *Schools and Inequality* (Cambridge, Mass.: Massachusetts Institute of Technology Press, 1971), pp. 119–121.

131. William B. Neenan, "Suburban-Central City Exploitation Thesis," *National Tax Journal*, June 1970, pp. 117–139. For a critical response to Neenan's thesis, cf. Peter Brown, "On Exploitation," *National Tax Journal*, March 1971, pp. 91–96.

132. Many public finance specialists argue that even though there are large differences in tax base among school districts, comparisons of differences in property value per pupil may overstate fiscal inequalities. This is so, they argue, because within any labor market area it seems safe to assume that communities housing families with equal economic means will have equal fiscal capacities, whatever their per-pupil property tax base. If a district enjoys a tax advantage, families living elsewhere will move into the area and bid up housing prices. Families in the community they left pay higher taxes, but the rest of their housing costs are lower.

As elegant as this deductive model may be, it suffers from one very faulty assumption: that families are free to move where they choose. Ignored are housing discrimination against minorities and exclusionary zoning and class pressures, which keep low-income families out of higher-income suburban areas.

133. *Detroit Free Press*, March 18, 1973.

134. State of Michigan, Department of Management and Budget, "Expiration of Detroit Board of Education Income Tax," Accounting Division Letter 81, November 5, 1973, Lansing, Mich.

135. Cf., for example, U.S. Advisory Commission on Intergovernmental Relations, *State Aid to Local Government* (Washington, D.C.: U.S. Government Printing Office, 1969); Committee for Economic Development, *Education for the Urban Disadvantaged: From Preschool to Employment* (New York: Committee for Economic Development, 1971).

136. *Detroit Free Press*, July 13, 1973.

137. *Detroit Free Press*, October 13, 1972.

138. *Michigan State News*, October 25, 1972.

139. Proposal C was defeated by a margin of 58 percent to 42 percent.

140. *Michigan State News*, October 25, 1972.

141. *Detroit Free Press*, October 16, 1971.

142. John Shannon, "The Property Tax: Reform or Relief?" in Peterson (ed.), *Property Tax Reform* (Washington, D.C.: The Brookings Institution, 1973), pp. 35–36.

143. Metropolitan Fund, Inc., "Regional Planning and Development Act; Regional Governance Opinion Survey; Regional Electoral Districting Study, 1974."

144. Citizens Research Council of Michigan, "Southeast Michigan" (1977 update), p. 93.

145. Metropolitan Fund, Inc., "Regional Planning." Quotes on p. 42. See also pp. 23–84.

146. *Detroit Free Press*, December 29, 1975, pp. 3a, 9a.

147. Citizens Research Council of Michigan, "Southeast Michigan" (1977 update), pp. 94–95.

148. Citizens Research Council of Michigan, "City-County Separation: Detroit and Wayne County" (a report to the Wayne County Efficiency Task Force, Detroit, Mich., March 1980), pp. i–v. See also *Detroit Free Press*, September 3, 1980.

149. Citizens Research Council of Michigan, "The Proposed Wayne County Charter," Report 275, September 1981, pp. iv–vi.

150. *Detroit Free Press*, April 26, 1981, June 17, 1981, September 4, 1981, October 12, 1981, and January 13, 1982.

151. *Detroit Free Press*, February 22, 1981.

152. *Detroit Free Press*, February 7, 1983.

153. See Metropolitan Affairs Corporation, *Annual Report, 1984;*and *Intergovernmental Cooperative Arrangements: Exploring Opportunities*, December 1982, which was prepared by the Southeast Michigan Council of Governments.

154. Southeast Michigan Council of Governments, *Annual Report, 1983* and *By-Laws*.

Chapter 7

1. Perhaps the best statement about this transition is in Robert Reich, *The Next American Frontier* (New York: Times Books, 1983).
2. Governor's Cabinet Council on Jobs and Economic Development, Task Force for a Long-Term Economic Strategy for Michigan, *The Path to Prosperity*, Lansing, Mich., 1984, p. 44.
3. *Ibid.*, pp. 55–56.
4. See Richard Child Hill, "Astronomy for the Unemployed: Reaping the Harvest of a Bidding War," *Detroit Metro Times*, April 1985, pp. 17–23.
5. Japan, it's worth noting, looks a lot like this already.
6. Governor's Cabinet Council on Jobs and Economic Development, Task Force for a Long-Term Economic Strategy for Michigan, *The Path to Prosperity*, p. 103.
7. *Ibid.*, p. 108.
8. *Ibid.*, p. 109.
9. See U.S. Advisory Commission on Intergovernmental Relations, *Fiscal Disparities: Central Cities and Suburbs, 1981* (Washington, D.C.; U.S. Government Printing Office, 1984), table 13, p. 34.
10. Detroit Planning Department, Master Plan Program Report, *The People of Detroit: Demographic and Socio-Economic Characteristics* January 1985, pp. 1.01–6.
11. Detroit Planning Department, Master Plan Program Report, *Neighborhoods and Housing*, January 1985, p. 5.
12. *Ibid.*, pp. 13–17.
13. *Ibid.*, p. 18.
14. Cassandra Spratling, "Jefferson Gets Three Cheers from Ten Years," *Detroit Free Press*, June 9, 1985, p. 3a.
15. *Detroit News*, January 11, 1985, p. 8a.
16. Thomasina Brown, interview, May 3, 1985.
17. Marsha Bruhn, director, Detroit Planning Commission, May 3, 1985, interview; Thomasina Brown and Ron Flies, Detroit Community Economic Development Department, interviews, May 3, 1985.
18. *Detroit News*, January 14, 1985.
19. Marsha Bruhn, interview, May 3, 1985.
20. *Detroit News*, January 8, 1985.
21. *Ibid.*
22. *Ibid.*
23. *Ibid.*
24. *Ibid.*
25. *Ibid.*
26. *Detroit News*, January 8, 1985; *Detroit News*, April 14, 1983.
27. Detroit Planning Department, *Federal, State, Regional Relations*, Master Plan Program Report, February 1985, p. vii.
28. *Ibid.*, pp. 5.00–2.

Index